Study Guide

For Plotnik's

INTRODUCTION TO PSYCHOLOGY

SIXTH EDITION

Matthew Enos
Harold Washington College

Language Workout by
Robert F. Keser
National-Louis University

WADSWORTH

THOMSON LEARNING

Australia • Canada • Mexico • Singapore • Spain • United Kingdom • United States

Sponsoring Editor: *Vicki Knight*
Assistant Editor: *Jennifer Wilkinson*
Editorial Assistant: *Dan Moneypenny*
Production Editor: *Scott Brearton*
Cover Design: *Christine Garrigan*
Print Buyer: *Micky Lawler*
Cover Printing: *Globus Printing Company*
Printing and Binding: *Globus Printing Company*

COPYRIGHT © 2002 the Wadsworth Group. Wadsworth is an imprint of the Wadsworth Group, a division of Thomson Learning, Inc. Thomson Learning™ is a trademark used herein under license.

For more information about this or any other Wadsworth products, contact:
WADSWORTH
511 Forest Lodge Road
Pacific Grove, CA 93950 USA
www.wadsworth.com
1-800-423-0563 (Thomson Learning Academic Resource Center)

All rights reserved. No part of this work may be reproduced, transcribed or used in any form or by any means—graphic, electronic, or mechanical, including photocopying, recording, taping, Web distribution, or information storage and/or retrieval systems—without the prior written permission of the publisher.

For permission to use material from this work, contact us by
www.thomsonrights.com
fax: 1-800-730-2215
phone: 1-800-730-2214

Printed in United States of America
10 9 8 7 6 5 4 3 2 1

ISBN: 0-534-58002-5

Contents

- Introduction 1
- 1 Discovering Psychology 6
- 2 Psychology & Science 22
- 3 Brain's Building Blocks 35
- 4 Incredible Nervous System 48
- 5 Sensation 62
- 6 Perception 77
- 7 Consciousness, Sleep, & Dreams 91
- 8 Hypnosis & Drugs 104
- 9 Classical Conditioning 120
- 10 Operant & Cognitive Approaches 133
- 11 Types of Memory 148
- 12 Remembering & Forgetting 162
- 13 Intelligence 175
- 14 Thought & Language 189
- 15 Motivation 204
- 16 Emotion 220
- 17 Infancy & Childhood 234
- 18 Adolescence & Adulthood 250
- 19 Freudian & Humanistic Theories 266
- 20 Social Cognitive & Traits 280
- 21 Health, Stress, & Coping 295
- 22 Assessment & Anxiety Disorders 310
- 23 Mood Disorder & Schizophrenia 325
- 24 Therapies 340
- 25 Social Psychology 355

Introduction

Welcome to Psychology

You are taking a challenging course. I think you will enjoy it, because psychology is one of the most exciting and relevant fields of college study today. An explosion of new ideas and research in psychology is creating a vast accumulation of knowledge that is radically changing the way we understand other people and ourselves. To participate fully and effectively in today's world, we need a kind of psychological literacy, just as we need computer literacy, Internet literacy, and other new technological abilities. This course can help you acquire the skills and information you need to become psychologically literate.

Let's Work Together

Forgive me for using the personal pronoun "I" in this Study Guide. As a teacher, I can't help imagining you working your way through psychology and Rod Plotnik's exciting new textbook, and I'd like to help. I want to speak to you as directly as I can. Even though I don't know you personally, I am sure I have had a student very much like you in my own classes. Happily, we can get to know each other — through e-mail. Throughout the Study Guide, I invite you to e-mail me! **Profenos@aol.com**

Rod Plotnik's New "Introduction to Psychology" (6th Edition)

I predict that you are going to enjoy using your new psychology textbook. My own students often ask, "Why can't *all* textbooks be like this?" Dr. Rod Plotnik, a psychologist and professor at San Diego State University, is an experienced teacher and writer who sees examples of psychology's importance everywhere he looks and loves sharing his observations with us. You'll find Rod Plotnik's book as fresh as your morning newspaper or your favorite talk show. At the same time, you'll see that his book is a work of solid scholarship. He covers the relevant research and carefully explains the major theories. It's how Rod tells it that I think you will find especially rewarding.

Rod's book is different. An expert in learning psychology, Rod knows we *understand* what we can visualize in a picture and *remember* what we can organize into a story. That's why he has filled his book with attractive pictures and compelling stories.

Excellent as his book is, I wouldn't want you to passively agree with everything Rod says. Instead, try to become actively involved in a dialogue with the book. You'll notice how often Rod *asks you a question*. Argue with him. Write notes in the margins. Highlight the important stuff. Make reading and studying this new textbook an adventure.

What Is a Module?

You may have noticed that Dr. Plotnik calls his units "Modules" instead of "Chapters," and that there are more of them than in most textbooks. Rod Plotnik wants his book to be as flexible as possible, so instructors and students can adapt it to their own needs.

Each module tackles an important aspect of psychology. If you mastered everything in every module, you would have a near-perfect understanding of modern psychology (you also might flunk your other courses!). When you read a single module, you learn the main facts and ideas about one area of interest in psychology.

Pay attention to the modules your instructor has assigned (our first job is to pass the course, after all), but remember that there's no law against reading an unassigned module that interests you. [Hint: if you do, tell your instructor about it and you'll make a good impression.]

How this Study Guide Works

The bottom line for this Study Guide is that it must help you earn the grade you want in your psychology course. I tried to include materials that have worked for my own students. Some information is highly specific, aimed straight at getting more questions right on the next test. There are observations about the field of psychology, because, as I explain in my Study Guide introduction for Module 1, if you can't see the forest because of the trees, you're lost. Still other parts have the general goal of helping you become a more effective student (and where better than in a psychology course?). The Study Guide is organized as follows:

Module Introduction

Each module in the Study Guide begins with an observation I think may help you tackle the module in the textbook more successfully. These introductions are not summaries, but thoughts about how to orient yourself toward understanding what you are reading in the textbook.

Effective Student Tip

Next, you will find a specific tip on how to become a more effective student. Some Effective Student Tips tell you how to study better, but most are general ideas about the psychology of effectiveness. Please read the first tip, which explains more about this feature of the Study Guide.

Key Terms

Rod Plotnik has carefully selected the words or phrases (I call them Key Terms) he believes are the most important for beginning psychology students to learn. He puts each Key Term in **boldface** type in the text and provides a brief, clear definition of the term. These terms are also collected in a Glossary at the end of the textbook.

If you did nothing but memorize the Key Terms, you would pass most psychology exams and have a pretty decent command of the vocabulary of the discipline. Of course, it wouldn't be much fun that way, and you need the story to understand psychology in any depth. Still, I can't stress enough the importance of learning the basic vocabulary.

To help you focus on these Key Terms, I have placed them (in alphabetical order) in the Study Guide right before my Outline of the module. I have also included each Key Term in the Outline and placed it in **boldface** type so you won't miss it.

Outline

Each module in the Study Guide includes a topic outline of the module in the text. My Outlines stick very close to Rod Plotnik's organization. I think working with the Outline will help you read and master the textbook.

There is one thing wrong with my Outlines: I wrote them instead of you. Much of the benefit of an outline comes from the process of building it. Therefore, your job is to turn each Outline into your own product by writing all over it and revising it as you study. Make each Outline a personal set of notes that will help you prepare for your tests. If you add your own notes and details to my Outlines, you will have an excellent summary of each module.

Notice that throughout the Outlines I have scattered questions for you to think about and answer. Why not write your answers right on the Outline?

For Psych Majors Only...

In some modules you will find a text box or a brief quiz titled "For Psych Majors Only...." The purpose of these exercises is to go a bit beyond what your course will require. I hope psychology majors will be interested. As you may have guessed, I won't mind a bit if an English major or chemistry major tries these materials!

Language Workout

Following each Outline, there is a special Language Workout section prepared by my colleague Professor Robert F. Keser of National-Louis University. This section is intended not only for non-native speakers, but also for all students who wish to strengthen their skills with the English language. We hope every user of the Study Guide will try the Language Workout materials. Since English is such a powerful and complicated language, anyone who reads these pages will gain greater insight into the intricacies of our wonderful language.

Even if you are quite skilled in English, I can assure you that going through the special language exercises Bob Keser has prepared not only will improve your skills, but will also deepen your understanding of how the English language works.

Bob has written a special introduction (see page 5) to help you make the best use of his exercises. Please read it. This material is too good to miss!

Self-Tests

In each module there are four sets of questions that will help you review and give you an idea of how well you are studying. These self-tests are the most immediate and practical part of this Study Guide. Be sure to use them.

- **The Big Picture**: This quiz is intended to test your overall understanding of the importance of the module. It presents you with five (well, four, really, as you will see!) general summary statements. Which statement best expresses the larger significance of the module? Circle the letter of your choice.

- **True-False**: Ten true-false questions are intended to indicate how well you understand the main ideas in the module.

- **Flashcards 1** and **Flashcards 2**: Two sets of ten matching questions each test your recall of the more important Key Terms in the module. I have quoted Rod Plotnik's definitions as closely as possible, so your results will be a good check on how well you know them. I call these questions "Flashcards" in the hope that you will study and test yourself on the Key Terms more than once.

- **Multiple-Choice**: Fifteen multiple-choice questions explore the important facts, concepts, and theories presented in the module. The multiple-choice questions are especially important because many of you will be taking multiple-choice exams in the course. In fact, some of my questions will be included in the test bank from which your instructor may construct exams.

- **Special Quizzes**: In several modules, you will find a special quiz. Some of these quizzes are serious, some not so serious. I hope you enjoy them.

- **Answers**: After marking your choices in the Study Guide, check your performance with the "Answers" page at the end of each module. No peeking!

Feedback Form

On the last page you will find a special mail-in form by which you can let us know how well this Study Guide worked for you and what suggestions you have for helping us make it better. Please send it in at the end of the semester. We would love to hear from you. (And see below for how to give me more immediate feedback.)

Enjoy Your Study Guide

I hope you enjoy working with the Study Guide. Think about the Effective Student Tips as you write your responses to them. Make real flashcards for the Key Terms, if you have time. Add your own notes and comments to the Outlines.

By the way, if an occasional question or comment of mine makes you laugh..., I'll be delighted. I don't believe learning has to be deadly serious all the time. So when I was writing and couldn't take it any longer, I sometimes indulged myself in what I hoped would be a bit of humor. The results may be too corny, but you be the judge.

"You've Got Mail!"

Music to my ears! I would love to have immediate feedback about the Study Guide. Use my e-mail address to ask questions, share your thoughts, make suggestions for improvements, and, darn it, tell me about those inevitable mistakes I know some of you will find. It will be fun to share ideas with you. My e-mail address is **Profenos@aol.com** and I am eager to hear from you!

Introduction

Introduction to the Language Workout (by Robert F. Keser)

Hey, students! If English is your second language, or even your first language, this feature of the Study Guide is for you. We want to help you with some of the words and special terms used in the book, and give you some practice with more advanced sentences and meanings. Some parts will be easier, some will be harder.

Let me explain the different parts. If you ask "What's that?", you probably want to know the meaning of a word or phrase. Our section called **"What's That?"** will give you meanings as they are used in the text. As you are reading the text, you can follow along in the Study Guide, page by page, to help you understand. (Our definitions are designed to help you understand one word in one particular sentence. However, many words in English have several meanings, so you'll still need a dictionary if you really want to master a word).

Sometimes it's easier to learn a family of words that have the same basic meaning. Our sections called **"Meet the Word Family"** and **"Wild Plurals"** will show you different forms of a word.

When you meet an unfamiliar word, you might be able to understand it from examining the parts of the word. You can work through the sections called **"Build Your Word Power"** and **"Flex Your Word Power"** to practice some of these word parts.

Some words are tricky because they are close in meaning but with an important difference. The section called **"What's the Difference?"** will help you study and practice these words.

"Making Connections" is a section to help you understand how we connect ideas with different meanings, while sections called **"Why a Comma?"** and **"Why a Colon?"** and **"Why a Semi-Colon?"** should help you understand how we use punctuation to show meaning.

Don't worry! Each module has only one or two of these sections, but we'll add some surprise sections, too, just to keep you interested. Remember, though, that this is not a complete grammar book that lists all the exceptions to all the rules. Instead, our job is to guide you to understanding the meaning as you read the textbook.

At the end, when you finish this book, you'll find a **"Language Workout Marathon"** that will help you review and pull together everything we have studied.

Finally, to help you learn and review the many new words you will encounter in the textbook and **"What's That"** sections, we have provided a special **"Word Saver"** form (see pages 15-16). If you make copies of the form and begin using them, you will soon have a valuable collection of new vocabulary flashcards. They will be especially valuable because they are personalized — the words you are adding to your new vocabulary.

Feel free to contact us anytime with questions, suggestions, or just feedback to let us know how the Language Workout is working for you. **Profenos@aol.com**

Let's get started!

Module 1

Discovering Psychology

An Explosion of Knowledge

One day I found a box of my old college textbooks. I was delighted to discover the textbook I used when I took my first psychology course, years ago. Would you believe I still remembered some of the pictures and lessons?

I was shocked, though, to see how slender a book it was. It had a chapter on the eye, another on the ear, and others on the rest of the senses. There was some material on Freud, but not much on anyone else. I was struck by how much less knowledge there was in the field of psychology back then.

The explosion of research and thinking in psychology has created a problem for teachers and students. Textbooks are four times as thick, and they apologize for leaving material out. In the newer textbooks, such as the one by Rod Plotnik that you are using, the writing is lively and the graphics are superb, but there still is much more material to cover. The problem is that colleges and universities, which change very slowly, still expect you to master it all in one semester!

How to Tell the Forest from the Trees

My experience as a teacher says the single greatest problem of introductory psychology is that the sheer mass of information thrown at students overwhelms them, no matter how diligently they study. What is really important? Where are the connections between all these facts and ideas and names? What must I remember for the tests? The study of introductory psychology presents a classic example of the old problem of not being able to see the forest because of the trees.

The solution is to develop a conceptual framework for understanding psychology. If you have an overview of what questions psychology attempts to answer, how it goes about seeking answers, and what the dominant themes in the answers have been, you will be able to fit any new fact, idea, or name into a coherent picture.

That's where Module 1 comes in. In addition to describing the kinds of work psychologists do, Rod Plotnik gives you an important tool: the six major theoretical approaches to psychology. As a student and consumer of psychology, you need to know how the major pioneers in the field have tried to answer our most important questions about human behavior. Module 1 is the road map for an exciting journey.

Effective Student Tip 1

Take a Tip from Me

I have been teaching psychology for many years, but that's not what makes me so smart (ahem!). I have learned from experience. The next tip, for example, owes a lot to my own checkered past. Have you ever heard of the "reformed drunk syndrome"? Guess who you call on if you want a really convincing lecture about the evils of Demon Rum? When I talk about the importance of good attendance, do as I say, not as I did!

But there's more to it. Not only does my experience as both a student and a teacher tell me that every student wants and needs to be effective (I tell you what the professor wants and needs in Tip 18), but I think the psychology of motivation says we all desire effectiveness in every aspect of our lives.

Meanwhile, I hope you will read all these Effective Student Tips, even the ones in the modules your professor does not assign. Some will touch you personally, others may give you something to think about, and some you won't agree with at all. Writing your answers to the "Your response..." questions should help you think about yourself as a student.

Please read the *next* tip and the *last* one right now. Tip 2 is the simplest, and yet the most important. Tip 25 says more about the underlying theme of all these Effective Student Tips.

Your response...
Do you consider yourself an effective person? In what ways "yes" and in what ways "no"?

Key Terms

Forget how big the textbook seems. You are not starting at square one in psychology. So much of psychology is becoming general knowledge these days that you already know quite a bit about it. Rod Plotnik defined 25 terms in this module he thought were especially important to know. How many of the following terms mean something to you right now, even without intensive study of the module?

approaches to understanding behavior
autism
behavioral approach
biological approach [psychobiology]
biological psychology [psychobiology]
clinical psychologist
cognitive approach

cognitive psychology
cross-cultural approach
developmental psychology
experimental psychology
functionalism
Gestalt approach
humanistic approach
introspection
personality psychology
procrastination

psychiatrist
psychoanalytic approach
psychologist
psychology
psychometrics
social psychology
structuralism
test anxiety

Outline

Reminder: Topic outline follows textbook closely. Key terms in boldface. Outline most useful for learning and review when you add your own notes and definitions. Try my questions, too (in italics with checkbox).

- *Introduction*
    1. Growing up in a strange world: Donna Williams' **autism**
    2. **Test anxiety**
    ☐ *Why do you think Rod Plotnik begins with one very rare and one quite common example?*
    A. *Definition & Goals*
        1. Definition of **psychology**
        2. Goals of psychology
            a. Describe
            b. Explain
            c. Predict
            d. Control
    B. *Modern Approaches*
        ☐ *Can you learn the six **approaches to understanding behavior**? Well enough to understand and remember them all through the course? If so, you will possess a master plan into which almost everything in psychology will fit.*
        1. **Biological approach** [psychobiology]
            a. Autism (Donna Williams)
            b. Test anxiety

2. **Cognitive approach**
   a. Autism (Donna Williams)
   b. Test anxiety
3. **Behavioral approach**
   a. Autism (Donna Williams)
   b. B. F. Skinner (strict behaviorism) and Albert Bandura (social learning)
   c. Test anxiety
4. **Psychoanalytic approach**
   a. Autism (Donna Williams)
   b. Sigmund Freud
   c. Test anxiety: example of **procrastination**
5. **Humanistic approach**
   a. Autism (Donna Williams)
   b. Abraham Maslow: dissatisfaction with both psychoanalysis and behaviorism
   c. Test anxiety
6. **Cross-cultural approach**
   a. How is autism diagnosed in other cultures?
   b. Test anxiety

C. *Historical Approaches*

❑ *Have you noticed that there is some overlap between the modern approaches (above) and the historical approaches (below)? Do you see how it's all part of the same story?*

1. **Structuralism**: elements of the mind
   a. Wilhelm Wundt
   b. **Introspection**
2. **Functionalism**: functions of the mind
   a. William James
   b. Purpose of mental activity
3. **Gestalt approach**: sensations versus perceptions
   a. Max Wertheimer, Wolfgang Köhler, Kurt Koffka
   b. Perception as more than the sum of its parts
   c. Apparent motion (phi phenomenon)
4. **Behavioral approach**: observable behaviors
   a. John B. Watson ["Give me a dozen healthy infants… and my own special world to bring them up in…"]
   b. Objective, scientific analysis of observable behaviors
   c. B. F. Skinner and modern behaviorism
5. Survival of approaches

D. Cultural Diversity: Early Discrimination
  1. Women in psychology
     a. Mary Calkins
     b. Margaret Washburn
  2. Minorities in psychology
     a. Ruth Howard
     b. George Sanchez
  3. Righting the wrongs
     a. APA efforts to help minority students
     b. State laws banning affirmative action programs

E. Research Focus: Taking Class Notes
  1. What's the best strategy for taking lecture notes?
  2. A research study of three techniques (which also illustrates the four **goals of psychology**)
  ☐ *Which technique worked best? Can you figure out why it was superior?*

F. Careers in Psychology
  1. Psychologist versus psychiatrist
     a. **Psychologist**
     b. **Clinical psychologist**
     c. **Psychiatrist**
  2. Many career settings

G. Research Areas
  1. Areas of specialization
     a. **Social psychology** and **personality psychology**
     b. **Developmental psychology**
     c. **Experimental psychology**
     d. **Biological psychology** (psychobiology)
     e. **Cognitive psychology**
     f. **Psychometrics**
  2. Decisions

H. Application: Study Skills
  1. Improving study habits
     a. Common complaint
     b. Poor judges
     c. Time management
  2. Setting goals
     a. Time goal
     b. General goal
     c. Specific performance goal

3. Rewarding yourself (self-reinforcement)
4. Taking notes
   a. In your own words
   b. Outline format [like this one]
   c. Associate new material with old [as in Concept/Glossary section]
   d. Ask yourself questions as you study
5. Stop procrastinating
   a. Stop thinking or worrying about final goal
   b. Break overall task down into smaller goals
   c. Write down a realistic schedule

For Psych Majors Only...

Contributors to Psychology: A matching exercise based on important people in psychology.

_____ 1. Albert Bandura   a. humanistic psychology movement
_____ 2. Mary Calkins   b. author of your psychology textbook
_____ 3. Ruth Howard   c. denied a doctorate in psychology by Harvard
_____ 4. William James   d. social learning theory
_____ 5. Abraham Maslow   e. founded Gestalt psychology movement
_____ 6. Rod Plotnik   f. strict behaviorism
_____ 7. B. F. Skinner   g. studied function of conscious activity
_____ 8. John B. Watson   h. first laboratory for psychological research
_____ 9. Max Wertheimer, Wolfgang Kohler, and Kurt Koffka   i. "Give me a dozen healthy infants... and my own special world to bring them up in..."
_____ 10. Willhelm Wundt   j. first African-American Ph.D. in psychology

Language Workout

What's That?

p. 3   "involuntarily **anesthetized**" = without feeling or sensations
students called her **"Zombie"** = a "walking dead" monster
figuring out the day of the week = identifying
getting through an ordinary day = completing the work of

p. 4   if they were **reared** by parents who were cold = raised
prevent **potential** abuse = possible in the future

p. 6   **inanimate** objects = without life, without movement
process human faces = organize information into clear identification
one **component** of test anxiety = part, factor
stressful thoughts **trigger** the emotional component = stimulate, start

p. 7   students who **channeled** their worry into studying = directed, redirected

p. 8   No making the fruit in the bowl **symmetrical** = orderly
rewards or punishment can **modify** behavior = change

p. 9   **rigid corpselike stance** = standing like a dead body, unmoving
procrastinators = people who wait until the last minute to do their work

p. 13 they **discriminated against** women = acted unfairly

p. 17 Psychologist **versus** Psychiatrist = compared to

p. 20 researchers have discovered a **startling** fact = surprising

p. 24 Dr. Rimland **downplayed** the finding = argued that it is not important

Build Your Word Power

Bio**logy** means the study of living things.
Psycho**logy** means the study of the mind.
Physio**logy** means the study of the body and its processes.
So, **-ology** means _____

Biology means the study of living things.
Biography means the story of a living being.
Biochemistry means the chemistry of living organisms.
So, **bio-** means _____

Psychology means the study of the mind.
Psychologists are persons who study the mind.
Psychotherapy is the treatment of disorders of the mind.
So, **psycho-** means _____

A psycholog**ist** is a person who studies the mind.
A biolog**ist** is a person who studies living organisms.
A scient**ist** is a person who works with science.
So, **-ist** means _____

Put it Together

Can you put together one word to describe the study of how the mind influences the body processes of a living organism? _____

Figure it Out!

Divide means separate into pieces.
Different means separate, not the same.
Discriminate means treat in a separate way.
Diverge means go in separate directions.

So, **di-** means _____

In**spect** means look at closely.
Spectator means a person who looks.
Intro**spect**ion means looking inside.

So, **-spect-** means _____

Flex Your Word Power

Potential means possible, or can be developed. Losing financial aid is a **potential** problem for some students.

One potential grade in this course is _____

Luis wants to get married, so he's looking for a potential _____.

I am studying for a potential career in _____.

Potential also means possible ability that can be developed in the future. We have to struggle to reach our potential (p.10) Every child has some kind of **potential**: some have **potential** in art or math, while others show **potential** for music.

Selling air conditioners in the Arctic Circle is a business with very little _____ for success.

Guo Ping likes to help his father work on car engines, so his family thinks he has good potential for a career as a _____.

A job interview is one way employers try to judge an applicant's _____.

Jackie's coach gave her special leg exercises to unlock her _____ as a runner.

See It And Say It

p. 13 **Gestalt** is a German word, so we pronounce it according to German rules.
Try it: geh - SHTAWLT
Sounds like: default

p. 19 **Psychometrics**
Try it: sy - ko - MET - riks

Meet the Word Family: perceive - perceptive - perception

Perceive

The following are all members of one word family: can you figure out the meaning from these sentences?

Maria **perceive**d that her boyfriend was angry because he didn't call her.

Maria **perceive**d that her boyfriend was angry because she read a letter where he explained his feelings.

Maria **perceive**d that her boyfriend was angry from the look on his face.

Maria **perceive**d that her boyfriend was angry because he told her so.

So, **perceive** means _____ (a) feel, (b) know, (c) understand

That's right: it means all of these, and more. See how it fits in the following sentences:

A person who is color-blind can't _____ the difference between red and green.

He lost his spectacles, so now he can only _____ the general outlines of big objects.

Dogs are able to _____ sounds and smells that humans cannot.

Everyone can taste the difference between coffee and tea, but it's harder to _____ the difference between Colombian and Hawaiian coffee.

Perceptive

A highly sensitive person who **perceive**s more than the ordinary person is called **perceptive**.

Helen made a good police officer because she was especially _____ about people and how to help them.

An especially _____ lawyer can usually guess whether the client is guilty or not.

Jorge notices more than the average person. That's why his teachers believe he is a _____ student.

Perception

The information you **perceive** is your **perception**.

The senator hid his marriage problems well, so the public _____ was that he was a good family man.

A doctor needs good powers of _____ because patients don't always reveal their problems directly.

Two people can see the same traffic accident but have different _____ s about what happened.

TEST YOURSELF: Read the following passage and choose the best word to fill the blank.

perceive - perceptive - perception - potential

Researchers have designed experiments to test perceptual differences between men and women. They wanted to establish whether men _____ colors differently from women. The popular _____ is that females can actually see smaller differences in color, so many people believe that women are more _____ in other areas as well. One theory is that both sexes have the same physical ability but that some cultures develop women's _____ to discriminate colors more than men's.

Answer Key

-ology means <u>study of</u>
bio- means <u>living</u>
psycho- means <u>mind</u>
-ist means <u>person</u>

Can you put together one word to describe the study of how the mind influences the body processes of a living organism? <u>Psychobiology</u>

-di means <u>separate</u>
-spect- means <u>look</u>

Researchers have designed experiments to test perceptual differences between men and women. They wanted to establish whether men **perceive** colors differently from women. The popular **perception** is that females can actually see smaller differences in color, so many people believe that women are more **perceptive** in other areas as well. One theory is that both sexes have the same physical ability but that some cultures develop women's **potential** to discriminate colors more than men's do.

Word Saver

How can I remember all these new words? Maybe you are asking yourself this question as you look through the textbook.

The answer is, you *can't* remember so many new words. The good news is that you don't have to remember them all; you only need to understand them in the text.

Of course, some words will come again and again in the text. These are the words that you should try to remember. But how?

The best way to remember a new vocabulary word is to focus your attention on the word from different angles: the meaning, the pronunciation, the context, and the related forms in the word family. Research also tells us that it is *especially important* to make your own sentences with the word: when you connect the word to your own life and thoughts, you will increase your ability to remember the word (Modules 11 and 12 of the text will explain a lot about memory).

To remember the words you choose, you need to organize this information. You can use the **Word Saver** form below to help you. Make photocopies of the blank **Word Saver** forms provided on the next page and then fill in as much information as you can. Be sure to make your own sentences with each word!

As you are reading, underline a word that you want to master. When you finish reading, go back and write the underlined word in the **Word Saver** form, and use an English language dictionary to fill out the rest of the information about the word. As you know, one word can have many meanings in English, but you should focus on the meaning in the text.

Here is an example of how you might fill out the **Word Saver** for the word "perceive":

Word Saver

Word _____*perceive*_____

Pronunciation _____*purr-SEEV*_____

Meaning(s) _____*become aware of through the senses*_____

Other forms in the word family? _____*perception, perceptive, perceptual, perceptible*_____

Example in the text _____*perceiving and analyzing objects in space (p. 77)*_____

Example in the dictionary? _____*Dogs can perceive sounds that humans cannot.*_____

My sentence _____*When it's quiet at night, I can perceive more sounds.*_____

STUDY GUIDE

Word Saver

Word _____

Pronunciation _____

Meaning(s) _____

Other forms in the word family? _____

Example in the text _____

Example in the dictionary? _____

My sentence _____

Word Saver

Word _____

Pronunciation _____

Meaning(s) _____

Other forms in the word family? _____

Example in the text _____

Example in the dictionary? _____

My sentence _____

Word Saver

Word _____

Pronunciation _____

Meaning(s) _____

Other forms in the word family? _____

Example in the text _____

Example in the dictionary? _____

My sentence _____

Word Saver

Word _____

Pronunciation _____

Meaning(s) _____

Other forms in the word family? _____

Example in the text _____

Example in the dictionary? _____

My sentence _____

The Big Picture

Which statement below offers the best summary of the larger significance of this module?

    A   Building on a long history that goes back to the ancient world, psychology today offers respect, honor, and financial security to those few who can complete medical school and post-doctoral training.

    B   There is no single "true" psychology because it is still a young and hotly debated science. At this stage in its growth, six theoretical approaches offer quite different but still valuable answers to life's complex problems.

    C   Psychology has not yet achieved the respect of the scientific community because there are so many answers and so many different specialties competing for our attention.

    D   A civil war has raged within psychology for more than a century, but the Freudian system is gradually emerging as the most convincing overall answer.

    E   How many psychologists does it take to change a light bulb, you ask? The answer is three: one to hold the ladder, one to change the bulb, and one to share the experience.

True-False

_____ 1. The goals of psychology are to explain, describe, predict, and control behavior.

_____ 2. There are as many different approaches to psychology as there are psychologists writing about psychology.

_____ 3. Techniques like free association and dream interpretation are products of the psychoanalytic approach to psychology.

_____ 4. Abraham Maslow wanted humanistic psychology to be a new way of perceiving and thinking about the individual's capacity, freedom, and potential for growth.

_____ 5. It is best to pick one of the general approaches to psychology and organize your thinking and work around it exclusively.

_____ 6. There has been ethnic discrimination in psychology, but at least women have always been equally represented.

_____ 7. Modern scientific psychology began with Wilhelm Wundt's attempt to accurately measure the conscious elements of the mind.

_____ 8. The key idea of behaviorism is that perception is more than just the sum of its parts.

_____ 9. Not only do you have several career choices in psychology — whichever one you choose, you are almost certain to make big bucks!

_____ 10. There is no special program for overcoming procrastination: just get off your duff and get to work.

Flashcards 1

____ 1. autism
____ 2. behavioral approach
____ 3. biological approach
____ 4. cognitive approach
____ 5. cross-cultural approach
____ 6. humanistic approach
____ 7. psychoanalytic approach
____ 8. psychology
____ 9. psychometrics
____ 10. test anxiety

a. systematic scientific study of behaviors and mental processes
b. rare problem with severe impairments in communication, motor systems, socialization
c. studies the influence of cultural and ethnic similarities and differences on functioning
d. physiological, emotional, cognitive problems in thinking, and reasoning caused by stress of exams
e. emphasizes individual freedom, capacity for personal growth, potential for self-fulfillment
f. interested in how we process, store, and use information; how information influences us
g. focuses on measurement of abilities, skills, intelligence, personality, abnormal behaviors
h. focuses on influence of unconscious fears, desires, and motivations on thoughts, behavior
i. examines how genes, hormones, and nervous system interact with environments
j. analyzes how organisms learn new behaviors through reward, punishment from environment

Flashcards 2

____ 1. clinical psychologist
____ 2. cognitive psychology
____ 3. developmental psychology
____ 4. experimental psychology
____ 5. functionalism
____ 6. Gestalt approach
____ 7. introspection
____ 8. psychiatrist
____ 9. psychologist
____ 10. structuralism

a. study of basic elements like perception which make up conscious mental processes
b. emphasized that perception is more than sum of its parts; how sensation becomes perception
c. has completed 4-5 years of postgraduate education; has obtained Ph.D. in psychology
d. includes areas of sensation, perception, learning, human performance, motivation, and emotion
e. study of function rather than structure of consciousness; how mind adapts to change
f. how we process, store, and retrieve information; how cognitive processes influence our behavior
g. medical doctor (MD) with additional years of clinical training in diagnosis, treatment
h. has Ph.D. plus specialization in clinical psychology and supervised work in therapy
i. method of exploring conscious mental processes by asking subjects to look inward
j. examines moral, social, emotional, cognitive development throughout a person's entire life

Multiple-Choice

_____ 1. Rod Plotnik tells the story of Donna's struggle with autism in order to make the point that psychology is
   a. the one science that has all the answers
   b. a rather grim science that involves lots of pain and suffering
   c. helpless when confronted with really severe human problems
   d. dedicated to answering questions about complex behaviors

_____ 2. Which one of the following is *not* a goal of psychology?
   a. to explain the causes of behavior
   b. to predict behavior
   c. to judge behavior
   d. to control behavior

_____ 3. The biological approach to psychology focuses on
   a. the workings of our genes, hormones, and nervous system
   b. conscious processes like perception and memory
   c. the effects of reward and punishment on behavior
   d. unconscious processes

_____ 4. The cognitive approach to psychology studies how we
   a. are motivated by unconscious processes
   b. are motivated by the need for self-fulfillment
   c. process, store, and use information
   d. program our behavior by seeking rewards and avoiding punishments

_____ 5. The major contributor to the behavioral approach to psychology was
   a. Sigmund Freud
   b. B. F. Skinner
   c. William James
   d. Abraham Maslow

_____ 6. The great importance of the unconscious is a key idea in the _____ approach
   a. psychoanalytic
   b. cognitive
   c. behavioral
   d. psychobiological

_____ 7. _____ was one of the major figures of the humanistic approach to psychology
   a. Sigmund Freud
   b. Abraham Maslow
   c. B. F. Skinner
   d. Erik Erikson

_____ 8. The cross-cultural approach to psychology studies the influence of _____ on psychological functioning
   a. brain chemistry
   b. information processing
   c. cultural and ethnic similarities and differences
   d. automatic behaviors and deeply ingrained habits

Module 1: Discovering Psychology   19

_____ 9. Once we understand the six approaches to psychology, Rod Plotnik advises us to
   a. make a personal decision about which approach is best
   b. combine and use information from all six approaches
   c. place our trust in the approaches that have stood the test of time
   d. judge each approach by the famous people who have supported it

_____ 10. The difference between "structuralism" and "functionalism" in the early years of psychology concerned a choice between
   a. British or American psychology
   b. Abraham Maslow or John B. Watson
   c. studying the brain or the cultural setting of behavior
   d. studying narrow sensations or general adaptations to our changing environment

_____ 11. By explaining perceptual phenomena like the phi phenomenon [apparent motion], Gestalt researchers gave psychology the idea that
   a. the whole is more than the sum of its parts
   b. research results could be profitable when applied to advertising
   c. Wundt and the structuralists had been right about the importance of the individual parts
   d. individual parts are more significant than resulting wholes

_____ 12. The early behaviorist John B. Watson wanted psychology to be a/n
   a. introspective investigation of how people understood the workings of their minds
   b. objective, scientific study of observable behavior
   c. philosophical study of the continuous flow of mental activity
   d. religious program for "building" moral children

_____ 13. The efforts of American psychology to overcome discrimination may be threatened by
   a. state laws banning affirmative action programs
   b. a steady decline in the numbers of men going into psychology
   c. wide-spread African-American and Latino disinterest in the subject of psychology
   d. a new policy of the American Psychological Association against affirmative action

_____ 14. After reading the material on careers and research areas, it would be reasonable to conclude that psychology
   a. requires so much education that few students should consider it
   b. will have fewer job opportunities in coming years
   c. offers a great variety of intellectual challenges and kinds of work
   d. is one of the best paid professions today

_____ 15. Which one of the following is *not* a good strategy for overcoming procrastination?
   a. stop thinking or worrying about the final goal
   b. break the final assignment down into a number of smaller goals
   c. write down a realistic schedule for reaching each of your smaller goals
   d. do not begin working until you have complete confidence that you will succeed

Answers for Module 1

True-False	Flashcards 1	Flashcards 2	Multiple-Choice
1. T	1. b	1. h	1. d
2. F	2. j	2. f	2. c
3. T	3. i	3. j	3. a
4. T	4. f	4. d	4. c
5. F	5. c	5. e	5. b
6. F	6. e	6. b	6. a
7. T	7. h	7. i	7. b
8. F	8. a	8. g	8. c
9. F	9. g	9. c	9. b
10. F	10. d	10. a	10. d
			11. a
			12. b
			13. a
			14. c
			15. d

The Big Picture

Statement B

"Contributors to Psychology" quiz

1. d   2. c   3. j   4. g   5. a   6. b   7. f   8. i   9. e   10. h

Hey You!

Yes you..., the one checking the answers! Whenever you turn to the Answers page, glance down at the bottom of the page (right here!). You will find a reminder about something in the textbook or Study Guide that I think is important, or a tip that you may find useful. Check it out! Then tell me what you think. **Profenos@aol.com**

Psychology & Science

Science and the Scientific Method

When we think of science, we imagine a person in a white lab coat working some kind of magic we can't understand. But that's not science. Science is a method of asking and answering questions about nature, including human nature. Science is only one of many ways of solving problems by answering questions through the analysis of gathered information. There are older and more widely used methods, such as reliance on tradition, custom, or authority. For much of our work, however, science is the most powerful intellectual tool yet invented.

Science offers a methodical procedure for the analysis of objective events. It is *not* simply the discoveries scientists make, or the techniques scientists use, or the beliefs that any scientists may hold. Instead, science is a way of approaching the task of gathering information and creating knowledge. It is a *method* of analysis.

Rules of Procedure and Basic Assumptions about Reality

Science consists of two related features: (1) a set of characteristics or rules of procedure, and (2) a set of basic assumptions about reality. The first feature constitutes the rules of the game that scientists follow in the laboratory. These rules require objectivity, freedom from bias, objective data collection, public procedures, precise definitions, careful measurements, logical reasoning, rigorous control of variables, systematic examination of relationships, and self-criticism. Through replication, scientists aim to create theories that allow prediction and control.

The second feature constitutes the starting point of science, what all scientists agree on about how nature works. These assumptions are that all events are naturally determined, that nature is orderly and regular, that truth is relative, and that knowledge is gained through empiricism, rationalism, and replication. Of course these basic assumptions about reality are assumptions rather than proven facts. Consequently, it is not necessary to believe that these assumptions are universally 'true' in order to use the scientific method.

Together the two features of the scientific method also serve as a checklist for the researcher. Any violation of or deviation from the rules of procedure or the basic assumptions about reality puts an investigation outside the realm of science and renders its results untrustworthy.

Effective Student Tip 2

Attend Every Class

I shudder when I hear about college teachers who advise, "Come to class if it helps, but attendance isn't required." That's such poor psychology and such destructive advice. Students should attend *every* class, even the dull ones, because regular attendance leads directly to involvement and commitment, the basic ingredients of effective college work.

We aren't talking morals here, we're talking the psychology of effectiveness. Here's why attendance is the basis of successful college work. (1) Good attendance makes you feel more confident, purposeful and in control. (2) Attendance is the one feature of college that is completely under your control. (3) The reason for an absence usually reveals some area in which you feel ineffective. (4) Whether they make a big deal of it or not, your professors want and need your good attendance. What if no one came? (5) There is more to a class than the lecture. Other good things happen when you attend class regularly. Your professor gets to know you. You become better acquainted with your classmates. You learn from them and you learn by helping them. (6) Most students can achieve perfect attendance if they try, and their professors will admire them for it. You can help make a good class a great one.

Your response…

What is your attendance history? Do you have an attendance goal for this class?

Key Terms

The vocabulary of science has become essential for any educated person. How many of these key terms do you know something about already, without further study?

animal model
Attention-deficit/hyper-
   activity disorder (ADHD)
case study
control group
correlation
correlation coefficient
debriefing
dependent variable
double-blind procedure

experiment
experimental group
hypothesis
independent variable
interview
laboratory experiment
laboratory setting
naturalistic setting
placebo
placebo effect

questionnaire
random selection
scientific method
self-fulfilling prophecy
standardized test
statistical procedures
survey
testimonial

Outline

- *Introduction*
    1. **Attention-deficit/hyperactivity disorder (ADHD)**
    2. Rhino horn and magnets
    ☐ In what possible way could rhino horn and vitamin C be connected?

A. *Answering Questions*
    1. Why the controversies about ADHD?
    2. Three research strategies for scientific investigation
        a. **Survey**
        b. **Case study**
        c. **Experiment**

B. *Surveys*
    1. Kind of information: hand washing, worries, ADHD
    2. Disadvantages
        a. How questions are worded
        b. Who asks the questions
    3. Advantages
    ☐ What are the main advantages and disadvantages of the survey method?

C. *Case Study*
    1. Kind of information in **case study**
    2. Personal case study: **testimonial**
    ☐ What are the main advantages and disadvantages of a testimonial?

3. Error and bias in testimonials
   a. Personal beliefs
   b. **Self-fulfilling prophecy**

D. *Cultural Diversity: Use of Placebos*
   1. Remarkable treatments
      a. **Placebo**
      b. **Placebo effect**
   2. Common world-wide placebos
      a. Rhino horn
      b. Bear gallbladders
      c. Tiger bones
      d. Magnets
   ☐ *What beliefs and practices in the United States might be thought of as our own "rhino horn?"*
   3. Conclusion: Testimonials and placebos

E. *Correlation*
   1. Definition
      a. **Correlation**
      b. **Correlation coefficient**
   2. Strength of relationship
      a. Perfect positive correlation coefficient (+1.00)
      b. Positive correlation coefficient (+0.01 to +0.99)
      c. Zero correlation (0.00)
      d. Negative correlation coefficient (-0.01 to -0.99)
      e. Perfect negative correlation coefficient (-1.00)
   3. Advantages and disadvantages
      a. Correlation versus causation
      b. Correlations as clues
      c. Correlation and predictions

F. *Decisions about Doing Research*
   1. Choosing research techniques
      a. **Questionnaires** and **interviews**
      b. **Standardized tests**
      c. **Laboratory experiment**
      d. **Animal model**
   2. Choosing research settings
      a. **Naturalistic setting** (case study)
      b. **Laboratory setting**
   ☐ *What are the main advantages and disadvantages of each setting?*

G. **Scientific Method: Experiment**
  1. Advantages of scientific method
     a. **Scientific method**
     b. **Experiment**
  2. Conducting an experiment: seven rules
     a. Rule 1: ask (**hypothesis**)
     b. Rule 2: identify variables
        (1) **Independent variable** (treatment)
        (2) **Dependent variable** (resulting behavior)
     c. Rule 3: choose subjects (**random selection**)
     d. Rule 4: assign subjects randomly
        (1) **Experimental group**
        (2) **Control group**
  ☐ Why is a control group needed in a scientific experiment?
     e. Rule 5: manipulate independent variable
        (1) administer treatment
        (2) **Double-blind procedure**
  ☐ What makes the double-blind procedure superior to the typical experiment?
     f. Rule 6: measure resulting behavior (dependent variable)
     g. Rule 7: analyze data
        (1) Sample
        (2) **Statistical procedures** (see Appendix in textbook)

H. **Research Focus: ADHD Controversies**
  ☐ Do you know a child who is hyperactive? What is he or she like?
  1. Why is there controversy after 30 years of research on ADHD?
     a. Controversy: diagnosis
     b. Controversy: treatment
        (1) Stimulants: advantages
        (2) Stimulants: disadvantages
  2. Controversy: long-term effects
  ☐ Do you have an opinion concerning the controversies surrounding ADHD?

I. **Application: Research Concerns**
  1. Concerns about being a subject
  ☐ Would you volunteer to be a subject in a psychological experiment?
  2. Code of ethics
     a. American Psychological Association ethical guidelines
     b. **Debriefing**
  3. Role of deception

4. Ethics of using animals as research subjects
   a. Pros, cons, and safeguards
   b. Striking a balance
☐ *Do you believe animals should be used in research?*

Language Workout

Build Your Word Power

Hyperactive means too active
Hypersensitive means too sensitive
Hypercritical means too critical
Hyper- means _____

What's the Difference?

AFFECT? EFFECT?

Affect means to change = Heat and cold **affect** water in different ways.
Effect means a result = Steam is one **effect** of heating water.

A bad grade can **affect** a student in different ways.

A positive **effect** could be to energize the student to study harder.

A negative **effect** could be depression.

Each student's own personality will **affect** his or her own reaction.

Now, you try it:

Other variables, such as family problems, money problems, and physical health, can also _____ the student's response.

Parents worry about the _____ of violent movies on young children.

Drinking coffee can _____ both mind and body. Increased energy is one good _____ but trouble going to sleep is a bad _____.

Flex Your Word Power

bias: means prejudice, a judgment distorted by personal feelings.

Job applicants for the police department are tested for **bias** against particular races or groups.

The chief of police has stated that racial **bias** and religious **bias** have no place in police work.

Max's years of eating in school cafeterias developed a **bias** in him against macaroni-and-cheese.

In a taste test, the taster puts on a blindfold to avoid **bias** from how the food looks.

School kids often judge each other by the kind of clothes they wear. School uniforms are one way to prevent this kind of **bias**.

Dracula has a **bias** for the color red.

biased: means distorted by personal feelings, influenced by bias

The public reaction to the politician's TV speech was **biased by** the bad lighting which made him look like a gangster.

You can't ask one of the mothers to judge a baby contest because she would be **biased toward** her own baby.

Muna loves hiking in the woods, so she is **biased in favor of** strong controls to protect the environment.

Jack's bad experiences as a cabdriver made him **biased against** ladies with lots of shopping bags and noisy children.

Alvaro complains that his parents are **biased against** rap music: they won't even listen to the songs!

The computer company's report was criticized for its **biased** perceptions about the need for schools to buy as many computers as possible.

See It and Say It

placebo *say* pluh-SEE-boh

hypothesis *say* hai-PAH-thi-sis

Meet the Word Family: deceive - deceptive - deception

deceive: means to mislead, make people think that something is true or good when it is actually false or bad.

The magician used tricks to **deceive** the audience that he had really pulled a rabbit out of his hat.

Not admitting that his drinking was a problem, Ray **deceive**d himself into thinking his life was fine.

Everyone in the office is **deceiv**ing the boss by secretly planning his surprise birthday party.

What do you think Shakespeare meant when he wrote:

"O, what a tangled web we weave
When first we practice to deceive"

deceptive: means ac**tive**ly misleading

"You can't tell a book by its cover" is one way to say that appearances can be **deceptive**: two people can weigh the same but one might look "fatter" than the other.

The critic wrote: "This movie is a tremendous waste of time." A week later, the movie ad quoted him as saying the movie was "tremendous", so the critic complained about this **deceptive** advertising.

The exam looked simple, but this was **deceptive**: the answers were more complicated than they looked.

deception: means the action of deceiving

Make-up is one kind of **deception** to make people think one is younger or less tired.

The magician used **deception** to make the audience believe that he had really sawed a woman in half.

Spies make their living out of **deception**.

Test Yourself

Read the following passage and choose the four best words to fill the blanks.

affect – effect / bias – biased / deceive – deceptive / deception

Why did the dinosaurs disappear? One hypothesis is that a giant meteor hit the earth. What sort of _____ would such an event have on animal life? Certainly the disaster would _____ the weather and the food sources for all animals, possibly leading to widespread death. In fact, scientists have found the crater of a giant meteor impact in the Gulf of Mexico, but other scientists say that this evidence is _____ because it proves nothing about the dinosaurs. Of course, these critics want to push their own theories, so their arguments could be _____.

Answer Key

Hyper- means too

Other variables, such as family problems, money problems, and physical health, can also **affect** the student's response.

Parents worry about the **effect** of violent movies on young children.

Drinking coffee can **affect** both mind and body. Increased energy is one good **effect,** but trouble going to sleep is a bad **effect**.

Why did the dinosaurs disappear? One hypothesis is that a giant meteor hit the earth. What sort of **effect** would such an event have on animal life? Certainly the disaster would **affect** the weather and the food sources for all animals, possibly leading to widespread death. In fact, scientists have found the crater of a giant meteor impact in the Gulf of Mexico, but other scientists say that this evidence is **deceptive** because it proves nothing about the dinosaurs. Of course, these critics want to push their own theories, so their arguments could be **biased**.

The Big Picture

Which statement below offers the best summary of the larger significance of this module?

- A The essence of scientific research in psychology necessarily is deception. Therefore, it probably would be wise not to volunteer to be a subject in a psychological experiment.

- B Psychology, because it sometimes uses the case study method and the survey method, is only partly a science. To be a true science, psychology would have to rely on the laboratory experiment alone.

- C When psychology at last becomes completely scientific, it will be able to answer any question we might have about the truth of our beliefs, the rightness of our behaviors, and the meanings of our lives.

- D Psychology uses several different research strategies and techniques. What makes psychology scientific, however, is that all of them have in common a devotion to *objectivity* (knowledge sought through the five senses).

- E On the other hand, some people would argue that it only takes one psychologist to change a light bulb — if the light bulb *really wants to change*.

True-False

_____ 1. Rod Plotnik's definition of psychology as the "scientific study of behaviors and mental processes" means that psychology is strongly linked to the power of the scientific method.

_____ 2. The scientific technique with the lowest potential for error and bias is the survey method.

_____ 3. Testimonials have a high potential for error and bias.

_____ 4. The main disadvantage of gathering information through surveys is that it takes so long and is so hard to do.

_____ 5. If it turns out that there is a *negative* correlation between studying the textbook and getting good grades, you just wasted a big chunk of money.

_____ 6. If you can establish a significant correlation between two variables, you have also determined the causal relationship between them.

_____ 7. Research in naturalistic settings has greater reality, but research in the laboratory has greater control.

_____ 8. What the experimenter manipulates is called the dependent variable; how the subjects react is called the independent variable.

_____ 9. Random selection is crucial in choosing subjects because you want them to accurately represent the larger population you are studying.

_____ 10. There is no way to justify doing research using animals.

Flashcards 1

_____ 1. case study
_____ 2. control group
_____ 3. correlation
_____ 4. dependent variable
_____ 5. experiment
_____ 6. experimental group
_____ 7. independent variable
_____ 8. random selection
_____ 9. scientific method
_____ 10. survey

a. identifying cause and effect relationships by following a set of rules that minimize error, bias and chance
b. composed of subjects who receive the experimental treatment
c. composed of subjects who undergo all the same procedures but who do not receive the treatment
d. an in-depth analysis of the thoughts, feelings, beliefs, experiences, behaviors or problems of a single person
e. a general approach to gathering information and answering questions so error, bias is minimized
f. a treatment or something that the researcher controls or manipulates
g. one or more of the subjects' behaviors that are used to measure the potential effects of the treatment
h. a way to obtain information by asking many individuals to answer a fixed set of questions
i. each subject in a sample population has an equal chance of being selected to participate in experiment
j. an association or relationship between the occurrence of two or more events

Flashcards 2

_____ 1. correlation coefficient
_____ 2. debriefing
_____ 3. double-blind procedure
_____ 4. hypothesis
_____ 5. laboratory setting
_____ 6. naturalistic setting
_____ 7. placebo
_____ 8. questionnaire
_____ 9. self-fulfilling prophecy
_____ 10. testimonial

a. a relatively normal environment in which researchers observe behavior but don't change or control it
b. neither the subjects nor the researchers know which group is receiving which treatment
c. some intervention (pill, injection) that resembles medical therapy but has no actual medical effects
d. a statement in support of a particular viewpoint based on observations of our personal experiences
e. studying individuals under systematic and controlled conditions, with real-world influences eliminated
f. a technique for obtaining information by asking subjects to check answers on a list of questions
g. having a strong belief or making a statement about a future behavior then acting to carry out the behavior
h. explaining the purpose and method of the experiment to subjects, helping them deal with doubts or guilt
i. an educated guess about some phenomenon stated in precise, concrete language to rule out confusion
j. a number that indicates the strength of a relationship between two or more events

Multiple-Choice

____ 1. Rod Plotnik begins this module with the example of Dusty, a hyperactive seven-year old, to show that
   a. often psychology must yield to medical science
   b. psychology needs accurate answers to highly complex problems
   c. science must recognize the problems for which it cannot find answers
   d. hyperactivity can be controlled by high doses of vitamin C

____ 2. The scientific method is defined as
   a. a general approach to answering questions that minimizes errors
   b. a faith that precise equipment will produce accurate information
   c. all of the findings of science in the modern era
   d. a set of guidelines published by the American Academy of Science

____ 3. Which one of the following has the *lowest* potential for error or bias?
   a. case study
   b. survey
   c. experiment
   d. testimonial

____ 4. When you encounter a testimonial, you know that it is
   a. true, if enough other people also report it
   b. false, because it is only a personal belief
   c. true, if the person conveying it has a good reputation for honesty
   d. possibly true, but not proven by science

____ 5. A good example of a self-fulfilling prophecy is the belief that
   a. there's no use studying for multiple-choice exams because the questions are tricky
   b. psychology requires more study than literature
   c. if you do all your studying the night before the exam you'll do better
   d. you don't have to take notes in class if you listen carefully

____ 6. One of the main disadvantages of the survey method is that
   a. many people won't go to the trouble of filling out the survey
   b. the results will be biased if the sample is not representative
   c. it is difficult to survey enough subjects to make the results valid
   d. it takes so long to conduct a survey that the method is impractical for most purposes

____ 7. When she wears her lucky socks, Gail wins three golf matches out of four, a _____ correlation between wearing the socks and winning
   a. perfect negative
   b. negative
   c. positive
   d. perfect positive

____ 8. Does this prove that the socks are the cause of Gail's winning?
   a. yes, because it cannot be just coincidence
   b. no, because correlation is not causation
   c. it would if she won *every* time she wore the socks
   d. which socks Gail wears cannot possibly have anything to do with the outcome of the matches she plays

9. You probably hope the correlation coefficient between using this Study Guide and getting an A in the course is
   a. +1.00
   b. -1.00
   c. 0.00
   d. +0.00

10. Whether to do research in a naturalistic or laboratory setting involves the issue of
    a. comprehensiveness versus cost
    b. testimonial versus science
    c. realism versus control
    d. objectivity versus subjectivity

11. The special treatment given to the subjects in the experimental group is called the
    a. hypothesis
    b. independent variable
    c. dependent variable
    d. control variable

12. Which one of the following is an example of random selection?
    a. winning numbers in the lottery
    b. annual National Football League player draft
    c. numbers people play in the lottery
    d. annual Miss America contest

13. The purpose of having a control group in an experiment is to
    a. show what results the opposite treatment would produce
    b. show how a different group would react to the treatment
    c. identify and rule out the behavior that results from simply participating in the experiment
    d. provide backup subjects in case any members of the experimental group are unable to continue

14. Should you volunteer to be a subject in a psychological experiment?
    a. no, because you are completely at the mercy of the researcher
    b. yes, because ethical guidelines protect subjects from danger or undue deception
    c. no, because they'll never tell you what the experiment was really about
    d. yes, because looking dumb or foolish occasionally makes us more humble

15. The attitude of most psychologists toward the use of animals in research is that
    a. scientists must have complete freedom to conduct research however they see fit
    b. ethical concerns are involved in research on humans but not on animals
    c. animals have no rights
    d. the issue is complicated and calls for a balance between animal rights and research needs

Answers for Module 2

True-False
1. T
2. F
3. T
4. F
5. T
6. F
7. T
8. F
9. T
10. F

Flashcards 1
1. d
2. c
3. j
4. g
5. a
6. b
7. f
8. i
9. e
10. h

Flashcards 2
1. j
2. h
3. b
4. i
5. e
6. a
7. c
8. f
9. g
10. d

Multiple-Choice
1. b
2. a
3. c
4. d
5. a
6. b
7. c
8. b
9. a
10. c
11. b
12. a
13. c
14. b
15. d

The Big Picture

Statement D

Are You Wired?

Rod Plotnik has an excellent page of electronic activities for you to try at the end of each module in his textbook. He calls them "Links to Learning." Try them. But first, you have to be wired. If you own a computer and are connected to the Internet, you already know what I mean. If you do not yet own a computer, its time to report to the campus Computer Center. Ask about obtaining an account and learning how to crawl the Web. If you don't have these skills, you are really doing school (and life) with one hand tied behind your back. Get wired! P.S. When you do, you can contact me directly by e-mail. **Profenos@aol.com**

Module 3

Brain's Building Blocks

Psychology as a Spectrum of Approaches

In the first module we got acquainted with psychology and learned some of its history. In the second module we saw how psychologists pursue knowledge. It is all interesting and important, yet you could say that psychology itself really begins in Module 3.

Remember the six approaches to psychology discussed in the first module? I find it useful to think of them as forming a spectrum, a rainbow of ideas. At one end there is the biological approach — the brain and nervous system Rod Plotnik describes in this module and the next. At the other end is the cross-cultural approach — the social interactions he covers in the last module, which examines social psychology.

I put the brain and nervous system at the beginning of the spectrum because the brain seems like the most obvious, most elemental starting point in psychology. You could just as well put social interaction first, however, because we become experts about other people long before we know anything about the brain. It doesn't really matter; the point is that the biological and cross-cultural approaches are polar opposites in how we think about psychology.

The other four approaches (psychoanalytic, cognitive, behavioral, and humanistic) fall somewhere within the spectrum. How you arrange them only reveals your biases about their relative importance. (Which process, for example, do you consider more dominant — thinking or feeling?)

Our Starting Point, Deep in the Fields of Biology and Chemistry

At the far extreme we are studying now, psychology is almost pure biology and chemistry. But when Rod Plotnik discusses social psychology in the last module, or whenever he brings in the cross-cultural approach on one of his Cultural Diversity explorations, you will see just how deeply psychology also reaches into the fields of anthropology and sociology.

Now you can appreciate why this module is not an easy one to master (and probably wasn't an easy one to write, either). It involves a mini-course in biology. You could easily get lost just trying to remember the key terms. My advice is to concentrate on the *processes* involved. Try to appreciate how the brain and nervous system stand between us and the rest of the world, helping us understand it and make the best use of it. I suppose loyal Trekkies could compare the brain to the Starship Enterprise, going bravely where no man has gone before, in the name of peace and the orderly regulation of our affairs.

Effective Student Tip 3

Meet Your New Friend, the Professor

Last semester it was Jason. Somewhat brash, but immediately likable, Jason came up to my desk after the first class and announced, "I'm getting an 'A' in your class!"

I like it when students make such pronouncements. For one thing, I learn their names right away. For another, we have the beginnings of a relationship. But most importantly, we have established a basis for working together. Now that I know Jason really wants an 'A,' I've got to pay attention to him and try to keep him on track. For his part, Jason has to make a genuine effort, unless he wants me to think he is just a blowhard. Some students may not have much of an investment in the class, but Jason and I know what we are doing. We're serious.

Meanwhile, that girl in the back who frowned all through the first lecture..., that guy who didn't take any notes..., and others who are just faces in the crowd for the first few weeks..., all these students could learn something useful from Jason.

Say hello to your professor right away. Let him or her get to know you. You need a friend in this new class, and what better person than the professor?

Your response...

What kind of relationship do you usually have with your teachers? Friendly? Formal? None at all?

Module 3: Brain's Building Blocks

Key Terms

Perhaps you know some of these terms from biology. Which will require the most study?

action potential	efferent [motor] neurons	neurotransmitters
afferent [sensory] neurons	end bulbs	Parkinson's disease
alcohol	genes	peripheral nervous system
all-or-none law	glial cells	phantom limb
Alzheimer's disease	interneuron	reflex
axon	ions	resting state
axon membrane	mescaline	reuptake
basal ganglia	mind-body question	sodium pump
cell body	myelin sheath	stereotaxic procedure
central nervous system	nerve impulse	synapse
curare	nerves	transmitters
dendrites	neuron	

Outline

- *Introduction*
    1. Losing one's mind (**Alzheimer's disease**)
    2. Diagnosis and causes
    - How does Alzheimer's disease illustrate the importance of the building blocks of the brain?
- A. *Overview: Human Brain*
    1. Development of the brain
        a. **Genes**
        b. Developmental stages
    2. Structure of the brain
        a. **Glial cells**
        b. **Neurons**
    3. Growth of new neurons
        a. Canary songs
        b. Primate brains
        c. Repairing the brain
    4. Brain versus mind
        a. **Mind-body question**
        b. How brain and mind influence each other
- B. *Neurons: Structure & Function*
    1. Three parts of the neuron
        a. **Cell body**

b. **Dendrites**

c. **Axon**

(1) **Myelin sheath**

(2) **End bulbs**

(3) **Synapse**

2. Alzheimer's disease and neurons

C. *Neurons versus Nerves*

1. Reattaching limbs

2. **Peripheral nervous system**

a. **Nerves**

b. Ability to regrow

3. **Central nervous system**

4. Regrowth or repair of neurons

D. *Sending Information*

1. Sequence: action potential

a. Feeling a sharp object

b. **Axon membrane**: chemical gates

c. **Ions**: charged particles

d. **Resting state**: charged battery

(1) Chemical batteries in the brain

(2) **Sodium pump**

e. **Action potential**: sending information

2. Sequence: nerve impulse

a. Sending information: **nerve impulse**

b. **All-or-none law**

c. Nerve impulse

d. Once begun, goes to end of the axon

e. Breaks in myelin sheath

f. End bulbs and neurotransmitters

E. *Transmitters*

1. Excitatory and inhibitory

a. **Transmitter**

b. Chemical keys and chemical locks

c. Excitatory transmitters and inhibitory transmitters

2. Neurotransmitters

a. **Neurotransmitters**

b. Chemical keys and chemical locks

c. Excitatory neurotransmitters and inhibitory neurotransmitters

3. Alcohol

   a. **Alcohol**

   b. GABA neurons

   c. GABA keys

4. New transmitters

   a. Endorphins

   b. Anandamide

   c. Nitric oxide

F. *Reflex Responses*

1. Definition and sequence of a **reflex**

2. Steps in a reflex

   a. Sensors

   b. **Afferent [sensory] neurons**

   c. **Interneuron**

   d. **Efferent [motor] neurons**

3. Functions of a reflex

G. *Research Focus: What Is a Phantom Limb?*

1. Case study

2. Definition and data

   (1) **Phantom limb**

   (2) Pain is real

3. Answers: old and new

H. *Cultural Diversity: Plants and Drugs*

   ❑ *If it is true that all human societies seem to discover or invent psychoactive drugs, what does this say about our species? Is there a lesson for psychology?*

1. Cocaine: blocking **reuptake**

2. **Curare**: blocking receptors

3. **Mescaline**: mimicking a neurotransmitter

I. *Application: Fetal Tissue Transplant*

1. **Parkinson's disease**

   a. Symptoms and treatment (L-dopa)

   b. **Basal ganglia**

2. Issues involving transplants

3. Fetal tissue transplants

   a. **Stereotaxic procedure**

   b. Results

   c. Brain scans

   d. Significance of fetal tissue transplant

Language Workout

What's That?

p. 47 prepare a full dinner **from scratch** = from the beginning
cognitive **deficits** = losses
the number of patients is **projected** to rise = predicted, expected
the worst is **yet to come** = coming in the future
the only **foolproof** test = certain

p. 48 the consistency of firm **Jell-O** = gelatin dessert

p. 49 **breeding** season = making babies
Nobel Prize winner = highest award in science

p. 50 myelin **sheath** = covering, protection
toxic substances = poisonous

p. 51 stringlike **bundles** = groups

p. 52 by using the **analogy** of a battery = comparison
very much like a lit **fuse** = starter to explode a bomb
segment by segment = part by part, piece by piece

p. 54 A transmitter is a chemical messenger that **transmit**s information = carries

p. 55 alcohol has **been around** for 3,000 years = existed, been available

p. 56 after eating **tainted** food = bad, full of harmful substances

p. 58 What is a **phantom** limb? = cannot be seen
like a ghost the brain **pieces together** a complete body image = organizes

p. 59 feelings of **euphoria** = great happiness
won a **Supreme Court** case = highest court in the United States

p. 60 A neuron from an 8-week-old **fetus** = unborn baby
the use of **fetal** brain tissue = from an unborn baby

p. 61 he still has **ups and downs** = good times and bad times

p. 64 **Quadriplegics** have damaged spinal cords = people who cannot use their arms or legs

Why a Comma?

The subject and verb are the heart of every sentence, the important action. So, any information that we put <u>before</u> the subject and verb needs to be separated by a comma. Look at the following sentences:

> Later, the millionaire counted his money.
> After dinner, the millionaire counted his money.
> With great enjoyment, the millionaire counted his money.
> Rubbing his hands with pleasure, the millionaire counted his money.
> Before he went to bed every night, the millionaire counted his money.

In all these sentences, the comma tells us that the first part is <u>not</u> the main action of the sentence. When we see the comma, it tells us that the <u>next</u> words — "the millionaire counted" — are the real action of the sentence.

So, the comma divides the introductory information from the main subject and verb. Try it yourself: read the following sentences. Each sentence needs one comma, so you decide where to put it:

Next to an elephant a mouse looks very small.

When she didn't see her mother the baby started crying.

After the war ended the soldiers all returned home.

Twenty-five years later he was released from prison.

With no warning at all to the students the teacher began to sing.

Carefully opening her umbrella Camilla stepped into the rain.

On the other hand the movie is three hours long.

Check your answers with the Answer Key at the end of this lesson.

Now, what happens if we reverse these sentences? Do we still need to use commas? What do you think?

A mouse looks very small next to an elephant.

The baby started crying when she didn't see her mother.

The soldiers all returned home after the war ended.

He was released from prison twenty-five years later.

The teacher began to sing with no warning at all to the students.

Camille stepped into the rain carefully opening her umbrella.

All these sentences are correct. In all of them, the important action — the main subject and verb — comes at the beginning of the sentence. This action is clear, so when the extra information comes at the end, we don't need to separate it with a comma. But what about the final sentence?

The movie is three hours long on the other hand.

This one is different. Here, we need the comma:

The movie is three hours long, on the other hand.

The information at the end — "on the other hand "— is <u>not</u> extra detail. It's not about time (like "after the war ended") or about place ("next to the elephant"). Instead, "on the other hand" is a phrase that organizes our thinking. It tells us that one fact is different from another fact. Words and phrases that help us to organize the ideas *must* be separated by commas, at the beginning of a sentence or at the end. Other words like this are: however, nevertheless, consequently, as a result, therefore, in addition, and others. We'll practice some of these in the next Module, and later too.

A Good Trick

Many people don't realize that we use commas when we speak. A comma is like a pause in speaking. Read the following sentences out loud, and see where you take a little break between words:

Running as fast as possible the mouse ran into its hole.

From beginning to end the movie was very funny.

As a result of his broken leg Tom could not play football for months.

You probably put in a little breath after the words "possible", "end", and "leg". Now, if you put in a pause when you are reading the sentence aloud, you will probably need to put in a comma when you are writing the sentence. The pause helps the listener make sense of the sentence. In the same way, a comma helps the reader understand the meaning. When you are not sure if you need a comma, try this trick: read your sentence aloud, and then put in a comma where you take a breath.

Answer Key

Next to an elephant , a mouse looks very small.
When she didn't see her mother , the baby started crying.
On the other hand , the movie is three hours long.
After the war ended , the soldiers all returned home.
Twenty-five years later , he was released from prison.
With no warning at all to the students , the teacher began to sing.
Carefully opening her umbrella , Camilla stepped into the rain.

The Big Picture

Which statement below offers the best summary of the larger significance of this module?

A No matter how much we discover about the structure and function of the brain, the workings of the mind will forever remain a mystery. Psychology should recognize that it must often yield to philosophy and religion.

B The widespread human craving for alcohol and drugs shows that while the brain may be essential to human survival, it can also be our biggest enemy. The brain is an ancient evolutionary left-over, but we are stuck with it.

C The brain could be described as an incredibly precise chemical and electrical information system. It is conceivable that brain science eventually will be able to decipher the composition and location of any single thought or idea.

D Alzheimer's disease and phantom limb pain illustrate the fragile nature of the brain and its tendency to malfunction and wear down. The conclusion is simply that we have to hope for the best.

E Having trouble learning all the terms in this module? Two words: brain transplant!

True-False

_____ 1. Science has determined that the mind is a separate entity from the brain.

_____ 2. If that ad "this is your brain on drugs" isn't scary enough, you can add the fact that damaged neurons are not regrown or replaced.

_____ 3. Most neurons have a cell body, dendrites, and an axon.

_____ 4. A reflex is an action you have learned to execute so fast you don't think about it.

_____ 5. The "all-or-none law" refers to the fact that ions are either positively or negatively charged.

_____ 6. Neurotransmitters are the keys that unlock the receptors of dendrites, cell bodies, muscles, and organs.

_____ 7. The steady reduction in an important neurotransmitter in the brain is part of the cause of Alzheimer's disease.

_____ 8. Nerves are located in the central nervous system; neurons are in the peripheral nervous system.

_____ 9. Drugs like cocaine and mescaline achieve their effects by interfering with the normal workings of neurotransmitters.

_____ 10. The stereotaxic procedure is the treatment of Parkinson's disease with a drug called L-dopa.

Flashcards 1

___ 1. action potential
___ 2. all-or-none law
___ 3. glial cells
___ 4. ions
___ 5. mind-body question
___ 6. nerve impulse
___ 7. neuron
___ 8. neurotransmitters
___ 9. phantom limb
___ 10. reflex

a. brain cell with specialized extensions for receiving and transmitting electrical signals
b. chemical keys with a particular shape that only fits a similarly shaped chemical lock or receptor
c. series of separate action potentials that take place segment by segment down length of axon
d. brain cells that provide scaffolding, insulation, chemicals to protect and support neuron growth
e. an unlearned, involuntary reaction to some stimulus; prewired by genetic instructions
f. if an action potential starts at the beginning of an axon, it will continue to very end of axon
g. asks how complex mental activities can be generated by physical properties of the brain
h. chemical particles that have electrical charges; opposite charges attract and like charges repel
i. vivid experience of sensations and feelings coming from a limb that has been amputated
j. tiny electrical current that is generated when positive sodium ions rush inside the axon

Flashcards 2

___ 1. Alzheimer's disease
___ 2. curare
___ 3. dendrites
___ 4. end bulbs
___ 5. mescaline
___ 6. Parkinson's disease
___ 7. reuptake
___ 8. sodium pump
___ 9. stereotaxic procedure
___ 10. synapse

a. a chemical process responsible for keeping axon charged by returning sodium ions outside axon
b. incurable, fatal disease involving brain damage, with memory loss, deterioration of personality
c. miniature containers at extreme ends of axon branches; store chemicals called neurotransmitters
d. a drug that enters bloodstream and blocks receptors on muscles, causing paralysis
e. tremors, shakes, progressive slowing of voluntary movements with feelings of depression
f. fixing a patient's head in a holder and drilling a small hole through the skull; syringe guided to a brain area
g. process of removing neurotransmitters from synapse by reabsorbtion into terminal buttons
h. branchlike extensions that arise from cell body and receive and pass signals to cell body
i. a drug that causes arousal, visual hallucinations; acts like neurotransmitter norepinephrine
j. very small space between terminal button and adjacent dendrite, muscle fiber, or body organ

Multiple-Choice

___ 1. Rod Plotnik begins with the example of Alzheimer's disease to illustrate the
   a. sad fact that the brain inevitably wears out
   b. hope offered by a new operation for those afflicted with the disease
   c. type of disease that could be prevented if people would take care of themselves
   d. key importance of the building blocks that make up the brain's informational network

___ 2. Is the mind the same as the brain? Rod Plotnik says that the
   a. the mind must be separate — otherwise there would be no soul
   b. brain and mind are closely linked, and researchers are studying these links
   c. physical brain is the only thing — there is no actual "mind"
   d. questions like this are best left to philosophers

___ 3. Believe it or not, your brain contains about _____ cells (neurons plus glial cells)
   a. one thousand
   b. 100 thousand
   c. a trillion
   d. a gad-zillion

___ 4. Unlike nerves, neurons
   a. are not replaced or regrown
   b. have the ability to regrow or reattach
   c. are located outside the brain and spinal cord
   d. have no dendrites or axons

___ 5. The purpose of the myelin sheath is to
   a. receive signals from neurons, muscles, or sense organs
   b. wrap around and insulate an axon
   c. protect the nucleus of the cell body
   d. drain dangerous electricity away from the brain

___ 6. An unlearned, involuntary reaction to a stimulus is called a/n
   a. explosion
   b. electrical burst
   c. conditioned reflex
   d. reflex

___ 7. The purpose of the ions in the axon's membrane is to
   a. generate a miniature electrical current
   b. plug up the tiny holes in the membrane's semipermeable skin
   c. pump excess sodium out of the neuron
   d. dry up the watery fluid that collects in the membrane

___ 8. On many nights you hear the cry "Let's party!" Odd, because actually alcohol
   a. increases tension and anxiety
   b. sharpens social judgment, therefore heightening inhibitions and self-doubt
   c. depresses activity of the central nervous system, dulling alertness
   d. improves memory, creating the ideal time to study

_____ 9. John Thomas' arms could be reattached because
   a. neurons have the ability to regrow, regenerate, or reattach
   b. neurons are part of the central nervous system
   c. nerves have the ability to regrow, regenerate, or reattach
   d. nerves are part of the peripheral nervous system

_____ 10. The "all-or-none law" explains what happens when
   a. positively and negatively charged ions meet
   b. an impulse starts at the beginning of an axon
   c. electrical impulses spread throughout the body
   d. your brain gets the idea of a six-pack

_____ 11. If receptors in muscle fibers are thought of as locks, the keys are
   a. the action potential of the axon
   b. synapses
   c. the resting state of the axon
   d. neurotransmitters

_____ 12. The effect of a neurotransmitter on an adjacent neuron, muscle, or organ is
   a. excitatory
   b. inhibitory
   c. either excitatory or inhibitory
   d. determined by the all-or-none law

_____ 13. Endorphin, a natural pain killer in the brain, offers an example of
   a. the key role that neurotransmitters play in regulating our lives
   b. the way neurotransmitters out of control can cause diseases like Alzheimer's
   c. hope for finding a cure for Parkinson's disease
   d. left-over entities in the brain (like the appendix in the body)

_____ 14. Donald, who had to amputate his own leg to survive an accident, now suffers from phantom limb pain. Researchers suspect that his pain comes from
   a. cut nerves in the stump
   b. a body image stored in the brain
   c. the spinal cord
   d. terrifying memories of the horrible ordeal

_____ 15. The newest hope for sufferers of Parkinson's disease is treating damaged cells with
   a. a new drug called L-dopa
   b. massive injections of dopamine
   c. genetically engineered cells grown in the laboratory
   d. transplanted human fetal brain tissue

Answers for Module 3

True-False
1. F
2. T
3. T
4. F
5. F
6. T
7. T
8. F
9. T
10. F

Flashcards 1
1. j
2. f
3. d
4. h
5. g
6. c
7. a
8. b
9. i
10. e

Flashcards 2
1. b
2. d
3. h
4. c
5. i
6. e
7. g
8. a
9. f
10. j

Multiple-Choice
1. d
2. b
3. c
4. a
5. b
6. d
7. a
8. c
9. c
10. b
11. d
12. c
13. a
14. b
15. d

The Big Picture

Statement C

Electronic Study Guide

The Study Guide you are reading is also available in an electronic version you can use on your computer. It is available in Macintosh or PC format. Ask at your bookstore, or use the order form on the last page of this book.

Module 4

Incredible Nervous System

A Golden Age of Biology

Not long ago a researcher commenting on a startling and provocative new idea about human functioning observed that we are living in "a Golden Age of biology." Hardly a week goes by without the media reporting a new breakthrough in genetics, evolutionary science, or human health. When early nineteenth-century scientists discovered the Rosetta stone, they suddenly had a blueprint that unlocked the secrets of ancient Egypt. Today's scientists are mapping the genes and discovering the blueprint for how we humans are constructed.

Progress in psychology has been no less dramatic. Neuroscientists, who study the brain and nervous system, are coming closer and closer to explaining human consciousness, perhaps the greatest mystery of all.

In the previous module, Rod Plotnik posed the question, are mind and brain two things, or the same thing? This is an old argument in psychology and philosophy. Plotnik gave you some of the reasoning on both sides. This debate is rapidly changing, however. For one thing, it is becoming less the province of philosophy and more the property of neuroscience. Philosophers continue to attempt to use logic and reason to find an answer, but for the first time neuroscientists are able to look into the functioning brain (Plotnik tells how) and conduct laboratory experiments on thinking in action.

The Biological Approach to Psychology

In the first module, Rod Plotnik carefully laid out six major approaches to psychology. It is hard to overstress the importance of becoming familiar with these six approaches. If you can learn them, and begin to see their reflections in all the facts and ideas you encounter in the textbook, you will be well on your way to having an overall view of the structure of the field of psychology and a real grasp of its organization.

The previous module, on the workings of the brain, and this one, on the functioning of the nervous system, contain the heart of the biological approach to psychology. Understand that the six approaches are not simply matters of the personal interests of researchers and practicing psychologists. They are bold claims to explain *everything* in psychology, and to have the best answers to our needs for specific health and therapeutic applications. Right now, the biological approach seems to be winning the debate. We live in an exciting time.

Effective Student Tip 4

Why You Must Be Effective in College

Effectiveness comes into play in all our endeavors, the most trivial as well as the most crucial. Consider a systems analyst, triumphant in the solution of a tricky problem (effectiveness confirmed), who then wheels around and fires a paper ball in a perfect jump shot into the wastebasket across the room (effective again). The urge behind each effort was effectiveness, but realistically it's more important that our systems analyst solve the problem than make the imaginary buzzer-beating shot.

If we were only dealing with office wastebasketball, we could afford to ignore the psychological factor of effectiveness. The stakes aren't very high. College is a different matter — probably the highest stakes in your life so far.

College is an essential rite of passage in our society, a critical bridge over which you cross into adulthood. College is more important today than ever, with at least two outcomes of great consequence: (1) College may determine whether you gain admittance to a technologically sophisticated world of commerce, industry, and the professions. (2) College helps shape your self-esteem and psychological health.

That's why you must handle your college experience effectively. Your future depends on it.

Your response...

Realistically, and aside from your "official" goals, what do you hope to get out of going to college?

Key Terms

There are more than the usual numbers of Key Terms in this module because it relies so heavily on biological concepts and ideas. If you have taken some biology, these terms will come fairly easily. If not, you will have to work harder on this module than on many others. Remind yourself that psychology is becoming an increasingly biological discipline. The work is difficult, but the rewards are great.

adrenal glands
amygdala
anencephaly
anterior pituitary
auditory association area
autonomic nervous system
Broca's area and Broca's aphasia
central nervous system
cerebellum
chromosome
cortex
endocrine system
fight-flight response
forebrain
fragile X syndrome
frontal lobe
frontal lobotomy
gene

gonads
hippocampus
homeostasis
hypothalamus
limbic system
medulla
midbrain
motor cortex
MRI scan (magnetic resonance imaging)
neglect syndrome
occipital lobe
pancreas
parasympathetic division
parietal lobe
peripheral nervous system
PET scan (positron emission tomography)
pituitary gland

pons
posterior pituitary
primary auditory cortex
primary visual cortex
sex or gender differences [in the brain]
somatic nervous system
somatosensory cortex
split-brain operation
sympathetic division
temporal lobe
thalamus
theory of evolution
thyroid
visual agnosia
visual association area
Wernicke's area and Wernicke's aphasia
zygote

Outline

- *Introduction*
    1. Lucy's brain: earliest ancestor
    2. Baby Theresa's brain: fatal flaw
    3. Steve's brain: cruel fate
    4. Scott's brain: Wrong instructions
    ☐ What do Rod Plotnik's wildly different examples of these four unusual brains tell us about the development and functioning of our own brains?

A. *Genes & Evolution*
   1. Genetic instructions
      a. Fertilization
      b. **Zygote**
      c. **Chromosome**
      d. Chemical alphabet (DNA)

e. **Genes** and proteins

f. Genome

g. **Fragile X syndrome**

2. Evolution of the human brain

   a. **Theory of evolution**

   b. Increases in brain size

B. *Studying the Living Brain*

1. New techniques

2. **MRI and fMRI brain scans (magnetic resonance imaging)**

3. **PET brain scans (positron emission tomography)**

4. Picturing thoughts (cognitive neuroscience)

C. *Organization of the Brain*

1. Divisions of the nervous system

   a. Major divisions of nervous system

      (1) **Central nervous system** (CNS)

      (2) **Peripheral nervous system** (PNS)

   b. Subdivisions of PNS

      (1) **Somatic nervous system**

         (a) Afferent (sensory) fibers

         (b) Efferent (motor) fibers

      (2) **Autonomic nervous system** (ANS)

   c. Subdivisions of ANS

      (1) **Sympathetic division**

      (2) **Parasympathetic division**

4. Major parts of the brain

   a. **Forebrain**

   b. **Midbrain**

   c. Hindbrain

      (1) **Pons**

      (2) **Medulla**

      (3) **Cerebellum**

D. *Control Centers: Four Lobes*

1. Overall view of the cortex

☐ *What is the anatomical problem for which the cortex is a clever solution?*

   a. Wrinkled **cortex**

   b. Four lobes

   c. Baby Theresa's brain: a fatal defect (**anencephaly**)

☐ *Why did baby Theresa live only nine days?*

2. **Frontal lobe**: functions
   a. A terrible accident (story of Phineas Gage)
   b. **Frontal lobotomy**
   c. Results of lobotomies
3. Frontal lobe: functions
   a. **Motor cortex**
   b. Organization and function of motor cortex
   c. Other functions of frontal lobe
4. **Parietal lobe**: functions
   a. Location of **somatosensory cortex**
   b. Organization of somatosensory cortex
   c. Other functions of parietal lobe
5. **Temporal lobe**: functions
   a. **Primary auditory cortex** and **auditory association area**
   b. **Broca's area** and **Broca's aphasia**
   c. **Wernicke's area** and **Wernicke's aphasia**
6. **Occipital lobe**: functions
   a. **Primary visual cortex** and **visual association area**
   b. **Visual agnosia**
   c. **Neglect syndrome**

E. *Limbic System: Old Brain*
  1. Structures and functions of **limbic system**
  ☐ Why is the limbic system sometimes called our "old brain" or our "animal brain"?
  ☐ What is the function of each of its four parts?
       a. **Hypothalamus**
       b. **Amygdala**
       c. **Thalamus**
       d. **Hippocampus**
  2. Autonomic nervous system
     a. Sympathetic nervous system
        (1) **Sympathetic division**
        (2) Increases physiological arousal
        (3) **fight-flight response**
     b. Parasympathetic nervous system
        (1) **Parasympathetic division**
        (2) Decreases physiological arousal
     c. **Homeostasis**

Module 4: Incredible Nervous System

F. Endocrine System
1. A hormonal system: **endocrine system**
   ☐ *In what way is the endocrine system similar to the nervous system?*
2. Endocrine system's glands
   a. **Hypothalamus**
   b. **Pituitary gland**
   c. **Posterior pituitary**
   d. **Anterior pituitary**
   e. **Pancreas**
   f. **Thyroid**
   g. **Adrenal glands**
   h. **Gonads**

G. Research Focus: Sex Differences in the Brain?
1. Science and politics: **sex or gender differences**
2. Differences in solving problems
   ☐ *What factors might explain the existence of sex differences in the brain?*
3. Differences between female and male brains
   ☐ *How important do you think these differences are in everyday life?*

H. Cultural Diversity: Brain Size and Racial Myths
1. Skull size and intelligence
   a. Results (Samuel George Morton)
   b. Reanalyzed (Stephen Jay Gould)
2. Brain size and intelligence
   a. Female brains
   b. Correlations

I. Application: Split Brain
1. **Split-brain operation**
   a. Seizures
   b. Major breakthrough
   c. Testing a patient
   ☐ *What does the split-brain operation reveal about how the brain works?*
2. Behaviors following split brain
3. Different functions
   a. Left hemisphere
      (1) Verbal
      (2) Mathematical
      (3) Analytical

b. Right hemisphere
      (1) Nonverbal
      (2) Spatial
      (3) Holistic
4. Left-brained or right-brained?
   a. Am I "left-brained" or "right-brained"?
   b. How is my brain organized?
   c. Does the brain get better with use?

For Psych Majors Only...

The Brain and Nervous System: Match each system or structure to its main components or functions.

___ 1. central nervous system
___ 2. peripheral nervous system
___ 3. somatic nervous system
___ 4. autonomic nervous system
___ 5. frontal lobe
___ 6. parietal lobe
___ 7. temporal lobe
___ 8. occipital lobe
___ 9. left hemisphere
___ 10. right hemisphere

a. sympathetic and parasympathetic divisions
b. verbal, mathematical, analytical
c. motor cortex
d. brain and spinal cord
e. primary auditory cortex
f. primary visual cortex
g. somatic and autonomic nervous systems
h. afferent (sensory) and efferent (motor) fibers
i. nonverbal, spatial, holistic
j. somatosensory cortex

Language Workout

What's That?

p. 67 **Anthropologists** think that Lucy did not make tools = scientists who study the customs and characteristics of different races and groups
He **babbled** = spoke nonsense sounds
The **press** called her Baby Theresa = newspapers and TV news

p. 68 Each **rung** of the DNA ladder = step
a **three-fold** increase = multiplied three times

p. 69 three major **milestones** = important events

p. 70 maximum **neural** activity = in the nervous system

p. 71 A person might go into a **coma** = complete loss of consciousness, the result of illness or injury

Module 4: Incredible Nervous System

the area of cognitive **neuro**science = study of the nervous system in relation to learning

p. 72 two major **nervous systems** = body system connecting brain, spinal cord, nerves and other parts

p. 73 a long column of **neurons** = cells of nervous system

p. 75 a Portuguese **neuro**logist = doctor who specializes in problems of nervous system

he did no controlled or **follow-up** studies = later, to check results

p. 76 emotional **swings** = changes, from very happy to very unhappy

p. 77 you can easily **tell** a key from a nickel = feel the difference
analyzing the positions of **chess pieces** on the board = objects used in a board game

p. 80 many kinds of **fleeting** memories = quickly disappearing

p. 81 **optimum** level, **optimum** functioning = top level

p. 82 Too little growth hormone produces **dwarfism** = condition where the body will not grow normally
too much causes **gigantism** = condition where the body continues growing beyond normal limits
the larger the brain the higher the **IQ** = Intelligence Quotient, a measurement of ability to learn, compared to other people

p. 90 they sort of **bumbled** through life = moved in a clumsy way, without plans

Figure It Out

(Experts think that) two forces are responsible.
= Two forces **are thought to be** responsible.

(Experts think that) she lived mainly on leaves and fruit.
= She **is thought to have** lived mainly on leaves and fruit.

(Experts think that) they added meat to their diets.
= They **are thought to have** added meat to their diets.

TRY IT

(Experts think that) the earth's temperature is rising.
= The earth's temperature _____ rising.

(Experts think that) cats are unable to see colors.
= Cats _____ unable to see colors.

(Many experts think) that Napoleon died from poison.
= Napoleon _____ from poison.

(Some experts think) that snakes evolved into birds.
= Snakes _____ into birds.

Build Your Word Power

Relatively means in comparison. For example: let's describe the weather in Toronto.

Compared to Mexico, the weather in Toronto is cold.
Compared to the North Pole, the weather in Toronto is not so cold.
So, we can say: The weather in Toronto is **relatively cold**.
This means it is fairly cold, in relation to other places.

Another example: let's describe Grandpa.

Compared to other people his age, Grandpa is strong.
So, we can say: Grandpa is **relatively strong**.

TRY IT

Plotnik's textbook is over 500 pages long.
That's fairly long, but not as long as an encyclopedia.
So, Plotnik's book is _____

A mouse looks small next to an elephant.
Still, a mouse is not as small as a spider.
So, a mouse is _____

It's fairly expensive to buy a computer.
Compared to buying a car, a computer is not so expensive.
Compared to buying a radio, a computer is quite expensive.
So, a computer is _____

Most nurses earn less money than most doctors.
Nurses earn less than many lawyers and engineers, too.
Of course, nurses earn more than street cleaners.
Therefore, nurses earn _____ money than other professionals.

NOTICE THE MEANING

a relatively new area [p. 71]
relatively more area... relatively less area [p. 76]
a relatively poor sense of smell [p. 79]
relatively simple [p. 87]

Answer Key

The earth's temperature **is thought to be** rising.
Cats **are thought to be** unable to see colors.
Napoleon **is thought to have died** from poison.
Snakes **are thought to have evolved** into birds.
So, Plotnik's book is **relatively long**.
So, a mouse is **relatively small**.
So, a computer is **relatively expensive**.
Therefore, nurses earn **relatively less** money than other professionals do.

The Big Picture

Which statement below offers the best summary of the larger significance of this module?

A   The "nervous system" is the name that is commonly given to a number of quite separate biological functions. It really should not be called a "system" at all.

B   The nervous system (including the brain) is an incredible regulatory arrangement that governs all the necessary functions and processes of human life. The nervous system makes us the most adaptable species on earth.

C   The finding that there are significant sex or gender differences in the brain suggests that there must be equally significant biological differences separating the various races and ethnic groups around the world.

D   The nervous system and the brain make up the two halves of the story of human biology: the brain gives the orders and the nervous system carries them out. We could live without a nervous system, but not without a brain.

E   The "nervous system" is the method by which psych students get ready for an exam.

True-False

_____ 1. The brain and the spinal cord make up the central nervous system.

_____ 2. The right and left hemispheres of the brain make up the peripheral nervous system.

_____ 3. More than any other part, it is the operation of the hindbrain that makes you a person.

_____ 4. When Igor hands Dr. Frankenstein a fresh brain, what we see quivering in his hands is the cortex.

_____ 5. As human society evolves, the limbic system incorporates cooperative and positive tendencies and feelings into the brain.

_____ 6. The general tendency of the autonomic nervous system is homeostasis.

_____ 7. In the endocrine system, glands secrete hormones that affect many important bodily processes.

_____ 8. Psychologists now know that human intelligence is determined by both skull size and brain size.

_____ 9. The need to perform split-brain operations for medical purposes gives science a rare look at the degree of specialization in the brain's two hemispheres.

_____ 10. Science has finally explained why people are so different: each human being is either left-brained or right-brained.

Flashcards 1

____ 1. autonomic nervous system
____ 2. central nervous system
____ 3. cortex
____ 4. forebrain
____ 5. frontal lobe
____ 6. gene
____ 7. MRI scan (magnetic resonance imaging)
____ 8. peripheral nervous system
____ 9. PET scan (positron emission tomography)
____ 10. somatic nervous system

a. measuring a radioactive solution absorbed by brain cells; shows the activity of various neurons
b. regulates heart rate, breathing, blood pressure, other mainly involuntary movements
c. a thin layer of cells covering the entire surface of the forebrain; folds over on itself to form a large area
d. passing nonharmful radio frequencies through brain and measuring how signals interact with brain cells
e. a network of nerves that connect either to sensory receptors or to muscles you can move voluntarily
f. the largest part of the brain; has right and left sides (hemispheres) responsible for many functions
g. made up of the brain and spinal cord; carries information back and forth between brain and body
h. a relatively large cortical area at the front part of the brain; involved in many functions; like an executive
i. a specific segment on the strand of DNA that contains instructions for building the brain and body
j. all nerves that extend from the spinal cord and carry messages to and from muscles, glands, sense organs

Flashcards 2

____ 1. amygdala
____ 2. cerebellum
____ 3. endocrine system
____ 4. fight-flight response
____ 5. gonads
____ 6. homeostasis
____ 7. limbic system
____ 8. occipital lobe
____ 9. parietal lobe
____ 10. temporal lobe

a. involved in processing visual information, which includes seeing colors and recognizing objects
b. keeping the body's level of arousal in balance for optimum functioning
c. involved in hearing, speaking coherently, understanding verbal and written material
d. core of the forebrain; involved in many motivational behaviors and with organizing emotional behaviors
e. located directly behind the frontal lobe; its functions include the sense of touch, temperature, and pain
f. a system of glands which secrete hormones that affect organs, muscles, and other glands in the body
g. glands (ovaries in females, testes in males) that regulate sexual development and reproduction
h. involved in forming, recognizing, and remembering emotional experiences and facial expressions
i. a state of increased physiological arousal that helps body cope with and survive threatening situations
j. located at back of brain; involved in coordinating (but not in initiating) voluntary movements

Multiple-Choice

_____ 1. Rod Plotnik introduces us to four very different persons — Lucy, baby Theresa, Steve, and Scott — to show that
   a. one side of the brain controls most human behavior
   b. brain damage can strike almost anyone at any time
   c. humans have evolved an incredibly complex nervous system
   d. the brain will never be fully understood

_____ 2. The behavioral problems plaguing Scott, the child who had inherited fragile X syndrome, illustrate the role of _____ in human development
   a. evolution
   b. genetic instructions
   c. fertilization
   d. skull size

_____ 3. The new techniques of brain scans have a great advantage:
   a. they permit a look inside the living, functioning brain
   b. the information they yield is more than worth the harm they do
   c. it is no longer necessary to perform frontal lobotomies in mental hospitals
   d. it's so hard to find volunteers for experimental brain surgery

_____ 4. Which one of the following is *not* included in the peripheral nervous system?
   a. somatic nervous system
   b. autonomic nervous system
   c. limbic nervous system
   d. sympathetic nervous system

_____ 5. Which one of the following is *not* one of the three main parts of the human brain?
   a. forebrain
   b. midbrain
   c. hindbrain
   d. topbrain

_____ 6. The cerebellum is an important part of the hindbrain that
   a. initiates voluntary movements
   b. influences social-emotional behavior
   c. coordinates voluntary movements and makes them graceful
   d. makes humans distinct from all other animals

_____ 7. The cortex is all folded and crinkled up because the human brain
   a. grows so fast during the first three years of life
   b. is divided into four separate lobes
   c. is protected by the skull
   d. evolved faster than the human skull that holds it

_____ 8. The incredible story of Phineas Gage's accident shows that
   a. the frontal lobe is critical to personality
   b. a person lives at best in a vegetative state after a frontal lobotomy
   c. the frontal lobe is wired to the opposite side of the body
   d. the frontal lobe receives sensory information from the body

_____ 9. Wernicke's aphasia and Broca's aphasia are evidence that
   a. language abilities are more inherited than acquired
   b. special areas of the lobes of the cortex control language abilities
   c. if one area is damaged, the other takes over for it
   d. human language is so complex that a number of things can go wrong with it

_____ 10. When you understand the limbic system, you begin to see why
   a. modern humans are so far advanced over their prehistoric ancestors
   b. a human can do so much more than an alligator
   c. modern society is still plagued by so many primitive behaviors
   d. the social life of human beings is so much more complex than that of alligators

_____ 11. If you saw a snake crawling out from under your car, what would happen next is an example of the
   a. fight-flight response
   b. homeostatic reaction
   c. parasympathetic push
   d. arouse-or-die response

_____ 12. Me Tarzan, you Jane. Therefore, according to research on sex differences in the brain:
   a. me spatial, you verbal
   b. me verbal, you spatial
   c. me emotional, you logical
   d. me lusty, you cold

_____ 13. The sad history of research on the relationship between intelligence and skull and brain size shows that
   a. when a Nobel Prize is involved, some scientists will fudge their data
   b. science can be influenced by the prejudices of the times
   c. science is not always the best way to answer a question about human behavior
   d. sloppy measurement can undercut a sound hypothesis

_____ 14. Which one of the following is *not* true about hemispheric specializations?
   a. left hemisphere – verbal
   b. right hemisphere – holistic
   c. left hemisphere – mathematical
   d. right hemisphere – analytic

_____ 15. Are you left-brained or right-brained? The best answer is that you are probably
   a. left-brained, since you are a college student
   b. constantly using both hemispheres
   c. right-brained if you are female and left-brained if you are male
   d. left-brained, since most people are

Answers for Module 4

True-False	Flashcards 1	Flashcards 2	Multiple-Choice
1. T	1. b	1. h	1. c
2. F	2. g	2. j	2. b
3. F	3. c	3. f	3. a
4. T	4. f	4. i	4. c
5. F	5. h	5. g	5. d
6. T	6. i	6. b	6. c
7. T	7. d	7. d	7. d
8. F	8. j	8. a	8. a
9. T	9. a	9. e	9. b
10. F	10. e	10. c	10. c
			11. a
			12. a
			13. b
			14. d
			15. b

The Big Picture

Statement B

"The Brain and Nervous System" quiz

1. d 2. g 3. h 4. a 5. c 6. j 7. e 8. f 9. b 10. i

> *Multiple-Choice Questions*
>
> Most multiple-choice questions have a stem and four alternatives. The first trick in handling multiple-choice questions is to know what the question is asking. One way to think about this is to ask yourself, "Which alternative turns the stem into a true statement?"

Talk to me! I love to hear "You've got mail!"   Profenos@aol.com

Module 5

Sensation

What is Real?

Back in the happy days before I studied psychology, I simply "knew" that there was a real world out there and that it came straight into my mind (I never thought to wonder what the "mind" is or how it works). When you study sensation (Module 5), perception (Module 6), and consciousness (Module 7), however, it gets confusing. If you don't watch out, you could find yourself in the predicament of poor Descartes, whose search for a proof of existence had him doubting his own existence, until he decided that just thinking about the problem must prove he was there to do it.

The story begins in this module, with the mechanisms of the sense organs (eye, ear, nose, tongue, and skin) and the processes by which they receive stimuli (light and sound waves, chemicals, and pressures) from the environment. But be prepared for a disappointment: it doesn't mean a thing.

How We Relate to the World

Suppose that right in the middle of writing a great paper your computer suddenly crashed and all you could recover was a data dump of everything it "knew" about your paper. You would experience a similar disappointment. All you would see on the printout would be a long succession of ones and zeros, the binary code in which computers work. It wouldn't mean a thing.

The processes of perception transform meaningless sensations into useful information. It's sort of like the word processing software that turns those ones and zeros in your paper into (hopefully) great prose. Now the raw sensations begin to take on meaning, as they are interpreted by the perceptual processes involved.

Are we finally in contact with the real world? In a way, but notice that we are also one step removed from that world, apprehending it second-hand through the possibly distorted mechanisms of perception. Even then, exactly *what* do the perceptions mean? The researchers in neuroscience we mentioned in the previous module are trying to find out. We could guess that the answer will involve a complex interaction of cognition and emotion, each enriching the information and making it more useful to us.

We could say that at last we have the real world, but now it is at least three steps removed, as we experience it in our conscious (and unconscious?) mind. How real is it anymore? Perhaps psychology must leave the question of reality to philosophers and theologians. I still believe it's out there, but now I know that what is in my mind is constructed, not real.

Effective Student Tip 5

Go Ahead, Ask Me

I am always astounded when I review my class lists early in the new semester. There are more than a few students who have not yet said a word in class.

For some, it is politeness. Heaven knows, I am flying, and they hesitate to interrupt. For others, it is modesty. Maybe the point they would make isn't all that brilliant. For still others it is excruciating shyness. If they did speak up, they just know the class would turn as one and sneer, "You idiot!"

For each of these students, an effective strategy would be to ask a simple question. A good question can be just the thing to begin your involvement in the class.

As you prepare for the next class, find something in the textbook or your lecture notes that really interests you. What more would you like to know? Think how you could ask about it in a short, clear question. Pick a moment when your question is relevant, then ask away. (If you feel you can't do it, ask your first question either before or after class. It's a start.)

What do you get out of it? Aside from the information you wanted, you have made contact with the professor and your fellow students. You have demonstrated to yourself that you can talk in class. And the class is more fun now.

Your response...

How comfortable do you feel in class? Do you talk? Is talking something you enjoy, or dread?

Key Terms

There are so many key terms in the module because it covers all the senses. The terms may be easier to learn if you organize them by the senses they help explain.

acupuncture	flavor	place theory
adaptation	frequency theory	placebo
afterimage	gate control theory of pain	placebo effect
auditory association area	hair cells	primary auditory cortex
auditory canal	iris	pupil
auditory nerve	lens	retina
basilar membrane	loudness	rods
cochlea	Meniere's disease	sensations
cochlear implant	middle ear	sense of touch
color blindness	monochromats	somatosensory cortex
conduction deafness	motion sickness	sound waves
cones	nearsightedness	taste
cornea	neural deafness	taste buds
decibel	olfaction	transduction
dichromats	olfactory cells	trichromatic theory
direction of a sound	opponent-process theory	tympanic membrane
disgust	ossicles	vertigo
double-blind design	outer ear	vestibular system
endorphins	pain	visible spectrum
external ear	perceptions	
farsightedness	pitch	

Outline

- *Introduction*
    1. Electric billboard in the brain
    2. Three characteristics of all senses

    ☐ *Can you explain how the three characteristics of all senses produce the experiences of seeing, hearing, smelling, touching, tasting, and position?*

    a. **Transduction**

    b. **Adaptation**

    c. **Sensations** versus **perceptions**

  A. *Eye: Vision*
    1. Stimulus
        a. Invisible: too short
        b. Visible: just right (**visible spectrum**)
        c. Invisible: too long

    ☐ *What is the visible spectrum and what makes it visible?*

2. Structure and function
- ☐ *What happens when you look at something? Can you explain the process of looking?*
    a. Image reversed
    b. Light waves
    c. **Cornea**
    d. **Pupil**
    e. **Iris**
    f. **Lens**
    g. **Retina**
    h. Eyeball's shape
        (1) Normal vision
        (2) **Nearsightedness**
        (3) **Farsightedness**
        (4) Eye surgery
3. **Retina**: a miniature camera-computer
    a. Photoreceptors
    b. **Rods**
    c. **Cones**
    d. Transduction
    e. Nerve impulses, optic nerve and blind spot
4. Visual pathways: eye to brain
    a. Optic nerve
    b. Primary visual cortex
        (1) Specialized cells
        (2) Stimulation or blindness
    c. Visual association areas
    d. PET scans reveal visual activity
5. Color vision
    a. Making colors from wave lengths
    b. **Trichromatic theory**
    c. **Opponent-process theory**
        (1) **Afterimage**
        (2) Excited or inhibited
    d. Theories combined
    e. **Color blindness**
        (1) **Monochromats**
        (2) **Dichromats**

B. *Ear: Audition*
   1. Stimulus: **sound waves**
      a. Amplitude and **loudness**
      b. Frequency and **pitch**
   2. Measuring sound waves
      a. **Decibel**
      b. Decibels and deafness
   3. Outer, middle, and inner ear
      a. **Outer ear**
         (1) **External ear**
         (2) **Auditory canal**
         (3) **Tympanic membrane**
      b. **Middle ear**
         (1) **Ossicles**
         (2) Hammer, anvil and stirrup
         (3) Oval window
      c. Inner ear
         (1) **Cochlea**
         (2) **Hair cells** and **basilar membrane**
         (3) **Auditory nerve**
      d. Auditory brain areas
         (1) **Primary auditory cortex**
         (2) **Auditory association area**
   4. Auditory cues
      a. Calculating **direction of a sound**
      b. Calculating pitch
         (1) **Frequency theory**
         (2) **Place theory**
      c. Calculating **loudness**
C. *Vestibular System*
   1. Position and balance: **vestibular system**
      a. Semicircular canals
      b. Sensing position of head, keeping head upright, maintaining balance
   2. **Motion sickness**
   3. **Meniere's disease** and **vertigo**

D. **Chemical Senses**
   1. **Taste**
      a. Four basic tastes: sweet, salty, sour, bitter
      b. Surface of the tongue
      c. **Taste buds**
      d. All tongues are not the same
      e. **Flavor**: taste and smell
   2. Smell or **olfaction**
      a. Stimulus
      b. **Olfactory cells**
      c. Sensations and memories
      d. Functions of olfaction
   ☐ *What is a recently discovered function of olfaction?*
E. **Touch**
   1. **Sense of touch**
      a. Skin
      b. Hair receptors
      c. Free nerve endings
      d. Pacinian corpuscle
   2. Brain areas: **somatosensory cortex**
F. *Cultural Diversity: Disgust versus Delight*
   1. Sensations and psychological factors
   ☐ *Although most foods cause delight, some cause disgust. Why?*
      a. **Disgust**
   ☐ *Why is this experience automatically translated into a facial expression?*
      b. Cultural influence
   2. What tastes good and what tastes bad
G. *Research Focus: Mind over Body?*
   1. Mind or medicine
      a. **Placebo**
      b. **Placebo effect**
   2. Method: **double-blind design**
   3. Placebo results: mind over body!
H. *Pain*
   1. **Pain** sensations
      a. Localized
      b. Generalized

2. **Gate control theory of pain**
   a. Competing messages to the brain
   b. Pain: physical and psychological
3. **Endorphins**
   a. Pain reduction and addiction
   b. Adrenal cell transplants
4. **Acupuncture**
   a. Competing stimuli
   b. Psychological factors

I. *Application: Artificial Senses*
   1. Artificial visual system
      a. Artificial photoreceptors
      b. Artificial eye and brain implant
      c. Functional vision
   2. Kinds of deafness
      a. **Conduction deafness**
      b. **Neural deafness**
      c. **Cochlear implant**
      d. Cochlear implants: how well do they work?

Language Workout

What's the Difference?

One way to show a difference is to use **although**. For example, the following pairs of sentences have exactly the same meaning:

> The outside of a pineapple is too tough to eat, **but** the inside is delicious.
> **Although** the outside of a pineapple is too tough to eat, the inside is delicious.

> Jerry has seen the movie already, **but** he wants to see it again.
> **Although** Jerry has seen the movie already, he wants to see it again.

> The weatherman predicted rain for today, **but** it's totally dry.
> **Although** the weatherman predicted rain for today, it's totally dry.

Notice how the sentence changes. Notice the comma.

TRY IT

> Cell phones are relatively new inventions, **but** many people have them now.
> **Although**_____

> Most vegetarians don't eat meat, but some will eat eggs and fish.
> **Although** _____

Module 5: Sensation 69

BE CAREFUL: Are you putting the comma in the right place?

TRY SOME MORE

    The family wanted Grandpa's money, **but** he left it all to his cat when he died.
    Although _____

    The earthquake destroyed many buildings, **but** the school is still standing.
    Although _____

    Chuck lifts weights in the gymnasium, **but** he can't open the ketchup bottle.
    Although _____

WHY A COMMA? Because the word "although" makes the following action weak. When we see the comma, we understand that the weak part has ended, and now the real action of the sentence — with the main subject and verb — is beginning.

Look at this sentence:

    Although the *Titanic* sank, some passengers were saved.
    Which action is weak? _____

Why is it weak? Because it can't stand alone as a full sentence. It must be connected to a strong sentence.

Which action is strong? _____ Why is it strong? Because it is a full sentence.

What does the comma tell us? _____

Read these sentences from the text again to make sure you understand the meaning:

    Although Kate is officially blind, she can still see (p. 93).
    Although your sense organs look different, they share three characteristics.
    Although radio waves are all forms of energy, they vary in wavelength (p. 94).
    Although most of us have good color vision, some have color blindness (p. 99).

Another way we can show a difference is by using "**however**". The following three sentences all have exactly the same meaning:

    The car is thirty years old, **but** it still runs well.
    Although the car is thirty years old, it still runs well.
    The car is thirty years old. **However,** it still runs well.

NOTICE that the first two are complete sentences. The last is actually a pair of independent sentences. The word "**however**" shows us that the second sentence is a different or surprising result of the first.

TRY IT

    Anya planted dozens of carrots in her garden, **but** the rabbits ate them all.
    Anya planted dozens of carrots in her garden _____

    Although more than 400 people applied for the job, only one was chosen.
    _____

    Romeo and Juliet wanted to get married, **but** their families stopped them.
    _____

Although the United States is the major producer of software, India is the second.

_____

BE CAREFUL! Did you remember to make two sentences? Did you remember to put the comma after **"however"**? Why a comma? Because "however" is an organizing word.

TRY making some more sentences with **"however"**

The alligator looked sleepy**,** **but** it jumped quickly when it smelled food.
The alligator _____

Although Greg carefully hid his passport in a safe place**,** now he can't find it.

_____

The concert wasn't very good**,** **but** it was free.

_____

Although Velma invited twenty guests to her party**,** over sixty people came.

_____

Make sure you put the commas in the right place. Check your answers in the Answer Key

What's That?

p. 97   the ability to **tell** night from day = see the difference

p. 100 pitch is our **subjective** experience of a sound = personal
       a **cheerleader's** yell = a shout to support your team
       opponent = enemy, fighter against

p. 101 **jackhammer** = noisy machine to break rocks and cement
       firecracker = toy bomb, party toy that explodes
       threshold of hearing = point where effect begins

p. 102 the music of **the Rolling Stones** = British rock group

p. 104 **less or fewer?** = fewer vibrations...less movement...less electrical force...fewer nerve impulses

p. 105 you rarely forget to **duck** (head) = move head to avoid danger
       a sensory **mismatch** = wrong combination
       feel a little **queasy** [KWEE-zee] = sick in the stomach
       malfunctioning of the vestibular system = wrong operation

p. 106 an **innate** preference for sweet and salt = natural, inborn
       humans avoid bitter-tasting substances, **presumably** because many poisonous substances taste bitter = most likely, most probably

p. 107 warm **brownies** = chocolate cake squares

p. 110 foods are judged **edible** = safe to eat
       sensors are **wound** around hair follicles = pull material in circle around object
       Note that **wound** [wow-ind] is the past tense of **wind** [wai-ind]

See It and Say It

p. 111 **placebo** = pluh-SEE-bo

p. 112 This competition creates a **bottleneck** = obstacle, like a traffic jam

p. 113 scientists trained in the **rigorous** methods of the West = extremely careful

p. 115 The signals **trigger** impulses = activate, cause a series of actions or effects

p. 118 **take full advantage of** the Mozart effect = use fully
     boosting general intelligence = increasing
     one **nursery** had positive proof = business that takes care of very young children

---

Answer Key

Although cell phones are relatively new inventions, many people have them now.
Although most vegetarians don't eat meat, some will eat eggs and fish.
Although the family wanted Grandpa's money, he left it all to his cat when he died.
Although the earthquake destroyed many buildings, the school is still standing.
Although Chuck lifts weights in the gymnasium, he can't open the ketchup bottle.
Which action is weak? **Although** the *Titanic* sank
Which action is strong? some passengers were saved
What does the comma tell us?
That the weak part has ended and the strong part is beginning.
Anya planted dozens of carrots in her garden. **However,** the rabbits ate them all.
More than 400 people applied for the job. **However,** only one was chosen.
Romeo and Juliet wanted to get married. **However,** their families stopped them.
The United States is the major producer of software. **However,** India is the second.
The alligator looked sleepy. **However,** it jumped quickly when it smelled food.
Greg carefully hid his passport in a safe place. **Howver,** now he can't find it.
The concert wasn't very good. **However,** it was free.
Velma invited twenty guests to her party. **However,** over sixty people came.

The Big Picture

Which statement below offers the best summary of the larger significance of this module?

    A   Sensation is the process by which the raw data we need for understanding the world around us comes into our brain. Perception is the process by which the brain makes the raw data meaningful.

    B   Study of the eye, ear, nose, tongue, and skin are traditional subjects in psychology. Today, however, it is becoming clear that these biological functions do not have much to do with psychology.

    C   Sensation is the collection of processes by which we understand what is happening in our world. For example, through vision we "make sense" out of what we see.

    D   Perception is how we gather data about the world. Sensation is how we make sense of that data. Therefore, in human psychology, sensation is more important than perception.

    E   Sensation is the excitement we feel when we see something really great, as in "I saw a sensational babe at the beach today."

True-False

_____ 1. All of the senses share three characteristics: transduction, adaptation, and the experience of "sensing" something.

_____ 2. The reason you can "see" a giraffe is that the animal emits light waves which humans can detect.

_____ 3. The retina performs the work called transduction.

_____ 4. The images you "see" are created by the primary visual cortex and related association area of the brain.

_____ 5. Sound waves vary in amplitude and frequency.

_____ 6. The vestibular system provides feedback on your body's position in space by interpreting sound waves from your environment

_____ 7. Motion sickness, Meniere's disease, and vertigo are disorders of the outer ear.

_____ 8. The tongue has receptors for only four basic tastes.

_____ 9. Humans won't eat just anything — we have biologically determined preferences for some foods and feelings of disgust at the thought of others.

_____ 10. Acupuncture often produces pain relief — probably by causing secretion of endorphins in the brain.

Module 5: Sensation

Flashcards 1

1. adaptation
2. frequency theory
3. opponent-process theory
4. place theory
5. sensations
6. sound waves
7. transduction
8. trichromatic theory
9. vestibular system
10. visible spectrum

a. says rate at which nerve impulses reach brain determine how low a sound is
b. says color vision is due to eye and brain responding to either red-green or blue-yellow
c. a sense organ changes physical energy into electrical signals that become neural impulses
d. location of basilar membrane vibrations determines medium and higher sounds
e. stimulus activates sensory receptors, producing electrical signals that are processed by the brain
f. stimuli for audition; resemble ripples on pond; have height (amplitude) and speed (frequency)
g. three semicircular canals in inner ear that determine our sense of balance and position
h. one particular segment of electromagnetic energy whose waves can be seen by human eye
i. says color vision is due to three kinds of cones in retina sensitive to blue, green, or red
j. prolonged or continuous stimulation results in a decreased responding by the sense organs

Flashcards 2

1. acupuncture
2. disgust
3. endorphins
4. gate control theory of pain
5. nearsightedness
6. olfactory cells
7. placebo effect
8. retina
9. sense of touch
10. vertigo

a. smell receptors located in nasal passages; use mucus into which volatile molecules dissolve
b. dizziness and nausea resulting from malfunction of semicircular canals of vestibular system
c. includes pressure, temperature, and pain; from miniature sensors beneath outer layer of skin
d. a universal facial expression (eyes closed, lips curled downward) indicating rejection of foods
e. chemicals produced by the brain and secreted in response to injury or stress cause reduced pain
f. may result when eyeball is too long; result is that near objects are clear but distant are blurry
g. thin film with three layers of cells located at back of eyeball; includes photoreceptor cells
h. inserting thin needles into various points on the body's surface and twirling them to relieve pain
i. says rubbing an injured area or becoming involved in other activities blocks pain impulses
j. change in patient's illness attributable to an imagined treatment rather than to a medical one

Multiple-Choice

_____ 1. Rod Plotnik says the experience of Katie, a blind woman who had tiny gold wires implanted into the back of her brain, raises the question
   a. are some cases of blindness actually hysterical?
   b. can blind persons regain their sight through intense practice?
   c. do you see with your eyes or with your brain?
   d. can science go too far in tampering with human capabilities?

_____ 2. The process by which a sense organ changes physical stimuli into impulses is termed
   a. transduction
   b. adaptation
   c. sensing
   d. experiencing

_____ 3. A decline in responding with prolonged or continuous stimulation is called
   a. transduction
   b. adaptation
   c. sensing
   d. experiencing

_____ 4. When you get that new road rocket for graduation, you may want a radar detector, too, because those things
   a. see the pulses of light that radar guns use
   b. hear the faint vibrations of radar guns
   c. see long wave lengths you can't
   d. make your car look cool

_____ 5. The function of the cornea is to
   a. bend and focus light waves into a narrower beam of light
   b. screen out irrelevant light waves
   c. prevent convergence from occurring too soon
   d. add color to light waves entering the eye

_____ 6. If you see close objects clearly but distant objects appear blurry, you are
   a. nearsighted
   b. farsighted
   c. normal
   d. abnormal

_____ 7. The work of the retina is to
   a. add sharp focus to what you are seeing
   b. transform light waves into impulses
   c. turn the inverted image we see right side up
   d. change impulses into light waves we can see

_____ 8. How loud a sound seems is determined by the _____ of the sound waves
   a. amplitude
   b. frequency
   c. pitch
   d. cycle

____ 9. If a tree falls in an uninhabited forest, does it make any sound?
   a. obviously, it does
   b. not if there is no human there to "hear" it
   c. it depends on whether we define "sound" as the waves of air or the subjective experience of hearing
   d. I thought this was psychology, not philosophy

____ 10. The widest range of human hearing is possessed by
   a. college students
   b. senior citizens
   c. infants
   d. members of rock bands (yeah, right!)

____ 11. The function of the cochlea is to
   a. turn vibrations into nerve impulses
   b. move fluid forward toward the oval window
   c. house the hammer, anvil, and stirrup
   d. house the band of fibers called the auditory nerve

____ 12. Our sense of movement and position in space is determined by
   a. movement of fluid in the three semicircular canals of the vestibular system
   b. the primary visual cortex and related association areas
   c. faint echoes from surrounding objects that the brain can decode
   d. the movement of fluid in the eardrum

____ 13. Which one of the following is *not* one of the four basic tastes?
   a. sweet
   b. sharp
   c. salty
   d. sour

____ 14. Our sense of touch comes from
   a. a half-dozen miniature sensors located in the skin
   b. millions of tiny nerves on the surface of the skin
   c. special glands for pressure, temperature, and pain
   d. stimulation of the tiny hairs that cover the body

____ 15. Can the ancient Oriental procedure called acupuncture actually relieve pain? Modern science says
   a. yes, because there are some mysteries Western science is not equipped to explain
   b. perhaps, because stimulation of certain points may cause the secretion of endorphins
   c. no, because there cannot be a relationship between twirling needles in the skin and pain caused by the nervous system
   d. no, because there is no research to date that supports acupuncture

Answers for Module 5

True-False
1. T
2. F
3. T
4. T
5. T
6. F
7. F
8. T
9. F
10. T

Flashcards 1
1. j
2. a
3. b
4. d
5. e
6. f
7. c
8. i
9. g
10. h

Flashcards 2
1. h
2. d
3. e
4. i
5. f
6. a
7. j
8. g
9. c
10. b

Multiple-Choice
1. c
2. a
3. b
4. c
5. a
6. a
7. b
8. a
9. c
10. c
11. a
12. a
13. b
14. a
15. b

The Big Picture

Statement A

Wanted!

I pass out a corny "Wanted" poster urging my students to look for any errors I make in writing (spelling, grammar, formatting). I offer a payoff to the first student who finds the particular error. Have you found any mistakes? I can't ask your instructor to pay off (it's my mistake, after all), but I will send you an e-mail you can show your teacher. Might make a good impression! Please e-mail me if you find a mistake! **Profenos@aol.com**

Module 6

Perception

How to Ruin a Professor's Day

When I took experimental psychology, years ago, our professor enjoyed bedeviling us with the same classic perceptual illusions that Rod Plotnik discusses in Module 6. The one that really got us was the famous Müller-Lyer illusion. It is so powerful that it fooled us every time, even after we already knew the lines were the same length. One day a troublemaker in the back row asked, "But *why* does it work?" Our professor hung his head and had to admit, "I don't know."

Today, cognitive psychology has an intriguing answer (it's in Module 6). Besides the fascination of discovering how sensing and perceiving work, understanding these processes can be personally liberating. Here's why.

The Task of Self-Management

Step on a rattlesnake and it whirls and strikes. Step on a human and... a hundred different things could happen. Instinct governs much of the snake's behavior, but almost none of the human's. That's why we humans constantly face the task of self-management, or self-regulation. We also face parallel tasks of managing physical objects and other people, but self-management is the most difficult because it's so subjective. As you will see in the modules on mental disorders, it's easy for things to get out of whack. Normally, the activity of self-management goes on so automatically it seems unconscious, but we are constantly working at it.

That's what I like about the module on perception. It helps us appreciate the incredibly complex processes of apprehending and interpreting reality, and in so doing can help us be more realistic about ourselves. There are many things in life to worry about and to fear. An important part of self-management is deciding which stimuli represent real threats and which do not. The disadvantage of our limitless freedom to create wonderful new things is our equally great ability to create fears where they are not appropriate. When we get a better handle on our processes of self-management, however, we begin to appreciate that some apparent perceptions are really glitches in the self-managing process, and we realize that we are scaring ourselves needlessly.

The modules on sensation and perception remind us that we are constantly creating our own reality. Just as illusions can fool us, we can torment ourselves with worries and fears about dangers that are illusory, not real.

Effective Student Tip 6

When You Participate, You Practice

My heart goes out to students who say "I would rather listen than talk...." They are invariably the quiet, supportive type of person the world needs a whole lot more of. (For a teacher, Hell would be a perpetual talk show, with everyone shouting at each other for all eternity and no one listening!) Yet I know that only listening is not really good for them.

Taking part in class discussion binds us to the group, satisfies deep social needs, and increases our sense of effectiveness. But it has a purely academic payoff as well. When you participate, you are practicing the facts and ideas of the course.

In class, you may have the strong feeling that you understand a point better than the student who is talking, maybe even better than the professor. When it's your turn to talk, you find out just how well you do understand it. As you struggle to put your ideas into words, you come to appreciate both what you have right and what you don't. The reactions of your professor and classmates further inform you how well you have grasped the material. Next time, you reword it, rework it, and begin to master it. The facts and ideas of the course are becoming more personal and more real. You aren't just sitting there waiting for the end of the period. You're really learning.

Your response...

Are you a talker or a listener in your classes? Is class discussion valuable, or a waste of time?

Module 6: Perception

Key Terms

Many of these key terms open up a whole new world. You'll never see things quite the same way after you learn the principles explained by these terms. This module can be fun.

absolute threshold (Gustav Fechner)
Ames room
apparent motion
atmospheric perspective
binocular depth cues
brightness constancy
closure rule
color constancy
continuity rule
convergence
cultural influences
depth perception
extrasensory perception (ESP)
figure-ground rule
Ganzfeld procedure

Gestalt psychologists
illusion
impossible figure
interposition
just noticeable difference (JND)
light and shadow
linear perspective
monocular depth cues
motion parallax
perception
perceptual constancy
perceptual sets
phi movement
proximity rule
psi
real motion

relative size
retinal disparity
rules of organization
self-fulfilling prophecies
sensation
shape constancy
similarity rule
simplicity rule
size constancy
structuralists
subliminal messages
subliminal stimulus
texture gradient
threshold
virtual reality
Weber's law

Outline

- *Introduction*
    1. Silent messages
    2. Nice dog, mean dog
    3. White spot
    4. Perceiving things
    ☐ *What are the three basic questions about perception Rod Plotnik says psychology tries to answer?*

A. *Perceptual Thresholds*
    1. Becoming aware of a stimulus
        a. **Threshold** (Gustav Fechner)
        b. **Absolute threshold**
        c. **Subliminal stimulus**
        d. Increasing accuracy
    2. Weber's law
        a. **Just noticeable difference (JND)** (E. H. Weber)
        b. **Weber's law**
    3. Just noticeable difference (JND) and soft towels

B. *Sensation versus Perception*
   1. Basic differences
      a. **Sensation**
      b. **Perception**
   2. Changing sensations into perceptions
      a. Stimulus
      b. Transductions
      c. Brain areas
      d. Sensations
      e. Personalized perceptions

C. *Rules of Organization*
   1. Structuralists versus Gestalt psychologists
      a. **Structuralists**
      b. **Gestalt psychologists**
      c. Evidence for rules: why Gestalt psychologists won the debate
   2. **Rules of organization**
      a. **Figure-ground rule**
      b. **Similarity rule**
      c. **Closure rule**
      d. **Proximity rule**
      e. **Simplicity rule**
      f. **Continuity rule**

D. *Perceptual Constancy*
   1. Size, shape, brightness, and color constancy
   2. **Perceptual constancy** in a potentially chaotic world
   - *How does perceptual constancy make our world understandable?*
      a. **Size constancy**
      b. **Shape constancy**
      c. **Brightness and color constancy**

E. *Depth Perception*
   1. Binocular depth cues
      a. **Depth perception**
      b. **Binocular depth cues**
   2. **Convergence**
   3. **Retinal disparity**

4. Organizational rules: **monocular depth cues**
   a. **Linear perspective**
   b. **Relative size**
   c. **Interposition**
   d. **Light and shadow**
   e. **Texture gradient**
   f. **Atmospheric perspective**
   g. **Motion parallax**

F. *Illusions*
   1. Strange perceptions
      a. **Illusion**
      b. **Impossible figure**
      c. Moon illusion
      d. **Ames room**
      e. Ponzo illusion
      f. Müller-Lyer illusion
   2. Learning from illusions?
   ☐ *How can an illusion help us understand the process of perception?*

G. *Research Focus: Subliminal Perception*
   1. Can "unsensed messages" change behavior (popcorn controversy)?
   2. Changing specific behaviors (experiment)
      a. **Subliminal messages**
      b. **Self-fulfilling prophecies**
   3. Changing perceptions (experiment)

H. *Cultural Diversity: Influence on Perceptions*
   1. What do cultural influences do?
   ☐ *How do cultural influences affect perception?*
   2. Perception of photos
   3. Perception of images
   4. Perception of motion
   5. Perception of 3-dimensions
   6. Perception of beauty
   7. **Perceptual sets**

I. ESP: Extrasensory Perception

- ☐ Tell the truth — do you believe that at least a few people possess the special power of perception we call ESP? If you answered "yes," doesn't that create a problem with psychology as a science? Can a science of behavior be valid if some human abilities may sometimes fall outside its scope?

1. Definition and controversy
    a. **Extrasensory perception**
        (1) Telepathy
        (2) Precognition
        (3) Clairvoyance
        (4) Psychokinesis
    b. **Psi**: believing in ESP
    c. Testimonials as evidence
2. Trickery and magic (the Amazing Randi)
3. ESP experiment: **Ganzfeld procedure**
4. Status of ESP
    a. Controversial experiment
    b. Replication

J. Application: Creating Perceptions

1. Creating movement: **phi movement**
2. Creating movies
    a. **Real motion**
    b. **Apparent motion**
3. Creating **virtual reality**
4. Creating first impressions

Language Workout

What's That?

p. 122 **threshold** = the dividing line (between inside and outside)
absolute value = basic, unquestioned
white spots that usually **stand out** = look distinct

p. 123 this **phenomenon** can be found = scientific event

p. 124 we'll **take the liberty of** calling = risk, take a chance
The **fetus** = unborn baby
exact **replicas** = copies

p. 125 a series of **discrete** steps = completely separate

p. 126 a **heated** debate = full of strong emotions
a set of **innate** rules = contained within, inseparable

Module 6: Perception

p. 127 The **closure** rule = act of closing, finishing the unfinished
The **proximity** rule = state of nearness, closeness

p. 128 Perceptual **constancy** = state of staying the same, unchanged value
chaotic world = completely confused, without organization

p. 129 so realistically that you **duck** = move your head to avoid injury
Convergence = act of coming together to unite
Retinal **Disparity** = fundamental difference

p. 130 **Linear perspective** = using lines to trick the eye into seeing depth
Interposition = putting one element between two others

p. 131 Texture **gradient** = a difference that changes in relation to another factor
Parallax = visual difference from two different angles

p. 132 illusion is created by **manipulating** the perceptual cues = changing
The moon illusion has **intrigued** people = interested

p. 133 a **fixed** peephole = unmoving
the United States Congress almost **outlawed** = made illegal

p. 135 **subliminal** advertising = hidden, outside our awareness
take **legislative** action = creating new laws
These results suggest **a self-fulfilling prophecy** = a prediction that makes itself happen

p. 136 Americans are much more likely to **zero in on** = immediately see
That's **where the money is** = the center of interest
analytical thinking = dividing the whole into parts
holistic thinking = emphasizing the whole (not the parts)
analytical **versus** holistic = against, compared to

p. 137 This custom eventually **declined** = lost popularity
modify our perceptions = change

p. 138 According to **Gallup** polls = famous American collector of statistics
26% believe in **psychics** = people who claim psychic powers
seeing the **auras** of people = invisible atmosphere around a person
the **scrutiny** of scientific investigation = close examination

p. 139 an **acoustically isolated** room = closed to outside sounds
extrasensory perception = from outside the senses
to **rule out** the potential for trickery = eliminate, prevent
psychic **hotlines** = telephone business giving advice
questions from **perfect strangers** = complete strangers
self-proclaimed psychics = self-called (not approved by experts)

p. 140 a **mind-blowing** three-dimensional world = amazing
modern **billboards** = large outdoor signs for advertising
a series of **stationary** images = unmoving
ingenious experiments = very clever
images that **vary** only slightly = differ
dissecting a frog = cutting into pieces (science exercise)

p. 141 virtual **cadavers** = dead bodies
maneuvering a tiny camera = guiding, putting into position
a pencil-thin **incision** = cut

84 STUDY GUIDE

a **debilitating** fear of spiders = weakening
duct tape = very heavy and strong tape
racial **stereotypes** = unfair generalizations

p. 144 you **scrawl** = write quickly and carelessly
A bit **peeved** = annoyed, angry
she was no **novice** = beginner
it wasn't going to be easy to **shake** her = upset, disturb
You're **all over the place** = without focus, going in different directions
Shoot = begin, tell me
Strike three = mistake number three

What's the Difference?

Our computer**'s** problems means = we have one computer
Our computer**s'** problems means = we have many computers

p. 135 consumers' buying habits = the buying habits **of** (many) consumer**s**
subjects' showing improvement = showing improvement **by** (many) subject**s**
listeners' beliefs = beliefs **of** (many) listener**s**

p. 138 the lab**s'** researchers = the researchers **of** (many) lab**s**

p. 141 actors' hair = the hair **of** (many) actor**s**

My brother**'s** ideas = one brother? or many?
His sister**s'** happiness = one sister? or many?
Your teacher**s'** offices = one teacher? or many?
The plant**s'** leaves = one plant? or many?
Our town**'s** history = one town? or many?
The movie**s'** success = one movie? or many?
The American**s'** choice = one American? or many?
The desk**'s** wood = one desk? or many?
Her parent**s'** reaction = one parent? or many?

Is That Clear?

Glass can be **clear** or opaque.

The windshield of a car should always be _____.
However, a bathroom window should be _____.

An explanation can be **clear** or confusing.

This study guide is excellent because the examples are so _____.
Learning many different theories can be _____.

Air can be **clear** or hazy.

The view from the mountaintop is especially _____.
The pollution from the factories makes everything look _____.

An action can look **clear** or blurry.

Keith's new digital camera takes pictures that are very _____.
Marci moved her head, so this photo looks _____.

Answer Key

My brother**'s** ideas = one brother
His sister**s'** happiness = many
Your teacher**s'** offices = many
The plant**s'** leaves = many
Our town**'s** history = one town
The movie**s'** success = many
The American**s'** choice = many
The desk**'s** wood = one desk
Her parent**s'** reaction = many
The windshield of a car should always be **clear**.
However, a bathroom window should be **opaque**.
This study guide is excellent because the examples are so **clear**.
Learning many different theories can be **confusing**.
The view from the mountain top is especially **clear**.
The pollution from the factories makes everything look **hazy**.
Keith's new digital camera takes pictures that are very **clear**.
Marci moved her head, so this photo looks **blurry**.

The Big Picture

Which statement below offers the best summary of the larger significance of this module?

A   Perception is the constant bombardment of sensory data on several specialized areas of the brain.

B   Both sensation and perception are inborn biological processes — once again demonstrating that psychology is basically just biology.

C   Through the several processes of perception, the mind creates the reality we take for granted. In a way, what is real is the picture of the world we create in our minds.

D   Considering how illusions and the various perceptual rules work, we can only conclude that there is no real world, and that psychology is little more than guesswork and shots taken in the dark.

E   The next time a teacher marks one of your answers "Wrong," just point out that, according to psychology, "it's all in how you look at it!"

True-False

_____ 1. A threshold is a point above which we are aware of a stimulus.

_____ 2. A biologist calls it "sensation" and a psychologist calls it "perception," but they are both talking about the same thing.

_____ 3. The brain follows a number of perceptual rules in order to make sense out of the mass of visual stimuli it receives.

_____ 4. If it were not for perceptual constancies, the world would seem ever-changing and chaotic.

_____ 5. In the Müller-Lyer illusion, one boy looks like a giant and the other like a midget.

_____ 6. Illusions are interesting because they remind us that perception is an active process.

_____ 7. Horses at the track, real motion; movie replay of the race, apparent motion.

_____ 8. A perceptual set is a kind of stubbornness that makes subjects stick to the first answer they give even if they realize they were wrong.

_____ 9. Anthropologists have discovered that how you see things depends at least in part on the culture in which you were raised.

_____ 10. There is a large body of accepted scientific evidence that supports the existence of ESP.

Module 6: Perception

Flashcards 1

1. closure rule
2. continuity rule
3. figure-ground rule
4. Gestalt psychologists
5. illusion
6. impossible figure
7. shape constancy
8. simplicity rule
9. size constancy
10. threshold

a. a point above which a stimulus is perceived and below which it is not perceived
b. our tendency to organize stimuli in the simplest way possible
c. found rules that specify how individual elements are organized into meaningful patterns or perceptions
d. tendency to perceive an object as remaining the same size even when its image on retina grows or shrinks
e. our tendency to favor smooth or continuous paths when interpreting a series of points or lines
f. a perceptual experience of perceiving a strange object as being so distorted that it could not really exist
g. tendency to see an object as keeping its same form in spite of viewing it from different angles
h. perceptual experience in which a drawing seems to defy basic geometric laws
i. our tendency to automatically identify an element of more detail, which then stands out from the rest
j. our tendency to fill in any missing parts of a figure in order to see the figure as complete

Flashcards 2

1. Ames room
2. apparent motion
3. convergence
4. extrasensory perception (ESP)
5. Ganzfeld procedure
6. perceptual sets
7. phi movement
8. self-fulfilling prophecies
9. subliminal messages
10. virtual reality

a. binocular cues for depth that depend on signals from muscles as they move both eyes inward to focus
b. a perceptual experience of being inside an object or environment or action that is simulated by computer
c. having strong beliefs about changing some behavior then acting, unknowingly, to change the behavior
d. a controlled method for eliminating trickery, error, and bias while testing telepathic communication
e. illusion that closely positioned stationary lights flashing at regular intervals seem to be moving
f. a group of presumed psychic experiences that lie outside the normal sensory processes or channels
g. learned expectations that are based on our personal, social or cultural experiences and change perceptions
h. a demonstration that our perception of size can be distorted by changing depth cues
i. brief auditory or visual messages that are presented below the absolute threshold
j. illusion that a stimulus or object is moving in space when, in fact, the stimulus or object is stationary

Multiple-Choice

_____ 1. An absolute threshold is the intensity level that you can
   a. detect every time it is presented
   b. guess is there, even if you can't quite detect it
   c. just barely detect
   d. detect 50 percent of the time

_____ 2. Weber's law of the just noticeable difference explains why
   a. your parents don't believe you really turned your stereo down
   b. kids like heavy metal and their parents like Montovani
   c. you study better if you have the radio on
   d. the Destiny's Child singers all have different names

_____ 3. Sensation is to perception as _____ is to _____
   a. grownup ... child
   b. complete ... unfinished
   c. word ... story
   d. movie ... reality

_____ 4. The perceptual rule that makes important things stand out is called
   a. closure
   b. proximity
   c. figure dominance
   d. figure-ground

_____ 5. Thank goodness for size constancy — without it you would
   a. never know for sure how big or small anything really was
   b. immediately get bigger after a single large meal
   c. think your honey is getting smaller and smaller while walking away from you
   d. see things change in size whenever the light changed in brightness

_____ 6. The advantage to the human species of having two eyes is
   a. figure-ground discrimination
   b. monocular cues
   c. retinal disparity
   d. glasses balance on the nose better

_____ 7. The reason people seem to change size as they change sides in the Ames room is that
   a. the room is not actually rectangular
   b. hidden mirrors distort the images you see as you look in
   c. a lens in the peephole forces you to view them upside down
   d. the subtle coloring of the walls creates a hypnotic trance in the viewer

_____ 8. The reason why you couldn't figure out the two-pronged/three-pronged gadget in the textbook is that
   a. seeing it in a textbook aroused test anxiety and that threw you off
   b. you were attempting to see it as an object in the real world
   c. Westerners aren't as good at this kind of puzzle as Africans are
   d. it was just a joke

9. A new explanation for why the lines in the Müller-Lyer illusion don't appear to be the same length is that
   a. our previous experience with arrows tells us they *aren't* all the same
   b. they really aren't quite the same — there is a tiny difference in length
   c. your experience with the corners of rooms makes you see the arrows differently
   d. this famous illusion remains unexplained (even Professors Müller and Lyer couldn't explain it)

10. Should you scrap this Study Guide and buy a subliminal message tape? Research suggests that any improvement you get with those tapes is probably due to
    a. a self-fulfilling prophecy
    b. turning the volume up too high
    c. the Ponzo illusion
    d. the effects of extra practice

11. Seeing buffalo as "insects" shows that size constancy and depth perception are strongly affected by
    a. cultural beliefs about animals
    b. seeing a black-and-white photo for the first time
    c. previous visual experience
    d. racial inheritance

12. Tops on the list of people *not* to invite to an ESP demonstration:
    a. Gustav Fechner
    b. E. H. Weber
    c. Max Wertheimer
    d. Amazing Randi

13. Despite the fact that many people believe in it, convincing evidence of ESP has been undercut by the
    a. hocus-pocus that surrounds ESP demonstrations
    b. refusal of psychologists to investigate it seriously
    c. inability to repeat positive results
    d. fact that some people have it and others don't

14. When John Wayne grabs the reins on the stagecoach, we see the horses as really flying because our brains
    a. apply the principle of closure and fill in the blanks between frames of the movie
    b. "suspend doubt" as we get more and more involved in the movie
    c. accept the data coming in from the retina and optic nerve
    d. know that the horses in the movie really were moving as they were being filmed

15. *Special question for tech-heads:* when "virtual reality" becomes an accomplished fact, you will be able to
    a. watch Star Trek reruns in 3-D
    b. dial up famous psychologists on your computer at home
    c. learn all the facts you need in psych while you sleep
    d. trade in your psych textbook for a headset and a computer disk

Answers for Module 6

True-False
1. T
2. F
3. T
4. T
5. F
6. T
7. T
8. F
9. T
10. F

Flashcards 1
1. j
2. e
3. i
4. c
5. f
6. h
7. g
8. b
9. d
10. a

Flashcards 2
1. h
2. j
3. a
4. f
5. d
6. g
7. e
8. c
9. i
10. b

Multiple-Choice
1. d
2. a
3. c
4. d
5. c
6. c
7. a
8. b
9. c
10. a
11. c
12. d
13. c
14. a
15. d

The Big Picture

Statement C

The "Language Workout"

Have you tried Bob Keser's "Language Workout" sections? Bob wrote this material especially for students new to English, but also for anyone who wants to use English more effectively.

I went through all of Bob's exercises myself. I found that they helped me understand English more fully, even when I already "knew" the right answers. Bob explains the construction of English grammar so clearly that you can't help but gain a better understanding of our wonderful language, even if you are good at it to begin with. That's why I am urging you to try Bob's lessons.

Please tell me how you like the Language Workout! Profenos@aol.com

Module 7

Consciousness, Sleep, & Dreams

Do Dreams Have Meaning?

Freud is dead... Freud is dead... Freud is dead.... Keep repeating it long enough, and maybe Freud will go away. He has a way of coming back, though, no matter how often psychology pronounces him dead wrong.

One of Freud's most provocative ideas is the notion that all dreams have meaning. He thought it was his most important discovery, and wrote, "Insight such as this falls to one's lot but once in a lifetime." Dreams were important to Freud because they allowed the best look into the workings of the unconscious. When you learn more about Freud's theory of personality (in Module 19) and his technique of psychoanalysis (in Module 24), you will see that he thought of dreaming, with unconscious meanings hidden behind innocent sounding or bizarre surface stories, as a model for all human psychic life. (See "For Psych Students Only" box for more on Freud's theory of dreams.)

The newer theories of dreaming discussed in Module 7 discount or reject Freud's theory, perhaps partly because — you knew this was coming — Freud says dreams represent sexual wishes. Building on laboratory research into sleep and brain biology, however, the new theories are filling in blanks Freud could only guess at.

Turn Your Bed into a Research Laboratory

The deciding evidence in the battle over the meaningfulness of dreams may be your own dreams. Why not use them as a research project? Many people find it useful to keep a dream journal, which helps them get down more details than we normally remember and also serves as a record that can be reviewed from time to time. The cares and worries of the day quickly chase dream details away, so try waking up slowly and peacefully. If you sense that you had a dream, keep your eyes closed and stay with it. Tell it to yourself a few times. Then get up (or grab your bedside pencil and pad if it is still night) and write down as much as you remember.

The hard part, of course, is trying to interpret the dream. Here's how. Review the story of the dream, then ask how it connects to your life. This is a process of indirection and confusion, and you have to go where the dream leads, no matter how apparently meaningless it seems. The *crucial clues* will be what Freudians call your *associations* to the dream, the things that come to mind as you think about each element of the dream. What feelings does it arouse? What thoughts (none sexual, of course) pop into your mind? How do the feelings and thoughts associated with the dream relate to issues in your psychological life? Is it possible that your dream does have meaning?

Effective Student Tip 7

Stay Focused

Everyone tells you how great it is that you are in college, but sometimes it seems like they don't really understand what you are up against. You may be away from home for the first time, trying to get along with your roommates, cheering on your college team, and worrying about how to get a date. Your parents and friends back home expect letters and phone calls. If you are a returning student, your children miss you, your spouse resents getting less attention, and your boss still asks you to stay late to finish that big project. In any case, you are discovering how easy it is to become distracted from your basic purpose for being in college.

No matter how important a party, your friend's need to talk all night, or extra work at the office may seem at the time, learning and succeeding are what college is really all about. The most important attributes of college are what happens in your classrooms and at your desk, when it's time to study.

Keep your emotional radar attuned to incoming distractions. When all you hear is the beep, beep, beep of threats to learning and succeeding, it's time to defend yourself. Remind yourself why you are in college. Then make the necessary adjustments to get back to the work you came to college to do.

Your response...
Think about a typical day in your college life. What distractions do you often face?

Key Terms

Everyone is fascinated by the topics in this module, especially sleep and dreaming. Learn these terms and you will be able to explain everything your friends want to know (well, enough to keep them listening).

activation-synthesis theory of dreams
adaptive theory
alpha stage
altered states of consciousness
automatic processes
benzodiazepines
biological clocks
circadian rhythm
consciousness
continuum of consciousness
controlled processes
daydreaming
dreaming
entering the spiritual world theory of dreams
evening persons

extension of waking life theory of dreams
Freud's theory of dreams
implicit memory
insomnia
interval timing clock
jet lag
light therapy
melatonin
morning persons
narcolepsy
night terrors
nightmares
non-REM sleep
questionnaire
REM behavior disorder
REM rebound
REM sleep

repair theory
reticular formation
seasonal affective disorder (SAD)
sleep
sleep apnea
sleepwalking
stage 1 sleep
stage 2 sleep
stage 4 sleep
stages of sleep
suprachiasmatic nucleus
unconscious (Freud)
unconscious (physical)
VPN (ventrolateral preoptic nucleus)

Outline

- *Introduction*
    1. Living in a cave
    ☐ What was the purpose of placing a person in a cave for four months?
    2. Chance discovery
- A. *Continuum of Consciousness*
    1. Different states
        a. **Consciousness**
        b. **Continuum of consciousness**
            (1) **Controlled processes**
            (2) **Automatic processes**
            (3) **Daydreaming**
            (4) **Altered states of consciousness**
            (5) **Sleep** and **dreaming**
            (6) **Unconscious** (Freud's theory) and **implicit memory**
            (7) **Unconscious** [physical]
    2. Several kinds

B. *Rhythms of Sleeping & Waking*
   1. Biological clocks
      a. **Biological clocks**
      b. **Circadian rhythm**
   2. Location of biological clocks
      a. **Suprachiasmatic nucleus**
      b. **Interval timing clock**
   3. Circadian problems and treatments
      a. Accidents
      b. **Jet lag**
      c. Resetting clock: **light therapy**
      d. **Melatonin**

C. *World of Sleep*
   1. **Stages of sleep**
      a. **Alpha stage**
      b. **Non-REM sleep**
         (1) **Stage 1 sleep**
         (2) **Stage 2 sleep**
         (3) Stage 3 and **Stage 4 sleep**
      c. **REM sleep**
         (1) Characteristics of REM sleep (**REM behavior disorder**)
         (2) REM: dreaming and remembering (**REM rebound**)
   2. Awake and alert
   3. Sequence of stages

D. *Research Focus: Circadian Preference*
   1. Research: are you a morning person or a night person?
      a. **Questionnaire**
      b. **Morning persons**
      c. **Evening persons**
   ☐ Are you a morning person or a night person?
   2. Body temperature
   3. Behavioral differences

E. *Questions about Sleep*
   1. How much sleep?
      a. Infancy and childhood
      b. Adolescence and adulthood
      c. Old age

☐ *What are your personal answers to questions 1 and 3 about sleep?*
   2. Why do I sleep?
      a. **Repair theory**
      b. **Adaptive theory**
   3. What if I miss sleep?
      a. Effects on the body
      b. Effects on the nervous system
   4. What causes sleep?
      a. Master sleep switch (**VPN [ventrolateral preoptic nucleus]**)
      b. **Reticular formation**
      c. Going to sleep

F. *Cultural Diversity: Incidence of SAD*
   1. Problem and treatment of **seasonal affective disorder (SAD)**
   2. Occurrence of SAD
   3. Cultural differences

G. *World of Dreams*
   1. Theories of dream interpretation
   2. The elevator dream
   ☐ *How would you explain the "elevator dream" Rod Plotnik offers as a sample?*
      a. **Freud's theory of dreams**
      b. **Extension of waking life theory of dreams** (Rosalind Cartwright)
      c. **Activation-synthesis theory of dreams** (J. Alan Hobson and Robert W. McCarley)
      d. **Entering the spiritual world theory of dreams**
   ☐ *What are the key differences in how the competing theories explain the elevator dream?*
   3. Typical dreams?

H. *Application: Sleep Problems & Treatments*
   1. Occurrence
   ☐ *Have you experienced a sleep problem? What was it like? What did you do about it?*
   2. **Insomnia**
      a. Psychological causes
      b. Physiological causes
      c. Non-drug treatment for insomnia (behavioral)
      d. Drug treatment for insomnia (**benzodiazepines**)
   3. **Sleep apnea**
   4. **Narcolepsy**
   5. **Night terrors** in children
   6. **Nightmares**
   7. **Sleepwalking**

96 STUDY GUIDE

> *For Psych Majors Only...*
>
> **How to Construct a Dream (Sigmund Freud):** If every dream represents a secret wish disguised as a jumbled, apparently meaningless story, how is the disguise constructed? Freud describes the "dream work" as four processes:
>
> 1. **Condensation** is the compression of several thoughts into a single element, which has the effect of making the dream seem *incoherent.*
>
> 2. **Displacement** is the transfer of psychical intensity from the actual dream thoughts to other ideas, which has the effect of making the dream seem *meaningless.*
>
> 3. **Symbolism** is the transformation of the dream thoughts into apparently unconnected pictorial arrangements or scenes, which has the effect of making the dream seem *illogical.*
>
> 4. **Secondary elaboration** is the interpretative revision of the dream content or scenes into stories, however absurd, which has the effect of making the dream seem *strange*, perhaps ridiculous or frightening, but *not connected to the dreamer.*
>
> The next time you remember a dream fairly clearly, try using these ideas to take it apart. It's not easy, but you may gain insight into the meaning of your dreams, and also into the provocative genius of Sigmund Freud.

Language Workout

What's That?

p. 147 a **hardy** subject = strong, not easily tired
stamina = strength, staying power
seemed to **come and go** = move from strong to weak
a publicity **stunt** = unusual act to get attention
correlation = proven relationship between two factors

p. 148 the **continuum** = a continuous sequence
we drive **on automatic pilot** = without paying attention
evasive action = avoiding
pondering some problem = thinking about
altered states = changed
all external **restraints** = controls
tactile dreams = touching
implicit memory = not directly expressed or seen
trauma = serious injury, physical or mental

p. 150 **mean** age 24 = middle, between oldest and youngest

p. 151 in a **lousy** mood = irritable, bad mood
to win **patents** = legal protection for inventions
(problems) that **plague** shift workers = disturb again and again
chronically disrupted = continuously, again and again

p. 152 levels of **metabolism**... = body process of using energy

p. 153 which **goes by** the initials REM = uses

p. 154 **recurring** stages = happening again and again

p. 155 Researchers **hypothesize** that = believe it may be true

p. 156 activities during the day **deplete** key factors = use until empty
that are **replenished** = refilled
immune cells = cells that protect the body from disease
nocturnal predators = night-time
large **predatory** animals = uses or eats other animals
(the) theories are not really **at odds** = conflicting, at war

p. 157 increased **vulnerability** = openness to injury
tasks that require **vigilance** = paying attention all the time
they **lapse into** (coma) = fall into

p. 159 explain this **discrepancy** = difference

p. 160 she says something about her **acne** = skin problem
swamis = religious persons, especially in traditions of India
Insights such as this **fall to one's lot** = are experienced
dream material is **sparse** = thin
stark nightmares = unpleasant, difficult
this still **leaves open** the question of meaning = does not answer

p. 161 the cortex tries to **make sense of** these random signals = organize
Inuit **shamans** = religious persons, especially who use magic
sighted people = people who can see

p. 163 **buckling** knees = losing support
anxiety or fear may **persist** = continue
while literally **sound asleep** = completely, deeply asleep

p. 166 the medical **establishment** = official leaders or authorities
I was operating **in a daze** = in a confused state
a **grueling** internship = very difficult, tiring

What's the Difference?

Why do you sleep? is a question.

> "**Why you sleep**" (p. 147) is not a question. It's a clause that does the same job as a noun.
>
> Like a noun, you can use it as the subject of a sentence: **Why you sleep** is an important topic.
>
> Like a noun, you can use it as the object of a sentence: Scientists are studying **why you sleep**.

STUDY GUIDE

Like a noun, you can use it as the <u>object of a preposition</u>: Experts have different explanations of **why you sleep**.

How much sleep do you need? is a question.
How much sleep you need is a noun clause.
How much sleep you need depends on _____

Where will we begin? is a question.
Where _____ is a noun clause.
The first page of the first chapter is **where** _____

How does a baby learn? is a question.
How _____ is a noun clause.
How _____ seems to be the same in all cultures.

When did Freud die? is a question.
When _____ is a noun clause.
The year 1939 is **when** _____.

Flex Your Word Power

deprive someone **of** something = take away something important: "they were **deprived of** REM sleep" (p. 153)

The baby cried when the mother deprived him of _____
Losing her job will deprive Lydia of _____
The heavy clouds today are depriving everyone of _____

deprivation

Feelings of hunger are the result of _____ deprivation.
Depression can be caused by deprivation of _____
Deprivation of _____ in childhood can lead to weakness in bones in adults.

See It and Say It

melatonin (p. 151) = mel-uh-TOH-nin

Answer Key
How much sleep you need depends on your age.
Where we'll begin is a noun clause.
The first page of the first chapter is **where we'll begin**.
How a baby learns is a noun clause.
How a baby learns seems to be the same in all cultures.
When Freud died is a noun clause.
The year 1939 is **when Freud died**.
The baby cried when the mother deprived him of **(his bottle) (his toy)**
Losing her job will deprive Lydia of **(her income) (money)**
The heavy clouds today are depriving everyone of **(sunlight)**
Feelings of hunger are the result of **food** deprivation.
Depression can be caused by deprivation of **(love) (light)**
Deprivation of **(milk) (vitamins)** in childhood can lead to weakness in bones in adults.

The Big Picture

Which statement below offers the best summary of the larger significance of this module?

   A   In everyday life, we seem to live in two states: awake and asleep. In actuality, there are many subtle degrees of consciousness which psychology is only beginning to explore and understand.

   B   A new spirit of common sense is coming into the psychological study of consciousness. We are either conscious or unconscious, dreams mean very little, and sleep disturbances are minor problems.

   C   This module raises disturbing questions about just how scientific the study of psychology really is. Most of what is presented comes from personal experience and insight, and very little from empirical research.

   D   The puzzling experience of living in a cave and the existence of morning persons and evening persons cast doubt on the existence of biological clocks and biological regulation. Humans are controlled by culture and learning.

   E   If we were all meant to be 'A' students, the Almighty would not have given us a need for sleep.

True-False

_____ 1. Human beings are always in one of two distinct states: awake and conscious or asleep and unconscious.

_____ 2. One adjustment problem faced by humans is that the circadian rhythm of our biological clocks is set closer to 25 hours than to 24.

_____ 3. Exposure to bright light is a fast way to reset our biological clocks.

_____ 4. Researchers study sleep by measuring brain waves.

_____ 5. Once you sink into true sleep, your bodily activity remains constant until you awake in the morning.

_____ 6. The existence of the REM rebound effect suggests that dreaming must have some special importance to humans.

_____ 7. Research on sleep deprivation and performance proves that the "repair theory" of sleep is correct.

_____ 8. Everyone dreams.

_____ 9. As with everything else in his theories, Freud's explanation of dreams has a sexual twist.

_____ 10. The activation-synthesis theory of dreams places great importance on getting to the underlying meaning of each dream.

Flashcards 1

____ 1. activation-synthesis theory of dreams
____ 2. adaptive theory
____ 3. circadian rhythm
____ 4. continuum of consciousness
____ 5. entering spiritual world theory of dreams
____ 6. extension of waking life theory of dreams
____ 7. Freud's theory of dreams
____ 8. REM rebound
____ 9. REM sleep
____ 10. repair theory

a. says dreaming represents the random and meaningless activity of nerve cells in the brain
b. says sleep replenishes key factors in brain and body depleted by activities during day; sleep as restorative
c. says dreams are ways of contacting souls of animals, supernaturals, departed relatives in search of help
d. wide range of experiences from being aware and alert to being unaware and unresponsive
e. an increased percentage of time spent in REM sleep when we are deprived of REM sleep on previous night
f. sleep during which eyes move rapidly back and forth behind closed eyelids; associated with dreaming
g. says sleep evolved to prevent energy waste and exposure to dangers of nocturnal predators
h. a biological clock that is genetically programmed to regulate physiological responses in a 24-25 hr day
i. says dreams are wish fulfillments, satisfaction of unconscious sexual or aggressive desires
j. says our dreams reflect the same thoughts, fears, concerns, and problems as are present when awake

Flashcards 2

____ 1. altered states of consciousness
____ 2. automatic processes
____ 3. controlled processes
____ 4. jet lag
____ 5. light therapy
____ 6. narcolepsy
____ 7. night terrors
____ 8. seasonal affective disorder (SAD)
____ 9. sleep apnea
____ 10. unconscious (Freud)

a. using meditation, drugs, or hypnosis to produce an awareness that differs from normal state
b. repeated periods during sleep when a person stops breathing for 10 seconds or longer; tiredness results
c. a mental place sealed off from voluntary recall where we place threatening wishes or desires
d. when one's internal circadian rhythm is out of step with external clock time; fatigue, disorientation
e. frightening child sleep experiences starting with a scream, followed by sudden waking in a fearful state
f. a chronic disorder marked by sleep attacks or short lapses of sleep throughout the day; muscle paralysis
g. a pattern of depressive symptoms beginning in fall and winter and going away in spring
h. use of bright artificial light to reset circadian rhythms and so combat insomnia and drowsiness from jet lag
i. activities that require full awareness, alertness, and concentration to reach some goal; focused attention
j. activities that require little awareness, take minimal attention, and do not interfere with other activities

Multiple-Choice

____ 1. Rod Plotnik opens the module on consciousness with the story of Stefania's four-month stay in a cave to illustrate the fact that
   a. body time runs slower than celestial time
   b. without sunlight, humans begin to lose their grip on reality
   c. without sunlight, Stefania's night vision became very acute
   d. we would all be much more cheerful if there were no clocks around

____ 2. We naturally think in terms of the two states called "conscious" and "unconscious," but actually there is/are
   a. three states, including the "high" from drugs
   b. four states: conscious, drowsy, dreaming, and unconscious
   c. a continuum of consciousness
   d. no measurable difference between consciousness and unconsciousness

____ 3. Psychologists call activities that require full awareness, alertness, and concentration
   a. automatic processes
   b. altered states
   c. comas
   d. controlled processes

____ 4. Have you noticed that you often wake up just before the alarm clock goes off? Credit it to the fact that we humans have a built-in
   a. aversion to jangling noise, which we try to avoid
   b. biological clock
   c. sense of responsibility
   d. brain mechanism that is always monitoring the external environment, even during sleep

____ 5. If human beings were deprived of all mechanical means of telling time (like clocks), they would
   a. still follow schedules and be punctual, thanks to their biological clocks
   b. follow a natural clock with a day about 30 hours long
   c. not stick to strict schedules the way we do now
   d. lose all sense of when things should be done

____ 6. The most promising new treatment for jet lag appears to be
   a. periods of bright light
   b. avoidance of food for 24 hours before a long flight
   c. surgical resetting of the biological clock
   d. drugs that induce sleep in the new time zone

____ 7. Dreams are most likely to occur during
   a. stage 1 (theta waves)
   b. EEG sleep
   c. non-REM sleep
   d. REM sleep

_____ 8. REM behavior disorder is a condition in which
   a. you appear to be looking around even though obviously you can't see anything
   b. you have dreams, but they don't make any sense
   c. voluntary muscles are not paralyzed and sleepers can and do act out their dreams
   d. voluntary muscles are paralyzed and you can't move no matter how hard you try

_____ 9. The VPN (ventrolateral preoptic nucleus) acts as a
   a. clue that makes it possible to tell if a sleeper is dreaming
   b. master on-off switch for sleep
   c. censor that disguises sexual and aggressive wishes in dreams
   d. light enhancer that combats feelings of depression during the winter months

_____ 10. Research in both Iceland and New Hampshire showed that seasonal affective disorder (SAD) is caused by
   a. an above average number of days of bright light
   b. a combination of diminished light and low temperature
   c. personal tragedy and family problems
   d. cultural factors as well as the amount of sunlight

_____ 11. According to Freud's famous theory, at the heart of every dream is a
   a. hate-filled thought
   b. clue to the future
   c. shameful sexual memory
   d. disguised wish

_____ 12. The activation-synthesis theory says that dreams result from
   a. a biological need to pull together and make sense of the day's activities
   b. "batch processing" of all the information gathered during the day
   c. random and meaningless activity of nerve cells in the brain
   d. the need to express hidden sexual and aggressive impulses

_____ 13. For thousands of years, the Inuit (Eskimo) people have believed that dreams are
   a. ways to enter the spiritual world, where the souls of animals, supernaturals, and departed relatives are made known
   b. solutions to practical, everyday problems that come to us during dreaming
   c. representations of evil forces that must never be spoken about
   d. tricks played on humans by mischievous gods, and therefore are meaningless

_____ 14. The best advice for combating insomnia is to
   a. get in bed at the same time every night and stay there no matter what happens
   b. get out of bed, go to another room, and do something relaxing if you can't fall asleep
   c. review the problems of the day as you lie in bed trying to go to sleep
   d. try sleeping in another room, or on the couch, if you can't fall asleep in your bed

_____ 15. Which one of the following is *not* a sleep problem?
   a. night terrors
   b. sleepwalking
   c. narcolepsy
   d. oversleeping

Answers for Module 7

True-False	Flashcards 1	Flashcards 2	Multiple-Choice
1. F	1. a	1. a	1. a
2. T	2. g	2. j	2. c
3. T	3. h	3. i	3. d
4. T	4. d	4. d	4. b
5. F	5. c	5. h	5. c
6. T	6. j	6. f	6. a
7. F	7. i	7. e	7. d
8. T	8. e	8. g	8. c
9. T	9. f	9. b	9. b
10. F	10. b	10. c	10. d
			11. d
			12. c
			13. a
			14. b
			15. d

The Big Picture

Statement A

Keep a Dream Journal

Many self-observing people have benefited from keeping dream journals. Have a notepad and pen on your nightstand. When you have a dream (see other material in this Study Guide module on catching and interpreting dreams), jot down the essential points. Later, write a fuller version in your Dream Journal. It is fascinating to re-read these dreams after you have accumulated a number of them. Patterns may emerge. Common themes will be revealed. You will learn more about yourself.

Module 8

Hypnosis & Drugs

We'll Have Ours Straight

Nature lovers have a kind of warped view of life. In general, we prefer it undiluted. When we're outdoors, we don't wear headsets because we would rather hear the birds, waves, and wind. When we're having fun, we would rather have all our senses set on normal, neither excited nor dulled by psychoactive agents, legal or otherwise.

For most humans, however, and apparently for most of human history, normal consciousness isn't quite satisfying. Sometimes we want it heightened, sometimes we need it muted. Hence the long history of human attempts to alter consciousness and mood through self-medication. Almost all of us have found some technique, or some substance, that adjusts our consciousness and mood to the point where it feels just right.

This module discusses two methods of altering consciousness. Hypnosis is either a state of great suggestibility or an alternate route to deeper truths about ourselves. Rod Plotnik discusses the debate over what hypnosis is, how it works, and what it can do. But regardless of your position in this debate, hypnosis is different from ordinary consciousness. Psychoactive drugs are a mind-altering power of a different sort.

Why Do We Use Drugs?

In textbook after textbook I've seen, the section on drugs reads like something you would get in pharmacy school. Good, solid technical information on psychoactive drugs, including the most recent illegal drugs to hit the streets, but nothing on the really important issue — why we use psychoactive drugs at all, let alone to such excess.

Rod Plotnik raises that question, and suggests provocative answers. Rod offers a balanced, dispassionate survey of contemporary drug use and abuse. Rather than succumbing to hysteria or personal beliefs, the common failing of so many politicians and public spokespersons, Rod carefully reviews the biological facts, the cultural connections, and the historical record of drug use and society's attempts to curtail it. If you read Rod's discussion carefully, you may discover that some of the things you always knew were "true" about drugs may not be true after all.

Personally, I'm dead set against any use of psychoactive drugs [...says he, after gulping down a can of caffeine-laced cola!], but I don't think it does any good to tell you that. Rod has it right. Instead of moralizing (as I did earlier), let's investigate the psychological processes by which almost all of us "self-medicate," in our continual attempt to control and manage our thoughts, feelings, and behavior. This is exciting stuff.

Effective Student Tip 8

People Power

One of my arguments for setting a goal of perfect attendance is that when you go to class every day the group takes over. It's not that you feel like a captive, but more like a member of a family that is determined not to let you fail. In a good class, I often notice that the regulars kind of take an informal attendance, not satisfied until all the other regulars have arrived, or pointedly worrying about the one who hasn't.

These friendships become the basis for study groups, invaluable for struggling students and even more valuable for the students helping them. (Here is a paradox of instruction: the teacher always learns more than the student, because in order to teach something to someone else you first have to really understand it yourself). Study groups give their members ten times more opportunities to ask questions and talk than class time allows. That adds up to lots more practice.

Another reason to get acquainted with your classmates is the opportunity to make new friends and expand your cultural horizons. Most colleges attract students from every part of the city and from all over the world. Finally, there is the fact that we humans may be the most social species on earth. Biologically speaking, other people replace our missing instincts. Practically speaking, friends make life fun.

Your response...

Do you talk to your classmates? How easily do you make new friends? Do you ever feel lonely?

Key Terms

Most of these key terms are as timely as today's news, where you are likely to find them. All you need to do is sharpen up your definitions.

- addiction
- age regression
- alcohol
- alcoholism
- altered state theory of hypnosis
- caffeine
- cocaine
- DARE (Drug Abuse Resistance Program)
- dependency
- designer drugs
- hallucinogens
- hypnosis
- hypnotic analgesia
- hypnotic induction
- imagined perception
- LSD
- marijuana
- MDMA ("ecstasy")
- mescaline
- methamphetamine
- nicotine
- opiates
- posthypnotic amnesia
- posthypnotic suggestion
- psilocybin
- psychoactive drugs
- socio-cognitive theory of hypnosis
- stimulants
- substance abuse
- tolerance
- withdrawal symptoms

Outline

- *Introduction*
  1. Hypnosis
  2. Drugs
  □ How are hypnosis and drug use somewhat alike?
- A. *Hypnosis*
  1. Definition of **hypnosis**
  2. Three often asked questions about hypnosis
     a. Who can be hypnotized?
     b. Who is susceptible?
     c. How is someone hypnotized?
        (1) **Hypnotic induction**
        (2) Method to induce hypnosis
  3. Theories of hypnosis
     a. **Altered state theory of hypnosis** (Milton Erickson)
     b. Hidden observer explanation (Ernest Hilgard)
  4. Socio-cognitive theory of hypnosis
     a. **Socio-cognitive theory of hypnosis**
     b. Social behaviors in conformity

5. Behaviors
   a. **Hypnotic analgesia**
   b. **Posthypnotic suggestion**
   c. **Posthypnotic amnesia**
   d. **Age regression**
   e. **Imagined perception**
6. Medical and therapeutic applications
   a. Medical and dental uses
   b. Therapeutic and behavioral uses

B. Drugs: Overview

1. Reasons for use (**psychoactive drugs**)
2. Definition of terms
   ❏ *Why is it significant that Freud had a problem? What does it say about drugs? About psychology?*
   a. **Addiction**
   b. **Tolerance**
   c. **Dependency**
   d. **Withdrawal symptoms**
3. Use of drugs
4. Effects on nervous system
   a. Drugs mimic neurotransmitters
   b. Drugs block removal of neurotransmitter (reuptake)

C. Stimulants

1. **Stimulants**
   ❏ *Rod Plotnik quotes a great marketing slogan used to sell amphetamines in Sweden in the 1940s. When we look back on our own times, what ad campaigns may seem equally irresponsible?*
2. Amphetamines: **methamphetamine**
   a. Nervous system
   b. Dangers
3. **Cocaine**
   a. Nervous system
   b. Dangers
4. **Caffeine**
   a. Nervous system
   b. Dangers
5. **Nicotine**
   a. Nervous system
   b. Dangers

D. *Opiates*
   1. Opium, morphine, heroin
   2. **Opiates**
      a. Nervous system
      b. Dangers

E. *Hallucinogens*
   1. **Hallucinogens**
   2. **LSD**
      a. Nervous system
      b. Dangers
   3. **Psilocybin** ("magic mushrooms")
      a. Nervous system
      b. Dangers
   3. **Mescaline** (peyote cactus)
      a. Nervous system
      b. Dangers
   4. **Designer drugs (MDMA "ecstasy")**
      a. Nervous system
      b. Dangers

F. *Alcohol*
   1. History and use
   2. Definition and effects
      a. Drug: **alcohol**
      b. Nervous system
      c. Dangers
   3. Risk factors
      a. Environmental/psychological risk factors
      b. Genetic risk factors
   4. Problems with alcohol

G. *Cultural Diversity: Alcoholism Rates*
   1. **Alcoholism**
   2. Cultural factors
      a. Genetic risk factors
      b. Cultural risk factors
      c. Across cultures

H. Marijuana
1. Use and effects
2. **Marijuana**
   a. Nervous system
   b. Dangers

I. Research Focus: Drug Prevention
1. Effectiveness of **DARE (Drug Abuse Resistance Program)**
2. Research on effectiveness of DARE Program
   a. Method and procedure
   b. Results and discussion
   b. Conclusion

J. Application: Treatment for Drug Abuse
1. Case history
2. **Substance abuse**
3. Treatment
   a. Step 1: Admit the problem
   b. Step 2: Enter a program
   c. Step 3: Get therapy
   d. Step 4: Remain drug free

Language Workout

What's That?

p. 169 all **filed out** = walked out
pieces of furniture assumed **grotesque** [forms] = strange, ugly
LSD's great **potency** = strength, power

p. 170 **verify** Mesmer's claims = prove as true
susceptibility to hypnosis = openness to an action
introversion = tendency to think and act inward, unsocial
extroversion = tendency to think and act outward, social
compliance = agreeing to follow other people's decisions
gullibility = tendency to easily believe lies
method to **induce** hypnosis = produce
[subjects] **retain** their ability = keep

p. 171 the world's leading **practitioner** = user, person who practices method
[followers] **hold to** the belief = strongly believe
plunge one hand into ice water = put
markedly increased suggestibility = greatly
has been duplicated and even **surpassed** = exceeded
Elvis Presley's **gyrations** = movements

p. 172 [Clients] had **undergone** hypnosis = experienced
After an **exhaustive** review = complete, with every detail
"Try to **swat** that fly" = hit
an armored **knight** = fighter, warrior
remove the **armor** = metal protection worn like a suit
not merely **faking** their responses = pretending false action
inhibit a variety of movements = physically restrain
authority figures = people in positions of importance

p. 173 **legitimate** uses of hypnosis = approved
a **terminal** disease = leading to death
lukewarm [water] = mildly warm
leads to successful **outcomes** = results
remove **warts** = skin growths
optimal functioning = highest level, best

p. 174 [Freud] tried to **cut down** = reduce his usage
an **overwhelming** and compulsive desire = impossible to fight
a strong tendency to **relapse** = return to harmful behavior
the original **dose** of the drug = measured amount of medicine
it was beyond his human power to **bear** = tolerate

p. 175 arrested for a drug **violation** = breaking the law
General Accounting Office = U.S. government collector of statistics
materially reduced the availability = strongly, directly
more **cost-effective** = with better results for less money
Drugs **mimic** neurotransmitters = imitate

p. 176 It resulted in **epidemic** usage = widespread
people **displaced** by the war = forced to leave their homes
stiffer penalties = stronger
available on **the black market** = illegal, hidden economy
amphetamines were **diverted** to illegal sales = redirected
authorities **raided** [laboratories] = attacked
its chemical **makeup** = composition, organization
can be smoked or **snorted** = inhaled through the nose
I **craved** it = felt strong desire for
Tara, who was a **heavy** amphetamine user = very frequent
a **crackdown** on amphetamines = strong action by police

p. 177 an **upsurge** in methamphetamine usage = increase
unlimited **access** to pure cocaine = freedom to use
to the point of **starvation** = dying from lack of food
they **overestimate** the quality of their work = have too high opinion of
damage to **cartilage** of the nose = rubbery material
Cocaine users often go through **a vicious circle** = a series of actions, where each solution makes a new problem

p. 178 **Abruptly** stopping the consumption of caffeine = without preparation
the **United States Surgeon General** = equivalent to Minister of Health
symptoms range in **severity** = serious effects
to **light up** again = light a cigarette
a **nicotine patch** = treatment applied to skin, like a bandaid

Module 8: Hypnosis & Drugs

p. 179 **gave rise to** a lucrative [market] = produced, created
a **lucrative** worldwide opium black market = profitable
constipation = inability of body to expel waste products
real floaty = very disconnected
the **gastrointestinal tract** = body system that uses food, stomach

p. 180 the **net** effect is increased stimulation = final
frightening **flashbacks** = surprise return of drug effects
a **whirlpool** of pictures = confusing mixture
[Effects] last **half as long** = 50% shorter

p. 181 use peyote as a **sacrament** = religious practice
Mescaline does not **impair** the intellect = hurt the operation of
the **setting** [influences] the experience = physical situation during drug-taking
anecdotal reports = popular stories, not accepted as scientific

p. 182 The first **brewery** appeared in Egypt = business producing beer
the Eighteenth **Amendment** = official change to the U.S. constitution
Congress **repealed** prohibition = negated the law
one **cocktail** = popular mixture of different alcohols
drink **hard** liquor = strong
a **fraternity pledge** died = college student trying to enter a social organization
Another serious problem is **blackouts** = periods that cannot be remembered

p. 183 **maladaptive** [traits] = not helpful to functioning
predispositions that increase the potential for alcoholism = **tendencies**
campus **rapes** = sexual attacks
the **assailant** = the attacker
manslaughter convictions = killing
husbands **batter** their wives = beat, hit
college women said they had **binged** = uncontrolled eating or drinking
suicides involve alcohol = cases of people who kill themselves
college freshmen who **drop out** = leave school
surpassing **apathy** = lack of interest

p. 185 the **Confucian moral code** = Chinese system of values, from the works of Confucius
strong cultural-religious **taboos** = laws forbidding actions
the average **duration** of alcoholism = time of existence
the overall **mortality** rate from alcoholism = death

p. 186 the leading U.S. **cash crops** = plants profitable to sell
associated with **chemotherapy** = treatment for cancer
This **federal-state conflict** = fight between U.S. government and state governments
researchers identified and **synthesized** THC = artificially produced
no **conclusive** evidence = certain
joints of marijuana = cigarette-like shape

p. 187 students were pretested to **determine** their attitudes = identify
politicians gave **glowing** testimonials = full of praise

p. 188 [Martin] felt **insecure** = uncertain, unsure
Martin's **knack** for learning helped him = ability
alcohol reduced his feelings of "**self-loathing**" = self-hating

his wife refused to **put up with** his heavy drinking = tolerate, live with
Martin sat home with his **booze** = liquor
treatment to **get straightened out** = stop harmful behavior
it represents a **hurdle** = obstacle, problem

p. 189 going out with drinking **buddies** = friends
cope with **stressors** = factors that cause stress

p. 192 evidence used by Kishline to **back up** the claims = prove

Wild Plurals

Language students know about irregular plurals of common words, like:

one **woman**, but many **women**
one **child**, but many **children**
one **mouse**, but many **mice**

Some formal words also have irregular plurals:

one **phenomenon**, but many **phenomena**
The bodily process that changes a child into an adult is a phenomen**on** found all over the world.
Earthquakes and volcanoes are phenomen**a** related to pressures within the earth.

one **datum**, but many **data**
To avoid lawsuits, a newspaper reporter must check every dat**um** in a story.
Computers are especially useful to store and analyze dat**a** from years of research.

one **stimulus**, but many **stimuli**
Next week's exam is a strong stimul**us** for Marisol to study harder.
Reward and punishment are both stimul**i** for actions, but which is more effective?

Test Yourself:

All the **dat___** from scientific experiments show that human activities are responsible for various **phenomen____** like rising temperatures and more storms.

The promise of food is a good **stimul____** to help an animal learn behavior. Humans use this **phenomen_____** to train dogs, horses, and elephants.

High blood pressure, the desire to fit in a new dress, and enjoyment are all **stimul___** to start an exercise program.

Not every **dat___** is important. For example, most people don't need to know the exact distance between Tokyo and Buenos Aires.

See It and Say It

p. 179 **methadone** = METH-uh-doan

p. 180 **hallucinogen** = huh-LOO-sin-uh-jen
hallucinogenic = huh-loo-sin-o-JEN-ik
peyote = pay-OH-tee

Meet the Word Family: abstain – abstinent - abstinence

abstain from drinking = decide to not do something *[verb]*
> Librarians always ask people to **abstain from** talking in the library.
> The doctor advised Halina to **abstain from** food for 24 hours before her operation.

clients remain **abstinent** *[adjective]*
> **Abstinent** guests are popular at parties because they can safely drive other people home.
> It's hard to stay **abstinent** when everyone around is eating and drinking.

the goal is total **abstinence** *[noun]*
> The war was a time of **abstinence** for everyone.
> In the month of Ramadan, Muslims practice **abstinence from** eating and drinking during daylight hours.

TEST YOURSELF

Darryl is very lazy; he _____ from exercise as much as possible. But he is not at all _____ when it's time for dinner. He prefers _____ from exercise, not from hamburgers. However, his friends try to _____ from criticizing him.

Answer Key

All the **data** from scientific experiments show that human activities are responsible for various **phenomena** like rising temperatures and more storms.

The promise of food is a good **stimulus** to help an animal learn behavior. Humans use this **phenomenon** to train dogs, horses, and elephants.

High blood pressure, the desire to fit in a new dress, and enjoyment are all **stimuli** to start an exercise program.

Not every **datum** is important. For example, most people don't need to know the exact distance between Tokyo and Buenos Aires.

Darryl is very lazy; he **abstains** from exercise as much as possible. But he is not at all **abstinent** when it's time for dinner. He prefers **abstinence** from exercise, not from hamburgers. However, his friends try to **abstain** from criticizing him.

For hip students only...

Special Quiz on Psychoactive Drugs: Sorry, but suspicious results may be sent home to your parents!

_____ 1. alcohol   a. America's number one cash crop
_____ 2. caffeine   b. creates a vicious circle of highs and intense craving for more
_____ 3. cocaine   c. most widely used drug in the world, relatively harmless
_____ 4. ecstasy   d. profound, long lasting sensory and perceptual distortions
_____ 5. heroin   e. responsible for the most drug deaths
_____ 6. LSD   f. designer drug
_____ 7. marijuana   g. oldest drug made by humans, still society's biggest drug problem
_____ 8. mescaline   h. reemerging as crystal meth or ice
_____ 9. nicotine   i. opium poppy
_____ 10. metham-   j. severe bad trips could lead to psychotic reactions
         phetamine

Scoring:

1 to 3 correct	*You've been in a monastery, right?*
4 to 6 correct	*I'm new on campus myself!*
7 to 9 correct	*This seems very suspicious.*
all 10 correct	*Report to Student Health immediately — you know too much!*

The Big Picture

Which statement below offers the best summary of the larger significance of this module?

A   This module comes right out and says it: the War on Drugs not only is a waste of time, but it may be contrary to human health. We need the pleasures that drugs provide and we can tolerate a few victimless crimes.

B   The material on hypnosis is a stage-setter for the message of this module. If we have so little control over our behavior, we cannot allow even the smallest existence of a drug culture. Zero tolerance is our only hope.

C   When we crack down on one psychoactive drug, people who are weak just find some other mood-altering substance. That's why the module concludes that government regulation of the drug trade is the only sensible answer.

D   As much as we might not like to admit it, drug use may be almost "natural." We seem driven to alter our consciousness, perhaps to make life more bearable, and history suggests that almost nothing will stop us.

E   Say something about this module? Well, its like totally awesome... you know what I mean?... like, you know?... whatever... oh man, I'm really wasted!

True-False

_____   1. Stage hypnotism really isn't so remarkable, since everyone can be hypnotized.

_____   2. According to the altered state theory, during hypnosis a person enters a special state of consciousness that is different from the normal waking state.

_____   3. The debate in psychology about hypnosis concerns whether entertainers should be allowed to exploit hypnosis for profit.

_____   4. One good use for hypnosis is to reduce pain during medical or dental procedures.

_____   5. Hypnosis is more effective than any other technique in helping people quit smoking.

_____   6. History shows that if our government would follow a consistent policy, one by one all illegal drugs could be eradicated.

_____   7. Psychoactive drugs create effects on behavior by interfering with the normal activity of neurotransmitters.

_____   8. The most harmful drugs are the illegal ones; the legal drugs may not be good for you, but they don't do any serious harm.

_____   9. Research proves that in DARE (Drug Abuse Resistance Program) we finally have a program that works — if only we had the resolve to use it in every school in the nation.

_____   10. Your risk for becoming an alcoholic rises significantly if members of your family were alcoholics.

Flashcards 1

____ 1. age regression
____ 2. altered state theory of hypnosis
____ 3. hypnosis
____ 4. hypnotic analgesia
____ 5. hypnotic induction
____ 6. imagined perception
____ 7. posthypnotic amnesia
____ 8. posthypnotic suggestion
____ 9. psychoactive drugs
____ 10. socio-cognitive theory of hypnosis

a. says hypnosis is a state during which a person experiences different sensations and feelings
b. experiencing sensations, perceiving stimuli, or performing behaviors from one's imagination
c. giving hypnotized subject an idea about performing a particular behavior upon coming out of hypnosis
d. not remembering what happened during hypnosis if hypnotist told you that you wouldn't
e. various methods to induce hypnosis, including asking subjects to close their eyes, go to sleep
f. reduction in pain after hypnosis, suggestions that reduce anxiety and promote relaxation
g. procedure for experiencing changes in sensations, perceptions, thoughts, feelings, or behaviors
h. says hypnosis is state of powerful social or personal influences and pressures to conform to suggestions
i. drugs that increase the activity of the nervous system and result in heightened alertness and arousal
j. subjects under hypnosis being asked to return or regress to an earlier period, such as early childhood

Flashcards 2

____ 1. addiction
____ 2. dependency
____ 3. caffeine
____ 4. designer drugs
____ 5. hallucinogens
____ 6. nicotine
____ 7. opiates
____ 8. stimulants
____ 9. tolerance
____ 10. withdrawal symptoms

a. change in nervous system so a person needs to take the drug to prevent painful withdrawal symptoms
b. a behavioral pattern marked by overwhelming and compulsive desire to use a drug; tendency to relapse
c. manufactured or synthetic illegal drugs designed to produce psychoactive effects
d. a mild stimulant that produces moderate physiological arousal; alertness, decreased fatigue
e. drugs that increase activity of nervous system and result in heightened alertness, arousal and euphoria
f. drugs that produce strange and unreal perceptual, sensory, and cognitive experiences
g. addictive drugs that come from the opium poppy, such as opium, morphine, heroin; highly addictive
h. dangerous drug that first produces arousal but then has calming effect [hint: it's legal!]
i. original dose of drug no longer produces the desired effect, so person must take increasingly larger doses
j. painful physical and psychological symptoms that occur after drug-dependent person stops using drug

Multiple-Choice

1. Rod Plotnik tells the story about attending a stage hypnotist's act to illustrate the point that
   a. a trained psychologist cannot be hypnotized
   b. hypnotism produces remarkable effects, but there is debate about what it really is
   c. hypnotism is an art that many have attempted to learn, but only a rare few have mastered
   d. entertainment pays better than psychology

2. Which one of the following is *not* a necessary part of inducing hypnosis?
   a. swing a watch (and it must be a pocket watch) slowly back and forth until the subject's eyes glaze over
   b. establish a sense of trust
   c. suggest that the subject concentrate on something
   d. suggest what the subject will experience during hypnosis

3. The main issue in the psychological debate over hypnosis is
   a. not whether it exists, but how it is induced
   b. why subjects tend to play along with the hypnotist
   c. whether hidden observers really can spot stage hypnotist's tricks
   d. whether it is a special state of consciousness

4. Which one of the following is *not* an effect claimed for hypnosis?
   a. age regression
   b. imagined perception
   c. hypnotic analgesia
   d. superhuman acts of strength

5. The hypnotist tells Janet, "When you wake up, you will not remember what you did on stage tonight." This instruction produces
   a. posthypnotic amnesia
   b. hypnotic suggestion
   c. posthypnotic ordering
   d. hypnotic analgesia

6. Research into the use of hypnosis to change problem behaviors suggests that hypnosis
   a. is a miracle treatment in changing behavior
   b. does not help in attempts to change behavior
   c. can be useful in combination with other treatments
   d. is useful in helping people quit smoking, but not in weight loss

7. Many students are shocked to learn that the great psychologist Sigmund Freud had a serious drug problem:
   a. cocaine
   b. nicotine
   c. alcohol
   d. marijuana

8. "Tolerance" for a drug means that the brain and the body
   a. adjust to the drug and use it with no ill effects
   b. no longer get any effect from using the drug
   c. shut out the drug, which passes harmlessly through the system
   d. require increasingly larger doses of the drug to achieve the same effect

9. Basically, all illegal drugs work by interfering with the normal operation of
   a. neurotransmitters in the brain
   b. glucose in the blood
   c. DNA in the genes
   d. sensory receptors in the eyes, ears, nose, tongue, and skin

10. All of the following are stimulants *except*
    a. cocaine
    b. caffeine
    c. alcohol
    d. nicotine

11. The main reason it is so tough to quit smoking is that
    a. tolerance for nicotine takes a long time to develop
    b. physical addiction can continue for years after quitting
    c. withdrawal symptoms are so painful
    d. psychological dependency is deepened by the fact that smoking solves problems

12. Studies of national rates of alcoholism around the world suggest that alcoholism is a/n
    a. partly genetic and partly cultural problem
    b. individual problem, relatively unaffected by where the individual lives
    c. genetic problem, independent of national origins
    d. family problem, passed down through the generations

13. Despite all the drug abuse horror stories we hear, the truth is that the two most costly and deadly drugs in our society are
    a. heroin and cocaine
    b. marijuana and crack cocaine
    c. angel dust and mescaline
    d. alcohol and tobacco

14. The clear lesson of the history of prohibition (1920 to 1933) is that
    a. it is almost impossible to ban a drug that is desired by a majority of the citizens
    b. we must abandon our on-again off-again enforcement strategies and declare an all-out war on drugs
    c. eventually people get tired of any drug
    d. legalization would reduce the problem to manageable dimensions

15. After years of studying the harmfulness of marijuana, scientists have concluded that it
    a. eventually causes brain damage
    b. often leads to mental illness
    c. typically leads to the use of hard drugs
    d. may or may not be dangerous in the long run — the research is not yet definitive

Answers for Module 8

True-False
1. F
2. T
3. F
4. T
5. F
6. F
7. T
8. F
9. F
10. T

Flashcards 1
1. j
2. a
3. g
4. f
5. e
6. b
7. d
8. c
9. i
10. h

Flashcards 2
1. b
2. a
3. d
4. c
5. f
6. h
7. g
8. e
9. i
10. j

Multiple-Choice
1. b
2. a
3. d
4. d
5. a
6. c
7. b
8. d
9. a
10. c
11. c
12. a
13. d
14. a
15. d

The Big Picture

Statement D

Special Quiz On Psychoactive Drugs

1. g   2. c   3. b   4. f   5. i   6. j   7. a   8. d   9. e   10. h

---

Test-Taking Tips 1

You don't have to remember *everything* in order to get the question right. Often the correct answer is revealed by carefully reading the question, plus relying on your own knowledge and intelligence.

- Be wary of answers stated in extreme terms like "always," "never," or "100 percent."
- Be wary of answers that defy all common sense.

Module 9

Classical Conditioning

The Paradox of Behaviorist Psychology

Most students begin reading about the psychology of learning with good intentions, but soon give up. It's just too darn complicated. They have run smack into The Paradox.

In truth, the basic principles of learning discovered by Pavlov, Skinner, and others (described in Modules 9 and 10) are elegantly simple, wonderfully powerful, and among the most useful products of psychology. Once you do understand them you'll say, "I sort of knew that already." The problem is the language they come wrapped in.

Ivan Pavlov was a pure scientist, a Nobel prize winner. Naturally, he used the precise, mathematical language of the laboratory. The psychologists who followed Pavlov, the ones we call behaviorists, also prided themselves on being laboratory scientists. One of the strongest points in favor of the behaviorist approach is its insistence that psychology stick to observable, measurable phenomena (no murky, mentalistic concepts like Freud's unconscious). We teachers can appreciate this approach, because we studied it thoroughly in graduate school. But when undergraduate students encounter behaviorism, they don't have much time to learn the technical language. Yet we expect them to gulp it all down in a couple of weeks. Most gag instead.

These poor beleaguered psychology students have a point. Reform in our terminology is long overdue. The first term we could do without is "conditioning." We're really talking about *learning*. Classical conditioning and operant conditioning are also learning, each by a different route, but learning all the same. Even the terms "stimulus" and "response" say more about Pavlov's fame than about how human life really works.

We're Mad As Hell and We're Not Going to Take It Anymore!

Your instructor will tell you which terms to learn, but as you study you can make some mental translations. Keep in mind that we're always talking about *learning*. When you read "classical conditioning," remind yourself that you are reading about Pavlov's kind of learning, where a dog's natural reflex to drool at meat got connected to something else (a bell). When you bump into a technical term like Skinner's "positive reinforcement," make up an everyday-life story that illustrates the term: "If my little brother cleans up his room and my parents reward him with extra allowance money, he will be more likely to clean up his room again next week."

Don't let yourself be cheated out of what may be the most useful ideas in psychology, just because the language is difficult. Fight back!

Effective Student Tip 9

Adopt a Strategy of Effectiveness

You're probably getting more advice about how to be successful in college than you know what to do with. By itself, any specific piece of advice tends to get lost in the crowd. You need a way to pull the really good advice together and put it to regular use. You need a *strategy* of success.

An overall strategy is important because it gives you a way of evaluating any particular suggestion and of adjusting to whatever conditions arise. It is more than a single game plan, because it is both more comprehensive and more flexible. If your game plan for the next test is to work like the devil, what do you do if hard work doesn't seem to be enough?

Any plan is better than no plan, but I suggest a special kind of strategy, a strategy of effectiveness. The strategy of effectiveness is simply this: (1) You recognize that you have a basic need to be effective in everything you do, especially your college work, since that's your most important task right now. (2) You measure everything you do in college by asking, "Is this procedure getting the job done?" (In other words, is it effective?) (3) Whenever a method isn't working, instead of continuing to do the same ineffective things you make a specific procedural change.

Your response...
Do you have an overall strategy for getting through college? [Most students don't.]

Key Terms

Fight back! Translate the technical terms into everyday language about learning.

adaptive value
anticipatory nausea
classical conditioning
cognitive learning
cognitive perspective
conditioned emotional response
conditioned response (CR)
conditioned stimulus (CS)

contiguity theory
discrimination
extinction
generalization
law of effect
learning
neutral stimulus
operant conditioning
preparedness

spontaneous recovery
stimulus substitution
systematic desensitization
taste-aversion learning
unconditioned response (UCR)
unconditioned stimulus (UCS)

Outline

- *Introduction*
    1. It's only aftershave
    2. It's only a needle
    3. It's only dish soap
        a. Conditioning
        b. **Learning**

    ❑ "Learning" is one of those everyday terms about which we say, "I know what it means...," until we attempt a formal definition. How would you define learning? Seriously... give it a try.

    A. *Three Kinds Of Learning*
    1. **Classical conditioning**
        a. Ivan Pavlov's famous experiment
        b. Conditioned reflex
        c. Learning through pairing stimuli
    2. **Operant conditioning**
        a. **Law of effect** (E. L. Thorndike)
        b. Consequences and learning (B. F. Skinner)
        c. Learning through effects or consequences of actions
    3. **Cognitive learning**
        a. Mental processes
        b. Observation and imitation (Albert Bandura)
        c. Learning through observing and thinking

B. Procedure: Classical Conditioning

1. Pavlov's experiment

☐ There is a beautiful logic to the way Pavlov worked out conditioning in his famous experiment with the drooling dog. Can you tell the story?

   a. Step 1: Selecting stimulus and response
      (1) **Neutral stimulus**
      (2) **Unconditioned stimulus (UCS)**
      (3) **Unconditioned response (UCR)**
   b. Step 2: Establishing classical conditioning
      (1) Neutral stimulus
      (2) Unconditioned stimulus (UCS)
      (3) Unconditioned response (UCR)
   c. Step 3: Testing for conditioning
      (1) **Conditioned stimulus (CS)**
      (2) **Conditioned response (CR)**

2. Terms in classical conditioning
   a. Step 1: Selecting stimulus and response
   b. Step 2: Establishing classical conditioning
   c. Step 3: Testing for conditioning

☐ See if you can apply Pavlov's logic to the example of poor Carla. Use the three steps above.

C. Other Conditioning Concepts

1. **Generalization**
2. **Discrimination**
3. **Extinction**
4. **Spontaneous recovery**

D. Adaptive Value and Uses

1. **Adaptive value**
2. **Taste aversion learning**
3. Explanation: **preparedness**
4. Examples of classical conditioning
   a. Bluejays and butterflies
   b. Hot fudge sundaes
5. **Conditioned emotional response**
6. Classical conditioning and dyslexia

E. Three Explanations
1. What is learned?
2. Stimulus substitution and contiguity theory
   a. **Stimulus substitution** (Pavlov)
   b. **Contiguity theory**
3. **Cognitive perspective** (Robert Rescorla)
   a. Predictable relationship
   b. Backward conditioning

F. Research Focus: Conditioning Little Albert
1. Can emotional responses be conditioned?
   a. John Watson and Rosalie Rayner (1920)
   b. "Little Albert"
2. Method: identifying terms
3. Procedure: establish and test for classical conditioning
4. Results and conclusions

G. Cultural Diversity: Conditioning Dental Fears
1. In the dentist's chair
2. Cultural practices
3. Origins of fears
4. Effects of fear

H. Application: Conditioned Fear & Nausea
1. Examples of conditioning
   a. Conditioned emotional response
   b. **Anticipatory nausea**
   c. Conditioning anticipatory nausea
2. **Systematic desensitization**
   a. Systematic desensitization procedure: three steps
      (1) Step 1: Learning to relax
      (2) Step 2: Making an anxiety hierarchy
      (3) Step 3: Imagining and relaxing
   b. Effectiveness of systematic desensitization

> *For Psych Majors Only...*
>
> **How Behaviorism Revolutionized Psychology:** Living in an age of scientific psychology, it is hard for us to comprehend how profoundly behaviorism revolutionized psychology. William James, the 'father' of American psychology, was more a philosopher than psychologist. He and others in the new field relied on the method of introspection, rather than on laboratory research, to figure out how the mind worked.
>
> Watson, extending Pavlov's scientific method to the study of human behavior, urged the following rule: Given the stimulus, predict the response; given the response, find the stimulus; given a change in response, find a change in the stimulus.
>
> My mother took a psychology course when she attended the University of Wisconsin in the early 1920s. Psychology was only a small part of the philosophy department, but the air was charged with Watson's crusade. She still remembers her young professor's challenge to his students: *"Stimulus and response, stimulus and response — learn to think in terms of stimulus and response!"*

Language Workout

What's That?

p. 195 I **assured** Carla = said it was true or possible
One [side effect] is severe **nausea** = sick feeling in stomach
its odor made her **salivate** = produce liquid in mouth (saliva)

p. 196 He has already won a **Nobel Prize** = highest award in science
this sort of **anticipatory** salivation = waiting for, in advance
an adult modeling **aggressive** behavior = forceful, attacking

p. 197 food **elicits** salivation = brings out, produces
salivation **is elicited by** food = produced

p. 199 **Spontaneous** recovery = without planning

p. 200 Taste-**aversion** = feeling of dislike
Rat **exterminators** = workers who destroy [rats]
bait poison = material used to catch or trap
Similarly, **quails** [have] poor olfaction = birds
They baited **grazing** areas = open areas of grass
where animals eat sheep flesh **laced** with a chemical = combined with

p. 201 For example, bluejays **feast on** butterflies = eat with pleasure
Unknown to a **naïve** bluejay = inexperienced
One purpose of salivation is to **lubricate** your mouth = make slippery

p. 202 a pizza [becomes] **bonded** = connected
this **contiguous** pairing = next to each other, side by side
Cognitive **perspective** = viewpoint

p. 204 John Watson was a strong **advocate of** behaviorism = supporter
was described as healthy, **stolid** = without emotion
which made a loud noise and elicited **startle** = surprise
he **crawled** away and cried = moved
a **rigorously** controlled experiment = very carefully
a **standardized** procedure = according to standard method
Watson's demonstration **laid the groundwork** = formed the basis

p. 205 free, universal dental **coverage** = availability of service
routine dental treatment = ordinary, common
counterconditioning = conditioning for opposite effect
this **intentional** relaxation = planned
how to relax her body **at will** = whenever she wants to
Making an anxiety **hierarchy** = system of lower and higher value

p. 210 stomach **cramps** = pains
demanded that olestra be **taken off the market** = removed from stores

What's the Result?

The more he eats, **the fatter** he looks.
The bigger my paycheck is, **the better** I like it.
The more books Luis reads, **the more** words he learns.
The faster the speed limit is, **the more** accidents will happen.

TRY IT

The easier the exam is, **the more** students will _____.
The less she eats, **the thinner** she _____.
The more he _____, **the more tired** Rakeem becomes.
The faster you _____, the **sooner** you will arrive.

Did you notice these lines in the text:

the more similar the new stimulus is to the original conditioned stimulus, **the larger** will be the conditioned response (p. 199).

the more painful their childhood dental experiences had been, **the greater** was their fear (p. 205).

Meet the Word Family: extinguish - extinction

extinguish = bring to a complete end

Marco blew hard **to extinguish** the candle.
The fireman **extinguished** the fire in my kitchen.
Every building should have a red fire **extinguisher** to use in case of fire.

extinction = the process of ending, erasing a conditioned response

Carla worked with a therapist on **the extinction of** her reaction to the aftershave.

The extinction of this conditioned response was a goal of her therapy.

Build Your Word Power

anticipate = expect, plan ahead

All the students **anticipated** a difficult exam, and they were correct.
No one can **anticipate** all the surprises that life might bring.

in anticipation of = expecting, before

Marta cleaned her house completely **in anticipation of** her mother's visit.
Ten minutes before his speech, Rob felt nervous **in anticipation** of speaking to a hundred people.

anticipatory = planned, before something happens

Dinner was not ready yet, but Toshio enjoyed the smells in the kitchen with **anticipatory** pleasure.
Calvin got a haircut and shined his shoes, **anticipatory** preparations for his job interview.

TRY IT

Mrs. Billings knew that she was pregnant, but she was surprised when the doctor told her to _____ the birth of twins. In the months before she had the babies, her husband made some _____ changes to their house; in fact, he built a new bedroom for the newcomers. Mrs. Billings kept a suitcase ready, with a nightgown and personal items, _____ of a sudden trip to the hospital.

Build the Word

sensit**ive** = full of feeling
sensit**ize** = make full of feeling
sensit**ization** = the action of making open to feeling
desensit**ization** = the action of removing feeling
systematic desensitization (p. 207) = methodical action, step by step

---

Answer Key

The easier the exam is, **the more** students will (pass)(get good grades)(be happy)
The less she eats, **the thinner** she (looks) (becomes) (gets).
The more he (works) (studies) (exercises), **the more tired** Rakeem becomes.
The faster you (drive) (walk), the **sooner** you will arrive.
Mrs. Billings knew that she was pregnant, but she was surprised when the doctor told her to **anticipate** the birth of twins. In the months before she had the babies, her husband made some **anticipatory** changes to their house; in fact, he built a new bedroom for the newcomers. Mrs. Billings kept a suitcase ready, with a nightgown and personal items, **in anticipation** of a sudden trip to the hospital.

The Big Picture

Which statement below offers the best summary of the larger significance of this module?

A   Begining with Ivan Pavlov's famous experiment with the salivating dog, behaviorists have performed remarkable feats of animal training. Almost all of their attempts to create such learning in humans, however, have failed.

B   Conditioning offers a powerful explanation of learning to fear things like rats, poisons, chemotherapy, etc. All that is lacking for a complete psychology of learning is a way to condition people to *like* things.

C   By demonstrating learning through "classical conditioning," Pavlov pioneered an objective, laboratory psychology. When Watson showed conditioning in humans, the stage was set for a scientific psychology of human behavior.

D   Although the behaviorists did demonstrate how simple behaviors can be taught and learned, behaviorist concepts cannot begin to explain the rich complexity of human behavior. Behaviorism is a very limited theory.

E   You think drooling to a bell was amazing? Wait 'til you hear what *my* dog did to my homework!

True-False

_____ 1. Learning is a relatively permanent change in behavior as a result of experience.

_____ 2. Ivan Pavlov's famous explanation of learning was so persuasive that no other theory has challenged it since.

_____ 3. The key to Pavlov's experiment was finding a reward that would make the dog salivate.

_____ 4. At first, UCS → UCR, but after the conditioning procedure, CS → CR.

_____ 5. Once conditioning has taken place, *generalization* may cause similar stimuli to elicit the response, but *discrimination* should work to establish control by the specified stimuli.

_____ 6. The cognitive perspective says classical conditioning happens when a new stimulus replaces an old one through association.

_____ 7. Bluejays avoid eating monarch butterflies because of taste-aversion learning.

_____ 8. In John Watson's classic experiment, Little Albert gradually learned to like a previously feared white rat when he was given candy for petting it.

_____ 9. If you are like most people, the sound of the dentist's drill has become an unconditioned stimulus.

_____ 10. The goal of systematic desensitization is to *uncondition* conditioned stimuli and make them neutral again.

Flashcards 1

1. conditioned response (CR)
2. conditioned stimulus (CS)
3. discrimination
4. extinction
5. generalization
6. neutral stimulus
7. spontaneous recovery
8. stimulus substitution
9. unconditioned response (UCR)
10. unconditioned stimulus (UCS)

a. tendency for the conditioned response to reappear after being extinguished
b. a formerly neutral stimulus that has acquired the ability to elicit the same response as UCS does
c. learning to make a particular response to some stimuli but not to others
d. explains classical conditioning as a neural bonding of a neutral and an unconditioned stimulus
e. an unlearned, innate, involuntary physiological reflex that is elicited by the unconditioned stimulus
f. failure of a conditioned stimulus to elicit a response when repeatedly presented without the UCS
g. new response elicited by a conditioned stimulus; similar to the unconditioned response
h. some stimulus that triggers or elicits a physiological reflex, such as salivation or eye blink
i. tendency for a stimulus that is similar to the original conditioned stimulus to elicit the same response
j. some stimulus that produces a response, but does not produce the reflex being tested

Flashcards 2

1. anticipatory nausea
2. classical conditioning
3. cognitive learning
4. conditioned emotional response
5. contiguity theory
6. law of effect
7. learning
8. preparedness
9. systematic desensitization
10. taste-aversion learning

a. procedure in which a person eliminates anxiety-evoking stimuli by relaxation; counterconditioning
b. a relatively enduring or permanent change in behavior that results from experience with stimuli
c. feeling fear or pleasure when experiencing a stimulus that initially accompanied a painful or pleasant event
d. learning in which a neutral stimulus acquires the ability to produce a response (Ivan Pavlov)
e. feelings of sickness elicited by stimuli that are associated with receiving chemotherapy treatments
f. if actions are followed by a pleasurable consequence or reward, they tend to be repeated (E. L. Thorndike)
g. explains classical conditioning as occurring because two stimuli are paired closely together in time
h. associating sensory cues (smells, tastes, sound, or sights) with getting sick, then avoiding those cues
i. a kind of learning that involves mental processes alone; may not require rewards or overt behavior
j. biological readiness to associate some combinations of conditioned and unconditioned stimuli

Multiple-Choice

_____ 1. Rod Plotnik begins this module with the story of Carla and the dentist's aftershave to show how
   a. learning often occurs when we least expect it
   b. learning is more likely to occur in some environments than in others
   c. we can learn a response simply because it occurs along with some other response
   d. we can like something very much, then turn against it for no clear reason

_____ 2. All of the following are approaches to understanding how learning occurs *except*
   a. classical conditioning
   b. operant conditioning
   c. cognitive learning
   d. physical learning

_____ 3. Since S → R, then obviously UCS → UCR, so naturally CS →
   a. UCS
   b. UCR
   c. CR
   d. neutral stimulus

_____ 4. In Pavlov's experiment, the actual learning took place when the
   a. neutral stimulus was paired with the unconditioned stimulus
   b. conditioned reflex was presented again and again
   c. unconditioned stimulus was paired with the conditioned stimulus
   d. paired unconditioned and neutral stimuli were presented together in several trials

_____ 5. John Watson was excited by Pavlov's discovery of the conditioned reflex because it
   a. provided the first look inside the thinking mind
   b. explained the operation of cognitive factors in learning
   c. explained learning in terms of behavior you could study in an objective way
   d. showed that canine and human brains work in much the same way

_____ 6. American children show more dental fear than Scandinavian children because
   a. American dentists are not as well trained
   b. health care systems in the two societies are different
   c. American children have seen many scary movies about cruel dentists
   d. Scandinavian dentists give their patients lots of candy for not crying

_____ 7. Now even the smell of her own shampoo can make Carla anxious: this is an example of
   a. generalization
   b. extinction
   c. discrimination
   d. spontaneous recovery

_____ 8. But the smell of her nail polish does not make Carla feel anxious; this is an example of
   a. generalization
   b. extinction
   c. discrimination
   d. spontaneous recovery

_____ 9. When a conditioned stimulus (e.g., a tone) is repeatedly presented without the unconditioned stimulus (e.g., meat), _____ eventually will occur
   a. generalization
   b. discrimination
   c. extinction
   d. spontaneous recovery

_____ 10. We seem to be biologically ready to associate some combinations of conditioned and unconditioned stimuli more easily than others, a phenomenon called
   a. conditioned nausea
   b. phobia
   c. taste-aversion learning
   d. preparedness

_____ 11. From the point of view of a behavioral psychologist, a phobia is a/n
   a. expression of an unconscious conflict
   b. representation of a hidden wish
   c. conditioned emotional response
   d. unconditioned response

_____ 12. According to Robert Rescorla's cognitive explanation of Pavlov's experiment, the conditioned reflex gets established because
   a. the dog wants to do what Pavlov seems to want it to do
   b. the dog learns that the tone predicts the presentation of the food
   c. Pavlov unwittingly tips off the dog by looking at the food tray
   d. Pavlov simply waits until the dog makes the right response

_____ 13. The reason for Little Albert's fame in psychology is the fact that
   a. Watson showed that emotional responses could be classically conditioned in humans
   b. Pavlov was unable to replicate his salivation procedure with Little Albert
   c. Rescorla used the Little Albert experiment to disprove Pavlov
   d. Carla learned not to fear the dentist through the example of this brave little boy

_____ 14. A classically conditioned response often observed in patients receiving chemotherapy is
   a. anticipatory nausea
   b. phobia
   c. taste-aversion learning
   d. preparedness

_____ 15. Which one of the following is *not* necessary to the systematic desensitization procedure
   a. learning to relax
   b. identifying unconscious conflicts
   c. making an anxiety hierarchy
   d. imagining and relaxing while moving up and down the anxiety hierarchy

Answers for Module 9

True-False
1. T
2. F
3. F
4. T
5. T
6. F
7. T
8. F
9. F
10. T

Flashcards 1
1. g
2. b
3. c
4. f
5. i
6. j
7. a
8. d
9. e
10. h

Flashcards 2
1. e
2. d
3. i
4. c
5. g
6. f
7. b
8. j
9. a
10. h

Multiple-Choice
1. c
2. d
3. c
4. d
5. c
6. b
7. a
8. c
9. c
10. d
11. c
12. b
13. a
14. a
15. b

The Big Picture

Statement C

Test-Taking Tips 2

Carefully reading the question, plus your own general knowledge and intelligence, often reveals the correct answer. Some hints:

- Be wary of answers that appear to be way off the point.
- Be wary of answers that contain nonsense statements or that do not make sense.

Module 10

Operant & Cognitive Approaches

B. F. Skinner and the Behavioral Approach

Which psychologist has had the greatest impact on twentieth-century thought? The only obvious alternative to B. F. Skinner is Sigmund Freud himself. Even then, many would credit Freud for the most provocative ideas but give Skinner the award for actual laws of behavior and their practical applications. Skinner made psychology a science and discovered a series of principles that have become a permanent part of psychology.

As a scientist, Skinner spent his career pursuing principles of behavior that could be demonstrated in the laboratory. But he was equally concerned with what psychology is *not*. Often criticized for a mechanistic approach to psychology, Skinner once protested, "I have feelings!" The point he was trying to make was that no matter how real and important feelings are, they are difficult to study objectively. No matter how tempting it might be, Skinner refused to speculate about any psychological phenomena that could not be subjected to rigorous laboratory investigation. Rod Plotnik tells a fascinating story about how Skinner stuck to his scientific guns to the end of his life, even at the cost of offending those who had come to admire him.

Is "Cognitive Learning" a Contradiction in Terms?

For B. F. Skinner and the "radical" or "strict" behaviorists, as they came to be called, learning meant the principles of acquiring and modifying behavior as explained *without* reference to any nonobservable phenomena like cognition or mind. "Cognitive" learning, which Plotnik covers in this module, brings in what Skinner called nonobservable, and hence nonscientific, mental activity.

For most psychologists, even many of Skinner's young disciples like Albert Bandura, this uncompromising stand seemed to require a deliberate turning away from factors that were obvious and suggestive of further insights about learning. They were unwilling to leave so much out. So, without rejecting Skinner's classic discoveries, they entered the forbidden territory of the mind anyway. The result has been a very fruitful combining of behavioral principles and cognitive processes. Because the combined cognitive-behavioral approach has been willing to speculate about mental processes, it has developed many innovative and effective therapeutic applications. When the Skinnerians were at the peak of their influence, they assumed that since they understood the laws of behavior, it would be a simple matter to apply those laws to curing human psychological suffering. It didn't work out that way, since real life is so much more complicated than the laboratory, and many of Skinner's frustrated followers drifted into the cognitive camp.

Effective Student Tip 10

Build Effective Routines

Anyone who loves computers also values orderly procedures. To get the most out of your computer, you must learn procedures and follow them.

Why not apply the same tactic to your college studies? When it comes to advice about how to do better in college, there are tons of useful techniques, hints, tips, tricks, and shortcuts out there. Become a consumer of useful procedures. Adapt them to your needs. Invent your own. Gather advice about how to be successful in school, but do it with a difference.

First, take a *procedural* point of view. Pay less attention to advice that is mainly sloganeering ("You *must* work harder!") and more to specific procedures (see Tip 19, "Three Secrets of Effective Writing," for example).

Second, gather all these useful procedures under the umbrella of *effectiveness*. Judge every procedure by whether it makes you a better student. If it works, keep it in your arsenal of useful procedures. If it doesn't, drop it. I once had a friend who decided to make himself lean and strong by eating *nothing but apples*. Excited about his new plan, for several days he was never without his bag of apples. It didn't work.

Your response...

What advice have you gotten that wasn't really very helpful? What was wrong with the advice?

Key Terms

Keep on fighting back! Here is more technical laboratory language, but each key term is still about how we learn stuff. Try to make up a little story for each one.

autism
behavior modification
biofeedback
biological factors
cognitive learning
cognitive map
continuous reinforcement
critical [sensitive] period
cumulative record
discrimination
discriminative stimulus
ethologists
extinction
fixed-interval schedule
fixed-ratio schedule
generalization

imprinting
insight
law of effect
learning-performance distinction
negative punishment
negative reinforcement
noncompliance
operant conditioning
operant response
partial reinforcement
pica
positive punishment
positive reinforcement
positive reinforcer

preparedness (prepared learning)
primary reinforcer
punishment
reinforcement
schedule of reinforcement
secondary reinforcer
self-injurious behavior
shaping
social cognitive learning
spontaneous recovery
superstitious behavior
time-out
variable-interval schedule
variable-ratio schedule

Outline

- *Introduction*
    1. Learning 45 commands: **operant conditioning**
    2. Learning to golf: cognitive learning (observation and imitation)

A. *Operant Conditioning*
    1. Background: Thorndike and Skinner
        a. Thorndike's law of effect
            (1) **Law of effect**
            (2) Effects strengthen or weaken behavior
        b. Skinner's operant conditioning
            (1) **Operant response**
            (2) Voluntary behavior and consequences
    2. Principles and procedures: operant conditioning
        a. Skinner box
        b. **Shaping**

3. Shaping: reinforcing close approximations
    a. Shaping: facing lever
    b. Shaping: touching lever
    c. Shaping: pressing lever
☐ *You could almost say that the process of shaping is at the heart of operant conditioning. Why?*
4. Shaping: importance of immediate reinforcement
    a. Power of reinforcers
    b. **Superstitious behavior**
5. Examples of operant conditioning
    a. Operant conditioning procedure
        (1) Target behavior
        (2) Preparation
        (3) Reinforcers
        (4) Shaping
    b. Toilet training and food refusal
6. Operant versus classical conditioning
☐ *How do classical conditioning and operant conditioning differ? What do they have in common?*
    a. Operant conditioning (Skinner)
        (1) Goal
        (2) Voluntary response
        (3) Emitted response
        (4) Contingent on behavior
        (5) Consequences
    b. Classical conditioning (Pavlov)
        (1) Goal
        (2) Involuntary response
        (3) Elicited response
        (4) Conditioned response
        (5) Expectancy

B. *Reinforcers*
1. Consequences
    a. **Reinforcement**
    b. **Punishment**
    c. **Pica**
2. Changing the consequences

3. Reinforcement
    a. Positive reinforcement
        (1) **Positive reinforcement**
        (2) **Positive reinforcer**
    b. Negative reinforcement
        (1) **Negative reinforcement**
        (2) Also increases frequency of behavior
4. Reinforcers
    a. **Primary reinforcer**
    b. **Secondary reinforcer**
5. Punishment
    a. **Positive punishment**
    b. **Negative punishment**
    c. **Self-injurious behavior**
    d. Positive punishment

C. *Schedules of Reinforcement*
   1. Skinner's contributions
       a. Operant conditioning and consequences
       b. **Schedule of reinforcement**
       c. Skinner box and cumulative record
   2. Measuring ongoing behavior
       a. **Cumulative record**
       b. Picture of responses and reinforcements
   3. Schedules of reinforcement
       a. **Continuous reinforcement**
       b. **Partial reinforcement**
   4. Partial reinforcement schedules
       a. **Fixed-ratio schedule**
       b. **Fixed-interval schedule**
       c. **Variable-ratio schedule**
       d. **Variable-interval schedule**

   ☐ Can you think of an example from everyday life for each of the four schedules of reinforcement?

D. *Other Conditioning Concepts*
   1. **Generalization**
   2. **Discrimination** and **discriminative stimulus**
   3. **Extinction** and **spontaneous recovery**

E. *Cognitive Learning*
   1. Three viewpoints on **cognitive learning**
      a. Against: B. F. Skinner
      b. In favor: Edward Tolman (**cognitive map**)
      c. In favor: Albert Bandura (**social cognitive learning**)
   2. Observational learning
      a. Bobo doll experiment
         (1) Procedure
         (2) Results
         (3) Conclusion
      b. Learning versus performance (**learning-performance distinction**)
   ☐ *Some psychologists say Bandura's classic Bobo doll experiment disproves Skinner. How so?*
   3. Bandura's social cognitive theory
   4. Social cognitive learning: four processes
      a. Attention
      b. Memory
      c. Imitation
      d. Motivation
   5. Social cognitive learning decreases the fear of snakes
      a. Background
      b. Treatment
      c. Results and conclusion
   6. Insight learning
      a. **Insight** (Wolfgang Köhler)
      b. Insight in animals (how Sultan got the banana)
      c. Insight in humans (the "ah ha" experience)

F. *Biological Factors*
   1. Definition
      a. **Biological factors**
      b. Biological predispositions to behave
   2. Imprinting
      a. **Ethologists**
      b. **Imprinting** (Konrad Lorenz)
         (1) **Critical [sensitive] period**
         (2) Irreversible
   3. Prepared learning in animals and humans
      a. Incredible memory (birds): **preparedness (prepared learning)**
      b. Incredible sounds (human infants)

G. Research Focus: Noncompliance
1. How can parents deal with "No!" (research on noncompliance)
   a. **Noncompliance**
   b. **Time-out**
2. Study: using time-out to reduce noncompliance

H. Cultural Diversity: East Meets West
1. Suzuki method (teaching violin) and Bandura's social cognitive learning
2. Different cultures but similar learning principles: teacher Suzuki and researcher Bandura
   a. Attention
   b. Memory
   c. Imitation
   d. Motivation

I. Application: Behavior Modification
1. Definition
   a. **Behavior modification**
   b. **Autism**
2. Behavior modification and autism
   a. Program (Ivar Lovaas)
   b. Results
3. **Biofeedback**
4. Pros and cons of punishment
   a. Spanking: positive punishment
   b. Time-out: negative punishment

☐ *Do you believe in spanking? Were you spanked as a child? Do you spank your own children?*

140 STUDY GUIDE

> *For Psych Majors Only...*
>
> **How to Trade Bad Habits for Good:** The central idea of behaviorism is that all human behavior is learned, the result of reinforcement through consequences. Your bad habits are not intrinsic parts of you, they are the result of learning. If that is true, then you can unlearn them, too, or crowd them out by learning new and better habits.
>
> How can you accomplish this? By keeping the focus on behavior, understanding behavior as a transaction with the environment, and constructing better environments that support better habits. Of course this is easier said than done, because you have a long and largely forgotten learning history and also because social environments are complicated structures.
>
> Have you noticed that nothing has been said about faults and weaknesses, blame or guilt? They have no place in behavior analysis. That's why the title of this box is not strictly accurate — habits are neither 'good' nor 'bad' in and of themselves. Behavior is simply behavior. How well any given behavior serves our purposes, however, leads to value judgments that can become guides to action.

Language Workout

What's That?

p. 213 a small bear **cub** = baby bear
So what? = Why is that important?
kills and eats any cub it **encounters** = meets
the learning process is **out in the open** = clear, not hidden
as a **toddler** = baby learning to walk
beaning his dad on the head = hitting
on the **Golf Channel** = TV station that shows only golf
On his own initiative = without help from other people

p. 214 training children to use the **potty** = child's toilet
analyzing **ongoing** behaviors = continuing
a mighty **jolt** = shock

p. 215 deliver food **pellets** = small pieces
a naïve rat does not usually **waltz over** = go directly
Shaping... **reinforce**s behaviors = strengthens
Immediate **reinforcement** = strengthening
that **approximated** the desired behavior = came near to
[behavior] that **just happens to occur** = occurs by chance
Superstitious behavior = not based on reason

Module 10: Operant & Cognitive Approaches

p. 216 give flowers to your **honey** = boyfriend or girlfriend
she or he has **persistently** refused to eat = again and again
Baseline = basic behavior, before attempts to change it

p. 217 something he would never do **in the wild** = in natural conditions

p. 218 **playing hookey** from school = being absent
eating **inedible** objects = not suitable for eating
the **preceding** response will occur again = earlier

p. 219 **coupon** [COO-pahn] = a ticket that promises payment
coupons could be **redeemed** for pizza = exchanged
the driver could **get rolling** = start driving
spanking = hitting child on backside as punishment
a child's **allowance** = weekly money given by parents to child
poking ears and eyes = pushing finger in
a special **Task Force** = group meeting to find solutions
eye and ear **gouging** = act of pushing, forcing
as **a last resort** = last possible solution, after others have failed

p. 220 **slot machine** = gambling machine
the pen moves up a **notch** = step, unit of measurement

p. 221 a different schedule of **payoff** = money paid to winner
the **odds** of winning = chance
a **fixed** number of responses = decided, chosen

p. 222 Although Bart was relatively **tame** = comfortable with people

p. 223 caused many in the audience to **gasp** = make sound of surprise
Tolman's position is **making a comeback** = becoming popular again

p. 224 a mildly **frustrating** situation = upsetting

p. 225 [the information] can be **retrieved** = recaptured
Bandura and colleagues **recruited** subjects = collected

p. 226 **chimpanzees, chimps** = monkeys
vainly grasp at the out-of-reach banana = unsuccessfully
he seemed to **hit on** the solution = find
something **critical** happened = very important

p. 228 **facilitate** or inhibit = make easy
minutes after **hatching** = breaking out of the egg
imprinting, which **promotes** their survival = helps
imprinting is essentially **irreversible** = cannot be changed

p. 229 **phenomenal** memories = extraordinary
humans' vocal **apparatus** = equipment

p. 230 **carry out** a request = perform
scolding = criticizing
pleading = begging
reprimanding = criticizing person for mistake
temper tantrums = child's outburst marked by losing control
the **pros and cons** of punishment = advantages and disadvantages

p. 231 instruments require more physical **dexterity** = skill in movement

p. 232 **grave** problems in developing spoken language = very serious
social and communication **deficits** = lack of skills
stop constant **rocking** = moving back and forth
interact with **peers** = other people of same age or position

p. 236 Dr. Den Trumbull, a **pediatrician** = doctor for babies and children
spanking may be **humiliating** = producing shame
lead to problems **down the line** = later
nonabusive spanking = not harmful, not damaging
the evidence isn't **that** strong = very

What's the Difference?

A **subjective** statement focuses on the **subject:** the person making the statement.
It is **subjective** because it expresses personal opinions, feelings, and biases.
Subjective = "This hamburger tastes good."

An **objective** statement focuses on the **object:** the thing or action that is observed.
It is **objective** because it reports only facts that can be measured or proved.
Objective = "This hamburger weighs 10.6 ounces."

Subjective statements often contain words of judgment, like "should" or "better".
Objective statements often contain words of description or measurement.

TRY IT

Subjective or Objective? *(Circle your answer)*

Textbooks cost too much.	Subjective	Objective
Apples have more vitamins than potatoes.	Subjective	Objective
Everyone should eat an apple every day.	Subjective	Objective
Most children like chocolate.	Subjective	Objective
It is better to be clean than dirty.	Subjective	Objective
American football is a more violent game than soccer.	Subjective	Objective

---

Answer Key

Subjective: Textbooks cost too much. = "too much" is an opinion
Objective: Apples have more vitamins than potatoes. = this can be proven
Subjective: Everyone should eat an apple every day. = "should" is an opinion
Objective: Most children like chocolate. = this can be proven with statistics
Subjective: It is better to be clean than dirty. = most people share this opinion (but it is still an opinion)
Subjective: American football is a more violent game than soccer. = what is or is not "violent" is an opinion, although it is possible to count the number of violent acts and compare them.

Module 10: Operant & Cognitive Approaches

The Big Picture

Which statement below offers the best summary of the larger significance of this module?

- A If B. F. Skinner is correct, most human behaviors are learned through the reinforcing powers of consequences. Because learning can be studied experimentally and objectively, psychology can become a science of behavior.

- B Skinner and the behaviorists reduced psychology to a study of rats and pigeons. They lost sight of the fact that humans are unique, individual, and not reducible to a set of laws organized around reinforcement.

- C Skinner thought his "operant conditioning" would replace Pavlov's "classical conditioning" as the fullest description of human behavior. Today we know that most human behavior is based on reflexes, and so Pavlov wins.

- D The behaviorists launched a revolution that led to a wealth of research in psychology. By the time he died, however, Skinner had turned to a belief in the importance of biological and cognitive factors to explain behavior.

- E Most research subjects are rats, pigeons, and psych students. A cynic once observed that the first two are not human, and the third *may* not be.

True-False

____ 1. Classical conditioning concerns involuntary (reflex) behavior while operant conditioning concerns voluntary behavior.

____ 2. The secret of successful shaping is waiting until the animal emits the desired final target behavior, then immediately applying reinforcement.

____ 3. The key to operant conditioning is making consequences contingent on behavior.

____ 4. Positive reinforcement makes behavior more likely to occur again; negative reinforcement makes it less likely to occur again.

____ 5. If you want effective learning, you must use primary reinforcers instead of secondary reinforcers.

____ 6. Schedules of reinforcement are payoff rules that govern different patterns of work done and payment given.

____ 7. Social cognitive learning shows how there is a difference between learning a behavior and performing that behavior.

____ 8. The difference between social cognitive learning and operant conditioning is that the former does not depend on external reinforcement.

____ 9. A good example of social cognitive learning was when Sultan piled up several boxes so he could reach the banana.

____ 10. The great power of reinforcement extends only so far — until it bumps into a biological restraint.

Flashcards 1

____ 1. continuous reinforcement
____ 2. negative punishment
____ 3. negative reinforcement
____ 4. partial reinforcement
____ 5. positive punishment
____ 6. positive reinforcement
____ 7. punishment
____ 8. reinforcement
____ 9. schedule of reinforcement
____ 10. shaping

a. the presentation of a stimulus that increases the probability of a behavior occurring again
b. a rule that determines how and when the occurrence of a response will be followed by a reinforcer
c. a consequence that occurs after behavior and decreases chance of that behavior occurring again
d. a situation in which responding is reinforced only some of the time
e. a procedure of successive reinforcement of behaviors that lead up to or approximate the desired behavior
f. a consequence that occurs after behavior and increases the chance of that behavior occurring again
g. removing a reinforcing stimulus (allowance) after response; decreases chances of response recurring
h. presenting an aversive stimulus (spanking) after a response; decreases chances of response recurring
i. every occurrence of the operant response results in delivery of the reinforcer
j. an aversive stimulus whose removal increases the likelihood of the preceding response occurring again

Flashcards 2

____ 1. behavior modification
____ 2. cognitive map
____ 3. fixed-interval schedule
____ 4. fixed-ratio schedule
____ 5. imprinting
____ 6. insight
____ 7. preparedness (prepared learning)
____ 8. superstitious behavior
____ 9. variable-interval schedule
____ 10. variable-ratio schedule

a. inherited tendencies or responses that are displayed by newborn animals encountering certain stimuli
b. a treatment or therapy that modifies problems by using principles of learning and conditioning
c. a reinforcer occurs only after a fixed number of responses made by the subject
d. an innate or biological tendency of animals to recognize and attend to certain cues and stimuli
e. a mental representation in the brain of the layout of an environment and its features
f. a reinforcer occurs following the first response that occurs after a fixed interval of time
g. a reinforcer occurs following the first response after a variable amount of time has gone by
h. a mental process marked by the sudden solution to a problem; the "ah ha" phenomenon
i. a subject must make a variable or different number of responses for delivery of each reinforcer
j. any behavior that increases in frequency because of accidental pairing with the delivery of a reinforcer

Module 10: Operant & Cognitive Approaches 145

Multiple-Choice

_____ 1. Rod Plotnik tells us about the starring performance of 1,800-pound Bart in *The Bear* to make the point that
   a. although animals cannot begin to match human intelligence, they do have some capacity for learning
   b. the key to learning (and teaching) is perseverance: keep working
   c. you shouldn't believe that what you see in the movies reflects actual behavior in the wild
   d. operant conditioning procedures are powerful (no other technique could have produced Bart's learning)

_____ 2. Skinner gets the credit for operant conditioning instead of Thorndike because
   a. Thorndike stated a general principle; Skinner's research explained precisely how it works
   b. Thorndike's Law of Effect was essentially a restatement of Pavlov's conditioned reflex
   c. Skinner realized that there were biological limits on learning
   d. Skinner studied rats, pigeons, and other animals instead of limiting himself to cats

_____ 3. You could argue that Skinner's discoveries are more important than Pavlov's in that
   a. beginning a quarter of a century later, Skinner could build on Pavlov's discoveries
   b. American science offers more freedom than Russian science
   c. almost all important human behavior is voluntary (not reflex) behavior
   d. the conditioned reflex isn't fully explained until you bring in the concepts of both positive and negative reinforcement

_____ 4. The shaping procedure succeeds or fails depending on
   a. how long you are willing to wait for the target behavior to occur
   b. exactly which behaviors you reinforce
   c. how many times you reinforce the target behavior
   d. selecting the best one of several reinforcers

_____ 5. The basic principle of operant conditioning is that
   a. consequences are contingent on behavior
   b. conditioned stimuli produce conditioned responses
   c. the performance of undesired behaviors brings swift consequences
   d. consequences are less important than feelings of guilt

_____ 6. The student on probation who finally buckles down and begins studying in earnest is under the control of an operant conditioning procedure called
   a. positive reinforcement
   b. negative reinforcement
   c. punishment
   d. extinction

_____ 7. The little child who gets a good hard spanking for running out into the street is experiencing an operant conditioning procedure called
   a. positive reinforcement
   b. negative reinforcement
   c. positive punishment
   d. extinction

_____ 8. When your date shakes your hand and says, "Thanks for a wonderful evening," you reply, "Gee, I was kind of hoping for a _____
   a. primary reinforcer
   b. secondary reinforcer
   c. token of your affection
   d. partial reinforcement

_____ 9. "Poor fool," you think to yourself when your friend tells you she lost on the lottery again, "another helpless victim of the _____ schedule of reinforcement"
   a. fixed-ratio
   b. variable-ratio
   c. fixed-interval
   d. variable-interval

_____ 10. Skinner opposed cognitive theories of learning to the end of his life because
   a. it is difficult to admit that the work of a lifetime was misguided
   b. they are based on philosophical speculation rather than on laboratory research
   c. they bring in the "mind," which he said couldn't be observed or measured directly
   d. you can't teach an old dog new tricks [just a joke!]

_____ 11. Although you haven't made a conscious effort to memorize the campus area, you probably can get to any point on it relatively easily; Edward Tolman would say you
   a. exhibited attention, memory, imitation, and motivation
   b. learned through observation as you moved around campus
   c. can call on the power of insight when necessary
   d. automatically developed a cognitive map

_____ 12. Which one of the following was *not* an important outcome in Albert Bandura's famous Bobo doll experiment?
   a. the children did not imitate the adult model until they were given a reward
   b. the children learned even though they did not receive tangible rewards
   c. the children learned even though they were not engaging in any overt behavior
   d. some subjects did not imitate the model (proving learning had occurred) until they were reinforced for doing so

_____ 13. Which one of the following is *not* a factor in Bandura's theory of social cognitive learning?
   a. attention
   b. memory
   c. rehearsal
   d. motivation

_____ 14. The important thing about the solution Sultan came up with for the out-of-reach banana problem was
   a. how an old conditioned reflex spontaneously recovered
   b. how he used trial and error
   c. how he built on previously reinforced behavior
   d. what was *missing* in his solution — namely, all the factors above

_____ 15. The Suzuki method of teaching violin to children closely resembles the processes of
   a. Pavlov's classical conditioning
   b. Bandura's social cognitive learning
   c. Skinner's operant conditioning
   d. Kohler's insight learning

Module 10: Operant & Cognitive Approaches

Answers for Module 10

True-False	Flashcards 1	Flashcards 2	Multiple-Choice
1. T	1. i	1. b	1. d
2. F	2. g	2. e	2. a
3. T	3. j	3. f	3. c
4. F	4. d	4. c	4. b
5. F	5. h	5. a	5. a
6. T	6. a	6. h	6. b
7. T	7. c	7. d	7. c
8. T	8. f	8. j	8. a
9. F	9. b	9. g	9. b
10. T	10. e	10. i	10. c
			11. d
			12. a
			13. c
			14. d
			15. b

The Big Picture

Statement A

Test-Taking Tips 3

More hints:

- Be wary of answers that seem way out of keeping for the subject involved.
- Be wary of answers that don't fit in with everything else you know about the subject.

Module 11

Types of Memory

Nothing in This Module Is True

The biological and cognitive approaches to psychology have made great strides in the last two decades. One of the results is a much clearer picture of how memory works. Even so, there is a sense in which none of it is true.

The answers we want are buried at least two layers down. First, how does the physical brain work? We are learning more about the brain every day, yet for all their discoveries neuroscientists have barely scratched the surface. The need to understand elusive electrical activity, not just gray matter, complicates the task. Second, how does the mind work? If the mind is an abstraction, a concept (unless you say mind and brain are the same thing), we cannot apprehend it directly, making it even more difficult to understand.

Today we are fond of comparing the mind to a computer, simply because the computer is the most powerful mechanical thinking device we know, and therefore makes a good comparison. Yet when we develop a *new* generation of thinking machines, perhaps based on liquid instead of silicone chips, we will stop comparing the mind to a computer and compare it to the new device instead, since the new device will seem much more like the human mind. The mind is not really a computer; the computer merely makes a good model for understanding the mind, at least today.

The Beauty of a Good Model

No wonder that dress looks so beautiful on the model sashaying down the runway in the fashion show. The model isn't an actual human being — obviously, no one could be that tall, that thin, that perfect! Consequently, when draped around this abstraction of a human, we can see much more clearly how the clothing itself really looks.

A model helps us understand the real world because it is an ideal against which we can compare specific phenomena. When we try to understand the workings of the mind, all we see are awkward elbows and knees. We need a model to help us visualize what it must really be like.

What we are struggling to understand is how the process of grasping the world and putting parts of it in our heads must work. Many of the formulations Rod Plotnik presents in Module 11 are models of what this process may be like. Because this is not yet certain knowledge, several theories, or models, compete for our acceptance. I think you can learn these theories better if you keep in mind the idea that they are models, not reality.

Effective Student Tip 11

High Grades Count Most

Here is a hard truth. Unfair, maybe, but true. Anyone who looks at your transcript, whether for admission to another school or for employment, is going to be looking for the *high* grades. It's difficult for them to tell exactly what 'C' means. In some schools, 'C' may mean little more than that you attended class. The grade 'B' begins to say more about your abilities and character, but it is an 'A' that is really convincing. No matter in what course or at what school, an 'A' says you did everything asked of you and did it well. That's a quality admissions people and personnel officers look for.

High grades have other rewards, too. You get on the school's honors list. You can join honors societies. You qualify for scholarships. With every 'A', your sense of effectiveness goes up a notch. You are more confident and enjoy greater self-esteem. (Keeps Mom and Dad happy, too!)

Tailor your work toward earning high grades. Take fewer courses, stay up later studying, write papers over, ruthlessly cut fun out of your life [just kidding].

Earning high grades in a few courses beats getting average grades in many courses. The fastest route toward your goal is a conservative selection of courses in which you do well, resulting in a good record and confidence in your effectiveness as a student.

Your response...

Can you remember a time when you thought you had an 'A', then didn't get it? What went wrong?

Key Terms

Many of these terms are based on a model of the mind. Get the model and it's easier to learn the terms.

automatic encoding
chunking
declarative memory
echoic memory
effortful encoding
eidetic imagery
elaborative rehearsal
encoding
episodic memory
flashbulb memories

iconic memory
interference
levels-of-processing theory
long-term memory
maintenance rehearsal
memory
photographic memory
primacy effect
primacy-recency effect

procedural or nondeclarative memory
recency effect
repression
retrieving
semantic memory
sensory memory
short-term (working) memory
storing

Outline

- *Introduction*
    1. Incredible memory
    2. Repressed memory
    3. Definitions
        a. **Memory**
        b. Three memory processes
            (1) **Encoding**
            (2) **Storing**
            (3) **Retrieving**
    A. *Three Types of Memory*
        1. Memory as three different processes
            a. **Sensory memory**
            b. **Short-term (working) memory**
            c. **Long-term memory**
        2. Role of attention
    B. *Sensory Memory: Recording*
        1. **Iconic memory**
        2. **Echoic memory**
        ☐ How do iconic and echoic memory work? What is their purpose?
        3. Functions of sensory memory
            a. Prevents being overwhelmed
            b. Gives decision time
            c. Provides stability, playback, and recognition

C. Short-Term Memory: Working
1. **Short-term (working) memory**
2. Two features
   a. Limited duration
      (1) From two to 30 seconds
      (2) **Maintenance rehearsal**
   b. Limited capacity
      (1) About seven items or bits (George Miller)
      (2) Memory span test
      (3) **Interference**
3. **Chunking**
4. Functions of short-term memory
   a. Attending
   b. Rehearsing
   c. Storing

D. Long-Term Memory: Storing
1. **Long-term memory**: steps in the memory process
   a. Sensory memory
   b. Attention
   c. Short-term memory
   d. **Encoding**
   e. **Long-term memory**
   f. **Retrieval**
2. Features of long-term memory
   a. Capacity and permanence
   b. Retrieval and accuracy
3. Separate memory systems
4. Primacy versus recency
   a. **Primacy effect** (first items)
   b. **Recency effect** (last items)
   c. **Primacy-recency effect**
   ☐ *Can you work out the logic of the memory processes involved in these concepts?*
5. Short- versus long-term memory
6. Declarative versus procedural or nondeclarative
   a. **Declarative memory**
      (1) **Semantic memory**
      (2) **Episodic memory**
   b. **Procedural or nondeclarative memory**

E. **Research Focus: Do Emotions Affect Memories?**
   1. Hormones and memories
   2. Memories of emotional events
      a. Procedure
      b. Results and conclusion

F. **Encoding: Transferring**
   1. Two kinds of **encoding**
      a. **Automatic encoding**
      b. **Effortful encoding**
   2. Effortful encoding
      a. **Maintenance rehearsal**
      b. **Elaborative rehearsal**
   4. **Levels of processing theory**

G. **Repressed Memories**
   1. Recovered memories of sexual abuse
   2. Definition of repressed memories: **repression**
   3. Therapist's role in recovered memories
   4. Implanting false memories
   5. Accuracy of recovered memories

H. **Cultural Diversity: Oral versus Written**
   1. United States versus Africa
   2. Remembering spoken information

I. **Application: Unusual Memories**
   1. **Photographic memory**
   2. **Eidetic imagery**
   3. **Flashbulb memories**
      a. Emotional events
      b. Most remembered events
      c. Recent study
      d. Flashbulb memories and hormones
      e. Memory: pictures versus impressions

Module 11: Types of Memory

> *For Psych Majors Only...*
>
> **Gloomy Psychology:** Here is a gloomy, possibly discouraging thought (considering how much you paid for your books): perhaps *nothing* in psychology is really true. Perhaps everything you are slaving so hard to learn is simply the best understanding we have now, soon to be replaced by better ways of understanding how psychology works.
>
> I suggested that the computer is merely a temporary model for understanding the mind. Let's go further and suggest that *all* the wonderful theories you study in psychology are models, none ultimately "true." There is no "unconscious" region of the mind, no pure "schedule of reinforcement," and no ethereal "self." They are all fictions — fictions we need in order to make sense of the facts.
>
> There is one happy possibility in this dismal thought. Think how eagerly psychology is waiting for the better model *you* may construct one day. Keep working on your favorite theories.

Language Workout

What's That?

p. 239 before the **packed** house = crowded with people
   He did not **err** = make a mistake
   such **gargantuan** memory powers = huge, great
   for **allegedly** molesting her as a child = reportedly [not proven]
   sexual **molestation** = unwanted physical attention
   subject to error and bias = have tendency to
   mental **representations** of information = pictures
   Admiral Nelson = British hero at the time of Napoleon

p. 239 memories ...can be **verified** = proven to be true

p. 240 walk through a big-city **mall** = shopping center
   you are **bombarded** = attacked
   a lone guitarist playing for **spare change** = extra money

p. 241 you are **absorbed in** reading a novel = completely interested

p. 242 **rehearsing** the information = practicing
   ZIP codes = numbers showing postal delivery areas in U.S.
   Maintenance = act of keeping something in good condition
   researchers have **confirmed** Miller's original finding = proven to be true

p. 243 **area code** = numbers showing telephone service areas in U.S.
   Ben Franklin = American statesman at time of independence
   John Adams = Second president of the U.S.
   driving along **with** your radio **on** = turned on, playing

information that is **relevant** = connected to the subject
and **disregard** everything else = ignore, not look at

p. 244 these different memory processes **interact** = influence each other
often **inflating** positive events = expanding importance of

p. 245 brain damage can **wipe out** long-term memory = destroy
while completely **sparing** short-term memory = not affecting, protecting
Primacy = position of first (primary) in time
Recency = position of close (recent) in time

p. 246 it was found **quite** by accident = completely
H.M. would **insist** that he had never seen = argue strongly, swear
show a **steady** improvement = continuing
Declarative = consciously known
Semantic = concerning language
pick up a **racket** = instrument used to play tennis
remember how to **serve** = begin tennis game with first hit
learning a **motor** skill = movement

p. 247 highly **charged** emotional situations = full of feeling
Because of safety **concerns** = worries
seeing a series of **slides** = photos
his feet were **severed** = cut off
McGaugh and his **colleagues** = co-workers, fellow researchers
lay the basis for similar studies = prepare, form

p. 247 "Let me tell you about **my day**" = my experiences today
at **a second-hand store** = store that sells used objects
avid sports fans = enthusiastic
watchers of daily TV **soap operas** = continuing dramatic stories
if you are **simultaneously** taking two or three = at the same time

p. 248 **Elaborative** = adding details
encoded at a **shallow** level = not deep, close to the surface
resulted in great **controversy** = argument

p. 249 Holly's memories first **surfaced** = came to conscious level
implanting false memories = introducing, creating
a state **appeals** court dismissed Holly's case = higher level court
truth-serum = drug that makes a person tell only the truth
it has been **barred** in California's courts = forbidden
survivors of **incest** = sexual relations with family members
The client was **dubious** at first = doubtful

p. 251 Do people believe **"fake"** memories? = false
comforted by an **elderly** woman = very old
she searched through his **things** = possessions
300 clients who later **retracted** charges = dropped
large **monetary** awards = money

p. 254 able to recall (notes) **verbatim** = perfectly, every word
Why eidetic imagery **drops out** = stops, leaves

p. 258 a **grand jury** = a jury studying accusations against people
teachers had **jabbed** scissors = hit, stab

after the not guilty **verdict** = official decision by jury
absolutely no **shred** of doubt = tiny piece

What Happens Next?

Once means **one time** = Wei-Ru went to a rock concert **once,** but her parents won't let her go again.

Once can also mean **after** = **Once** the professor finished grading the exams, he returned them to the students.

Once the movie begins, latecomers will not be admitted.

TRY IT: Use **once** meaning **after**:

    Once the war ended, the soldiers _____.

    Once _____, we washed the dishes.

    Once her visit to the dentist was over, Anna _____.

    Once summertime begins, the children _____.

    Once _____, the class could begin.

Did you notice these sentences in the text:

    Once a limited amount of information is transferred into short-term, or working memory, it will remain there for up to 30 seconds (p. 240).

    Once the song title is encoded in long-term memory, it has the potential to remain there for your lifetime (p. 244).

Make a Connection

Thus means **for this reason**, connecting a reason and a result:

    Reason = Joel had an important job interview on Wednesday morning.
    Result = **Thus,** he ironed his tie and shirt on Tuesday night.

    Reason = Jeff drank a cup of coffee late at night.
    Result = **Thus,** he could not fall asleep until dawn.

    Reason = Chicago's airport closed because of a heavy snowstorm.
    Result = **Thus,** airplanes coming from other cities could not land.

TRY IT

    The boss gave Elena a raise in salary.
    Thus, she _____.

    Mustapha ran faster than all the other racers.
    Thus, he _____.

    The library books were overdue.
    Thus, when Jason returned them, he _____.

Bad weather and fires destroyed much of the coffee produced in Brazil last year. **Thus,** this year, the price of coffee has _____.

The washing machine takes only quarters, but Vincent had no small change. **Thus,** he _____.

p. 250 There are also many examples of therapists who have helped clients recover and deal with terrible repressed memories. **Thus,** therapists are in the difficult position of trying to distinguish accurate accounts of repressed memories from those that may have been shaped or reinforced by the suggestions or expectations of the therapist.

One or Many?

Take a look at these quotes from the text. Decide if the **word** means one or many, then circle ONE *or* MANY. Check your answers in the Answer Key.

The **guitarist's** music sounds familiar (p. 240)	ONE *or* MANY
resulted in **subjects'** remembering fewer letters (p. 241)	ONE *or* MANY
others' research (p. 251)	ONE *or* MANY
clients' later retractions (p. 251)	ONE *or* MANY
implanted by **therapists'** suggestions (p. 251)	ONE *or* MANY

Answer Key

Once the war ended, the soldiers (came home) (were happy)
Once (we finished dinner) (dinner ended), we washed the dishes.
Once her visit to the dentist was over, Anna (felt happy) (received the bill)
Once summertime begins, the children (will not be in school) (will be free to play)
Once (the teacher arrived) (the students were quiet), the class could begin.
The boss gave Elena a raise in salary. **Thus,** she (felt happy) (thanked him) (went shopping)
Mustapha ran faster than all the other racers. **Thus,** he (won the race) (was the winner)
The library books were overdue. **Thus,** when Jason returned them, he (had to pay a fine)
Bad weather and fires destroyed much of the coffee produced in Brazil last year. **Thus,** this year, the price of coffee has (risen) (increased) (gone up)
The washing machine takes only quarters, but Vincent had no small change. **Thus,** he (could not do his laundry) (had to find change)
the **guitarist's** music sounds familiar = one guitarist
resulted in **subjects'** remembering fewer letters = many
others' research = many
clients' later retractions = many
implanted by **therapists'** suggestions = many

The Big Picture

Which statement below offers the best summary of the larger significance of this module?

    A   The study of memory shows that humans are destined to disappointment in their endeavors to learn. The best we can achieve is a fragmentary and temporary grasp of facts and ideas that are of importance to us.

    B   The human brain is like a vast container, which we fill with facts and ideas from birth to death. Every time we attend to something in our environment, it goes into the box to be saved for later use.

    C   In the future, psychology will use electrical and chemical examination to locate and identify every specific memory in the brain. Until then, we really can't say anything definitive about what memory is or how it works.

    D   Although we are just beginning to find the precise mechanisms of memory in the brain, several theories, or models, of memory illustrate the processes that seem to be occurring as we perceive, learn, and remember.

    E   Types of memory: long-term, short-term, and examination (real-short-term).

True-False

____ 1. Memory involves three basic processes: encoding, storing, and retrieving.

____ 2. There are four basic kinds of memory: flashbulb snapshots, temporary, impermanent, and permanent.

____ 3. Without the stage called sensory memory, we would drown in a sea of visual and auditory sensations.

____ 4. Short-term memory is capable of holding several dozen bits of information for several minutes.

____ 5. When you attempt to remember a list of animals, the recency effect takes precedence over the primacy effect.

____ 6. If you are studying for the next psych exam, elaborative rehearsal will be a more effective strategy than maintenance rehearsal.

____ 7. Encoding is transferring information from short-term to long-term memory.

____ 8. The best way to get information into long-term memory is to repeat it over and over again.

____ 9. A good strategy for remembering something is to associate it with some distinctive visual image.

____ 10. When you find someone who has unusual powers of memory, you can be fairly certain that the person possesses a photographic memory.

Flashcards 1

____ 1. declarative memory
____ 2. echoic memory
____ 3. encoding
____ 4. iconic memory
____ 5. long-term memory
____ 6. procedural memory
____ 7. retrieving
____ 8. sensory memory
____ 9. short-term (working) memory
____ 10. storing

a. a form of sensory memory that holds auditory information for one or two seconds
b. another process that can hold only a limited amount of information (7 items) for short period (2-30 sec)
c. memories for performing motor tasks, habits, conditioning; not conscious or retrievable
d. an initial process that holds information in raw form for a brief period of time (instant to several seconds)
e. a form of sensory memory that holds visual information for about a quarter of a second
f. the process of getting or recalling information that has been placed into short-term or long-term storage
g. the process of placing encoded information into relatively permanent mental storage for later recall
h. memories for facts or events (scenes, stories, faces, etc.); conscious and retrievable
i. the process of storing almost unlimited amounts of information over long periods of time
j. making mental representations of information so that it can be placed or put into our memories

Flashcards 2

____ 1. chunking
____ 2. effortful encoding
____ 3. eidetic imagery
____ 4. elaborative rehearsal
____ 5. flashbulb memories
____ 6. interference
____ 7. maintenance rehearsal
____ 8. photographic memory
____ 9. primacy-recency effect
____ 10. repression

a. the ability to form sharp, detailed visual images of a page, then to recall the entire image at a later date
b. better recall of information presented at the beginning and at the end of a task
c. vivid recollections, usually in great detail, of dramatic or emotionally charged incidents of great interest
d. process of pushing memories of threat or trauma into the unconscious, from which it cannot be retrieved
e. transfer of information from short-term into long-term memory by working hard to do so
f. results when new information enters short-term memory and overwrites information already there
g. making meaningful associations between information to be learned and information already stored
h. simply repeating or rehearsing the information rather than forming any new associations
i. the ability to examine material for 10-30 seconds and retain a detailed visual image for several minutes
j. combining separate items of information into a larger unit, then remembering the unit as a whole

Module 11: Types of Memory   159

Multiple-Choice

_____ 1. Rod Plotnik discusses Rajan Mahadevan, who memorized more than 30,000 digits of pi, because Rajan's rare abilities
   a. show that extreme concentration of mental ability in one area is usually accompanied by significant mental deficiencies in other areas
   b. are possessed only by people who are otherwise retarded or autistic
   c. could be duplicated by any of us... if we put our minds to it
   d. offer an extreme example of the memory processes we all use

_____ 2. Which one of the following is *not* one of the three processes of memory?
   a. encoding
   b. storing
   c. deciphering
   d. retrieving

_____ 3. The function of sensory memory is to
   a. hold information in its raw form for a brief period of time
   b. make quick associations between new data and things you already know
   c. weed out what is irrelevant in incoming information
   d. burn sensations into long-term memory for later retrieval and inspection

_____ 4. _____ memory holds visual information for about a quarter of a second
   a. Chunking
   b. Iconic
   c. Pictorial
   d. Echoic

_____ 5. Thanks to _____ memory, incoming speech sounds linger just long enough so we can recognize the sounds as words
   a. chunking
   b. iconic
   c. verbal
   d. echoic

_____ 6. Which statement below best describes what short-term or working memory is?
   a. your perceptual processes react to it
   b. you freeze it briefly in order to pay attention to it
   c. you work with it to accomplish some immediate task
   d. you retrieve it later when you need it again

_____ 7. Out of change at the pay phone, you frantically repeat the 11-digit number you just got from Information over and over again; that's called
   a. chunking
   b. maintenance rehearsal
   c. memory span stretching
   d. duration enhancement

_____ 8. But wait a minute... You already know the "1" and the area code, so you need only find something to associate with the prefix and the number; that's called
   a. chunking
   b. maintenance rehearsal
   c. memory span stretching
   d. duration enhancement

_____ 9. Why doesn't information in short-term memory simply become permanent? Probably because of
   a. limited storage space in the brain
   b. fascination with the new and different
   c. incompatibility with previously processed information
   d. interference caused by newly arriving information

_____ 10. If you attempt to remember a list of animal names, you will be more likely to remember
   a. the first few names
   b. the last few names
   c. both the first and last few names
   d. neither the first or last few names, but the ones occurring in the middle of the list

_____ 11. Remembering how you did on your last psych test involves _____ memory
   a. episodic
   b. semantic
   c. consequential
   d. procedural

_____ 12. The actual knowledge required for that test involves _____ memory
   a. episodic
   b. semantic
   c. consequential
   d. procedural

_____ 13. Your manual ability to write out the answers on the test involves _____ memory
   a. episodic
   b. semantic
   c. consequential
   d. procedural

_____ 14. The main problem with repressed memories of childhood abuse is that
   a. very few people can remember that far back
   b. we now know that the "unconscious" does not exist
   c. therapists may unwittingly help patients form memories which seem to explain their key problems
   d. so far, all the claimed cases of abuse in childhood have been proven to be lies

_____ 15. Rod Plotnik puts psychology to good use in his textbook by providing _____ to help you encode the material you must learn
   a. distinctive visual associations
   b. flashbulb memories
   c. maintenance rehearsal drills
   d. chunking strategies

Answers for Module 11

True-False
1. T
2. F
3. T
4. F
5. F
6. T
7. T
8. F
9. T
10. F

Flashcards 1
1. h
2. a
3. j
4. e
5. i
6. c
7. f
8. d
9. b
10. g

Flashcards 2
1. j
2. e
3. i
4. g
5. c
6. f
7. h
8. a
9. b
10. d

Multiple-Choice
1. d
2. c
3. a
4. b
5. d
6. c
7. b
8. a
9. d
10. c
11. a
12. b
13. d
14. c
15. a

The Big Picture

Statement D

Test-Taking Tips 4

More hints:

- Be on the lookout for any *part* of an answer that makes the *whole* answer untrue.
- When you find an answer that sounds correct, you must also check the others — to make sure there isn't another answer that is even *more* true.

Module 12

Remembering & Forgetting

What If You Could Remember Nothing?

Can you imagine how terrifying it must be to suffer from amnesia? In one form of amnesia, you can't remember back before a certain point. In a less common form, you can't construct new memories. In either case, you are rootless, adrift in a world with no clear sense of past, present, and future. You wouldn't really know who you are, why you exist, or what will happen to you.

What if you could *forget* nothing? Happily, there is no such psychiatric condition (although you could use such powers, along about now, with mid-term exams coming up). If you were incapable of ever forgetting anything you would be immobilized in a sea of indistinguishable bits and pieces of information, incapable of ever making a decision or taking action because the necessary review of past information and action would be never-ending.

The processes of remembering and forgetting are so immediate and so crucial that we take them for granted. But science, of course, takes nothing for granted. Rod Plotnik shows us what the science of psychology has learned about these vital memory processes.

Forget About It

When something is too painful to endure, a common psychiatric reaction is to forget it, in part or completely. Often victims of auto accidents experience temporary amnesia for the immediate events of the crash. All of us "forget" bad grades and other humiliating defeats.

As we have learned more about child abuse, we have come to realize how its victims often repress their trauma, in order to go on living. Uncovering these repressed memories has become an important part of psychotherapy. Many therapists are convinced that the suffering child cannot become well again unless the painful memories are dug out and worked through.

But memory is ever so much more complicated. Now we are also learning that it is quite possible to "remember" things that never happened. Rod Plotnik reveals the interesting and disturbing dangers of false memories, both those of eyewitness testimony in court cases and childhood memories in psychotherapy. Is it really possible that an eyewitness to a crime could make the wrong identification, or that a child could be wrong about having been sexually abused? Must we not believe what children and good people say when they testify in court? Forget about it!

Effective Student Tip 12

Manage Your Grade

True, we professors set the course standards and assign the final grades. Since most professors stick to the rules once they are established, however, *you* have almost total control over what that grade will be. But wishing doesn't make it so: you have to know how to make it happen. The trick is to take a management attitude toward your grades.

Taking charge and managing your grade involves six steps: (1) Understand your inner motivation concerning grades, to guard against self-sabotage. (2) Understand the details and logic of your professor's grading system. (3) Keep accurate records of your scores and grades (all of them, including any assignments or quizzes you missed). (4) Project your final grade from your current performance. (5) Determine what immediate steps you must take. (6) Make whatever adjustments seem necessary for effective pursuit of your goal.

Don't underestimate the importance of grades to your mental health. Rightly or wrongly, we interpret grades, like earnings, as powerful messages about our effectiveness.

You can passively allow your grades to happen to you, as many students do, or you can take charge and make them what you want.

Your response...

How important are grades to you? How much control do you seem to have over the grades you get?

Key Terms

These key terms touch on an area of psychology that researchers are just beginning to understand. But what could be more important than the way we orient ourselves to time and place?

amnesia
cognitive interview
eyewitness testimony
forgetting
forgetting curve
interference
long-term potentiation (LTP)
method of loci

mnemonics
network hierarchy
network theory
neural assemblies
nodes
peg method
proactive interference
recall

recognition
repression
retrieval cues
retroactive interference
source misattribution
state-dependent learning
tip-of-the-tongue
   phenomenon

Outline

- *Introduction*
    1. Watching a crime
    - ☐ Were you surprised when you tried Rod Plotnik's quiz about the assault?
    2. **Recall** versus **recognition**
    - ☐ Can you see how essay exams and multiple-choice exams require different study techniques?
    3. Eyewitness testimony

    A. *Organization of Memories*
    1. Trash can versus **network theory**
    2. Network theory of memory organization
        a. Nodes
        b. Associations
        c. Network
    3. Organization of network hierarchy
        a. **Nodes**
        b. **Network hierarchy**
        c. Searching
    4. Categories in the brain

    B. *Forgetting Curves*
    1. Early memories
    2. Unfamiliar and uninteresting
        a. **Forgetting curve** (Hermann Ebbinghaus)
        b. Nonsense syllables
    3. Familiar and interesting

C. *Reasons for Forgetting*
1. Overview: four reasons for **forgetting**
    a. **Repression** (Freud)
    b. **Retrieval cues** [poor]
    c. **Amnesia**
    d. **Interference**
2. **Interference**
    a. **Proactive interference**
    b. **Retroactive interference**
    c. Why did viewers forget the mugger's face?
3. **Retrieval cues**
    a. Forming effective retrieval cues
    b. **Tip-of-the-tongue phenomenon**
4. **State-dependent learning**

D. *Biological Bases of Memory*
1. Location of memories in the brain
    a. Cortex: storing short-term memories
    b. Cortex: recalling long-term memories
    c. Amygdala: adding emotional associations
    d. Hippocampus: transferring into long-term memory
    e. Brain: memory model
2. Mechanisms of memory
    a. Making short-term memory (**neural assemblies**)
    b. Genetically altering a long-term memory
    c. Making a long-term memory (**long-term potentiation [LTP]**)

E. *Mnemonics: Memorization Methods*
1. Improving your memory: **mnemonics**
2. **Method of loci**
3. **Peg method**
4. Effectiveness of methods

F. *Cultural Diversity: Aborigines versus White Australians*
1. Retrieval cues
2. Visual versus verbal retrieval cues
    a. Using visual cues
    b. Better performance
    c. Culture and retrieval cues

166 STUDY GUIDE

G. Research Focus: False Memories
1. Can false memories be implanted?
2. Research method to create false memories
   a. Procedure
   b. Results
   c. Conclusions
   ☐ What are the implications of this research for psychologists and legal professionals?

H. Application: Eyewitness Testimony
1. How accurate is **eyewitness testimony**?
2. Can eyewitnesses be misled?
3. Can questions change answers (Elizabeth Loftus research on biasing factors)?
4. Is what you say, what you believe (**source misattribution**)?
5. Which interview technique works best (**cognitive interview**)?

Language Workout

What's That?

p. 261 **instinctively**, you threw out your hands = automatically, without thinking
tried to **ward off** the oncoming threat = push away
with a **menacing** gesture = threatening
the **assailant's** face = attacker's
the **mugger's** jacket = attacker's
the **trash can** theory = garbage can

p. 262 Norman's **train of thought** = direction of thinking
smoke detectors on the ceilings = devices to warn about fire

p. 263 very **concrete** information = specific
general or **abstract** information = without details or specific facts
categories for **sorting** and filing information = classifying

p. 264 our earliest memories are usually **sketchy** = without details
A forgetting **curve** = measurement of performance
He **got around** the fact = avoided the problem
the **ticking** of a metronome = repeating sound
the ticking of a **metronome** = device that keeps rhythm (see picture on p. 12)
He used only **rote** memory = mechanical, routine
something you were **exposed to** for several years = shown

p. 265 **prominent** memory researchers = well-known
if you study primarily by **cramming** = studying the night before the exam
Wanting to **show off** = attract attention

p. 267 later **roamed** around the huge lot = wandered
long list of related past **annoyances** = disturbing things

p. 268 **sea slugs** = simple, formless sea animals

p. 269 activates a neural **assembly** = structure, organization
long-term **potentiation** = activating or developing the potential

p. 271 **at my fingertips** = easily available (in memory)
The rhymes act like **pegs** = hooks, nails
as rare as duck's teeth = impossibly rare, extremely rare

p. 272 **barren** desert world = empty, without trees or plants
using visual **landmarks** = structures that identify area
thimble = small metal protector for finger (when sewing)
when questioned about their **strategies** = methods (of remembering)

p. 273 her conviction was **overturned** = reversed
a wide range of social classes = (rich, middle, poor)
a trip to **Disney World** = children's amusement park
some of which were **fictitious** = false stories
stammering = stopping-and-starting speech, stuttering

p. 274 **a DNA test** = scientific test that can identify person from sample of skin
she did not **get a good look** = see clearly
the more **confident** a witness is = sure
a series of **armed** robberies = using guns
The police had few **leads** = clues, information
After being **prompted** to look = encouraged
wearing a **clerical** collar = for priests or religious leaders

p. 275 a memory **impairment** = problem
a **hit-and-run** accident = driver escapes, does not stop to help
without holding anything back = showing all information openly
police **interrogation** = questioning
life or death decisions = decisions which could result in death

p. 278 Kim **stuck by her** = stayed with her
against all odds = despite little chance of success
they **courted** = dated
I was **devastated** = shocked
surroundings might **jog** her memory = stimulate
fingering her **china** = dishes
Nothing **clicked** = was recognizable
How did I **do the wife thing**? = function as a wife
Valentine's Day = holiday celebrating love

Build Your Word Power

mistaken identity = identifying the **wrong** person
misleading questions = questions leading in the **wrong** direction
misinformation = **wrong** information
people do **mis**remember = remember **wrong**ly
source **mis**attribution = giving credit to the **wrong** cause

So, **mis-** means _____

Here (on the left) are some more words that begin with **mis-** . On the right are definitions of these words, but they are **mis**ordered. In each group of five, *draw a line connecting the word to its definition.*

misclassify	identify illness wrongly
miscount	send in the wrong direction
misdiagnose	put in wrong category
misfit	write 223 when the answer is 227
misguide	person who is in the wrong group
mishandle	give the wrong name
mishear	give the wrong facts
misidentify	receive wrong auditory information
misinform	use resources in the wrong way
mismanage	treat in the wrong way
misnomer	forget (remember wrongly) a location
misplace	give wrong words of another person
misprint	see "filling" when the word is "filing"
misquote	type "here" when the word is "hear"
misread	a wrong name
misshape	believe a person or fact might be wrong
mistranslate	apply talent for criminal (wrong) purposes
mistrust	give wrong word from a foreign language
misunderstand	form in the wrong way
misuse	hear "concert" when the word is "concept"

What's the Difference?

One meaning of **while** is "at the same time", as in the following sentences:

Romeo washed the dishes **while** Juliet dried them.
While Eric was studying Module 12, he kept an eye on the baseball game on TV.

However, **while** has another meaning to show a difference:

His father is a smoker, **while** Luis is not.

The sentence above shows a difference with <u>exactly</u> the same meaning as "but" and "although" sentences. So, we have three ways to show a difference:

His father is a smoker, **while** Luis is not.
His father is a smoker, **but** Luis is not.
Although his father is a smoker, Luis is not.

We can also use **while** at the beginning of the sentence:

While Yan Lian can speak Chinese, she is unable to read it.

Again, the sentence above shows a difference in the same way as "but" and "although" sentences. So, we have three ways to show a difference:

While Yan Lian can speak Chinese, she is unable to read it.
Yan Lian can speak Chinese, **but** she is unable to read it.
Although Yan Lian can speak Chinese, she is unable to read it.

TRY IT: *Change the following information to make **while** sentences:*

Although Bill is rich, he is also unhappy.
While _____

Although the movie is three hours long, it is very entertaining.
While _____

Although the library is crowded today, it is usually empty.
While _____

BE CAREFUL! *Did you remember to use the comma? Try some more:*

Texas is big, **but** Alaska is even bigger.
While _____

This experiment is complicated, **but** the results will be useful.
While _____

The doctor can see you at noon, **but** he is busy right now.
While _____

The firemen are here, **but** the fire is still out of control.
While _____

Look at this sentence from the text (p. 272): "Aborigines used visual retrieval cues, **while** the white Australians used verbal retrieval cues." Do you think Rod Plotnik wrote **while** in this sentence to mean "at the same time" or to show a difference?

Answer Key

misclassify	=	put in wrong category
miscount	=	write 223 when the answer is 227
misdiagnose	=	identify illness wrongly
misfit	=	person who is in the wrong group
misguide	=	send in the wrong direction
mishandle	=	treat in the wrong way
mishear	=	receive wrong auditory information
misidentify	=	give the wrong name
misinform	=	give the wrong facts
mismanage	=	use resources in the wrong way
misnomer	=	a wrong name
misplace	=	forget (remember wrongly) a location
misprint	=	type "here" when the word is "hear"
misquote	=	give wrong words of another person
misread	=	see "filling" when the word is "filing"
misshape	=	form in the wrong way
mistranslate	=	give wrong word from a foreign language
mistrust	=	believe a person or fact might be wrong
misunderstand	=	hear "concert" when the word is "concept"
misuse	=	apply talent for criminal (wrong) purposes

While Bill is rich, he is also unhappy.
While the movie is three hours long, it is very entertaining.
While the library is crowded today, it is usually empty.
While Texas is big, Alaska is even bigger.
While this experiment is complicated, the results will be useful.
While the doctor can see you at noon, he is busy right now.
While the firemen are here, the fire is still out of control.

The Big Picture

Which statement below offers the best summary of the larger significance of this module?

  A   Research has demonstrated that eyewitness testimony is not very reliable and that false memories can be implanted. These discoveries throw our whole understanding of memory up for grabs.

  B   We may be stuck with the cognitive models that now describe remembering and forgetting, since a biological understanding of the neural basis of memory appears to be beyond the reach of neuroscience.

  C   The subtle operations of acquiring (and then sometimes losing) memories suggest that remembering and forgetting work together in a reciprocal balance to meet the changing demands of our environments.

  D   The fact that aborigines remember in a different way than white Australians suggests that the mechanisms of memory are entirely cultural, and have no common biological or evolutionary basis.

  E   Would a psych instructor *dare* expect us to remember all this complicated stuff for an exam? We think not!

True-False

_____ 1. Of the two ways to remember, recall is easier than recognition.

_____ 2. According to network theory, memory is organized like a gigantic map on which roads connect cities of related information.

_____ 3. Forgetting curves measure the length of time that pieces of information will remain in long-term memory.

_____ 4. Rod Plotnik says Freud's theory of repression best explains why his sister can't remember what she did on her 9th birthday — something very embarrassing happened!

_____ 5. Proactive interference occurs when you are trying too hard to remember new information.

_____ 6. Amnesia is the loss of memory that may occur following drug use, damage to the brain, or after severe psychological stress.

_____ 7. Although it is the brain that does the "thinking," the spinal cord stores the actual memories.

_____ 8. Both the method of loci and the peg method are mnemonic strategies.

_____ 9. It turns out that people *are* different in mental ability — aborigines, for example, score lower than white Australians on intelligence tests.

_____ 10. Psychologists have discovered that introducing misleading information during questioning can distort eyewitness testimony.

Flashcards 1

____ 1. amnesia
____ 2. forgetting
____ 3. interference
____ 4. long-term potentiation (LTP)
____ 5. network theory
____ 6. nodes
____ 7. recall
____ 8. recognition
____ 9. repression
____ 10. retrieval cues

a. memory files that contain related information organized around a specific topic or category
b. mental reminders we create by forming vivid mental images or creating associations between information
c. identifying previously learned information with the help of more external cues
d. a common reason for forgetting; recall of a particular memory is blocked by other related memories
e. says we store related ideas in separate categories or files called nodes, all linked together in a network
f. the inability to retrieve, recall, or recognize information that was stored in long-term memory
g. loss of memory caused by a blow or damage to the brain or by drug use or by severe psychological stress
h. a neuron becoming more sensitive to stimulation after it has been repeatedly stimulated
i. retrieving previously learned information without the aid of or with very few external cues
j. a Freudian mental process that automatically hides emotionally threatening information in unconscious

Flashcards 2

____ 1. cognitive interview
____ 2. forgetting curve
____ 3. method of loci
____ 4. network hierarchy
____ 5. peg method
____ 6. proactive interference
____ 7. retroactive interference
____ 8. source misattribution
____ 9. state-dependent learning
____ 10. tip-of-the-tongue phenomenon

a. when new information (learned later) blocks the retrieval of related old information (learned earlier)
b. encoding technique that creates visual associations between memorized places and items to memorize
c. a technique for questioning eyewitnesses by having them imagine and reconstruct details of event fully
d. encoding technique that creates associations between number-word rhymes and items to be memorized
e. when old information (learned earlier) blocks the remembering of new information (learned later)
f. despite great effort, temporary inability to recall information we absolutely know is in our memory
g. easier to recall information when in same emotional or physiological state or setting as when first learned
h. a memory error that results when a person has difficulty in deciding where a memory came from
i. measures amount of previously learned information that subjects can recall or recognize across time
j. arranging nodes so concrete information is at bottom of hierarchy, with abstract ideas at top level

Multiple-Choice

_____ 1. Your brow beading with perspiration, you struggle to answer these questions, desperately summoning your best powers of
   a. recall
   b. reflection
   c. recognition
   d. recollection

_____ 2. If you only glanced through the chapter, pray that the snap quiz will be
   a. essay
   b. multiple-choice
   c. short essay
   d. oral

_____ 3. According to _____ theory, memory is organized by nodes, associations, and hierarchies of information
   a. network
   b. trash can
   c. script
   d. abstraction

_____ 4. Which of the following groups of items would provide the best material for scientific research on memory over time?
   a. names and faces of childhood friends
   b. commonly studied facts, such as state capitals
   c. foreign language vocabulary
   d. nonsense syllables

_____ 5. Analysis of the data yielded by such research (above) would yield
   a. rates of retention
   b. memory percentages
   c. forgetting curves
   d. cognitive charts

_____ 6. You know you said something terribly embarrassing, but you can't remember what it was — this is an example of
   a. repression
   b. poor retrieval cues
   c. amnesia
   d. interference

_____ 7. You were introduced to your friend's professor recently, but there was no time to chat and now you can't recall the professor's name — this is an example of
   a. repression
   b. poor retrieval cues
   c. amnesia
   d. interference

____ 8. Proactive interference is when
   a. information learned later now disrupts retrieval of information learned earlier
   b. learning positive information interferes with the retrieval of negative information
   c. information learned earlier now disrupts retrieval of information learned later
   d. retrospective thinking interferes with potential learning

____ 9. Retroactive interference is when
   a. information learned later now disrupts retrieval of information learned earlier
   b. learning positive information interferes with the retrieval of negative information
   c. information learned earlier now disrupts retrieval of information learned later
   d. retrospective thinking interferes with potential learning

____ 10. Darn! I know it as well as I know my own name, but I just can't remember it right now — sounds like a case of
   a. false memory
   b. source misattribution
   c. state dependent learning
   d. tip-of-the-tongue phenomenon

____ 11. The process in which a neuron becomes more sensitive to stimulation after it has been repeatedly stimulated is called
   a. long-term potentiation (LTP)
   b. state dependent learning
   c. neural assembly formation
   d. interference

____ 12. Both the method of loci and the peg method work by
   a. causing learning to be strengthened through repeated practice
   b. creating strong associations that will serve as effective retrieval cues
   c. connecting material to be learned to the purpose it will be used for
   d. considering material to be memorized as easy and pleasant to learn

____ 13. Aborigine children performed significantly better than white Australian children on memory tasks when
   a. only Aborigine objects were used
   b. the task involved auditory cues
   c. testing was done outdoors in a natural setting
   d. the task involved visual cues

____ 14. Recent research on false memories of abuse in young children has shown that
   a. children can be coached to lie about trivial matters, but not about sexual abuse
   b. false memories can be created through repeated suggestions
   c. children make things up because they really can't remember very well at that age
   d. children tend to lie about most things if they can get something out of it

____ 15. When evaluating eyewitness testimony, pay close attention to
   a. whether the eyewitness has anything to gain or lose by testifying
   b. how confident the eyewitness appears to be
   c. how the questions to the eyewitness are worded
   d. whether the eyewitness seems biased in favor of or against the defendant

174 STUDY GUIDE

Answers for Module 12

True-False
1. F
2. T
3. T
4. F
5. F
6. T
7. F
8. T
9. F
10. T

Flashcards 1
1. g
2. f
3. d
4. h
5. e
6. a
7. i
8. c
9. j
10. b

Flashcards 2
1. c
2. i
3. b
4. j
5. d
6. e
7. a
8. h
9. g
10. f

Multiple-Choice
1. c
2. b
3. a
4. d
5. c
6. a
7. b
8. c
9. a
10. d
11. a
12. b
13. d
14. b
15. c

The Big Picture

Statement C

Test-Taking Tips 5

More hints:

- Trust your common knowledge and don't choose an answer that is obviously not the way the world really works.
- Often the question itself contains a strong hint about the right answer.

Module 13

Intelligence

The Social Psychology of Psychology

Perhaps no single topic reveals the interconnectedness of psychology and society more clearly than the complicated issue of intelligence. Delineating the nature and quality of human thought, captured in the concept of intelligence, has always been a primary goal of psychology. Yet few other subjects have entangled the science of psychology more controversially in the needs and passions of society.

Few would argue the importance of addressing the special needs of the super bright and the severely retarded. It seems obvious that something real is going on in both cases. But what about the rest of us, the great majority? How real are the differences among us that psychology measures with such precision, and, until recently, with such confidence? Questions like these evoke the central question of the social sciences.

The Nature-Nurture Debate in the Social Sciences

Heredity or environment? Personality or experience? Are we best explained by reference to our nature (what is built in) or to our nurture (how we are raised)? This is the essence of the nature-nurture debate, an old argument over basic assumptions that continues to rage in the social sciences. Two controversies illustrate the nature-nurture debate: (1) How important is what we inherit (genetics) compared to what we experience (learning)? (2) To what extent can we control our thoughts, feelings, and actions (free will) compared to control over us by outside forces (determinism).

You will find echoes of the nature-nurture debate in almost everything you read about psychological research and theory. Your basic orientation toward nature or nurture will influence what major theories in psychology you find most convincing, what giants of psychology you like and dislike, what research you believe or doubt, and even what "facts" you accept or reject. Whenever you come across an idea in psychology that arouses your strong interest, whether positive or negative, try examining the idea from the perspective of the nature-nurture debate. Odds are, the idea strongly supports or challenges your basic assumptions about life.

In the long run, thoughtful study of psychology will drive us more and more toward a middle position, an 'interactionist' point of view which sees humans as products of the interplay of heredity and environment, individual uniqueness and group pressure, rational choice and force of habit. Still, I am willing to bet that most of us will continue to feel the pull of our basic adherence either to the argument of nature or the argument of nurture.

Effective Student Tip 13

Risk a New Idea

You didn't come to college to stay the same. You intend to be a better and more fully developed person when you leave. You hope to grow in many ways, and one of the most important is mental. Intellectual growth requires a spirit of openness to change, of willingness to risk new ideas.

If you don't try out a new idea in college, you probably never will. As time goes on, work, family and responsibility all conspire to make most of us more cautious and more conservative. Never again will you encounter as many new and different ideas as in college. In one sense, the very mission of colleges and universities is to hit us with new ideas. If everything was dandy just the way it is now, we really wouldn't need colleges and universities.

When a professor or student throws out a challenging idea, seriously consider whether it might be true. If true, how would it change what you believe? If false, how do your own beliefs disprove it?

Accepting intellectual challenges will strengthen your ideas and your ability to defend them. You might even solve a problem you have been puzzling over. Most of the time, however, you will augment and improve your understanding of the world and yourself only slightly. This is a great victory. We call it growth.

Your response...

What startling new idea have you encountered recently? What was your reaction to that idea?

Key Terms

Understanding the controversies over intelligence will make these key terms easier to learn.

Binet-Simon Intelligence Scale
cultural bias
cultural-familial retardation
culture-free tests
ecological psychology
fraternal twins
Gardner's multiple-intelligence theory
gifted
heritability
identical twins
intelligence quotient
intervention program
mental age
mental retardation
nature-nurture question
non-intellectual factors
normal distribution
organic retardation
psychometric approach
psychometrics
reaction range
reliability
Sternberg's triarchic theory
two-factor theory
validity
Wechsler Adult Intelligence Scale (WAIS-III)
Wechsler Intelligence Scale for Children (WISC-III)

Outline

- *Introduction*
    1. How would you rank these five on intelligence?
    2. Measuring intelligence (**psychometrics**)

A. *Defining Intelligence*

   1. Problem: definition

   ☐ *Consider both the advantages and disadvantages of the following definitions of intelligence. Which theory makes the most sense to you?*

   2. Two-factor theory (Charles Spearman)
       a. **Psychometric approach**
       b. **Two-factor theory**
       c. Advantages and disadvantages
   3. Multiple-intelligence theory (Howard Gardner)
       a. **Gardner's multiple-intelligence theory**
       b. Advantages and disadvantages
   4. Triarchic theory (Robert Sternberg)
       a. **Sternberg's triarchic theory**
       b. Advantages and disadvantages
   5. Current status

B. Measuring Intelligence
  1. Earlier attempts
     a. Head size and intelligence (Francis Galton)
     b. Brain size and intelligence (Paul Broca)
     c. Brain size and achievement
     d. Brain size, sex differences, and intelligence
     e. Measuring intelligence
  2. Binet's breakthrough (Albert Binet)
     a. **Binet-Simon Intelligence Scale**
     b. **Mental age**: measure of intelligence
  3. Terman's formula for IQ (Lewis Terman)
     a. **Intelligence quotient**
     b. Ratio IQ replaced by deviation IQ
  ☐ What is the essential difference between Binet's and Terman's approach to intelligence?
  4. Examples of IQ tests
     a. **Wechsler Adult Intelligence Scale (WAIS-III)**
     b. **Wechsler Intelligence Scale for Children (WISC-III)**
  5. Two characteristics of tests
     a. **Validity**
     b. **Reliability**
  ☐ The two terms above are absolutely essential to an understanding of science, and therefore to an appreciation of the basis of psychology. Can you define each term? Give an example of each?

C. Distribution and Use of IQ Scores
  1. **Normal distribution** of IQ scores
  2. **Mental retardation**: IQ scores
     a. Borderline mentally retarded
     b. Mild/moderately mentally retarded
     c. Severe/profoundly mentally retarded
     d. Causes
        (1) **Organic retardation**
        (2) **Cultural-familial retardation**
  3. Vast majority: IQ scores
     a. Do IQ scores predict academic achievement?
     b. Do IQ scores predict job performance?
  4. Gifted: IQ scores
     a. **Gifted**
     b. How do gifted individuals turn out? (Lewis Terman)

D. *Potential Problems of IQ Testing*
   1. Binet's two warnings
      a. Intelligence tests do not measure innate abilities or natural intelligence
      b. Intelligence tests, by themselves, should not be used to label people
   2. Racial discrimination
      a. Definition of mental retardation
      b. Educational decisions
   3. **Cultural bias**
   4. Culture-free
      a. **Culture-free tests**
      b. **Ecological psychology**
   5. **Non-intellectual factors**

E. *Nature-Nurture Question*
   1. Definitions: the **nature-nurture question**
   2. Twin studies
      a. **Fraternal twins**
      b. **Identical twins**
      c. Definition of intelligence
      d. Influence of genetic factors
   3. Adoption studies
   4. Interaction: nature and nurture
      a. **Heritability**
      b. **Reaction range**
   5. Racial controversy (*The Bell Curve* by Richard Herrnstein and Charles Murray)
      a. Difference between IQ scores
      b. Cause of IQ differences

F. *Cultural Diversity: Races, IQs, and Immigration*
   1. Innate intelligence (Lewis Terman)
   2. Classify races (Robert Yerkes)
   3. Immigration laws United States Congress: IQ scores as the basis for laws
      a. Immigration Law of 1924
      b. Mismeasurement examined (Stephen Jay Gould)

G. *Research Focus: New Approaches*
   1. Can genius be found in the brain?
   2. Can Spearman's "g" be found in the brain?

180 STUDY GUIDE

H. Application: Intervention Programs
1. Definition of **intervention program**
   a. Abecedarian Project
   b. Head Start
2. Raising IQ scores
3. Importance of intervention programs

Language Workout

What's That?

p. 281 how would you **rank** these five = put in order of importance
win the **prestigious** tennis tournament = honored, respected
in his 20s he **founded** Microsoft = established the business
the math part of the **SAT** = Scholastic Aptitude Test (for students)
she **made a big stir** = caused excitement

p. 282 not always **clear cut** = clearly defined, easy to see
devoted an entire issue = used
quantifies cognitive abilities = describes by using quantities

p. 283 argues for **broadening** the definition = making wider, including more factors
spatial intelligence = ability to perceive differences in terms of space
a person may be "**street smart**" = with practical knowledge about living

p. 284 efforts to measure intelligence began **in earnest** = with serious work
Galton **switched gears** = changed methods
the head size of **Cambridge** students = British university

p. 285 By a strange **twist of fate** = unexpected result
be able to **recite** the days of the week = say the names of
retarded in intellectual development = developing later than normal
intelligence **quotient** = a ratio, comparing a test score to age
a child's **chronological** age = measured in time

p. 286 A trained examiner **administers** the Wechsler scales = uses
on a **one-to-one basis** = one examiner with one student (not group)
from a **deprived** environment = without necessary support (such as money)
rule out other cultural or educational problems = exclude

p. 287 this characteristic **makes or breaks** a test = decides the success of
knowledge that a person has **accumulated** = collected
handwriting remained **constant** over time = unchanging
verbal IQ scores are quite **stable** = unchanging

p. 288 **borderline** mental retardation = not definite
outside an institution = in normal life (not in hospital)
the **vast** majority = very large
provided they are in a family = if, with this condition
a greatly **impoverished** environment = very limited, without necessities

Module 13: Intelligence

p. 289 memorized the **top tunes** = most popular songs
high school equivalency exam = successful score on exam gives high school diploma without attending classes
the **gifted** end of the normal curve = having special abilities
labeled as **nerds** = unattractive, unfashionable persons
geeks = unfashionable persons, often working with computers
How do gifted individuals **turn out**? = are they successful or not?
2% actually **flunked out** = left school because of bad grades

p. 290 neither of Binet's warnings were **heeded** = used, noticed
the judge's **ruling** = official decision
considered a **dead end** = hopeless, with no hope of success
a **class action suit** = lawsuit with group of people suing one company
on behalf of = for the benefit of
federal **court of appeals** = high court
children **of color** = non-white
overrepresented = more than normal (expected) number
predominately White school districts = mostly, primarily

p. 291 may **penalize** them = punish (unfairly lower scores)
dairy workers = milk producer
bartenders = workers who mix and serve liquor
navigational skills = directing boats across distances
(intelligence) might not **show up** = be seen
the psychologist tries to **put her at ease** = make her comfortable
that may help or **hinder** performance on tests = prevent (not help)

p. 292 **insightful** intelligence = full of understanding, thoughtful
written in stone = cannot be changed, permanent

p. 293 children who had been **abandoned** = given away, left without protection
disadvantaged homes = without benefits (culture, money, education)

p. 294 **no matter** the color of one's skin = with no influence from
only "**skin deep**" = on the surface (not deep)

p. 296 one of psychology's **sorriest** moments = worst, saddest
the **guiding force** = leader
for **an effective moral life** = life of careful decisions about right and wrong
a **meager** 13 years = very small number
unconstrained breeding = uncontrolled, unlimited
feebleminded = with weak mental ability
The **fair** peoples = with blond hair and light skin
congressmen **sought** a way = looked for (were **seek**ing)
render useless = make

p. 297 performed the **autopsy** = medical examination of dead body

p. 298 Why might a child need a **head start**? = extra help at beginning
combating poverty = fighting
retained a small gain = kept
health **screening** = examining to find and identify problems

p. 299 this decline **has to do with** = is related to, concerns
below the **poverty line** = standard of income that classifies people as poor or not-poor

>   lowered **aspirations** = hopes or goals for the future
>   increased **apathy** = lack of emotion ("I don't care")

p. 302 police have **seized** $700,000 = taken control of
>   He leaves gambling **slips** = tickets, pieces of paper
>   he was **committed** to a state school = placed (by legal order)
>   that's a **sure thing** = a certain result

See It and Say It

p. 283 **triarchic** = try-ARR-kik

p. 285 **Binet** = bee-NAY
>   **imbeciles** = IHM-bih-sillz
>   **quotient** = KWOH-shint

p. 286 **Wechsler** = WEHK-slurr

p. 287 **validity** = vuh-LID-ih-tee

p. 291 **ecological** = ee-kuh-LAH-ji-kull

p. 292 **nurture** = NURR-churr

p. 296 **Yerkes** = YURR-keez

p. 298 **Abecedarian** = ay-bee-see-DAIR-ee-uhn

Make the Connection

We can use **which** to connect two sentences:

>   Americans like to eat fast food. Fast food can be unhealthy.
>   Americans like to eat fast food, **which** can be unhealthy.

In the same way, we can use **which** to connect and to measure (with words like "some", "all", "many" or any number).

>   Rado has a lot of work tonight. Some of the work is important
>   Rado has a lot of work tonight, **some of which** is important.

In this example, we replaced the subject of the second sentence (some of the work) with some of which.

TRY IT

Jenny has a lot of research to do. Some of it requires a computer.
>   Jenny _____
>   _____

Sharella bought a dozen eggs. Three of them were cracked.
>   Sharella _____
>   _____

The library has 85,000 books. Most of them are about technical subjects.
>   The library _____
>   _____

BE CAREFUL! Did you remember to put in the comma after the first sentence? You need the comma to show that the two are connected, not joined into one.

TRY SOME MORE

Mr. and Mrs. Smith have a lot of problems. 90% of them can be solved.
    Mr. and Mrs. Smith _____

Chang-Woo had ten math problems to solve. All ten of them required a calculator.
    Chang-Woo _____

Ford makes fourteen models of automobiles. A few of them are built for right-hand driving.
    Ford _____

Now look at the following example:

Rado has a lot of work tonight. He has finished <u>some of the work</u>.
    Rado has a lot of work tonight, **some of which** he has finished.

In this example, <u>some of the work</u> is the object of the sentence, but we can still replace it with **some of which**. Try connecting the following sentences:

Jenny has a lot of research to do. The professor wants all of it tomorrow.
    Jenny _____

Ernie wrote a 27-page paper. His dog ate half of it.
    Ernie _____

Ella earned a hundred dollars for her work. The government will take thirty dollars of it for taxes.
    Ella _____

Marco read 135 pages of the textbook. He remembered none of it the next morning.
    Marco _____

This is tricky, so check your answers in the Answer Key below.

Do you understand this sentence now?

    Along with using IQ scores to label individuals came racial and cultural discrimination, **some of which** continues to the present (p. 290).

Answer Key

Jenny has a lot of research to do, **some of which** requires a computer.
Sharella bought a dozen eggs, **three of which** were cracked
The library has 85,000 books, **most of which** are about technical subjects
Mr. and Mrs. Smith have a lot of problems, **90% of which** can be solved.
Chang-Woo had ten math problems to solve, **all ten of which** required a calculator.
Ford makes fourteen models of automobiles, **a few of which** are built for right-hand driving.
Jenny has a lot of research to do, **all of which** the professor wants tomorrow.
Ernie wrote a 27-page paper, **half of which** his dog ate.
Ella earned a hundred dollars for her work, **thirty dollars of which** the government will take for taxes.
Marco read 135 pages of the textbook, **none of which** he remembered the next morning.

The Big Picture

Which statement below offers the best summary of the larger significance of this module?

A Intelligence is a real dimension along which people do vary, but it must be measured and used with great sensitivity because we do not know with certainty how it is formed and how it influences a person's life.

B From Binet to the present, psychology has refined the measurement of intelligence to a degree of precision where IQ scores can and should be used in a wide variety of personal and social decisions.

C Psychology has wasted great energy and resources pursuing the nature-nurture question, when it should have been obvious all along that we get our smarts from an irreversible throw of the genetic dice.

D The measurement of intelligence has been so riddled with bias and discrimination that most psychologists are ready to abandon the concept of intelligence altogether.

E My psych instructor must think I'm real stoopid. She just handed out a page of questions and thought I wouldn't notice there are no answers on it!

True-False

_____ 1. The key issue in defining intelligence is whether it is essentially cognitive abilities or a combination of cognitive abilities and other skills.

_____ 2. It is generally true that the larger the brain the more intelligent the person.

_____ 3. Alfred Binet gave us the concept of an intelligence quotient (IQ).

_____ 4. Lewis Terman's formula for determining IQ was mental age divided by chronological age times 100.

_____ 5. If you use a precise doctor's scale in an attempt to measure your intelligence, your results will be reliable, but not valid.

_____ 6. As a result of protest movements, all the major intelligence tests are now culture-free.

_____ 7. Measurements of intelligence have been used to support racial and ethnic discrimination.

_____ 8. Twin studies suggest that we inherit only a small percentage of our intelligence.

_____ 9. Adoption studies suggest that environment plays a significant role in determining intelligence.

_____ 10. Research shows that intervention programs like Head Start, while well meaning, have few long-term benefits.

Flashcards 1

1. Binet-Simon Intelligence Scale
2. Gardner's multiple-intelligence theory
3. intelligence quotient
4. mental age
5. nature-nurture question
6. psychometrics
7. reliability
8. Sternberg's triarchic theory
9. two-factor theory
10. validity

a. says intelligence is three skills — analytical thinking, problem solving, practical thinking
b. says there can be at least seven different kinds of intelligence: verbal, musical, logical, spatial, body...
c. estimating intellectual progress by comparing child's score on an IQ test to average children of same age
d. computed by dividing a child's mental age (MA) by the child's chronological age (CA) then times 100
e. degree to which a test measures what it is supposed to measure
f. says that intelligence is based on a general mental abilities factor (g) plus specific mental abilities (s)
g. asks how much genetic and environmental factors each contribute to the development of intelligence
h. area of psychology concerned with developing tests that assess abilities, skills, beliefs, and traits
i. consistency; a person's test score on a test at one time should be similar to score on a similar test later
j. first intelligence test; items of increasing difficulty measured vocabulary, memory, common knowledge

Flashcards 2

1. cultural bias
2. culture-free tests
3. ecological psychology
4. gifted
5. heritability
6. intervention program
7. mental retardation
8. normal distribution
9. organic retardation
10. reaction range

a. substantial limitation in functioning characterized by sub-average intellectual functioning, other limits
b. question wording and background experiences more familiar to some social groups than to others
c. says intelligence should be measured by observing how people solve problems in their usual settings
d. extent to which traits, abilities, or IQ scores increase or decrease as result of interaction with environment
e. a statistical arrangement of scores so that they resemble the shape of a bell; the bell shaped curve
f. amount or proportion of some ability, characteristic, or trait that can be attributed to genetic factors
g. impressive cognitive abilities; moderate defined by IQ scores of 130 to 150, profoundly by 180 and above
h. vocabulary, experiences, social situations in test same as those of individual taking test
i. creates environment that offers more opportunities for intellectual, social, personal development
j. mental deficits resulting from genetic problems or brain damage

Multiple-Choice

____ 1. Rod Plotnik is interested in Supreme Court Justice Clarence Thomas and his sister Emma Mae Martin because their stories
   a. show that some individuals seem destined for greatness
   b. illustrate the unpredictability of human abilities and behaviors
   c. show how unevenly intelligence is spread, even within one family
   d. illustrate the nature-nurture question in psychology

____ 2. Charles Spearman's two-factor theory says that intelligence is a
   a. general factor (g) plus specific mental abilities (s)
   b. group of separate and equally important mental abilities
   c. set of processes for solving problems
   d. combination of biological functions of the brain and nervous system

____ 3. An advantage of both Howard Gardner's multiple-intelligence theory and Robert Sternberg's triarchic theory is that they
   a. yield a single score that is useful for predicting academic performance
   b. measure each of the five known areas of intelligence
   c. take into account abilities not covered by standard IQ tests
   d. define intelligence in a way that is completely culture free

____ 4. The simplest yet most accurate indication of intelligence in humans is
   a. head size
   b. skull size
   c. brain size
   d. (none of the above has much relationship to intelligence in humans)

____ 5. The first intelligence test was devised by
   a. Charles Spearman
   b. Louis Terman
   c. Alfred Binet
   d. Howard Gardner

____ 6. The formula for IQ is
   a. level of schooling divided by actual age
   b. chronological age divided by mental age
   c. test score divided by grade in school plus 100
   d. mental age divided by chronological age times 100

____ 7. Ten times your sister jumps on the scale and ten times it reads 115 pounds. "Wow," she exclaims, "I'm taller than the average American woman!" Her results are
   a. both reliable and valid
   b. neither reliable nor valid
   c. reliable, but not valid
   d. valid, but not reliable

_____ 8. If you measured the intelligence of everyone in the United States, a distribution of all the scores would look like a
   a. curve sloping gently upward to the right
   b. bell-shaped curve
   c. flat horizon line with a skyscraper in the middle
   d. curve that rises and falls at regular intervals

_____ 9. Terman's 35-year study of gifted persons revealed their lives to be
   a. no different from the average American's life
   b. plagued by the mental instability that goes with high intelligence
   c. much lonelier, sadder, and more eccentric than average
   d. somewhat healthier, happier, and more successful than average

_____ 10. The problem with IQ tests is that they are
   a. completely culture-free
   b. seldom used to get children into the right classes in school
   c. sometimes used to label people and discriminate against them
   d. unable to predict how well a child will do in school

_____ 11. In the matter of intelligence, the answer to the nature-nurture question is that
   a. twin studies prove the predominance of nurture
   b. adoption studies prove the predominance of nature
   c. intervention programs show that intelligence is fixed at birth
   d. both nature and nurture contribute about equally to the formation of intelligence

_____ 12. Twin studies suggest that intelligence is
   a. about 90% inherited
   b. only slightly influenced by heredity
   c. about 50% determined by genetics
   d. a random phenomenon unaffected by heredity

_____ 13. Adoption studies suggest that intelligence
   a. can be positively affected by improved environmental conditions
   b. is essentially fixed at birth by heredity
   c. is lessened by the loss of one's biological parents
   d. does not change much, regardless of family environment

_____ 14. The story of IQ tests and immigration shows that
   a. good research can be used for bad purposes
   b. scientific research often reflects the prejudices of the times
   c. good research can be used to right injustice
   d. scientific research is politically neutral

_____ 15. Studies of the effectiveness of intervention programs like Head Start suggest that
   a. however well-intentioned, intervention programs don't work
   b. the main benefits of these programs go to the middle-class professionals they employ
   c. the short-term benefits fail to justify the high costs of these programs
   d. even if differences in IQ fade over time, there are other social benefits that justify continuing these programs

188 STUDY GUIDE

Answers for Module 13

True-False
1. T
2. F
3. F
4. T
5. T
6. F
7. T
8. F
9. T
10. F

Flashcards 1
1. j
2. b
3. d
4. c
5. g
6. h
7. i
8. a
9. f
10. e

Flashcards 2
1. b
2. h
3. c
4. g
5. f
6. i
7. a
8. e
9. j
10. d

Multiple-Choice
1. d
2. a
3. c
4. d
5. c
6. d
7. c
8. b
9. d
10. c
11. d
12. c
13. a
14. b
15. d

The Big Picture

Statement A

Test-Taking Tips 6

More hints:

- Use everything you know. Even if you can't recall the specific information needed, think about what you *do* remember concerning the subject.
- Don't jump to the conclusion that an answer is correct just because it uses the right word. The entire statement must be true.

Module 14

Thought & Language

Can We Study Ourselves Scientifically?

Historians of science have pointed out that the accumulation of human knowledge seems backwards. We understood the far-away phenomena of astronomy centuries ago, gradually grasped the principles of physics and biology in modern times, but only now are beginning to penetrate the mysteries of the brain and the mind. The closer we are to something, the harder it is to study it objectively. Add to this difficulty an even greater one — we *are* the very thing we want to study. Natural scientists say this problem alone dooms the social sciences to be inherently subjective and therefore not really scientific. Social scientists disagree, of course, but they admit that being objective about ourselves presents enormous challenges.

Processes That Make Us Human

As an animal lover, I welcome every discovery of animals engaging in behavior (like tool-using) previously thought to be the exclusive property of *Homo sapiens.* Those of us who observe animals in the wild know they communicate very effectively. New research shows that elephants communicate at a decibel level we can't even hear. Still, is it really language? (See Rod Plotnik's fascinating review of whether apes can acquire language.)

In our efforts to win greater respect for the rights and inherent value of other animals, some of us argue that we humans aren't so different and shouldn't consider ourselves morally superior. Nevertheless, we have to admit that humans have strikingly unique skills and abilities in three areas that perhaps define our species. We have unmatched intellectual potential, unrivaled flexibility in exploiting that potential, and a system of communication that preserves and extends those mental powers. In this module, Rod Plotnik continues the story of these quintessential human properties, helping us appreciate how interrelated they are.

Science is never easy, however. We all know what thought and language are, yet how do we describe and explain them? Our own subjective experience seems to get in the way of objective understanding. We have to fight for every piece of knowledge. Further complicating matters is the sad fact that science is not always neutral. In the previous module, Rod Plotnik described times in our history when racial prejudice distorted the measurement of intelligence. After weighing all the evidence on whether other primates can acquire language, most psychologists have concluded that, however remarkable, the linguistic abilities of apes are not true language. So says science. Or is it our human prejudice?

Effective Student Tip 14

What Can You Do?

Some students freeze up when they get an assignment, fearing that, unless they instantly know what to do and how to do it, they're dead. The solution, if only they realized it, is right at hand. One of the best ways to tackle a new challenge is to draw on what you already do well. Step away from the course for a moment. What can you do competently right now?

Perhaps your work relates to the course (a business student at a bank, or a psychology student in a day-care center). Your experiences and observations would make great examples to use in class discussion or in written reports. Most professors delight in having students relate the subject matter of the course to the realities of the working world. If you learned how to operate a word processor at work, can you use it after hours to prepare papers so beautiful they will knock your professor's socks off? If you are an athlete, can you use your knowledge of effective training techniques to work out a schedule for gradually building up your academic skills?

You only start from square one once, and that was years ago. By now you have acquired many competencies, some quite special. Don't hesitate to use them.

Your response...

What are you really good at? Could that skill be used in your schoolwork? (Don't say "no" too quickly!)

Module 14: Thought & Language

Key Terms

Oh, oh... another tough set of key terms. This module covers two areas of psychology, thought and language, which are related but also separate and complete fields of study in their own right. Both are complicated and offer some highly technical facts and concepts [that's one of the terms]. Buckle down!

algorithms
analogy
availability heuristic
babbling
basic rules of grammar
Chomsky's theory of language
cognitive approach
communication
concept
convergent thinking
creative individual
creative thinking
critical language period
deductive reasoning
deep structure
definition theory
divergent thinking
dyslexia
environmental language factors
functional fixedness
grammar
heuristics
inductive reasoning
innate language factors
insight
language
language stages
morpheme
morphology
overgeneralization
parentese [motherese]
phonemes
phonology
problem-solving
prototype theory
reasoning
savants
semantics
sentences
single words
social learning approach
subgoals
surface structure
syntax [grammar]
telegraphic speech
theory of linguistic relativity
thinking
transformational rules
two-word combinations
word

Outline

- *Introduction*
    1. Concepts
    2. Creativity
    3. **Cognitive approach**
        a. **Thinking**
        b. **Language**

    A. Forming Concepts
        1. **Concept**
        ☐ "Concept" is another of those deceptively simple common terms. Can you define it formally?
        2. Definition theory
            a. **Definition theory**
            b. Problems with definition theory
        3. Prototype theory
            a. **Prototype theory**
            b. Advantages of prototype theory

4. Early formation of concepts
5. Concepts in the brain
6. Two functions of concepts
   a. Organize information
   b. Avoid relearning

B. *Solving Problems*
   1. **Problem-solving**
   2. Different ways of thinking
      a. **Algorithms**
      b. **Heuristics**
         (1) Playing chess
         (2) Daily life: **availability heuristic**
      c. Artificial intelligence
   3. Three strategies for solving problems
      a. Changing one's mental set
         (1) **Functional fixedness**
         (2) **Insight**
      b. Using an **analogy**
      c. Forming **subgoals**

C. *Thinking Creatively*
   1. Definition
      a. **Creative thinking**
      b. **Creative individual**
   ☐ *Do you consider yourself a creative person? How do you express your creativity?*
      c. Psychometric approach
         (1) **Convergent thinking**
         (2) **Divergent thinking**
      d. Case study approach
      e. Cognitive approach
   2. Is IQ related to creativity?
      a. **Savants**
      b. Creativity and IQ
   3. How do creative people think and behave?
      a. Focus
      b. Cognition
      c. Personality
      d. Motivation
   4. Is creativity related to mental disorders

D. *Language: Basic Rules*
   1. **Language**
      a. **Word**
      b. **Grammar**
   2. Four rules of language
      a. **Phonology** and **phonemes**
      b. **Morphology** and **morpheme**
      c. **Syntax [grammar]**
      d. **Semantics**
   3. Understanding language (Noam Chomsky)
      a. Mental grammar
      b. Innate program
   4. Different structure, same meaning
      a. **Surface structure**
      b. **Deep structure**
      c. **Transformational rules**
      d. **Chomsky's theory of language**

E. *Acquiring Language*
   1. Four stages in acquiring language (**language stages**)
      a. **Babbling**
      b. **Single words** and **parentese [motherese]**
      c. **Two-word combinations**
      d. **Sentences**
         (1) **Telegraphic speech**
         (2) **Basic rules of grammar**
         (3) **Overgeneralization**
      e. Going through the stages
   2. Learning a particular language
      a. Innate factors
         (1) **Innate language factors**
         (2) **Critical language period**
      b. Environmental factors
         (1) **Environmental language factors** (B. F. Skinner)
         (2) **Social learning approach**

F. *Reason, Thought, & Language*
   1. Two kinds of **reasoning**
      a. **Deductive reasoning**
      b. **Inductive reasoning**

2. Why reasoning fails
3. Words and thoughts (**theory of linguistic relativity** [Benjamin Whorf])
   a. Inuit versus American words for snow
   b. Thinking in two languages

G. *Research Focus: Dyslexia*
   1. Research question: what kind of problem is **dyslexia**?
   2. Why can't dyslexics read?
   3. Can training help?

H. *Cultural Diversity: Influences on Thinking*
   1. Differences in thinking
   2. Male-female differences
      a. Males and females use language differently
      b. Brains process words differently

I. *Application: Do Animals Have Language?*
   1. **Communication**
   2. Four criteria for **language**
      a. Abstract symbols
      b. Express thoughts
      c. Complex rules of grammar
      d. Generate endless number of meaningful sentences
   ☐ *What is the difference between communication and language?*
   3. Dolphins (Louis Herman)
   4. Gorilla and chimpanzee
      a. Koko (Francine Patterson)
      b. Washoe (Beatrice and Allan Gardner)
      c. Criticisms (Herbert Terrace)
   5. Bonobo: star pupil
      a. Kanzi (Sue Savage-Rumbaugh)
      b. New attention

Language Workout

What's That?

p. 305 **shorthand** = quick way to explain
No one thought Parks would **amount to much** = be successful
He was **out on the streets** at age 15 = living alone (without family)
you're gonna be **porters** = laborers
worst of all, **lynchings** = illegal hangings (murders)
That man didn't want to **take me on** = take responsibility for me
lived in **flophouses** = cheap hotels

p. 306 would **tax** the best of memories = be difficult for
the large brown **mutt** = common street dog

p. 307 children can **early on** perform these tasks = from an early age
helping us **make sense of** our world = understand, organize

p. 308 Kasparov looks very **glum** = unhappy
The match **was all about** thinking = concerned
novices become bogged down = newcomers
novices become **bogged down** = slowed (or stopped)
rules that lead to specific **outcomes** = results
Heuristics are **rules of thumb** = quick rules
basic rules of **checkers** = board game (easier than chess)
In no time = after a very short time

p. 309 the experience of **getting stuck** = stopping, unable to continue
without **retracing** any lines = rewriting
the sudden **grasp** of a solution = understanding
mount a candle on the wall = attach, fix

p. 310 a time of **segregation** = forced separation of different races in public
produce **innovative** ideas = new and creative
A creative individual **fashions** products = designs
Convergent thinking = moving toward one point
Divergent thinking = moving out in different directions

p. 311 **unconventional** = outside ordinary behavior
committed to their work = emotionally connected
they tend to have large **egos** = feelings of self-importance
intrinsic motivation = coming from inside
extrinsic motivation = coming from outside factors
their creative **fires are fueled** = energies are powered, stimulated
achieved creative **breakthroughs** = new solutions

p. 312 A word is an **arbitrary** pairing = random, without a reason
"Did Pat **pat** a caterpillar's back?" = touch

p. 313 how do we **acquire** this mental grammar? = learn, get
we **convert** our ideas = change

p. 315 shows **warmth** = friendly, loving quality
a rather large language **leap** = advance (jump) to higher state

p. 316 father **strapped** her to a potty chair = tied
period of social deprivation **left its mark** = had long-lasting effects

p. 318 only a drunk person would **gleefully** walk into the ocean = very happily
there is only one correct conclusion to **draw** = make
Based on these **particulars** = specific details
provided you're aware of their pitfalls = if
provided you're aware of their **pitfalls** = traps
downward **velocity** = rate of speed
it often **runs counter to** our experiences = opposes, goes against

p. 319 Whorf's story **lives on** = continues (is not forgotten)
very **temperamental** = moody, sensitive, unpredictable
which would not **be the case** if = be true

p. 320 Dyslexia is now **regarded** as a neurological problem = explained
faulty neural connections = not working correctly

p. 321 use language to **share concerns** = discuss worries

p. 322 the answer **hinges on** the difference = depends on
understand my commands and **act accordingly** = obey the commands
four **criteria** = standards for judgment [plural of one **criterion**]
to **probe** the sea = explore, investigate
Frisbee = plastic disk used in game
sophisticated ability to use language = highly developed
some scientists remain **skeptical** = doubtful, unbelieving

p. 323 the most **devastating** criticism = damaging, destroying
research **monies** = funds, money for projects
a kind of **primitive** grammar = undeveloped

p. 326 **singsong crooning** = making sounds with definite rhythm (like singing a song)
patronizing **gibberish** = nonsense words

Flex Your Word Power

The following pairs of words are opposites in meaning. These words follow the same pattern of using prefixes. Test yourself: can you make the opposite of each word?

inhale means the opposite of **ex**hale

internal means the opposite of _____

introvert means the opposite of _____

intrinsic means the opposite of _____

_____ means the opposite of **ex**clude

_____ means the opposite of **ex**tensive

import means the opposite of _____

implode means the opposite of _____

_____ means the opposite of **ex**plicit

What's the Difference?

As Plotnik explains (on p. 313), most of us can see the difference between **active** sentences ("You picked up a caterpillar") and **passive** sentences ("A caterpillar was picked up by you"). But how can we choose which one to use?

Most sentences are active: someone does/did something. For example,

Darwin wrote the first book about evolution.

So, if your focus is Darwin, his many actions and achievements, then you will want to keep Darwin **active** in your sentence: you will have the person writing.

On the other hand, sometimes you will want to write about an object. For example,

The first book about evolution was written by Darwin.

If your focus is evolution, the development and importance of the idea, then you will want to make your reader think about evolution and the first book about it. In this case, you will probably choose to keep Darwin **passive** in your sentence.

Which of the two sentences would fit best in the following passage? *Check the best one.*

_____ Charles Darwin is often called the father of evolution. As a naturalist, he studied a variety of plants and animals before he took his famous trip to the Galapagos Islands.

_____ On this voyage, Darwin first conceived his theory of how all living things develop, or "evolve".

Which of the two sentences is appropriate to end the next passage? *Check the best one.*

_____ One of the most important concepts in twentieth-century science was the idea that living things, both plants and animals, tend to continuously develop in a process of adapting to their surroundings.

_____ When this concept was first presented in 1851, it changed the thinking of scientists throughout the world.

Do you see how the two paragraphs focus on different factors? The first is clearly about a person, so the active sentence is more suitable. The second focuses on the idea, so the passive sentence keeps the reader's attention on the idea.

Sometimes, in an active sentence, the person or force performing the action is obvious or not important, so we choose to use a passive sentence. For example, look at the following sentence:

The police arrested the criminal.

This active sentence is correct in grammar, and it might be suitable in a paragraph about police activities. However, who else arrests criminals? The police are usually the only ones with the power to make arrests, so we don't need to waste words to say this.

Now look at the passive sentence:

The criminal was arrested.

Everyone who reads this sentence will understand that it means **by the police**, so it is not necessary to say it (unless there is some unusual situation).

Because we don't need to identify the actor in a **by** phrase **(by the police, by Darwin)**, some writers use a passive sentence as a way to hide responsibility. For example, if you were an office worker, which of these two sentences would you say to escape punishment? **"I broke the copy machine"** or **"the copy machine was broken"**?

Answer Key

internal means the opposite of **external**
introvert means the opposite of **extrovert**
intrinsic means the opposite of **extrinsic**
include means the opposite of **ex**clude
intensive means the opposite of **ex**tensive
import means the opposite of **export**
implode means the opposite of **explode**
implicit means the opposite of **ex**plicit

The Big Picture

Which statement below offers the best summary of the larger significance of this module?

    A   There you go again, Rod Plotnik! You didn't have enough space in your textbook, so you crammed two subjects into this module even though they have very little in common.

    B   Both subjects are interesting, but the material on thought is more philosophical than psychological and could have been omitted from a textbook in general psychology.

    C   Thought and language, while technically separate topics in psychology, are intimately connected. In their sophisticated human form, each would be impossible without the other. It is likely that they developed together.

    D   Both subjects are interesting, but the material on language has more to do with child development and could have been omitted from a textbook in general psychology.

    E   What do I think about this module? Gee, I don't know..., I can't put it into words.

True-False

_____ 1. According to prototype theory, we form a concept by constructing a complete list of all the properties that define an object, event, or characteristic.

_____ 2. Today computer programs can beat all but the very best human chess players because they employ such powerful heuristics.

_____ 3. Good thinking: insight, analogy, subgoals. Bad thinking: functional fixedness.

_____ 4. Divergent thinking is a popular psychometric measure of creativity.

_____ 5. There is no scientific data to back up the common belief that creativity is related to an increased risk of mental instability.

_____ 6. Noam Chomsky bases his theory of language on the premise that humans have inborn language capabilities.

_____ 7. It is easier to learn a foreign language in grade school than in college.

_____ 8. Children complete the essential tasks of learning language during the three-word stage.

_____ 9. Eskimos probably think differently about snow because they have so many more words for it than other people do.

_____ 10. Despite fascinating research on dolphins, chimpanzees, and gorillas, so far it appears that only humans clearly meet the four criteria for true language.

Flashcards 1

___ 1. concept
___ 2. convergent thinking
___ 3. creative thinking
___ 4. deductive reasoning
___ 5. definition theory
___ 6. divergent thinking
___ 7. functional fixedness
___ 8. heuristics
___ 9. inductive reasoning
___ 10. prototype theory

a. says you form a concept by creating a mental image based on the average characteristics of an object
b. flexibility in thinking plus reorganization of thought to produce innovative ideas and solutions
c. a mental set characterized by inability to see an object having a function different from its usual one
d. beginning with a problem and coming up with a single correct solution
e. drawing a specific conclusion from a general assumption believed to be true; general to particular
f. rules of thumb or clever short-cuts that reduce the number of operations needed to solve a problem
g. beginning with a problem and coming up with many different solutions
h. a way to group objects, events, etc., on the basis of some characteristics they all share in common
i. says you form a concept of an object or event by making a mental list of its essential characteristics
j. making particular observations then drawing a broader conclusion form them; particular to general

Flashcards 2

___ 1. critical language period
___ 2. dyslexia
___ 3. morpheme
___ 4. overgeneralization
___ 5. parentese (motherese)
___ 6. phonemes
___ 7. semantics
___ 8. telegraphic speech
___ 9. theory of linguistic relativity
___ 10. transformational rules

a. the smallest meaningful combination of sounds in a language
b. applying a grammatical rule to cases where it should not be used ("I goed to store")
c. a way adults speak to young children; slower, higher than normal voice, simple sentences, repeats words
d. procedures for converting our ideas from surface structures into deep structures and back again
e. the basic sounds of consonants and vowels (any word can be broken down into these units)
f. a distinctive pattern of speaking in which the child omits articles, prepositions, and parts of verbs
g. specifies the meaning of words or phrases when they appear in various sentences or contexts
h. reading, spelling, and writing difficulties that may include reversing or skipping letters and numbers
i. says differences among languages result in similar differences in how people think and perceive world
j. the time from infancy to adolescence when language is easier to learn; more difficult to learn after period

Multiple-Choice

_____ 1. Concepts are crucial to effective thinking because without them
   a. we would not know the rules for logical thought
   b. we would be overwhelmed by apparently unrelated pieces of information
   c. our cognitive processes would be just like those of a dog or cat
   d. our motivation to think would be greatly reduced

_____ 2. Most psychologists favor the _____ theory of concept formation because it _____
   a. definition ... is based on good, sound definitions
   b. definition ... accounts for the exceptions to the rule
   c. prototype ... is based on complete listings of essential properties
   d. prototype ... accounts for more objects using fewer features

_____ 3. A computer program finally has defeated a top human chess player, primarily because
   a. increasingly more powerful algorithms finally won
   b. good heuristics finally won
   c. computers don't have to take breaks for food and drink
   d. there is an element of luck in any game

_____ 4. When your friend remarks pessimistically that crime is increasing ("Did you see that gruesome murder on the news last night?"), you recognize the operation of the
   a. accuracy algorithm
   b. availability heuristic
   c. prototype theory
   d. self-fulfilling prophecy

_____ 5. If you were not able to solve the nine-dot problem, it probably was because of
   a. functional fixedness
   b. lack of insight
   c. using poor analogies
   d. failure to establish subgoals

_____ 6. One of the best ways to finish your assignment on time is to
   a. have the problem in the back of your mind, and wait for a sudden flash of insight
   b. use the analogy of other, similar assignments you have done before
   c. fix your thoughts on the function that is involved in the assignment
   d. break the assignment down into subtasks and subgoals

_____ 7. A serious problem with too many college courses is that they place all the emphasis on _____ thinking
   a. creative
   b. convergent
   c. divergent
   d. brainstorm

_____ 8. From most *particular* to most *general* in the rules of language, the correct order is
   a. morpheme, phoneme, syntax or grammar, semantics
   b. syntax or grammar, phoneme, semantics, morpheme
   c. phoneme, morpheme, syntax or grammar, semantics
   d. semantics, syntax or grammar, morpheme, phoneme

_____ 9. Which is the correct sequence of stages in children's acquisition of language?
   a. crying, begging, asking, reasoning
   b. senseless noises, listening, imitation, original productions
   c. babbling, one-word, two-word, three-word, four-word, etc.
   d. babbling, single word, two-word combinations, sentences

_____ 10. According to Noam Chomsky, language operates at two levels:
   a. spoken words and censored words
   b. surface structure and deep structure
   c. obvious meaning and implied meaning
   d. sentences and telegraphic speech

_____ 11. The theoretical debate between Chomsky and B. F. Skinner concerns whether language abilities are _____ or _____
   a. innate ... learned through shaping by the environment
   b. universal ... different from one cultural group to another
   c. superficial ... deep-seated
   d. individual ... common to the group

_____ 12. "I goed to store" is an example of
   a. babbling
   b. parentese
   c. overgeneralization
   d. telegraphic speech

_____ 13. When you use particular observations in order to draw a broader conclusion, you use
   a. deductive reasoning
   b. inductive reasoning
   c. convergent thinking
   d. divergent thinking

_____ 14. Benjamin Whorfs' theory of linguistic relativity theory might be proved by the observation that Eskimos have many more words for snow... except for the fact that
   a. they also have fewer words for rain
   b. snow is obviously such a crucial factor in their lives
   c. there is no relationship between language and thought
   d. the claim turned out to be untrue

_____ 15. The bottom line in the debate over whether other animals can acquire true language seems to be that
   a. dolphins may possess a system of communication far superior to human language
   b. only humans clearly meet the four criteria for true language
   c. the pygmy chimp is the only animal able to learn true language
   d. several of the higher primates can acquire the language skills of five-year-old children

Module 14: Thought & Language   203

Answers for Module 14

True-False
1. F
2. F
3. T
4. T
5. F
6. T
7. T
8. F
9. F
10. T

Flashcards 1
1. h
2. d
3. b
4. e
5. i
6. g
7. c
8. f
9. j
10. a

Flashcards 2
1. j
2. h
3. a
4. b
5. c
6. e
7. g
8. f
9. i
10. d

Multiple-Choice
1. b
2. d
3. a
4. b
5. a
6. d
7. b
8. c
9. d
10. b
11. a
12. c
13. b
14. d
15. b

The Big Picture

Statement C

The Beauty of Linguistics

A subtle advantage of reading the Language Workout sections of the Study Guide is that you are learning more than how the English language works. In a way, you are learning how all languages work. That's the exciting study of linguistics, which explores the foundations of our human ability to communicate. Bob Keser, the author of the Language Workout materials, knows several languages and has taught English to students in other countries. You can learn a lot from him.

Module 15

Motivation

Does Learning Interest You?

Studying psychology offers a wonderful extra payoff: learning how to become a more effective student. Sometimes Rod Plotnik gives you an outright suggestion and sometimes you have to make the connection yourself, but each module contains a fact or an insight you can apply to becoming more effective in your college work. One of the most important ideas concerns motivation.

Module 15 introduces the idea of intrinsic motivation, the kind of motivation that goes beyond working for a specific, immediate, tangible payoff. Not that there's anything wrong with motivation through rewards. That's what gets us to work and makes us meet specific goals. In the long run, however, sustained pursuit of complex goals requires that extrinsic reinforcement be replaced by intrinsic motivation. That's why you get smiley faces on your papers in grade school, but not in college.

It is important to understand your motivation for attending college. If the real reason you enrolled was to please your parents or because all your friends went, you may have a difficult time mustering the energy and finding the time college work demands. If you find the activity of learning itself interesting, however, your college studies should be exciting and fun.

Our Motivation to be Effective

I think the most significant of all motivations may be the need to be effective. Oh sure, thirst, hunger, and sex are more immediate and can be insanely demanding, but what is it that we want all the time? We want to be effective in our dealings with the world, in our interactions with other people, and in managing our personal lives. Some call this a sense of mastery or control, but I like the word "effectiveness" to convey our broad need to do things that work.

The idea comes from Robert W. White, who wrote persuasively about "competence motivation" forty years ago. Unfortunately, his idea of competence has become so deeply woven into the fabric of modern psychology that we tend to overlook it. I think effectiveness is such a significant need that it deserves explicit recognition.

Perhaps you see why it is so important to do well in college. Success in college is the crucial measure of effectiveness at this point in your life. Examine your thoughts, feelings, and behavior. Doing something well — being effective — makes you pleased and happy, but when you are ineffective, you feel awful. Everything in your psychological makeup says you want to be effective in college.

Effective Student Tip 15

The One Day You Must Not Miss Class

The day the term paper is due? The day a surprise quiz is likely? The big exam? All these are important days to attend, but there is one day when you absolutely must not miss class. That's the day you don't have the assigned paper ready or aren't prepared for the test.

Of course this is exactly the day you are most tempted to cut. The embarrassment! The humiliation! Yet that's the very day when you can profit most from attending.

What you dread probably won't happen. Turns out you weren't the only one who goofed, and no one is taken out and shot. Not planning to read the papers until the weekend anyway, the professor may take yours later. Some professors will reassign a tough paper, reschedule an exam, or even allow a retake.

One especially good thing can happen when you attend on that agonizing day: you learn more about yourself. Why did you procrastinate? Why did you trip yourself up by not leaving enough time? What are your true feelings about the teacher, and how did they come into play? If you go to class and discuss it, all of this becomes more clear, your relationship becomes more honest, and you take an important step toward becoming a more effective student. If you stay in bed, everything just gets worse.

Your response...

Have you ever avoided a class when there was a problem? What happened?

Key Terms

There are lots of key terms in this module because Rod Plotnik discusses several major areas of motivation, like hunger, sex, and aggression. But many of these terms are already part of your general knowledge.

achievement need	gender identity disorder	paraphilias
AIDS (Acquired Immune Deficiency Syndrome)	gender roles	peripheral cues
	genetic hunger factors	premature [rapid] ejaculation
anorexia nervosa	genetic sex factors	psychological factors
biological hunger factors	high need for achievement	psychological sex factors
biological needs	HIV positive	psychosocial hunger factors
biological sex factors	homeostasis	self-handicapping
bulimia nervosa	incentives	set point
central cues	inhibited female orgasm	sex chromosome
cognitive factors in motivation	instincts	sex hormones
double standard for sexual behavior	interactive model of sexual orientation	sexual dysfunctions
	intrinsic motivation	sexual orientation [preference] (heterosexual, bisexual, homosexual)
drive-reduction theory	male hypothalamus	
evolutionary theory	Maslow's hierarchy of needs	social needs
extrinsic motivation	metabolic rate	social role theory
fat cells	motivation	Thematic Apperception Test (TAT)
fear of failure	need	
female circumcision	obesity	underachievers
female hypothalamus	optimum [ideal] weight	weight-regulating genes
fixed action pattern	organic factors	
gender identity	overweight	

Outline

- *Introduction*

    1. **Motivation**

    2. Achievement

    ☐ What was the hardest thing you have ever done? The greatest victory you have ever achieved? How do you explain your behavior in these extreme situations?

    A. *Theories of Motivation*

    ☐ It may help to think of four basically different explanations of motivation. Which theory makes the most sense to you?

    1. Instinct theory

        a. **Instincts**

        b. **Fixed action pattern**

2. Drive reduction theory
   a. **Need**
   b. **Homeostasis**
   c. **Drive-reduction theory**
3. Incentive theory
   a. **Incentives**
   b. Pull rather than push theory
4. Cognitive theory
   a. **Extrinsic motivation**
   b. **Intrinsic motivation**
5. Explaining human motivation

B. *Biological & Social Needs*
1. **Biological needs**
2. **Social needs**
3. Satisfying needs
   a. Humanistic approach of Abraham Maslow
   b. **Maslow's hierarchy of needs** [from lowest to highest]
      (1) Physiological needs
      (2) Safety needs
      (3) Love and belongingness needs
      (4) Esteem needs
      (5) Self-actualization

C. *Hunger*
1. Optimal weight
   a. **Optimum [ideal] weight**
   b. Natural regulation
2. Overweight
   a. **Overweight**
   b. **Obesity**
3. Three hunger factors
   a. **Biological hunger factors**
   b. **Psychosocial hunger factors**
   c. **Genetic hunger factors**
4. Biological hunger factors
   a. **Peripheral cues**
   b. **Central cues**

5. **Genetic hunger factors**
   a. **Fat cells**
   b. **Metabolic rate**
   c. **Set point**
   d. **Weight-regulating genes**
6. **Psychosocial hunger factors**
   a. Learned associations
   b. Socio-cultural influences
   c. Personality traits

D. *Sexual Behavior*

☐ Does sex, which Freud claimed was central to human psychology, cause any particular concerns or problems in your life? Good..., I thought not!

1. Three factors
   a. **Genetic sex factors**
   b. **Biological sex factors**
   c. **Psychological sex factors**
2. Genetic sex factors
   a. **Sex chromosome**
   b. Differentiation: male and female
   c. Importance of testosterone
3. Biological sex factors
   a. **Sex hormones**
   b. **Male hypothalamus**
   c. **Female hypothalamus**
   d. Sexual motivation
4. **Psychological sex factors**
   a. 1st step: gender identity
      (1) **Gender identity**
      (2) **Gender identity disorder**
   b. 2nd step: **gender roles**
      (1) Stereotypic behaviors and roles
      (2) Two qualifications
   c. 3rd step: **sexual orientation [preference]**
      (1) **Homosexual, bisexual**, and **heterosexual orientation**
      (2) **Interactive model of sexual orientation**

5. Male-female sex differences
    a. **Social role theory**
        (1) Division of labor
        (2) Social and cultural factors
    b. **Double standard for sexual behavior**
☐ *Is the "double standard" still operating among the people you know?*
    c. **Evolutionary theory**
        (1) Reproductive goals
        (2) Genetic and biological factors
6. Homosexuality
    a. Genetic/biological factors
    b. Psychological factors
7. Sexual response: problems and treatments
    a. **Paraphilias**
    b. **Sexual dysfunctions**
    c. **Organic factors**
    d. **Psychological factors**
    e. Four-stage model of human sexual response (William Masters and Virginia Johnson)
        (1) Excitement
        (2) Plateau
        (3) Orgasm
        (4) Resolution
    f. **Premature [rapid] ejaculation**
    g. **Inhibited female orgasm**
8. AIDS: Acquired Immune Deficiency Syndrome
    a. **HIV positive**
    b. **AIDS (Acquired Immune Deficiency Syndrome)**
        (1) Risk for AIDS
        (2) Progression of disease
        (3) Treatment

E. *Cultural Diversity: Female Circumcision*
   1. Worthwhile tradition or cruel mutilation?
☐ *If you value the ideal of cultural diversity, can you still condemn the practice of female circumcision in those cultures that believe in it?*
   2. Issues involved in **female circumcision**
       a. What is its purpose?
       b. Are there complications?
       c. Is there a solution?

F. **Achievement**
   1. **Social needs**
   2. **Achievement need**
   ☐ *Do you feel a strong need for achievement? How does achievement influence your life?*
   3. How is the need for achievement measured?
      a. **Thematic Apperception Test (TAT)**
      b. David McClelland and John Atkinson
   4. What is **high need for achievement**?
   5. **Fear of failure**
      a. Motivation
      b. **Self-handicapping**
   6. Underachievement
      a. **Underachievers**
      b. Characteristics
   7. Three components of success
   8. Cognitive influences
      a. **Cognitive factors in motivation**
         (1) **Intrinsic motivation**
         (2) **Extrinsic motivation**
      b. Intrinsic motivation

G. *Research Focus: Immigrant Students*
   1. Why did immigrant children do well?
   2. A study of academic performance
      a. Procedure
      b. Results
      c. Conclusions

H. *Application: Eating Problems & Treatment*
   1. Dieting: problems, concerns, and benefits
   ☐ *Why are eating problems so common?*
   2. Serious eating disorders
      a. **Anorexia nervosa**
         (1) Personality and genes
         (2) Treatment
      b. **Bulimia nervosa**
         (1) Risk factors
         (2) Treatment

Language Workout

What's That?

p. 329 a nearly vertical **slope** = mountain
the slope's crumbly **granite** = stone
Mark fell 50 feet into a **crevice** = opening
paralyzed from the waist down = lost all power and feeling
sleeping bags **anchored** to the granite wall = attached
never **underestimate** a person with a disability = doubt the strength
Victor grew up with an **obstacle** = problem

p. 330 **sightseers** = tourists
a half-dozen instincts, such as **flight** = escape, fleeing
repulsion = feeling disgust
pugnacity = eagerness to fight or argue
self-abasement = denying value of self, shaming self
seeking excitement or **novelty** = new experiences
predisposes an organism to behave = influences, pushes
raiding the refrigerator = eating snacks

p. 331 **perplexing** behaviors = difficult to understand, puzzling
complaining of being **stuffed** = full of food (not hungry at all)

p. 332 **critical** to our survival = extremely important, necessary
individuals may **starve themselves to death** = kill themselves by not eating
psychological factors can **override** biological needs = overpower, dominate
nurturance = taking care of another person's needs
dominance = having power over another person
an **ascending** order = moving upward, rising

p. 333 we face **roadblocks** = problems
into a single **framework** = system
a list of **priorities** = most important matters (must be done first)
or **vice versa** = the opposite

p. 334 **home-bound** pets = not allowed to go outside
surplus calories = extra, not used
clogged arteries = condition causing heart attacks
being a **couch-potato** = lazy person

p. 335 the stomach **monitors** the amount = watches, controls
our **depleted** stores of food = low or empty
the stomach's walls are **distended** = pushed out

p. 336 the body **compensates** = acts to create a balance
can stay **trim** = in good shape, at suitable weight

p. 337 allows me to **rationalize** = give self false explanation or reasons
prefer large **portions** = servings, amounts of food
examples may be **cited** = given as proof
gourmet ice cream = extra rich, high fat
overestimate = make a guess above the real facts
sensitive to **rejection** = other people refuse relationship

p. 338   the female is **in heat** = period of sexual need

p. 339   you are **destined** to be = forced
        on a **cyclic** basis = repeating again and again
        some **yet** unknown signal = still

p. 340   **exerts** a powerful influence = works
        mannerisms of the other sex = ways of moving and speaking
        society **designates** as masculine = names
        stereotypic male behaviors = typical, standard
        rough and tumble play = not polite, with possible violence

p. 341   how **subtly** we were rewarded = indirectly, cleverly
        inconclusive sex organs = not clearly one gender

p. 342   **virtually** every sex survey = almost
        men were traditionally **providers** = suppliers of food and necessities
        extramarital affairs = sex outside the marriage relationship
        it **maximized** their chances = most increased
        indiscriminate and frequent mating = uncontrolled, random
        offspring of low quality = children

p. 343   **gay** = homosexual
        if genetic predisposition was **decisive** = the controlling factor

p. 344   **ejaculation** of sperm = shooting out, ejecting
        premature ejaculation = too soon, before ready
        shortly after **penetration** = entering
        inhibited female orgasm = not freely expressed, blocked
        using a **vibrator** = device used to stimulate sexual feeling

p. 345   **pneumonia** *noo-MOH-nyuh* = dangerous disease (of lungs)
        HIV **antibodies** = signs that body is fighting disease
        through **casual** contact = common, ordinary (not close)
        1,000 times more **infectious** = able to spread disease
        a walking **time bomb** = danger that might activate at any time
        especially **susceptible** to infections = open (unprotected)

p. 346   men want to marry **virgins** = women who have never had sex
        ancient **rite of passage** = custom to mark new stage of life
        fight this cruel **mutilation** = cutting, destroying body part
        Muslim **clerics** = religious leaders
        serves no **hygienic** purpose = health, cleanliness
        amputation of the male's penis = removal, cutting off
        bleeding, and even **hemorrhaging** = losing large amounts of blood
        cysts = abnormal growths on the body
        maintain female **chastity** = pure state (without sexual experience)
        their **disfigured** genitals = made unnatural, ugly
        organizations have **endorsed** anti-circumcision laws = approved
        success in **drumming up** support = building
        they have **encountered** considerable resistance = met

p. 348   frustrations, and **setbacks** = problems
        people in **ambiguous** situations = without clear meaning
        games that most children **take for granted** = value too lightly
        careers that require **initiative** = energy

most of **exhibit** varying degrees = show
striving for social recognition = working

p. 349 Rich is a computer **wizard** = expert
the **paradox** of underachievement = puzzle, contradiction

p. 350 get a **doctorate** in chemistry = Ph.D. degree (Doctor of Philosophy)
very little **charitable work** = unpaid volunteer helping poor

p. 351 they **pass along** a negative attitude = teach to others
making teachers more **accountable** = responsible for results

p. 352 hired a **personal trainer** = exercise coach

p. 353 her weight **plummeted** = fell rapidly and in large amount
everyone thought I was so nice and so **sweet** = lovable, pleasant
use of **laxatives** = medicines to force cleaning of digestive tract

p. 356 a **"wonder drug"** = drug that can perform "miracles", cure disease
scientists figured out the **plumbing** = physical system
the most successful prescription drug **ever** = in history
Viagra appears to be a very **good deal** = an effective product

Make the Connection

Look at these two sentences:

Abraham Lincoln was born in a house. The house no longer exists.

Short sentences like these are correct, but they always sound a little childish, probably because children speak that way. It always seems more adult to put such information into one sentence. Look at the following sentence:

The house <u>in which Abraham Lincoln was born</u> no longer exists.

This sentence seems more exact and professional and formal in English. That's why it is preferred for writing, but in speaking we can say:

The house <u>where Abraham Lincoln was born</u> no longer exists.

This sentence is easier to make, but students have to practice the more formal **in which** sentence because this is the language of textbooks and professional work.

Did you notice the following sentence in this textbook?

Thousands of people train for months to run grueling 26-mile-long marathons, **in which** only the top two or three receive any prize money (p. 331).

This is really two sentences. The first sentence is:

Thousands of people train for months to run grueling 26-mile-long **marathons**.

The second sentence is:

In these marathons only the top two or three receive any prize money.

Notice that the word **marathons** is repeated. We don't want to repeat unnecessarily, so we replace the second **marathons** with **which**. We can join two sentences with any preposition and **which** in combinations like **with which, at which, for which, to which, from which,** and many others.

NOW YOU TRY IT

See if you can put together sentences in the same way. Read the following sentences, and then use the suggested **which** form to make one sentence:

The chair is going to collapse. The professor is sitting in the chair.
Use **in which** : _____

The strength surprised me. The child shook my hand with strength.
Use **with which** : _____

The temperature is zero degrees centigrade. Water freezes below this temperature.
Use **below which** : _____

Not so easy, is it? You aren't using commas, are you? None of these sentences need commas because the two sentences are very closely locked together, so we don't want commas to separate them. If you're not sure of your answers, check the Answer Key at the end. Now try some more:

The factory is closed for repairs. Miguel's father works at the factory.
Use **at which** : _____

The letter never arrived. Anya was waiting for the letter.
Use **for which** : _____

The club is planning a picnic. David and his neighbors belong to the club.
Use **to which** : _____

The company went out of business. We bought our computers from the company.
Use **from which** : _____

The land lies in an earthquake zone. The nuclear power plant is built on the land.
Use **on which** : _____

Now check your answers in the Answer Key.

Answer Key

The chair **in which the professor is sitting** is going to collapse.
The strength **with which the child shook my hand** surprised me.
The temperature **below which water freezes** is zero degrees centigrade.
The factory **at which Miguel's father works** is closed for repairs.
The letter **for which** Anya was waiting never arrived.
The club **to which David and his neighbors belong** is planning a picnic.
The company **from which we bought our computers** went out of business.
The land **on which the nuclear power plant is built** lies in an earthquake zone.

The Big Picture

Which statement below offers the best summary of the larger significance of this module?

- A   One day we may have a single explanation of human motivation, but for now there seem to be several useful ways of looking at it. These different approaches to motivation parallel the general approaches to psychology.

- B   Rod Plotnik gives us several different areas of motivation (hunger, sex, achievement) to show that each area of human behavior has its own particular kind of motivation. There is no overall theory of motivation.

- C   In areas like hunger, sex, and achievement, human motivation is radically different from animal motivation. Thus the study of motivation shows that humans are far above the lower animals, a fact psychology should recognize.

- D   After years of exploring the reasons how and why humans pursue their goals, it seems to come down to "mind over matter." Once again, cognitive psychology is shown to be superior to the other approaches.

- E   Oh sure, I *could* learn all the stuff in this module. But why bother?

True-False

_____ 1. Animals have instincts; humans have fixed action patterns.

_____ 2. The concept of homeostasis supports the drive reduction theory.

_____ 3. The concept of intrinsic motivation rests on a recognition of the importance of external factors.

_____ 4. Maslow's hierarchy of needs nicely brings together both biological and social needs.

_____ 5. Humans are the only animal for whom learned cues to eating are more powerful than biological cues.

_____ 6. As one might expect, the male lion gets sex whenever he wants it.

_____ 7. A sexual attraction to particular articles of clothing, such as shoes, is classified as a paraphilia.

_____ 8. The percentage of people who are homosexual is rising rapidly.

_____ 9. Researchers believe they will find a cure for AIDS in the next year or two.

_____ 10. The dull truth is that the only realistic solution to weight problems is a combination of better eating habits and exercise.

Flashcards 1

___ 1. achievement need
___ 2. extrinsic motivation
___ 3. fear of failure
___ 4. fixed action pattern
___ 5. homeostasis
___ 6. instincts
___ 7. intrinsic motivation
___ 8. Maslow's hierarchy of needs
___ 9. self-handicapping
___ 10. underachievers

a. innate tendencies or biological forces that determine behavior
b. the tendency of the body to return to, and remain in, a more balanced state
c. engaging in certain behaviors because the behaviors are personally rewarding or fulfill our beliefs
d. a motivation to avoid failure by choosing easy, nonchallenging tasks where failure is unlikely
e. individuals who score relatively high on tests of ability but perform more poorly than scores predict
f. an ascending order in which biological needs are placed at the bottom and social needs at the top
g. engaging in certain behaviors that either reduce biological needs or help us obtain external rewards
h. an innate biological predisposition toward a specific behavior in a specific environmental condition
i. a tendency to do things that contribute to failure and then to use these things as excuses for failure
j. your desire to set challenging goals and to persist in pursuing those goals in the face of obstacles

Flashcards 2

___ 1. anorexia nervosa
___ 2. bulimia nervosa
___ 3. double standard for sexual behavior
___ 4. female circumcision
___ 5. gender identity
___ 6. gender roles
___ 7. inhibited female orgasm
___ 8. paraphilias
___ 9. set point
___ 10. sexual dysfunctions

a. problems of sexual arousal or orgasm that interfere with adequate functioning during sexual behavior
b. traditional or stereotypic behaviors, attitudes, and personality traits designated masculine or feminine
c. a set of beliefs, values, or expectations that subtly encourages sexual activity in males (not females)
d. a certain level of body fat that our body strives to maintain constant throughout our lives
e. characterized by binge-eating and purging and an excessive concern about body shape and weight
f. a serious eating disorder characterized by refusing to eat, an intense fear of fat, and a distorted body image
g. sexual deviations characterized by repetitive or preferred sexual fantasies about nonhuman objects
h. a persistent delay or absence of orgasm after becoming aroused and excited
i. the individual's subjective experience and feelings of being either a male or a female
j. practice in some traditional African cultures of cutting away the female's external genitalia

Multiple-Choice

____ 1. Rod Plotnik tells the story of Mark Wellman's incredible climb to illustrate the fact that
   a. you can do anything you really put your mind to
   b. you should take risks in life, but also have strong ropes!
   c. the causes of human actions are complex, yet important to understand
   d. there must be a single source of motivation, as yet undiscovered

____ 2. Early in this century, most psychologists believed that motivation was explained by
   a. drives and needs
   b. instincts
   c. environmental incentives
   d. beliefs and expectations

____ 3. The newest theory of motivation places greatest emphasis on
   a. drives and needs
   b. instincts
   c. environmental incentives
   d. beliefs and expectations

____ 4. The key idea of Maslow's hierarchy of needs is that
   a. unless social needs like esteem are satisfied, one cannot deal effectively with biological needs like safety
   b. basic biological needs must be satisfied before higher social needs can be dealt with
   c. unless you achieve level five, you are a defective person
   d. the higher needs are essential; the lower needs are incidental

____ 5. Which one of the following is *not* a biological cue for hunger?
   a. glucose in the blood
   b. the hypothalamus
   c. learned associations
   d. the walls of the stomach

____ 6. Which one of the following is *not* a genetic factor that influences body weight?
   a. fat cells
   b. metabolic rate
   c. set point
   d. responsiveness to food cues

____ 7. Which one of the following is the best explanation of the common tendency of dieters to regain the weight they lose?
   a. fat cells
   b. metabolic rate
   c. set point
   d. weight-regulating genes

____ 8. Lions never go on talk shows; their sexual behavior is kept in line by the fact that
   a. females do most of the hunting
   b. hormones and pheromones prevail
   c. social roles and rules predominate
   d. a lioness's bite can be fatal

_____ 9. Which one of the following is the correct order of human sexual response?
   a. excitement – plateau – orgasm – resolution
   b. plateau – excitement – orgasm – resolution
   c. excitement – orgasm – plateau – resolution
   d. orgasm – excitement – resolution – plateau

_____ 10. The term "double standard" means the
   a. added burden modern women face of both working and caring for their families
   b. biological fact that women want one man but men want more than one woman
   c. social expectation that men will be more sexually active than women
   d. new idea that a woman can ask a man out and still expect him to pick up the check

_____ 11. What makes a person homosexual? Much of the new evidence points to
   a. social factors like having homosexual teachers
   b. biological factors like inherited tendencies
   c. family factors like overbearing mothers
   d. intellectual factors like fascination with art

_____ 12. The influence of culture in sexuality is clearly seen in the debate over
   a. celibacy
   b. paraphilias
   c. female circumcision
   d. sexual dysfunctions

_____ 13. The best motivation for superior academic performance is having a
   a. high need for achievement
   b. high fear of failure
   c. very efficient self-handicapping strategy
   d. reasonable excuse for occasional failure

_____ 14. Which of the following is the best example of self-handicapping?
   a. choosing easy, nonchallenging tasks where failure is unlikely
   b. performing more poorly on an exam than IQ scores would predict
   c. getting plenty of sleep before the exam, but doing poorly anyway
   d. having a hangover during the exam, then blaming drug use for poor results

_____ 15. Remember Oprah Winfrey's public battle with weight a few years ago? She eventually gained back all the weight she lost, because, as she later realized, she
   a. had secretly been bulimic for years
   b. had always been terrified that she was potentially anorexic
   c. had not made a long-term commitment to change her lifestyle
   d. never did have much will power

Answers for Module 15

True-False	Flashcards 1	Flashcards 2	Multiple-Choice
1. F	1. j	1. f	1. c
2. T	2. g	2. e	2. b
3. F	3. d	3. c	3. d
4. T	4. h	4. j	4. b
5. T	5. b	5. i	5. c
6. F	6. a	6. b	6. d
7. T	7. c	7. h	7. c
8. F	8. f	8. g	8. b
9. F	9. i	9. d	9. a
10. T	10. e	10. a	10. c
			11. b
			12. c
			13. a
			14. d
			15. c

The Big Picture

Statement A

Our Need for Effectiveness

Go back a few pages and re-read what I wrote about effectiveness. I really think I have an important message here, even though I may not have explained it well. Can you see what I am getting at? Could the key to a happier and more successful life begin with recognition of our universal need to be effective?

Module 16

Emotion

A Gift of Nature

If visitors from outer space dropped in for a visit, what would impress them most about us? Not our powers of logic and reason (theirs would be superior). Perhaps our emotions, which add the vitality to our life experience, would impress them as truly marvelous. "What a wonderful gift nature has given you," they might tell us. We would be surprised, because feelings seem to create such problems for us.

In this module, Rod Plotnik carefully unravels the most important theories about what emotion is and how it works. All the theories keep coming back to two questions: (1) Does the body's reaction to a stimulus cause an emotion, or does an emotion trigger a physiological response? (2) Does a thought cause an emotion, or does an emotion trigger a thought? Plotnik shows us the competing answers psychology has offered.

Still, something seems to be missing. No one of these classic theories of emotion has triumphed, and none seems fully satisfying, no matter how intriguing the research findings are. What if the *answers* are correct, but the *questions* are wrong? What if emotion is not separate from the mental process, but an integral part of it?

A Different View of Emotion

New discoveries in neuroscience are beginning to suggest that sensory data doesn't really become thought until it is charged by the force of emotion. A dual mental system both transforms sensory experience to tell us what's out there and also uses emotion to tell us how important it is. Feelings and thoughts are inseparable.

The new discoveries fit nicely with a different view of emotion, discovered by psychotherapist and writer Kenneth Isaacs. In his recent book *Uses of Emotion: Nature's Vital Gift* (Praeger: 1998), Isaacs says feelings are always benign and potentially useful parts of mental activity. Emotion comes and goes almost instantaneously, and therefore cannot build up in us. We may remember a feeling, but the actual emotion is already gone and cannot possibly harm us. The mistaken idea that feelings are dangerous entities that must be "gotten out," or at least controlled, robs many people of a rich emotional life and cripples others with extreme fear of emotion expressed in a wide variety of symptoms. The real danger is our misunderstanding and fear of emotion.

Instead of fighting to control emotion, says Isaacs, we should welcome feelings as useful sources of information. We couldn't get along without our emotions any more than we could do without other information. If Kenneth Isaacs is correct, many ideas in psychology will have to be reconsidered. Try his new web page: **Usesofemotion.com**

Effective Student Tip 16

How to Beat Test Anxiety

In a famous experiment, dogs that received shocks in a closed box did not even try to escape when given shocks in an open box. The experimenter called it "learned helplessness." If we could ask them, the dogs might tell us that 'test anxiety' made them fail to jump over to the safe side.

Sometimes school can be like the shock box. Too many painful defeats, and you learn to accept failure as a normal part of life. You don't like it, but you have no experience of escaping it. So don't be too quick to say you are no good at tests. You may have learned to think so, but you can't really know until you take a test *for which you have prepared effectively.*

Scratch the surface of most test anxiety and you find ineffective techniques. The first thing to do is stop blaming yourself. Next, discard the idea that you simply have to try harder. Finally, dissect your weaknesses in note-taking, studying, and test-taking and replace them with better techniques.

You will begin to feel effective when you begin to be effective. As your sense of effectiveness increases, your ability to work out winning strategies will also increase. You may still experience some jitters (phobic effects linger), but who cares? Test anxiety will no longer rule your life.

Your response...

If you were brutally honest with yourself, what steps could you take to improve your test preparation?

Key Terms

Try to understand the battle of psychological theories that is reflected in many of these key terms.

adaptation level theory
affective-primacy theory
cognitive appraisal theories of emotions
cognitive appraisal theory
Control Question Technique
display rules
emotion
emotional intelligence
facial expressions
facial feedback theory
galvanic skin response
happiness
James-Lange theory
lie detector [polygraph]
peripheral theories of emotions
primacy question
psychoevolutionary theory of emotions
universal emotional expressions
Yerkes-Dodson law

Outline

- *Introduction*
    1. Emotional experience (**emotion**)
        a. Appraise stimulus
        b. Subjective feeling
        c. Physiological responses
        d. Overt behaviors
    ☐ Psychologists can't agree on how emotion works. What is your understanding of emotion?
    2. Staying happy

- A. *Peripheral Theories*
    1. Sequence for emotions
        a. **Peripheral theories of emotions**
        b. **Cognitive appraisal theories of emotions**
    ☐ In both of the two famous peripheral theories of emotion, the key is the sequence. Be sure to work it out for each theory.
    ☐ What do modern research findings say about each of the two theories?
    2. **James-Lange theory**
        a. Physiological changes
        b. Interpretation of changes
        c. Emotional feeling
        d. James-Lange: sequence for emotional components
        e. Criticisms
    3. **Facial feedback theory**
        a. Physiological changes
        b. Interpretation of changes
        c. Emotional feeling

d. Sequence for emotions

e. Criticisms

B. *Cognitive Appraisal Theory*

1. **Cognitive appraisal theory**

2. Schachter-Singer experiment

   a. Physiological arousal

   b. Interpretation of cues

   c. Emotional feeling

   d. Sequence for emotions

   e. Criticisms

3. **Primacy question**: which comes first, feeling or thinking?

❏ Why will your answer to the primacy question dictate which of the following two theories you tend to agree with more?

   a. **Cognitive appraisal theory**

      (1) Stimulus

      (2) Appraise or interpret

      (3) Emotional feelings

      (4) Bodily responses

      (5) Thinking before feeling (Richard Lazarus)

   b. **Affective-primacy theory**

      (1) Stimulus

      (2) Emotional experience

      (3) Appraise or think

      (4) Bodily responses

      (5) Feeling before thinking (Robert Zajonc)

C. *Universal Facial Expressions*

1. Definition: **universal emotional expression**

❏ What does it mean when you tell someone, "I can read you like a book"?

2. Cross-cultural evidence

3. Genetic evidence

❏ Why are some emotions universal? Why doesn't each culture have its own unique emotions?

D. *Functions of Emotions*

1. Emotions: send social signals

   a. **Facial expressions**

   b. More accurate than words

2. Emotions: adapt and survive

   a. **Psychoevolutionary theory of emotions**

   b. Signal intentions

3. Emotion: arouse and motivate
   a. **Yerkes-Dodson law**
   b. Arousal and performance

E. *Happiness*
   1. Kinds of **happiness**
   2. **Adaptation level theory**
   3. Influences on long-term happiness

F. *Cultural Diversity: Emotions Across Cultures*
   1. Showing emotions
      a. **Display rules**
      b. Belief systems
   2. Perceiving emotions
      a. Display rules about intensity
      b. Which emotion is the most intense?

G. *Research Focus: Emotional Intelligence*
   1. What is **emotional intelligence** (Daniel Goleman)?
   2. How to measure emotional intelligence?
   3. Is emotional intelligence important?

H. *Application: Lie Detection*
   1. What is the theory?
      a. **Lie detector [polygraph]**
      b. **Galvanic skin response**
   2. What is a lie detector test?
      a. **Control Question Technique**
      b. Assessing galvanic skin responses
   ☐ *Have you ever taken a lie detector test? Would you do so willingly if asked?*
   3. How accurate are lie detector tests?
      a. Error rates
      b. Employment and court restrictions

For Psych Majors Only...

Emotion — Myths and Actualities: Which statements about emotion are true and which are false? Don't worry about your score, because these statements are more the foundation of a theory than a quiz. When you check the "answers," see if you can understand the theory (it was described in my module introduction).

_____ 1. Emotions can be dangerous.

_____ 2. Emotions have no constructive function.

_____ 3. Emotions, once evoked, remain in a kind of pressured storage until discharged.

_____ 4. Emotions, while in storage, become a source of damage to the person.

_____ 5. The necessary discharge of emotions must be accomplished very carefully so as to cause the least amount of damage.

_____ 6. Emotions are vital aspects of human functioning.

_____ 7. Emotions are automatic subjective responses to internal and external events.

_____ 8. Emotions serve the vital function of informing us of qualities of internal and external events.

_____ 9. Emotions are fleeting and in their initial reactive form are impossible to store or accrue.

_____ 10. Because emotions are fleeting, their discharge is not mandatory and their expression is optional.

Language Workout

What's That?

p. 359 fright and **apprehension** = fear for future
appraise some stimulus = judge, estimate the effect
frantic swimming = very nervous, out of control
playing **poker** = card game
winning **big bucks** = a lot of money
the emotional **high** = experience of pleasure
such an enormous **windfall** = unexpected good fortune

p. 362 explanation **flip-flopped** your emotional state = reversed direction
their **groundbreaking** experiment = moving in new direction
a **confederate** of the researchers = co-worker, helper

p. 363 the **primacy** question = which comes first?
somewhat **complementary** answers = supporting each other
the **spokesperson** for this position = official representative
thinking obviously **precedes** feeling = comes before

p. 364 **biologically determined** facial expressions = controlled by biological factors
smiling is **biologically programmed** = controlled by biological factors
foul tastes or odors = offensive, very unpleasant

p. 365 **What good are emotions?** = What is the value of emotions?
may **elicit** a variety of responses = produce

p. 366 **holding down** two jobs = working
going on a **buying spree** = burst of activity (buying)
I thought I'd **drop everything** = change all my plans
hang out at my brother's house = spend time, visit
indecision about what to do = no certainty about which action to take
in-laws who are **envious** = jealous
will **fade** with time = become weaker
a **daily diet of little highs** = small experiences of pleasure every day
a good **dose** of hope = amount

p. 367 **display** = showing feelings openly
seen as **dishonorable** = shameful
my **fellow citizens** = other Americans

p. 369 the chance to **come up with** new ideas = create
maintaining hope after **setbacks** = disappointments, problems
this book **sparked** tremendous interest = stimulated
I couldn't think **straight** = clearly

p. 370 Ames **pleaded** guilty = answered in court
espionage = spying
serving a **life sentence** = punishment continuing until end of life
skin **conductance** = ability to transmit
They had a **warrant** and arrested him = court order, permission to arrest
the **prosecutor** offered = lawyer responsible for starting lawsuit
Floyd **jumped at the chance** = eagerly agreed to cooperate
several years **behind bars** = in prison
his lawyer **tracked down** the real robbers = found

p. 371 from **field** studies = practical (not in lab)
processing **oddball** stimuli = unusual, strange

p. 372 **bucking** cultural traditions = opposing, breaking
customers are getting **choosy** = selective, hard to satisfy
a **radical** change = extreme, serious
Japanese salespeople are very **reserved** = do not show emotions
smiling was totally **frowned upon** = not approved, discouraged
reluctant and **bashful** students = shy
building **morale** = enthusiasm (especially of workers)
racking up the most sales = making
such a high **premium** on smiling = value

What about Whom?

Your English teachers probably made you practice using **whom** in sentences like the following:

The rock star whom I interviewed has a new hit song.

This sentence is perfectly correct, but modern grammar experts agree that this way to use **whom** is dying. Why? Because it is hard to use it correctly, so it slows down our communication. Most grammar teachers now believe that it is perfectly acceptable to say or write:

The rock star who I interviewed has a new hit song.

Still, this doesn't mean that **whom** is completely dead! We still must use **whom** after a preposition like **of, for, with, to,** and **from**. This is a very useful way to join sentences. For example, look at the following two sentences:

The man works for the government. Ludmila is married **to him.**

Short sentences like these are correct, but they sound too simple, like a children's book. It always seems more adult to join them into one sentence. Look at the following sentence:

The man **to whom Ludmila is married** works for the government.

This sentence seems more exact and professional and formal in English, although it is also troublesome to put together. That's why it is preferred for writing, but in everyday speaking we can say:

The man **Ludmila is married to** works for the government.

This sentence is easier to make, but students still need to practice the more formal **to whom** sentence because textbooks and professional work use this language. This is exactly the same problem we practiced in Module 15: in the last lesson we joined two sentences with **to which** (an object), while in this lesson we'll practice **to whom** (a person), **for whom, with whom, on whom, in whom,** and **from whom**. The changes you need to make are the same as we made in the last lesson.

Now you try it. See if you can put together sentences in the same way. Read the following sentences, and then use the suggested **whom** form to make one sentence:

The fireman saved the lives of 14 people. The mayor gave a medal to him.
Use **to whom** : _____

The grandmother comes from Amsterdam. Peter inherited his blue eyes from her.
Use **from whom** : _____

The tourists spent a lot of money. Mrs. Lopez traveled with them to Disney World.
Use **with whom** : _____

No need for commas because the two sentences are very closely locked together: we want to join them, not separate them. If you're not sure of your answers, check the Answer Key at the end. Now try some more:

The new nurse never smiles. All the patients are complaining about her.
Use **about whom** : _____

The fat man is called Santa Claus. Many children believe in him.
Use **in whom** : _____

_____

The rock star will arrive in five minutes. All the fans are waiting for him.
Use **for whom** : _____

_____

The dancer injured her leg. The ballet cannot begin without her.
Use **without whom** : _____

_____

Now check your answers in the Answer Key.

Do you understand this sentence from the textbook better now?

> After we have acquired a gender identity, gender role, and sexual orientation, there remain sometimes difficult decisions about when, where, and **with whom** sexual behavior is appropriate (p. 342).

Answer Key

The fireman **to whom the mayor gave a medal** saved the lives of 14 people.
The grandmother **from whom Peter inherited his blue eyes** comes from Amsterdam.
The tourists **with whom Mrs. Lopez traveled to Disney World** spent a lot of money.
The new nurse **about whom all the patients are complaining** never smiles.
The fat man **in whom many children believe** is called Santa Claus.
The rock star **for whom all the fans are waiting** will arrive in five minutes.
The dancer **without whom the ballet cannot begin** injured her leg.

The Big Picture

Which statement below offers the best summary of the larger significance of this module?

A   There is a reason why Rod Plotnik talks about sharks, primitive peoples, and greed in this module: emotion almost seems to be left over from an earlier period in our evolution, something we would be better off without.

B   Nothing is more basic to our common psychological experience than emotion processes, yet science has not yet agreed on how to explain emotion. In science, that which is closest to us is often the last to be understood.

C   Emotions provide startling evidence for the cultural and environmental side of the nature-nurture debate. All over the world people treat emotions very differently, with little evidence of commonality.

D   Emotions are not terribly important in human affairs, but they add a much-needed drama and spice to life. The best way to handle emotions is not to pay too much attention to them.

E   Sheesh! This $&!# module really ticks me off! All those %!$# theories to learn! Why is emotion important, anyhow?

True-False

_____ 1. Psychologists now agree that the James-Lange theory provides the best explanation of how emotions work.

_____ 2. Psychologists do not agree on whether feeling or thinking comes first in the process of experiencing emotions.

_____ 3. People all over the world recognize the expression of a few universal emotions.

_____ 4. Emotions are essential to our survival.

_____ 5. Human emotions, like the human appendix, are left over from our primitive past and are not really needed today.

_____ 6. There is a universal language of emotion expression that helps people understand each other.

_____ 7. The reason the joy of winning the lottery doesn't last is that taxes soon take most of the winnings.

_____ 8. Display rules are cultural expectations that govern the presentation and control of emotional expression in specific situations.

_____ 9. People all over the world rate happiness as the most intense emotion.

_____ 10. Lie detector tests determine whether a statement is true or false.

Flashcards 1

____ 1. affective-primacy theory
____ 2. cognitive appraisal theories of emotions
____ 3. emotion
____ 4. facial expressions
____ 5. facial feedback theory
____ 6. James-Lange theory
____ 7. peripheral theories of emotions
____ 8. primacy question
____ 9. psychoevolutionary theory of emotions
____ 10. universal emotional expression

a. has four components: (1) appraisal (2) subjective feeling (3) physiological responses (4) overt behaviors
b. says brain interprets specific physiological changes as feelings or emotions; see bear, run, feel fear
c. must thinking come before we can experience an emotion, or can feeling come before any thinking?
d. emphasize how your interpretations or appraisals of situations give rise to your emotional feelings
e. emphasize how physiological changes in the body give rise to your emotional feelings
f. says sensations from movement of facial muscles and skin are interpreted by brain as different feelings
g. a number of specific inherited facial patterns or expressions that signal specific feelings
h. says in some situations you feel an emotion before having time to interpret or appraise the situation
i. communicate state of your personal feelings and provide different social signals to others around you
j. says we evolved basic emotional patterns to adapt and solve problems important for our survival

Flashcards 2

____ 1. adaptation level theory
____ 2. cognitive appraisal theory
____ 3. Control Question Technique
____ 4. display rules
____ 5. galvanic skin response
____ 6. happiness
____ 7. lie detector [polygraph]
____ 8. Yerkes-Dodson law
____ 9. *lottery ticket*
____ 10. *money*

a. *maybe it can't buy happiness, but it sure finances the illusion!*
b. specific cultural norms that regulate how, when, and where we should express emotion (and how much)
c. abnormal changes in sweating of fingers or palms that accompanies emotional experiences
d. says performance on a task is an interaction between the level of arousal and the difficulty of the task
e. *Go ahead, punk. Pay my taxes!*
f. feeling a positive emotion, being satisfied with one's life, and not experiencing negative emotions
g. says we quickly become accustomed to receiving some good fortune [lottery], so the initial joy fades
h. says your interpretation of situation, object, or event can contribute to experiencing different feelings
i. based on theory that a person telling a lie feels guilt or fear and exhibits involuntary physical responses
j. lie detection procedure that utilizes both neutral questions and critical (emotional) questions

Multiple-Choice

_____ 1. Rod Plotnik tells us about the surfer who was attacked by a shark [where does he *get* these stories?] to show that
   a. emotions play a major role in our lives
   b. sometimes you can feel all the emotions at once
   c. sometimes survival depends on having no emotions
   d. emotions (like the joy of surfing) can get in the way of common sense

_____ 2. Which one of the following is *not* a component of an emotion?
   a. appraising a stimulus
   b. physiological responses
   c. overt behaviors
   d. genetic variation

_____ 3. The _____ theory says emotions result from specific physiological changes in the body
   a. primacy
   b. James-Lange
   c. facial feedback
   d. cognitive appraisal

_____ 4. The _____ theory says emotions result from our brain's interpretation of muscle and skin movements that occur when we express an emotion
   a. primacy
   b. James-Lange
   c. facial feedback
   d. cognitive appraisal

_____ 5. The _____ theory says that your interpretation of a situation, object, or event can contribute to, or result in, your experiencing different emotional states
   a. primacy
   b. James-Lange
   c. facial feedback
   d. cognitive appraisal

_____ 6. The answer to the primacy question, as determined by research, is that
   a. thinking comes first
   b. feelings come first
   c. thinking comes first for men; feelings come first for women
   d. (the debate is not yet resolved)

_____ 7. Evidence for the universality of emotional expression comes from the fact that people all over the world
   a. consider happiness to be the most intense emotion
   b. follow the same rules about how to show emotions
   c. recognize facial expressions of certain basic emotions
   d. make up rules about how to show emotions

_____ 8. Which one of the following is *not* a universally recognized emotion?
   a. indecision
   b. happiness
   c. surprise
   d. anger

_____ 9. Which one of the following is *not* something emotions do for us?
   a. help us adapt and survive
   b. help us answer questions of fact
   c. motivate and arouse us
   d. help us express social signals

_____ 10. Adaptation level theory explains why people who win big in the lottery
   a. don't come forward to claim their prizes right away
   b. often spend lavishly until they are right back where they started
   c. don't feel much happier than anyone else after a while
   d. often report that winning permanently changed them from discontented to happy persons

_____ 11. Cultural rules that govern emotional expression in specific situations are called
   a. display rules
   b. feelings guides
   c. primacy rules
   d. intensity rules

_____ 12. Cross-cultural research reveals that the most intense emotion is
   a. happiness
   b. disgust
   c. anger
   d. (it differs from culture to culture)

_____ 13. Lie detector tests measure
   a. whether a statement is true or false
   b. how much physiological arousal the subject feels
   c. whether the subject is basically honest or dishonest
   d. how much character a person has

_____ 14. In most courtrooms, lie detector test results are
   a. admissible, because they give scientifically derived evidence
   b. admissible, because the jury must hear any evidence available
   c. inadmissible, because of their potential for error
   d. inadmissible, because they would put lawyers out of work

_____ 15. [*For Trekkies only*] The subject matter of this module helps us understand why, in a perverse way, we find the character of _____ so fascinating
   a. Spock
   b. Uhuru
   c. Kirk
   d. Scotty

Answers for Module 16

True-False
1. F
2. T
3. T
4. T
5. F
6. T
7. F
8. T
9. F
10. F

Flashcards 1
1. h
2. d
3. a
4. i
5. f
6. b
7. e
8. c
9. j
10. g

Flashcards 2
1. g
2. h
3. j
4. b
5. c
6. f
7. i
8. d
9. e
10. a

Multiple-Choice
1. a
2. d
3. b
4. c
5. d
6. d
7. c
8. a
9. b
10. c
11. a
12. d
13. b
14. c
15. a

The Big Picture

Statement B

Emotion — Myths and Actualities Quiz

1. F 2. F 3. F 4. F 5. F 6. T 7. T 8. T 9. T 10. T

The first five items represent what Kenneth Isaacs calls *myths* about feelings, false beliefs that cause us to misunderstand emotion. The second five items represent what Isaacs sees as *actualities* of emotion, truths that could make us healthier and happier.

An Important Book about Emotion

Ask if your library has the book I discussed on the introductory page of this module. Look for *Uses of Emotion: Nature's Vital Gift*, by Kenneth S. Isaacs (Praeger: 1998). I wrote the Foreword for this book. If you are interested in emotion, you should also check out Kenneth Isaacs' web site. **Usesofemotion.com**

Module 17

Infancy & Childhood

The Competent Child

One of the most striking changes in psychological thinking about child development in recent years has been the emerging view of the child as a competent person, right from the beginning. It had been thought that human infants were essentially helpless, completely dependent on the care of adults. Rod Plotnik shows how current research on newborns' abilities, and better understanding of how children interact with adult caregivers, has given us a fresh picture of childhood. We now see children as incredibly active, responsive persons who spend much of their day "working" at building relationships and creating environments most conducive to growth. If the little rugrats could talk, they would probably even claim that *they* are in charge, not us.

The Importance of Childhood in Psychology

One of psychology's most important contributions to modern knowledge is the idea of childhood as a separate, special phase of human life, with processes of development crucial for the rest of life. That idea seems obvious today, but not long ago most people thought of children simply as small adults, not really different in any special way, or as happy innocents enjoying a carefree period of freedom before the onset of adult concerns.

Once psychology recognized the importance of childhood, every comprehensive theory had to attempt to explain it. Not surprisingly, most of the 'big' theories in psychology are also theories of childhood. Sigmund Freud argued that in the first five years children struggle through a series of conflicts that essentially shape personality. Erik Erikson placed the most fundamental developmental tasks in the early years and showed how they affected all later growth. Jean Piaget claimed that mature thinking evolves just as obviously as the physical body, and illustrated the many ways in which children think differently than adults. Albert Bandura demonstrated that children learn even from the simple act of observing, and have a powerful tendency to imitate what they see around them. If you can master this module, with its heavy involvement of psychology's most famous names, you can congratulate yourself on learning the major theories of modern psychology.

Thinking about childhood inevitably leads to ideas about psychology in general. In order to explain what children are like, it is necessary to say what humans are like. In no time at all, we are back debating the nature-nurture question. If we find a strong urge in children to be competent, must that not mean we all have a need to be effective?

Effective Student Tip 17

Overstudy!

My favorite myth about tests is the often-heard lament, "I studied too hard!" The idea seems to be that what you learn has only a fragile and temporary residence in your head, and studying too much disorganizes it or knocks it right back out again. A sadder myth is the belief so many students have that they are "no good at tests," when the truth is that, for whatever reasons, they have not yet *done* well. No less misguided is the teeth-clenching determination to "do better next time," with no idea of what specific steps to take to bring that about.

A closer look would reveal that each of these misguided students is making the same mistake: not studying hard enough, or effectively enough. When I am able to persuade students to read the assigned chapters three or four times (they thought once was enough), the results amaze them. Almost invariably, their test grades go from 'D' or 'C' to 'B' or 'A.' Why? Because with more study, and better study, they are really mastering the material.

Determine how much studying you think will be enough for the next test. Then do more. Lots more. The single best way to improve your test scores is to overstudy the material.

Your response...

Have you ever studied much harder for a test than seemed necessary? What happened?

Key Terms

The inclusion of four major psychological theories in this module brings in many key terms. Group the terms by the famous psychologists who used them to build their theories.

accommodation
amniocentesis
anal stage
assimilation
attachment
cephalocaudal principle
child abuse and neglect
cognitive development
cognitive developmental theory
conception [fertilization]
concrete operations stage
conservation
cross-sectional method
developmental norms
developmental psychologists
Down syndrome
egocentric thinking
embryonic stage
emotional development
evolutionary theory
fetal alcohol syndrome (FAS)
fetal stage
formal operations stage
gender identity
gender roles
gender schemas
genital stage
germinal stage
inhibited children
insecure attachment
latency stage
longitudinal method
maturation
motor development
nature-nurture question
object permanence
oral stage
ovulation
phallic stage
Piaget's cognitive stages
placenta
prenatal period
preoperational stage
principle of bidirectionality
prodigy
proximodistal principle
psychosexual stages
psychosocial stages
resiliency
secure attachment
sensorimotor stage
separation anxiety
social cognitive theory
social development
social role theory
temperament
teratogen
theory theory
visual cliff
vulnerability

Outline

- *Introduction*
    1. **Nature-nurture question**
    - ☐ The nature-nurture question may be the most fundamental issue in the social sciences. It comes up again and again in psychology. Do you know the basic issues?
    2. **Developmental psychologists**

A. *Prenatal Influences*

   1. Nature and nurture
      a. **Prodigy**
      b. Nature-nurture interaction
   2. Genetic and environmental factors

3. **Prenatal period**: three stages
   a. **Germinal stage**
      (1) **Ovulation**
      (2) **Conception [fertilization]**
   b. **Embryonic stage**
   c. **Fetal stage**
4. Placenta and teratogens
   a. **Placenta**
   b. **Teratogen**
5. Birth defects and amniocentesis
   a. **Amniocentesis**
   b. **Down syndrome**
6. Drugs and prenatal development
   a. Multiple drug/cocaine usage
   b. Alcohol: **fetal alcohol syndrome (FAS)**

B. *Newborn's Abilities*
   1. Genetic developmental program
      a. Genes
      b. Brain development
   2. Sensory development
      a. Faces
      b. Hearing
      c. Touch
      d. Smell and taste
      e. Depth perception (**visual cliff**)
   3. **Motor development**
      a. **Proximodistal principle**
      b. **Cephalocaudal principle**
      c. **Maturation**
      d. **Developmental norms**

C. *Emotional Development*
   1. Definition and kinds of **temperament**
      a. Easy babies (40%)
      b. Slow-to-warm-up babies (15%)
      c. Difficult babies (10%)
      d. No-single-category babies (35%)
   2. Temperament and emotions (**emotional development**)

3. **Attachment**
    a. How does attachment occur (**separation anxiety**)?
    b. Are there different kinds of attachment?
        (1) **Secure attachment**
        (2) **Insecure attachment**
    c. What are the effects of attachment?

D. *Research Focus: Temperament*
    1. Research methods for studying developmental changes (Jerome Kagan)
        a. **Longitudinal method**
        b. **Cross-sectional method**
    2. Procedure (**inhibited children**)
        a. Results
        b. Conclusions

E. *Cognitive Development*
    1. Jean Piaget's theory of **cognitive development**
        a. **Assimilation**
        b. **Accommodation**
    ☐ When you are with young children, does their thinking seem like ours, except less developed, or does it seem quite different from adult thought?
    2. **Piaget's cognitive stages**
        a. **Sensorimotor stage**
            (1) Sensory experiences and motor actions
            (2) **Object permanence**
        b. **Preoperational stage**
            (1) Symbols
            (2) **Conservation**
            (3) **Egocentric thinking**
        c. **Concrete operations stage**
            (1) Mental operations
            (2) Conservation and classification
        d. **Formal operations stage**
            (1) Adult thinking and reasoning
            (2) Abstract ideas and hypothetical constructs
        e. Piaget's key ideas

3. Evaluation of Piaget's theory
    a. Criticisms
        (1) Four stages
        (2) Description versus explanation
        (3) Current status
    b. Current directions
        (1) Genetic factors
        (2) Basic concepts
        (3) New theories (**theory theory**)

F. *Social Development*
  1. **Social development**
  2. Freud's **psychosexual stages**
  ☐ *The heart of Freud's theory is the conflict at each stage. Do you buy his descriptions?*
      a. **Oral stage**
      b. **Anal stage**
      c. **Phallic stage**
      d. **Latency stage**
      e. **Genital stage**
  3. Erikson's **psychosocial stages**
  ☐ *The heart of Erikson's theory is the potential problem at each stage. Do his ideas make sense?*
      a. Stage 1: trust versus mistrust
      b. Stage 2: autonomy versus shame and doubt
      c. Stage 3: initiative versus guilt
      d. Stage 4: industry versus inferiority
      e. Stage 5: identity versus role confusion
      f. Evaluation of Erikson's and Freud's theories
  4. Bandura's **social cognitive theory**
  5. Resiliency
      a. **Vulnerability**
      b. **Resiliency**
  6. Gender differences
      a. **Gender identity**
      b. **Gender roles**
  7. **Social role theory**
  8. **Cognitive developmental theory** and **gender schemas**
  9. Differences in gender traits
      a. Career choices?
      b. Are there gender differences in aggression?

c. Are there gender differences in cognitive abilities?

d. Conclusion: what do gender differences mean?

☐ *What position do you take in the debate over gender differences?*

8. Review: the big picture

G. *Cultural Diversity: Gender Roles*

1. Identifying gender roles

2. Gender roles across cultures

3. Acquiring gender roles: two theories

a. **Social role theory**

b. **Evolutionary theory**

H. *Application: Child Abuse*

1. Kinds of abuse (**child abuse and neglect**)

2. Who abuses children (**principle of bidirectionality**)?

3. What problems do abused children have?

4. How are abusive parents helped?

Language Workout

What's That?

p. 377   **put** Jessica **up** for adoption = offered
courts have **sided with** biological parents = agree with
awarding **custody** of an adopted child = legal control
they have **a good bond** in the home = a strong relationship
supreme court justices = high judges
the **age-old** question = long-time

p. 378   **prenatal** influences = before birth
He **walks on the waves** = He makes miracles

p. 379   the ovum is **sloughed off** = separated, removed
when most **miscarriages** occur = death of fetus inside mother

p. 381   **"crack"** cocaine = very addictive and destructive form of cocaine
somewhat less **drastic** = violent, serious change
short **stature** = height
the baby gets a **pat on the backside** = slap (from the doctor) at birth
ready **to take on the world** = for the future

p. 382   **grasping** = using fingers to hold
very **keen** hearing = good, well-developed
a **citrus** odor = lemon or orange
and a **floral** odor = flower

p. 383   they can control their **trunks** = bodies (from shoulders to hips)
developmental **norms** = standards for average behavior
rather than **absolute** ages = pure (with no other influences)

Module 17: Infancy & Childhood 241

p. 384   my first baby was very **fussy** = irritable, hard to satisfy
        my new baby is **a dream** = well-behaved
        Caucasian babies = from the white race
        neonatal smile = newborn

p. 385   **squirm** and push away = twist body

p. 386   **fretting** = worrying behavior

p. 387   fearfulness and **timidity** = shy behavior

p. 388   an infant is soon ready to **creep** = move on the floor
        natural settings, such as **cribs** = beds for infants

p. 389   children may get angry or **pout** = show annoyance

p. 390   some **trail mix** = food (combination of nuts and dried fruits)
        computer **hackers** = users who break into private information
        if **going steady** is a good idea = dating only one person exclusively

p. 391   stages that all children **go through** = experience
        in the face of conflicting information = in spite of
        intertwined with social development = connected

p. 392   she may become **fixated** = locked
        these stages will **hinder** her development = slow
        seek oral **gratification** = satisfaction
        being very neat, **stingy** = unwilling to share or spend money
        latency = condition of undeveloped or "sleeping" potential

p. 393   **downplay** the importance = minimize
        autonomy = independence
        she is **bound** to get into conflict = sure
        industry = desire to work

p. 394   the theories are **complementary** = support each other
        her father was rarely **around** = present
        vulnerability = unprotected, open to hurt or danger
        resiliency = ability to recover from shock

p. 396   not **mutually exclusive** = unable to exist together
        armed forces = soldiers, army
        society rewards boys for **acting out** = expressing their impulses
        viewing women as less intellectually **bright** = intelligent

p. 399   **meek** = weak, afraid to object
        jolly = happy, laughing
        steady = stable, unchanging
        their chances for **reproduction** = producing children

p. 400   all the **trappings** of being perfect = outward signs
        a **pillar** of the Denver community = leader
        until she **confronted** her father = openly opposed

p. 401   a number of **compensatory** factors = balancing
        the principle of **biodirectionality** = going in two directions

p. 404   **bullying** = forcing others to do what you want
        truancy = avoiding school

their lives go **irretrievably** wrong = permanently

no **putdowns** = hurtful or critical remarks

See It and Say It

p. 378 **prodigy** = PRAH-dih-djee

p. 383 **proximodistal** = PRAHK-sih-moh-DISS-tul
cephalocaudal = SHE-fuh-loh-KAW-dul

p. 386 **longitudinal** = lawn-djih-TOO-dih-nul

p. 388 **Piaget** = pyah-ZHAY

p. 395 gender **schemas** = SKEE-muhz

What's the Difference?

Concept / Principle / Theory

About now you might be a little uncertain about the difference between a **concept** and a **principle** and a **theory**. Yes, all three are kinds of thoughts, the result of thinking, but how are they different?

A concept is an idea: Before Darwin, few people believed that biology had a direction. Then, Darwin produced **the concept of evolution**. In the same way, before Freud, few people believed that our behavior might be influenced or controlled by hidden drives and feelings. Then, Freud formulated his **concept of the unconscious**. These two contributions were new ideas, claims that such forces really exist.

A principle is a law: it says that some behavior always happens or usually happens. For example, Darwin took his concept of evolution and described how it works in nature. This resulted in the **principle of natural selection**: this said that evolution works to preserve useful attributes and eliminates ones that are not useful. Thus, when Darwin took his concept and showed how it works, he was describing a principle.

A theory is a system that explains how principles work together, in relation to each other in a bigger framework. So, Freud put together his concept of the unconscious and his belief that unresolved sexual conflicts are stored in the unconscious, with his idea that anxiety arises from such unexpressed conflicts and that psychoanalysis can be useful to resolve these problems. All of this interaction can be described as Freud's **theory of the unconscious** (there's more about Freud's theories in Module 19).

Be careful, though: different writers can use these words differently, and certain subject areas — like philosophy or physics — can give them special meanings.

Make the Connection

When you are reading, it's vitally important to understand all the logical help that writers give you. Certain words will help you by showing you the connection between one sentence and the next one.

> Is the next sentence about <u>more</u> of the same? The writer should tell you with words like:
> **moreover, furthermore, in addition, besides.**

Or is it something <u>different</u>? If so, you'll know from words like:
however, nevertheless, on the other hand, conversely.

Or is the second sentence a <u>result</u>? Certain words will give you this information: **consequently, as a result, thus, for this reason**.

Or is what follows an <u>example</u>? You will know from words like:
for example, for instance.

As a reader, when you see one of these words, you expect a certain meaning to follow in the next sentence. Look at this sentence: **Faysal never eats meat.** Now see how different the next sentence will be if you follow the meaning of the following logic words. Try it: in the sentence below, how do you think the story will continue?

Esmeralda just signed a contract to play in a movie.
As a result, _____

There is no one right answer. You could have written any of the following:

As a result, she is excited.
As a result, she is planning to move to Hollywood.
As a result, she might become rich and famous.

Try another one:

Esmeralda just signed a contract to play in a movie.
Nevertheless, _____

You probably wrote a sentence similar to one of these:

Nevertheless, she is not at all excited.
Nevertheless, she will probably not move to Hollywood.
Nevertheless, she is not giving up her job at the bank.

Practicing this kind of thinking will help you understand what you read more quickly and more deeply. Let's try some more:

Faysal never eats meat. **Moreover,** _____

Faysal never eats meat. **However,** _____

Faysal never eats meat. **Consequently,** _____

Faysal never eats meat. **For example,** _____

Many answers are possible. Look at the Answer Key to see some of them. Let's try some more:

It rained all night. **Thus,** _____
It rained all night. **Furthermore,** _____
The movie is almost four hours long. **For this reason,** _____
The movie is almost four hours long. **Still,** _____
Bogdana works hard during the week. **Conversely,** _____
Bogdana works hard during the week. **As a result,** _____
Bogdana works hard during the week. **In addition,** _____
Arthur's father is a strict disciplinarian. **Consequently,** _____
Arthur's father is a strict disciplinarian. **Nevertheless,** _____

244 STUDY GUIDE

Now, let's see what difference it makes if we reverse the order. In many cases, you'll have a completely different story:

_____. **Consequently,** Faysal never eats meat.

_____. **Thus,** it rained all night.

_____. **For this reason,** the movie is four hours long.

_____. **As a result,** Bogdana works hard during the week.

_____. **Nevertheless,** Esmeralda just signed a contract to play in a movie.

_____

Answer Key:

Faysal never eats meat. **Moreover,** he (never eats eggs)(wears a cloth belt) (does not wear leather).
Faysal never eats meat. **However,** sometimes he eats fish (milk) (eggs).
Faysal never eats meat. **Consequently,** he (is thin) (eats a lot of rice) (saves money).
Faysal never eats meat. **For example,** he never eats (hot dogs) (hamburgers).
It rained all night. **Thus,** (the streets are wet) (the roads are flooded).
It rained all night. **Furthermore,** (it is still raining now) (it might rain later).
The movie is almost four hours long. **For this reason,** (no one wants to see it) (you should buy lots of popcorn) (go to the bathroom before).
The movie is almost four hours long. **Still,** it (is very interesting) (is popular) (seems like an hour).
Bogdana works hard during the week. **Conversely,** she (does nothing at all on the weekend) (sleeps late on Saturday).
Bogdana works hard during the week. **As a result,** she (is tired by Friday) (has a lot of money) (has no extra time).
Bogdana works hard during the week. **In addition,** she (has a weekend job) (goes to school on Saturdays).
Arthur's father is a strict disciplinarian. **Consequently,** Arthur (is afraid of him) (never does anything wrong) (is afraid to take risks).
Arthur's father is a strict disciplinarian. **Nevertheless,** (he is not strict with himself) (Arthur loves him).

(He loves animals) (He thinks vegetarianism is healthy). **Consequently,** Faysal never eats meat.
(A storm began) (It's the rainy season). **Thus,** it rained all night.
(It's a long story) (The film covers 100 years). **For this reason,** the movie is four hours long.
(She needs money for her education) (She's saving to buy a car) (She has bills to pay). **As a result,** Bogdana works hard during the week.
(She has no acting experience) (She doesn't want to be an actress). **Nevertheless,** Esmeralda just signed a contract to play in a movie.

The Big Picture

Which statement below offers the best summary of the larger significance of this module?

A   It is in areas like infancy and childhood that psychology risks losing the respect of the general public. If we present theories as outrageous as Freud's and as strange as Piaget's, how can we expect to be taken seriously?

B   The fact this module ends with a section on child abuse is sad testimony to the state of childhood today. If you read it carefully, you realize that this module is mostly about the injuries and misfortunes suffered by children.

C   In the ongoing argument over nature and nurture, the pendulum is clearly swinging toward nurture. All the major theories (Freud, Erikson, Piaget) say that our personalities are shaped mainly by our environment.

D   The processes of development that take place during infancy and childhood reveal the complex and subtle interaction of the forces of nature and nurture, suggesting that this interplay probably continues throughout life.

E   This theory of Freud's is really a crock! Say, get me another brewski, would you?

True-False

_____ 1. The nature-nurture question asks how much development owes to inheritance and how much to learning and experience.

_____ 2. The "visual cliff" is the distance beyond which infants cannot see clearly.

_____ 3. The cephalocaudal principle of motor development says that the parts closer to the head develop before the parts closer to the feet.

_____ 4. The concept of maturation is closer to "nature" than to "nurture."

_____ 5. Attachment is the close emotional bond that develops between infant and parent.

_____ 6. In Piaget's first stage of cognitive development, the child relates sensory experiences to motor actions.

_____ 7. When Piaget used the word "operations," he meant behaviors such as walking and talking that accomplish important tasks for the child.

_____ 8. In Erikson's scheme, each stage of life contains a "test" that, if failed, prevents you from entering the next stage.

_____ 9. Studies of "resilient" children tend to support Erikson's idea that later positive experiences can compensate for early traumas.

_____ 10. Ninety percent of abusive parents were themselves abused children.

Flashcards 1

____ 1. anal stage
____ 2. concrete operations stage
____ 3. formal operations stage
____ 4. genital stage
____ 5. latency stage
____ 6. nature-nurture question
____ 7. oral stage
____ 8. phallic stage
____ 9. preoperational stage
____ 10. sensorimotor stage

a. Freud's 1st stage; age 0-18 mo; infant's pleasure seeking is centered on the mouth
b. Freud's 2nd stage; age 1-3; infant's pleasure seeking centered on anus and its functions of elimination
c. Freud's 3rd stage; age 3-6; child's pleasure seeking is centered on the genitals
d. Piaget's 4th stage; from age 12; adolescents develop ability to think about and solve abstract problems
e. Piaget's 2nd stage; age 2-7; children learn to use symbols like words to think about things not present
f. Piaget's 3rd stage; age 7-11; children perform logical mental operations on physically present objects
g. Freud's 4th stage; age 6-puberty; child represses sexual thoughts and engages in nonsexual activities
h. Freud's 5th stage; after puberty; individual has renewed sexual desires fulfilled through relationships
i. asks how much genetic factors and environmental factors each contribute to a person's development
j. Piaget's 1st stage; birth-age 2; infant interacts with environment by sensory experience and motor action

Flashcards 2

____ 1. attachment
____ 2. cephalocaudal principle
____ 3. gender schemas
____ 4. maturation
____ 5. proximodistal principle
____ 6. resiliency
____ 7. separation anxiety
____ 8. temperament
____ 9. teratogen
____ 10. visual cliff

a. any environmental agent (such as a disease, drug, or chemical) that can harm a developing fetus
b. personality, family, other factors that compensate for increased life stresses to prevent expected problems
c. states that parts closer to center of infant's body develop before parts farther away
d. an infant's distress (loud protests, crying, and agitation) whenever the parents temporarily leave
e. a close fundamental emotional bond that develops between the infant and the parent or caregiver
f. developmental changes that are genetically or biologically programmed rather than learned
g. states that parts of the body closer to the infant's head develop before parts closer to the feet
h. stable behavioral and emotional reactions that appear early and are influenced largely by genetics
i. a glass tabletop with checkerboard and clear glass surfaces to create the illusion of a drop to the floor
j. sets of information and rules organized around how either a male or a female should think and behave

Multiple-Choice

____ 1. Applying the nature-nurture question to Yehudi Menuhin, the child violin prodigy, we would ask whether his special abilities
   a. are a gift of God or an accident of nature
   b. are inborn or the product of learning and experience
   c. will stay with him or fade as he gets older
   d. are genuine or the result of good publicity

____ 2. The briefest period of prenatal development is the
   a. germinal period
   b. embryonic period
   c. fetal period
   d. baby-making period [just kidding!]

____ 3. If you believe what the textbook says about teratogens, you would tell all pregnant women to
   a. watch their weight gain very carefully
   b. get plenty of rest — even more as they approach delivery
   c. avoid alcohol entirely
   d. avoid becoming overly stressed

____ 4. Infants first use their more developed arms, and then their fingers, whose control develops later — this is the
   a. cephalocaudal principle
   b. proximodistal principle
   c. principle of maturation
   d. principle of normal development

____ 5. A longitudinal study of infant temperament found that
   a. infants develop a distinct temperament in the first two to three months
   b. infants' temperaments tend to mirror their parents' temperaments
   c. temperament is determined by the emotional state of the mother during pregnancy
   d. temperament fluctuates widely during infancy

____ 6. The research on infant temperament tends to support the
   a. prenatal influences theory
   b. nature side of the nature-nurture question
   c. concept of gradual maturation
   d. nurture position in child development

____ 7. The essence of Piaget's theory of cognitive development is that
   a. through thousands and thousands of mistakes, the child gradually builds a factual picture of the world
   b. a child's picture of the world is slowly, gradually shaped by a steady succession of learning experiences
   c. each stage is characterized by a distinctly different way of understanding the world
   d. the mind of a child is like the mind of an adult — there just isn't as much information in it

_____ 8. The concept of object permanence develops during the _____ stage
   a. sensorimotor
   b. preoperational
   c. concrete operations
   d. formal operations

_____ 9. Watching juice poured from a short, wide glass into a tall, narrow glass, the child cries, "I want [the tall] glass!" thus illustrating the problem of
   a. object permanence
   b. egocentric thinking
   c. classification
   d. conservation

_____ 10. If there is one idea Erikson's theory clearly modifies, it is
   a. Freud's emphasis on the critical importance of the first five years
   b. the idea that childhood development takes place in stages
   c. Piaget's emphasis on how children see the world
   d. Bandura's idea that children learn through social interaction

_____ 11. All of the following are positive outcomes in Erikson's first four stages, but which list is in the correct chronological order?
   a. trust – autonomy – industry – initiative
   b. trust – initiative – industry – autonomy
   c. trust – autonomy – initiative – industry
   d. autonomy – initiative – industry – trust

_____ 12. Perhaps the most attractive aspect of Erikson's theory is that he sees development as
   a. continuing throughout life, with many opportunities for reworking and rebuilding personality traits
   b. biologically predetermined in a positive direction, so that only extreme trauma results in negative personality traits
   c. arising from a foundation of essential human goodness and positiveness
   d. packed into the formative years, so that a happy child almost automatically becomes a happy adult

_____ 13. Which one of the following is *not* an essential ingredient of resiliency?
   a. a positive temperament
   b. parents free from mental and financial problems
   c. a substitute caregiver
   d. social support from peers

_____ 14. The text asks, "When do you know whether you're a boy or a girl?" The answer is
   a. early in the first year
   b. between the ages of 2 and 3
   c. when you first observe other kids (as in bathing) and notice the obvious anatomical differences
   d. it's never really "learned" — it's something you always know

_____ 15. Treatment for child abuse involves at least two goals:
   a. arresting the abusing parent and removing the child from the home
   b. placing the child in a temporary foster home and enrolling the parent in counseling
   c. teaching the parent to substitute verbal for physical punishment and helping the child learn how to read the parent's moods
   d. overcoming the parent's personal problems and changing parent-child interactions

Answers for Module 17

True-False
1. T
2. F
3. T
4. T
5. T
6. T
7. F
8. F
9. T
10. F

Flashcards 1
1. b
2. f
3. d
4. h
5. g
6. i
7. a
8. c
9. e
10. j

Flashcards 2
1. e
2. g
3. j
4. f
5. c
6. b
7. d
8. h
9. a
10. i

Multiple-Choice
1. b
2. a
3. c
4. b
5. a
6. b
7. c
8. a
9. d
10. a
11. c
12. a
13. b
14. b
15. d

The Big Picture

Statement D

A Day in the Nursery

You know that little brat who gets in the way and makes it difficult for you to study? Instead of muttering "rugrat" under your breath, think "research subject" instead! The theories you are studying are somewhat abstract when presented in a textbook, but you've got the real article right in front of you. Put on your mental lab coat and look at this child coolly and dispassionately (i.e., scientifically). Does the behavior you observe support or contradict the theories you are studying? All right! Now psychology is getting real.

Module 18

Adolescence & Adulthood

All About You

If there is one module in the textbook that clearly is about *you*, this is it. If you are in college, you've just been an adolescent and now you're an adult. Therefore, it will be the hardest module to learn.

Say what?

When studying something like the brain or memory or language, even though it's all right on top our shoulders, it seems removed from our everyday knowledge. In a way, that makes it easier to objectify, and hence to learn.

The facts and theories of adolescence and adulthood, on the other hand, are so close to our everyday experience that it is difficult to obtain sufficient distance to allow getting a handle on them. As you read, you say "yes...," "yes...," yes...," but later it's hard to remember what ought to stand out as important to learn.

I suggest a three-step process in studying this material. First, give yourself credit for what you have learned from your own experience. Don't expect every idea in the module to be new to you. Second, recognize that many of the new ideas discussed in the module may be interesting, but have not yet been accepted as permanent contributions to knowledge. Find out from your professor what to master. Third, have one simple question in mind as you read and study: is this idea helpful? In other words, does what you are reading seem true about yourself, add to your knowledge, and deepen your understanding? Pay special attention to those facts and ideas that do.

The Elegance of Erik Erikson

In this module Rod Plotnik concludes his review of Erik Erikson's fascinating theory of development across the lifespan. (Erikson, considered a "neo-Freudian," does appear again in Plotnik's discussion of psychoanalytic personality theories in Module 19.)

To win a place in the educated public's understanding, a theory needs sharp edges and distinctive, even shocking, premises. We all remember Pavlov's confused dog, Freud's obsession with sex, Piaget's surprising ideas about how children think, and Skinner's untiring lever-pressing rats. Erik Erikson's elegant, almost poetic saga of human life lacks all that. Consequently, although psychologists respect Erikson highly, the educated public does not know his outlook very well. That's a shame, because it might be the most true-to-life theory of all.

Re-read Rod Plotnik's thoughtful discussion of Erikson in Modules 17 and 18. Put Erikson on your list of authors to read in the original.

Effective Student Tip 18

What the Professor Wants

I remember a student who would walk me to class and offer an admiring comment on my shirt, or some such, but then fail to turn in the assignment. Professors love compliments and admiring students. They're human, after all. That isn't what they really want, though.

Every professor wants to be an effective teacher. What your professor wants from you personally is that you really do *learn*. The best thing you can do for your professor is also the best thing you can do for yourself: learn, achieve your goals, and be successful.

Professors sometimes deceive themselves and each other by saying, "If I can help just one student, it's all worth while...," but they don't really believe it. Deep down, they wish *every one* of their students would learn and progress. Then they would know what they are doing is right, which would satisfy their own urge to be effective.

Like you, your professor wants to be effective, but because the measure of that effectiveness is your learning, only you can bring it about. Does it occur to you that you and the professor really need each other? Both of you want to be effective in life, and you can help each other achieve that effectiveness. Don't underestimate your power. The professor's fate is in your hands!

Your response...

Of all the teachers you have known, which one meant the most to you? Explain why.

Key Terms

The key terms for this module are a mixed bag. Some are important terms from well-established theories, while others are interesting concepts from new research and thinking about adolescence and adulthood.

adolescence	formal operations stage	permissive parents
aging by chance theory	gender roles	personality and social development
aging by design theory	personal identity [self-identity]	postconventional level
authoritarian parents	justice orientation	preconventional level
authoritative parents	male secondary sexual characteristics	processing speed
BioPsychoSocial model	menarche	puberty
care orientation	menopause	reaction time
cognitive development	normal aging	schema
companionate love	passionate love	self-esteem
conventional level	pathological aging	testosterone
estrogen	perceptual speed	triangular theory of love
female secondary sexual characteristics		

Outline

- *Introduction*
    1. **Adolescence**
       ☐ What was your own adolescence like? Was it the best of times or the worst of times?
    2. Adulthood
    3. Major periods of change

  A. *Puberty & Sexual Behavior*
    1. Definition: **puberty**
       ☐ Do you remember a time when you were confused or troubled by how your body was changing? What were your thoughts and feelings about it at the time?
    2. Girls during puberty
       a. Physical growth
       b. Female sexual maturity (**menarche** and **estrogen**)
       c. **Female secondary sexual characteristics**
       d. Early versus late maturing
    3. Boys during puberty
       a. Physical growth
       b. Male sexual maturity (**testosterone**)
       c. **Male secondary sexual characteristics**
       d. Early versus late maturing

4. Adolescents: sexually mature
   a. Conflicting answers: **BioPsychoSocial model**
   b. Decisions about becoming sexually active

B. *Cognitive & Emotional Changes*
   1. Definition: **cognitive development**
   2. Piaget's cognitive stages: continued
      a. Stage 4: formal operations
         (1) **Formal operations stage**
         (2) Thinking abstractly
      b. Brain development: reason and emotion
   3. Kohlberg's theory of moral reasoning
      a. Three levels of moral reasoning
         (1) **Preconventional level**
         (2) **Conventional level**
         (3) **Postconventional level**
      b. Evaluating Kohlberg's theory
         (1) Stages
         (2) Criticisms (Carol Gilligan)
            (a) **Care orientation** (females)
            (b) **Justice orientation** (males)
            (c) Importance of gender roles and cultural values
   4. Parenting styles and effects
      a. Personal experiences
      b. Different styles of parenting (Diana Baumrind)
         (1) **Authoritarian parents**
         (2) **Authoritative parents**
         (3) **Permissive parents**
      c. Effects of parenting styles
   ☐ *Which of Diana Baumrind's parenting styles describes your family?*
   5. Adolescence: Big picture
      a. Girls during puberty
      b. Boys during puberty
      c. Sexual maturity
      d. Piaget's stages: continued
      e. Brain development, reason, and emotion
      f. Kohlberg's theory of moral reasoning
   6. Beyond adolescence
      a. Changes in cognitive speed

                (1) **Processing speed**
                (2) **Perceptual speed**
                (3) **Reaction time**
        b. Changes in memory
C. *Personality & Social Changes*
    1. Definition
        a. **Personality and social development**
        b. **Personal identity [self-identity]**
    2. Development of **self-esteem**
        a. High self-esteem
        b. Low self-esteem
        c. Reversals
        d. Forces shaping self-esteem
        e. Importance of self-esteem
    3. Adulthood: Erikson's psychosocial stages
        a. Stage 5: identity versus role confusion
        b. Stage 6: intimacy versus isolation
        c. Stage 7: generativity versus stagnation
        d. Stage 8: integrity versus despair
    4. Personality change
D. *Gender Roles, Love & Relationships*
    1. Definition: **gender roles**
        a. Current gender roles: USA and worldwide
        b. Gender roles: development and function
    2. Expectations
    3. Kinds of love
        a. **Passionate love**
        b. **Companionate love**
        c. **Triangular theory of love** (Robert Sternberg)
        d. Combinations and common types of love
            (1) Passion
            (2) Intimacy
            (3) Commitment
    4. Choosing a partner (**schema**)
    5. Long-term relationship: success or failure
E. *Research Focus: Happy Marriages*
    1. Key to a happy relationship
    2. Method, results, and conclusions

F. *Cultural Diversity: Preferences for Partners*
   1. Measuring cultural influences
   2. Desirable traits
   3. Reasons for marrying

G. *Physical Changes: Aging*
   1. Definition
      a. **Normal aging**
      b. **Pathological aging**
   2. Reasons for aging
      a. **Aging by chance theory**
      b. **Aging by design theory**
   3. Sexual changes with aging
   4. Sexual changes in women (**menopause**)
   5. Sexual changes in men

H. *Application: Suicide*
   1. Teenage suicide
   ☐ *If you are like most of us, you know someone who committed suicide (or tried to). What happened?*
   2. Problems related to teenage suicide
      a. Problems and symptoms
      b. Precipitators
   3. Preventing teenage suicide
      a. Identify risk factors
      b. Crisis management
      c. Hotline services
   4. Suicide in the elderly
      a. Risk factors
      b. Assisted and legal suicide
      c. Opponents and proponents of doctor assisted suicide
   ☐ *Are you in favor of doctor assisted suicide?*

Language Workout

What's That?

p. 407 five-cent **Bazooka gums** = brand of chewing gum
from a **7-Eleven** = convenience store
Stay in there = keep trying
After **making it through** adolescence = finishing
elected **prom** queen = yearly dance in high school or college
levelheaded person = with good judgment
cocky-type person = happy, risk-taking
she did not **figure on** a divorce = predict

p. 408 the **onset** of puberty = beginning
this growth **spurt** begins = sudden increase
go through puberty earlier = experience

p. 409 girls had not **appreciated** the risks of pregnancy = understood
all the **dimensions** of having a sexual relationship = factors
not using **contraceptives** = devices to prevent pregnancy

p. 410 the **Pledge of Allegiance** = promise of loyalty to the United States government, repeated daily by schoolchildren
I'm very **outspoken** = open, not afraid to give opinion
hypothetical concepts = in imaginary situations

p. 411 developing **in fits and starts** = unevenly
venereal diseases = resulting from sexual activity
condoms = contraceptives used by males
getting a tongue pierced **on a dare** = because of a challenge from friend
being **ecstatic** = extremely happy

p. 412 may involve **making bargains** = balancing good and bad effects
all the **alternatives** = possibilities
striking a balance = achieving
issues of law and equality = factors

p. 413 I **get around** them = avoid the rules
I don't **do** drugs = use
I'm asking for **the world** = too much
My parents never **make** their punishments **stick** = enforce
I play right into it = I use their feelings to my advantage
encourage verbal **give-and-take** = equal exchange of viewpoints
different **costs** and benefits = disadvantages

p. 414 a **surge** in physical growth = sudden increase

p. 415 young adults **excel** at encoding = are excellent
doing **crosswords** = word puzzles

p. 416 a **chronically** low sense of self-esteem = continuing for a long time
problems **present for some time** = longtime (not new)

p. 417 **stagnation** = lack of growth or development
mentoring at work = helping and advising younger people

p. 418 the city's **futile** exercise = useless, hopeless
arrogant = self-important, rude
ambitious = actively trying to reach goals
colleagues = co-workers
women are trying to **assume** some traits = take

p. 419 never had much **passion** = strong feeling
a friend **fixed me up with** Charlie = introduced me to
abrasive = annoying
I knew he was **the one** = the right choice
love **at first sight** = immediate, when seeing person for the first time
physical attraction has **waned** = become weak
Why doesn't romantic love **last**? = continue

p. 420 we usually **turn a deaf ear** = refuse to listen
stonewalling = rejecting any discussion (like a stone wall)
love is **grand** = enjoyable

p. 422 cannot be explained, **much less** predicted = and even less it cannot be
his claim is **nothing but** amazing = completely, totally
a known **sore point** = cause of disagreement
it's **not uncommon** = common
husbands who were **autocratic** = controlling
dismissed their wives' advice = rejected

p. 423 a **prospective** partner = potential, possible
virginity is **indispensable** = absolutely necessary
simply **out of the question** = not considered
women expressed more **stringent** standards = strict
the most common reason to **dissolve** marriages = break

p. 424 **pathological** aging = not normal
wear and tear = injury from using every day
life expectancy is **projected** to reach about 100 = predicted

p. 425 results in **cessation** of ovulation = ending, stopping of a process
baby boomers = people born soon after Second World War, from 1945 to 1960.
women experience **hot flashes** = sudden feeling of heat
a society that **glorifies** being young = honors, praises

p. 426 suicide for teenagers almost **quadrupled** = increased four times
the **class clown** = student known for making jokes
considered teenage **histrionics** = dramatic behavior
listen to **oldies** = old songs
I've finally **slipped over the edge** = moved into dangerous situation
gregarious = friendly, sociable
"**preacher** boy" = tiresome, giving advice to everyone
take such talk **seriously** = consider carefully
bouts of depression = periods
may be hard to **spot** = see

p. 427 **Centers for Disease Control and Prevention** =
U.S. government agency that studies causes, cure and prevention of diseases.
family **turmoil** = disorder, confused state
in **imminent** danger = close, ready to begin

       hotline services = telephone line available 24 hours/day to help with problems
       a **lethal** dose of drugs = deadly, causing death
       safeguards to protect patients = protections

p. 430 in a **Social Security** office = U.S. government program of economic insurance
       give even a simple **presentation** = speech, giving information
       With her memory **going** = failing

See It and Say It

p. 408 **puberty** = PYOO-burr-tee
       menarche = MEN-arr-key
       estrogen = ESS-truh-jen
       testosterone = tess-TAHS-tuh-roan

p. 415 **gingko biloba** = GIHNK-koh bai-LOH-buh

p. 424 **gerontology** = djair-ahn-TAHL-oh-jee

p. 426 **precipitators** = prih-SIP-ih-tay-turz

p. 427 **euthanasia** = yoo-thuh-NAY-zhuh

Wild Plurals

Here are some more irregular plurals from the last few modules:

    one **cris<u>is</u>**, two **cris<u>es</u>**

    one **criteri<u>on</u>**, several **criteri<u>a</u>**

    one **ov<u>um</u>**, many **ov<u>a</u>**

TEST YOURSELF

The president has had to solve many public **cris___**, but the problem of global warming may be the most difficult **cris___**.

Cost and convenience are two of the **criteri___** used by most students when they are choosing a college, yet a more important **criteri___** should be the program of studies.

One of the world's most expensive foods is caviar, which is actually the **ov___** from a large fish called a sturgeon. Each **ov___** is so small that a spoon can hold fifty or more.

Now check your answers in the Answer Key.

Build Your Word Power

What's the Count?

You have certainly learned that some nouns in English are non-count, which means that we cannot count them directly. Many second-language students are surprised that we cannot count the following words in English (because their languages can count the equivalent words).

research - advice - equipment - information - knowledge - evidence

So, we can <u>never</u> use "a" or "an" with any of these words. Also, we can <u>never</u> add an "s" to make a plural with any of the words above.

But isn't there some way to count research? Yes, but we need to use another word: it's possible to say **a piece of research** or **a research project**. We can also say:

> The professor assigned **some research** or **a lot of research** or **too much research** or **several pieces of research** or **three research projects**.

If you think that you are hearing people say "researches", you are right. But they are not counting their research. Instead, they are reporting an action:

> "What does she do? <u>She researches</u> the influence of alcohol on fetal development."

To practice these non-count nouns, read the following sentences. *Choose the correct form of the <u>underlined word</u> and circle it:*

Grandpa enjoys giving <u>advice / advices</u> to young people.

Maryam is spending hours in the library on her <u>research / researches</u>.

Willard stopped at the Tourist Office to get some <u>information / informations</u>.

The failed business sold all its <u>equipment / equipments</u> to pay its bills.

The team of lawyers presented surprising <u>evidence / evidences</u> about the crime.

A lot of <u>knowledge / knowledges</u> disappeared when the library burned down.

Now check your answers in the Answer Key.

Answer Key:

The president has had to solve many public **crises**, but the problem of global warming may be the most difficult **crisis**.

Cost and convenience are two of the **criteria** used by most students when they are choosing a college, yet a more important **criterion** should be the program of studies.

One of the world's most expensive foods is caviar, which is actually the **ova** from a large fish called a sturgeon. Each **ovum** is so small that a spoon can hold fifty or more.

Grandpa enjoys giving <u>advice</u> to young people.

Maryam is spending hours in the library on her <u>research</u>. (You could say "projects")

Willard stopped at the Tourist Office to get some <u>information</u>. (You could say "facts")

The failed business sold all its <u>equipment</u> to pay its bills. (You could say "machines")

The team of lawyers presented surprising <u>evidence</u> about the crime. (You could say "facts")

A lot of <u>knowledge</u> disappeared when the library burned down. (You could say "facts" or "ideas")

Flashcards for the fun of it...

A Special Rock 'n' Roll Quiz on Adolescence: Teenagers have always been aware of living in an emotional pressure cooker, and the music they listen to reflects their concerns. Can you match these worries of adolescence with the Golden Oldies that expressed them so memorably? After you try this quiz, how about making up one of your own? Perhaps you could base it on current hits.

____ 1. masculinity   a. Why Do Fools Fall in Love?
____ 2. femininity   b. Fifty Ways to Leave Your Lover
____ 3. self-esteem   c. Walk Like a Man
____ 4. vulnerability   d. Get a Job
____ 5. chastity   e. Big Girls Don't Cry
____ 6. intimacy   f. Sweet Little Sixteen
____ 7. romantic love   g. Lonely Girl
____ 8. career   h. Where Did My Baby Go?
____ 9. marriage   i. Under the Boardwalk
____ 10. commitment *(not!)* j. Going to the Chapel

Module 18: Adolescence & Adulthood   261

The Big Picture

Which statement below offers the best summary of the larger significance of this module?

A   There is at least one compensation for the physical, cognitive, and emotional upheaval of adolescence — it is followed by adulthood, a period of calm and psychological smooth sailing while waiting for the end.

B   Although psychological theories of development tend to place great importance on infancy and childhood, it must be remembered that adolescence and adulthood are also periods of great change.

C   Rod Plotnik wants us to understand that Erikson's psychosocial stage theory of human development is the best, because it is the only one that takes into account adolescence, adulthood, and old age.

D   Once again psychology challenges the popular notion that men and women are equal. Discoveries in every area — physical, cognitive, and personality — reveal significant differences between the way men and women function.

E   Have you noticed that your parents are getting smarter as you get older?

True-False

_____   1. New research shows that adolescence is a period of great psychological turmoil and severe emotional stress.

_____   2. Girls normally experience the physical changes of puberty about two years earlier than boys.

_____   3. For obvious reasons, early maturing girls are more confident and outgoing than late maturing girls.

_____   4. Erik Erikson saw the key developmental issue of adolescence as the acquisition of a positive sense of identity.

_____   5. The good news (too late for you) is that the happiest, best adjusted adolescents come from families using the permissive style of parenting.

_____   6. Enjoy it while you can! The sad fact is that *all* cognitive abilities decline with age.

_____   7. According to Erikson, the main task of young adulthood is to find intimacy by developing loving relationships.

_____   8. Robert Sternberg's triangular theory of love explains why romantic love doesn't last — it has passion and intimacy, but it lacks commitment.

_____   9. Regardless of culture, young adults all over the world ranked traits desirable in a potential mate in almost exactly the same way.

_____   10. Most women report a kind of relief after menopause — at least they don't have to have sex anymore.

Flashcards 1

____ 1. adolescence
____ 2. care orientation
____ 3. estrogen
____ 4. formal operations stage
____ 5. personal identity [self-identity]
____ 6. justice orientation
____ 7. menarche
____ 8. puberty
____ 9. self-esteem
____ 10. testosterone

a. the major male hormone; stimulates growth of genital organs and development of sexual characteristics
b. the first menstrual period; a signal that ovulation may have occurred; potential to conceive child
c. the last of Piaget's cognitive stages (12-adulthood), when adolescents develop the ability to think logically
d. how we describe ourselves, includes our values, goals, traits, interests, and motivations
e. how much one likes oneself; includes feelings of self-worth, attractiveness, and social competence
f. making moral decisions based on issues of caring, avoiding hurt, and concerns for others
g. a developmental period (9-17) of significant biological changes resulting in secondary sexual characteristics
h. making moral decisions based more on issues of law and equality and individual rights
i. one of the major female hormones; at puberty, stimulates development of sexual characteristics
j. developmental period from 12-18 during which many characteristics change from childlike to adultlike

Flashcards 2

____ 1. aging by chance theory
____ 2. aging by design theory
____ 3. authoritarian parents
____ 4. authoritative parents
____ 5. companionate love
____ 6. gender roles
____ 7. menopause
____ 8. passionate love
____ 9. permissive parents
____ 10. triangular theory of love

a. traditional or stereotypic behaviors, attitudes, and personality traits adults expect of males and females
b. continuously thinking about loved one: accompanied by warm sexual feelings and powerful emotions
c. less controlling; nonpunishing and accepting attitude; make few demands on their children
d. having trusting and tender feelings for someone whose life is closely bound up with one's own
e. attempt to control behavior of their children in accordance with an absolute standard of conduct
f. says our bodies age because of preset biological clocks that are like blueprints controlling cell death
g. says your body ages because of naturally occurring problems or breakdowns in the body's cells
h. gradual stoppage in secretion of estrogen, causing cessation of ovulation, menstrual cycle
i. says love has three components: passion, intimacy, and commitment
j. attempt to direct their children's activities in a rational way; supportive, loving; discuss their rules

Multiple-Choice

_____ 1. Experts now believe that adolescence is *not* a period of
   a. great psychological turmoil
   b. considerable biological, cognitive, and social changes
   c. searching for personal identity
   d. dramatic positive or negative changes in self-esteem

_____ 2. When you compare the development of sexual maturity in girls and boys during puberty, you find that the changes are
   a. radically different in girls and boys
   b. gradual in girls but sudden in boys
   c. essentially the same, but occur about two years earlier in girls
   d. somewhat similar, except that the difference between a boy and a man is far greater than the difference between a girl and a woman

_____ 3. In terms of enjoying a psychological advantage in adjustment, it is better to be a/n
   a. early maturing girl
   b. late maturing girl
   c. early maturing boy
   d. late maturing boy

_____ 4. The stage during which adolescents develop the ability to think about abstract or hypothetical concepts and solve problems in a logical way is
   a. Freud's stage four: the latency stage
   b. Erikson's stage eight: integrity versus despair
   c. Piaget's stage four: formal operations
   d. Kohlberg's stage two: conventional level

_____ 5. Probably the most disturbing finding about self-esteem during adolescence is that
   a. boys' self-esteem plunges unless they are good at athletics
   b. girls are more likely to show declining or low self-esteem
   c. both boys' and girls' self-esteem rises rapidly, then falls during adulthood
   d. once self-esteem declines, it almost never recovers or increases

_____ 6. Lawrence Kohlberg based his theory of moral development on research into
   a. the behaviors that children of different ages listed as "good" or "bad"
   b. stories children made up when asked to illustrate good and bad behavior
   c. the correlation between how children rated their own behavior and how their teachers rated it
   d. the reasoning children used to solve problems that posed moral dilemmas

_____ 7. Your new friend seems to be competent, independent, and achievement oriented; you guess that she had _____ parents
   a. authoritarian
   b. authoritative
   c. permissive
   d. protective

_____ 8. Which one of the following cognitive abilities does *not* decrease with aging?
   a. processing speed
   b. perceptual speed
   c. reaction time
   d. interpretation

_____ 9. In Erikson's psychosocial stage theory, an adolescent who does not develop a positive sense of identity is likely to suffer from
   a. role confusion
   b. stagnation
   c. a sense of inferiority
   d. isolation

_____ 10. What we need in late adulthood [Stage 8], says Erikson, is
   a. recognition, respect, and honor from our family and colleagues
   b. a sense of pride in our acquisitions and our standing in the community
   c. a sense of contentment about how we lived and what we accomplished
   d. mainly good health — without it there is despair

_____ 11. What is this thing called love? Sternberg's triangular theory says love is a mix of
   a. romantic love, respect, and companionship
   b. romance, sharing, and loyalty
   c. infatuated love plus companionate love
   d. passion, intimacy, and commitment

_____ 12. Research suggests that one important key to the success or failure of marriage is
   a. how couples decide on major purchases
   b. how couples handle conflicts
   c. whether both partners maintain good physical appearance
   d. whether both partners remain faithful

_____ 13. According to the _____ theory, our bodies age because of naturally occurring problems or breakdowns in the body's cells
   a. aging by chance
   b. aging by design
   c. biological limit
   d. chronological aging

_____ 14. When a young person commits suicide, our typical reaction is an anguished "Why? Why?"... but the truth is that
   a. nothing can stop a person who has decided to commit suicide
   b. there probably were signs of psychological problems and behavioral symptoms long before
   c. psychology has no answer to the riddle of why adolescents, with their whole lives before them, sometimes take their own lives
   d. adolescents who are contemplating suicide go to great lengths to disguise their intentions

_____ 15. Perhaps the main reason why the debate over assisted suicide is intensifying is that
   a. a doctor has invented a machine that makes it relatively easy
   b. psychologists, as scientists, are unwilling to become involved in a moral question
   c. morals in our country are breaking down
   d. so many Americans are living so much longer

Answers for Module 18

True-False	Flashcards 1	Flashcards 2	Multiple-Choice
1. F	1. j	1. g	1. a
2. T	2. f	2. f	2. c
3. F	3. i	3. e	3. c
4. T	4. c	4. j	4. c
5. F	5. d	5. d	5. b
6. F	6. h	6. a	6. d
7. T	7. b	7. h	7. b
8. T	8. g	8. b	8. d
9. F	9. e	9. c	9. a
10. F	10. a	10. i	10. c
			11. d
			12. b
			13. a
			14. b
			15. d

The Big Picture

Statement B

"A Special Rock 'n' Roll Quiz on Adolescence"

1. c   2. e   3. g   4. h   5. f   6. i   7. a   8. d   9. j   10. b

---

More about My Mother

I love the story my mother recalled from her college days way back in the 1920's (see "How Behaviorism Revolutionized Psychology" in Module 9). My mother is a remarkable person in many ways. Very much in the spirit of Erik Erikson's life span development theory, she and others like her are redefining our understanding of old age. After retirement, my mother discovered the joys of running. She goes out six days a week for a run/walk of two or three miles. To celebrate her birthday, she goes five miles. She is 96! I hope you, too, are learning wonderful lessons from your parents.

Module 19

Freudian & Humanistic Theories

Big Theories to Answer Big Questions

In Modules 19 and 20, Rod Plotnik discusses personality theory, one of the most absorbing areas in all of psychology. Personality theories tackle the big questions, the questions we think about when we try to understand who we are and what meaning and purpose our lives have. We feel that we are unique individuals, but aren't we essentially like everyone else? We know we are growing and developing, but aren't we also somehow very much the same from year to year? We would like to change some things about ourselves, but why does that seem so difficult to do?

A theory of personality is necessarily comprehensive. The better it is, the more of our questions about ourselves it answers. As you study these two modules, pay attention to each theory's basic assumptions about human nature. Do you agree with them? To what extent can you see yourself in each theory? Does it describe you and explain your life?

But Do They Explain You?

I've said it before, but it's especially true for the two modules on personality: *challenge every new idea you meet.* Ask yourself, is that idea really true? Does that concept explain my own experience accurately? Does this theory capture how I feel about myself and life in general?

When Sigmund Freud says you have inborn sexual and aggressive tendencies, do you find them in yourself? When Abraham Maslow and Carl Rogers portray humans as fundamentally good, does that square with people as you know them? When Albert Bandura (next module) suggests that we are what we have learned to expect ourselves and the world to be, ask yourself if you are something more than a collection of past experiences. When Gordon Allport (also next module) paints your personality as a complex mosaic of tendencies to behave in certain ways, ask yourself if that captures all you are.

Finally, you might think about your own theory of personality. You do have one, even though you probably haven't tried to work it out in any detail. Anyone who studies psychology inevitably comes to have some sort of theory of personality — a global view of how all the facts and ideas in psychology fit together, and how they apply to everyday life. Reflecting on your own ideas about human nature will help you understand psychology's famous theories of personality.

Effective Student Tip 19

Three Secrets of Effective Writing

Too many students think the ability to write well is something you have to be born with. The truth is just the opposite. Any student can become a good writer. The *art* of writing requires curiosity and creativity, but we all have those qualities. The *craft* of writing is as learnable as cooking or carpentry. Three secrets of effective writing reveal how any serious student can get started on becoming a better writer.

Secret #1: Tell a *story* that is important to you. We organize our memory around stories. A well-told story is the most effective way to convey information.

Secret #2: Paint *word pictures*. We understand best what we can visualize. A beautifully worded description is the most effective way to create understanding in writing.

Secret #3: Think of writing as a *craft* (the artistry will come naturally, flowering as you work). One by one, learn the skills of good writing. Start by learning how to type a beautiful paper, the easiest procedure to learn and the one that has the most immediate effect on your reader.

When you think of writing as a craft, you realize that the goal is progress, not perfection. It doesn't really matter how good your next paper is, as long as it is a little bit better than the last one. That's progress.

Your response...
What was the best paper you ever wrote? What made it so good?

Key Terms

Many of the key terms for this module have crossed over into the general vocabulary of the educated person. All the more reason to make sure you learn them!

- ability tests
- anal stage
- anxiety
- cognitive unconscious
- collective unconscious
- conditional positive regard
- conscious thoughts
- defense mechanisms
- deficiency needs
- denial
- displacement
- dream interpretation
- ego
- fixation
- free association
- Freud's psychodynamic theory of personality
- Freudian slips
- genital stage
- growth needs
- holistic view
- humanistic theories
- id
- ideal self
- Maslow's hierarchy of needs
- Oedipus complex
- oral stage
- personality
- personality tests
- phallic stage
- phenomenological perspective
- pleasure principle
- positive regard
- projection
- projective tests
- psychological assessment
- psychosexual stages
- rationalization
- reaction formation
- real self
- reality principle
- reliability
- repression
- Rogers' self-actualizing tendency
- Rorschach inkblot test
- self theory [self-actualization theory]
- self [self-concept]
- self-actualization
- shyness
- sublimation
- superego
- Thematic Apperception Test (TAT)
- theory of personality
- unconditional positive regard
- unconscious forces
- unconscious motivation
- validity

Outline

- *Introduction*
    1. Personality
        a. **Personality**
        b. **Theory of personality**
    2. Changing personality
- A. *Freud's Psychodynamic Theory*
    1. Definition: **Freud's psychodynamic theory of personality**
    2. Conscious versus unconscious forces
        a. **Conscious thoughts**
        b. **Unconscious forces**
        c. **Unconscious motivation**

3. Techniques to discover the unconscious
   a. **Free association**
   b. **Dream interpretation**
   c. **Freudian slips**

B. *Divisions of the Mind*
   1. Id, ego, and superego
      a. Id: pleasure seeker
         (1) **Id**
         (2) **Pleasure principle**
      b. Ego: negotiator between id and superego
         (1) **Ego**
         (2) **Reality principle**
      c. Superego: regulator
         (1) **Superego**
         (2) Guilt feelings

   ☐ *How do Freud's twin concepts of the pleasure principle and the reality principle make conflict inevitable in his personality theory?*

   2. **Anxiety**
   3. **Defense mechanisms**

   ☐ *Freud didn't mean that defense mechanisms are bad. Can you think of an everyday life example for each defense mechanism that also shows how it promotes our adaptation and survival?*

      a. **Rationalization**
      b. **Denial**
      c. **Repression**
      d. **Projection**
      e. **Reaction formation**
      f. **Displacement**
      g. **Sublimation**

C. *Developmental Stages*
   1. Development: dealing with conflicts
      a. **Psychosexual stages**
      b. Conflict
   2. Fixation: potential personality problems
      a. **Fixation**
      b. Too little or too much gratification

3. Five psychosexual stages

☐ For this theory to make any sense, you must appreciate the conflict in each stage. Think about children you have known (including yourself!) and try to come up with examples for each stage.

   a. **Oral stage**
   b. **Anal stage**
   c. **Phallic stage** and the **Oedipus complex**
   d. Latency stage
   e. **Genital stage**

D. *Freud's Followers & Critics*

☐ Why did Freud's most creative followers eventually become critics?

1. Carl Jung and the **collective unconscious**
2. Alfred Adler
3. Karen Horney
4. Neo-Freudians (Erik Erikson)
5. Freudian theory today
   a. How valid is Freud's theory?
   b. How important are the first five years?
   c. Are there unconscious forces?
      (1) A major Freudian assumption
      (2) A different explanation: **cognitive unconscious**
   d. What was Freud's impact?

E. *Humanistic Theories*

1. Three characteristics of **humanistic theories**
   a. **Phenomenological perspective**
   b. **Holistic view**
   c. **Self-actualization**

☐ The humanistic theories are a more varied collection than other major approaches to personality. What assumptions and characteristics do they have in common?

2. Abraham Maslow: need hierarchy and self-actualization
   a. **Maslow's hierarchy of needs**
      (1) **Deficiency needs**
      (2) **Growth needs**
   b. **Self-actualization**
   c. Characteristics of self-actualized individuals
3. Carl Rogers: self theory
   a. **Self theory** [self-actualization theory]
      (1) **Rogers' self-actualizing tendency**
      (2) **Self** [self-concept]

b. Real self versus ideal self
   (1) **Real self**
   (2) **Ideal self**
c. **Positive regard**
d. Conditional and unconditional positive regard
   (1) **Conditional positive regard**
   (2) **Unconditional positive regard**
e. Importance of self-actualization
4. Applying humanistic ideas
5. Evaluation of humanistic theories
   a. Impact
   b. Criticisms

F. Cultural Diversity: Unexpected High Achievement
1. Boat people: remarkable achievement
2. Values and motivation
3. Parental attitudes

G. Research Focus: Shyness
1. What is **shyness** and what causes it?
2. Psychodynamic approach
3. Social cognitive theory

H. Application: Assessment — Projective Tests
1. **Psychological assessment**
   a. **Personality tests**
   b. **Ability tests**
2. Examples of **projective tests**
   a. **Rorschach inkblot test**
   b. **Thematic Apperception Test (TAT)**
4. Two characteristics
   a. **Validity**
   b. **Reliability**
5. Usefulness of projective tests
   a. Advantages
   b. Disadvantages

Language Workout

What's That?

p. 433 he **had it all** = all advantages and success
why **did he end it all**? = kill himself
I feel guilty **beyond words** = cannot be expressed
manic roar of the crowd = excited noise
Freddie Mercury = British rock star, leader of Queen
someone with **so much going for him** = so many advantages
typify how we react = is typical of
Cobain's **rocket to stardom** = fast rise to rich and famous state
horrendous problems = terrible
reform schools = semi-prison for troubled young people
sent to prison for **manslaughter** = killing, possibly by accident
possession of a **firearm** = gun
punished with **solitary confinement** = imprisoned alone in cell
after his **parole** = release from prison
culminating in = ending
his inner **demons** = serious emotional problems (devils)

p. 434 he was skinny and **frail** = weak, thin
Kurt lived **sporadically** with his father = sometimes, for irregular periods
life was full of **inconsistencies** = illogical factors
as a **backhanded** response = sarcastic, bitterly backward

p. 435 more truth than **jest** = joking
Monkey see monkey do = animals imitate any behavior they see
hinted at a person's unconscious wishes = suggested

p. 436 one of those **narcissists** = people fascinated by their own selves
It's better to **burn out than fade away** = die quickly than slowly
analogous to an iceberg = similar to

p. 437 if they **disregarded** the scientific evidence = ignored
a best friend or **spouse** = husband or wife

p. 438 acted out imaginative **skits** = little stories
lays the groundwork for personality growth = prepared the basis
to a large extent = mostly
he was **eerily** moody = strangely

p. 439 fears of **castration** = removal of sexual organs
Freud's **assertion** = idea, claim

p. 440 Adler **resigned** as president = quit the position
vain and submissive = too proud of physical appearance
she especially **took issue with** Freud's idea = objected to
she changed and **renovated** Freud's theory = renewed

p. 441 his concepts **have been incorporated** = become part of, swallowed by

p. 442 a unique and total **entity** = an independent being

p. 443 achievements **exemplify** the humanistic idea = are a good example of

Module 19: Freudian & Humanistic Theories

p. 444 a **glaring** contradiction = clear, impossible to ignore
discrepancies between our ideal and real selves = differences

p. 445 **grouchy** = irritable
nursing homes = private hospitals giving care to old and very ill people
abide by their fashion standards = obey, follow
foster the development = encourage
blocked by situational **hurdles** = problems, obstacles

p. 446 **hang out** on the streets = spend time
instill a sense of pride = produce, teach
mainstream psychology = accepted by most experts

p. 447 **refugees** = immigrants escaping dangerous situations
boat people = refugees who escape in small boats
astonishing **scholastic** success = in school, academic
metropolitan area = city, urban

p. 450 extremely **intimidating** = causing nervousness and fear in others
ambiguous photo = without clear meaning

p. 454 a **loner** = person who avoids other people, prefers to be alone
an aggressive **hothead** = person with quickly becomes angry
had no **run-ins** with the law = experiences, problems

Why a Colon?

Did you notice this heading in the text?

p. 436 Superego **:** Regulator

The punctuation mark between the words is a **colon**. When you see a colon, you are seeing a kind of **equal sign**. It has the same meaning as Superego **=** Regulator

The colon tells you that both sides — the words before the colon and the words after the colon — are the same. When you see the colon, the words that follow will **define or explain**. Look at the definitions in these examples from the text:

p. 442 She reached her lifelong dream **:** a gold medal in figure skating at the Winter Olympics.

p. 448 Equally noteworthy was the children's overall performance in math **:** almost 50% of the children earned A's, while another 33% earned B's.

A colon also can introduce a **list**, as in the following examples:

p. 443 Maslow divided our needs into two general categories **:** deficiency and growth needs.

p. 442 We'll describe each of the three characteristics unique to humanistic theory **:** having a phenomenological perspective, a holistic view, and a goal of self-actualization.

Try it yourself. Read the following sentences. Each one needs a colon to make the meaning clear. *Decide where the colon is needed, then write it in:*

The airline offered three drink choices coffee, tea, and juice.

To open a childproof bottle, you must do the following actions push down on the cap, align the arrows, and then turn the cap.

After her argument with Richard, Betty knew what she had to do give back the engagement ring and cancel the wedding plans.

The coach explained that there were only two ways to play the game his way and the wrong way.

Anorexics have a disturbed body image they are thin but see themselves as fat.

When asked if she was a person or an animal, Koko the gorilla used sign language to answer with three words "fine animal gorilla".

Vietnamese culture values respect for elders a child should never show disrespect for adults.

One symbol of America is now found throughout the world blue jeans.

In her magazine, Oprah Winfrey started a new idea in publishing she puts her own picture on the cover of every issue.

Now check your answers in the Answer Key.

Answer Key

The airline offered three drink choices : coffee, tea, and juice.
To open a childproof bottle, you must do the following actions : push down on the cap, align the arrows, and then turn the cap.
After her argument with Richard, Betty knew what she had to do : give back the engagement ring and cancel the wedding plans.
The coach explained that there were only two ways to play the game : his way and the wrong way.
Anorexics have a disturbed body image : they are thin but see themselves as fat.
When asked if she was a person or an animal, Koko the gorilla used sign language to answer with three words : "fine animal gorilla".
Vietnamese culture values respect for elders : a child should never show disrespect for adults.
One symbol of America is now found throughout the world : blue jeans.
In her magazine, Oprah Winfrey started a new idea in publishing : she puts her own picture on the cover of every issue.

Module 19: Freudian & Humanistic Theories

The Big Picture

Which statement below offers the best summary of the larger significance of this module?

A The space problems of any textbook are evident in this module. Humanistic psychology has nothing in common with psychoanalytic psychology and belongs in a separate module. These theories are completely different.

B Behaviorists have always been skeptical about the concept of personality, and the two theories in this module show why. Many Freudian ideas are outlandish and humanistic ideas often seem naive and idealistic.

C Psychoanalytic and humanistic personality theories are essentially the same. Freud talks about ego, Rogers about self. Freud's unconscious motivation is like Maslow's hierarchy of needs. Superego could be self-actualization, etc.

D Both psychodynamic and humanistic theories of personality describe processes that go on inside us. But where Freud finds childhood all important, Maslow and Rogers emphasize the challenges of the future.

E "I made an awful Freudian slip when I was having dinner at my mother's house the other day," one psychologist told another. "I meant to say 'Please pass the butter,'" but what I actually said was, 'You [rhymes with witch], you ruined my life!'"

True-False

_____ 1. Freud's famous personality theory is provocative, but hard to test scientifically.

_____ 2. Freud's key concept is the idea of conscious processes — how we understand reality.

_____ 3. Because almost all of Freud's main followers broke with him, today his ideas have little influence.

_____ 4. Free association is necessary because we cannot know the unconscious directly.

_____ 5. For Freud, most personality development takes place during the first five years of life.

_____ 6. Maslow and Rogers are pessimistic about the degree to which personality can change.

_____ 7. The hierarchy of needs helps explain why children who come to school hungry don't learn well.

_____ 8. Self-actualization means honestly recognizing your actual faults and weaknesses.

_____ 9. Rogers warns that a child who receives only unconditional positive regard will grow up spoiled and unrealistic about life.

_____ 10. For a personality test to be scientifically useful, it must possess the twin characteristics of reliability and validity.

Flashcards 1

____ 1. anxiety
____ 2. dream interpretation
____ 3. ego
____ 4. fixation
____ 5. id
____ 6. Oedipus complex
____ 7. pleasure principle
____ 8. reality principle
____ 9. superego
____ 10. unconscious motivation

a. operates to satisfy drives and avoid pain, without concern for moral restrictions or society's regulations
b. the influence of repressed thoughts, desires, or impulses on our conscious thoughts and behaviors
c. an unpleasant state that is associated with feelings of uneasiness, apprehension, and physiological arousal
d. being locked into an earlier psychosexual stage because wishes were overgratified or undergratified
e. based on assumption that dreams contain hidden meanings and symbols; yield clues to unconscious
f. contains biological drives of sex and aggression that are the source of all psychic or mental energy
g. goal is to find safe and socially acceptable ways of satisfying id's desires and superego's prohibitions
h. goal is applying the moral values and standards of one's parents and society in satisfying one's wishes
i. process where child competes with same-sex parent for affections and pleasures of opposite-sex parent
j. has a policy of satisfying a wish or desire only if there is a socially acceptable outlet available

Flashcards 2

____ 1. collective unconscious
____ 2. conditional positive regard
____ 3. free association
____ 4. Freudian slips
____ 5. phenomenological perspective
____ 6. rationalization
____ 7. self [self-concept]
____ 8. self-actualization
____ 9. sublimation
____ 10. unconditional positive regard

a. our inherent tendency to develop and reach our true potentials
b. redirecting a threatening or forbidden desire, usually sexual, into a socially acceptable one
c. mistakes that we make in everyday speech; supposed to reflect our unconscious thoughts or wishes
d. the warmth, acceptance, and love that others show you because you are valued as a human being
e. Jung's theory of inherited ancient memory traces and symbols shared by all peoples in all cultures
f. clients talking about any thoughts or images that enter their head, providing clues to their unconscious
g. how we see or describe ourselves; our self-perceptions, abilities, and personality characteristics
h. idea that how you perceive the world, whether or not it is accurate, becomes your reality
i. positive regard if we behave in certain, acceptable ways, such as living up to the standards of others
j. making up acceptable excuses for behaviors that cause us to feel anxious

Multiple-Choice

1. In psychology, the term "personality" means
   a. a fixed way of responding to other people that is based on our inherited emotional makeup
   b. a combination of long-lasting and distinctive behaviors, thoughts, motives, and emotions that typify how we react to other people and situations
   c. favorable and unfavorable personal characteristics
   d. how interesting and attractive we are to other people

2. In Sigmund Freud's psychodynamic theory of personality, the unconscious contains
   a. everything we are aware of at a given moment
   b. feelings and thoughts we remember from long ago
   c. material that can easily be brought to awareness
   d. repressed wishes, desires, or thoughts

3. Saying whatever comes to mind, even if it seems senseless, painful, or embarrassing, is part of the Freudian technique known as
   a. a defense mechanism
   b. a Freudian slip
   c. free association
   d. projection

4. The ability to create feelings of guilt gives the _____ its power
   a. superego
   b. ego
   c. id
   d. unconscious

5. A student who blames poor test performance on "tricky questions" — rather than admit to poor preparation — is using the defense mechanism of
   a. compensation
   b. denial
   c. projection
   d. rationalization

6. The defense mechanism in which unacceptable wishes are turned into their opposites is known as
   a. projection
   b. reaction-formation
   c. compensation
   d. rationalization

7. Which one of the following shows the correct order of Freud's psychosexual stages?
   a. oral, anal, phallic, latency, genital
   b. anal, latency, phallic, oral, genital
   c. genital, phallic, oral, anal, latency
   d. latency, anal, oral, phallic, genital

_____ 8. The concept of the collective unconscious was proposed by
   a. Carl Jung
   b. Alfred Adler
   c. Karen Horney
   d. B. F. Skinner

_____ 9. Unlike psychodynamic theories, humanistic theories of personality emphasize
   a. the continual operation of contradictory forces buried deep in our unconscious minds
   b. our capacity for personal growth, the development of our potential, and freedom to choose our destiny
   c. how difficult it is — even with therapy — to change personality significantly
   d. the importance of perceptions and beliefs

_____ 10. At the first level of Abraham Maslow's hierarchy, we find _____ needs
   a. self-actualization
   b. esteem
   c. love and belongingness
   d. physiological

_____ 11. By self-actualization, Maslow meant
   a. fulfillment of our unique potential
   b. having our deficiency needs satisfied
   c. being loved and loving someone in return
   d. gaining recognition and status in society

_____ 12. Why are so many people unhappy? Carl Rogers says it is because
   a. happiness is only possible when we become self-actualized
   b. happiness is only an illusion
   c. we have both a real self and an ideal self, and often they are in conflict
   d. we have a positive self and a negative self, and one always dominates

_____ 13. The story of the Indochinese "boat people" illustrates the basic assumption of _____ psychology that all humans possess _____
   a. humanistic ... a hierarchy of needs
   b. humanistic ... a tendency toward self-fulfillment
   c. psychodynamic ... a fierce determination to survive
   d. psychodynamic ... a tendency toward love as well as toward aggression

_____ 14. The old warning, "Of course Mommy loves you... when you're good!" is an example of Rogers' concept of
   a. self-actualization
   b. self-esteem needs
   c. conditional positive regard
   d. unconditional positive regard

_____ 15. Because they use _____ , projective tests often bring out unconscious material
   a. pictures of people
   b. simple materials
   c. ambiguous stimuli
   d. computer analysis

Module 19: Freudian & Humanistic Theories

Answers for Module 19

True-False
1. T
2. F
3. F
4. T
5. T
6. F
7. T
8. F
9. F
10. T

Flashcards 1
1. c
2. e
3. g
4. d
5. f
6. i
7. a
8. j
9. h
10. b

Flashcards 2
1. e
2. i
3. f
4. c
5. h
6. j
7. g
8. a
9. b
10. d

Multiple-Choice
1. b
2. d
3. c
4. a
5. d
6. b
7. a
8. a
9. b
10. d
11. a
12. c
13. b
14. c
15. c

The Big Picture

Statement D

A Freudian Slip

I have heard (and made) some dandy Freudian slips, but I'm not going to tell them, not here! They can be so revealing. A Freudian slip is saying something you didn't mean to say, breaking something, losing something, etc. The trick is to interpret the hidden meaning lying beneath the actual mistake. Treat the slip as you would a dream: carefully examine the manifest content and try to decipher the latent content (see introductory page of Study Guide Module 24). Start listening for the Freudian slips people make. Listen for your own, too! You may be amazed by what you discover!

Module 20

Social Cognitive & Traits

The Story of a Cold-Blooded Killer

Did you know that you are reading the work of a cold-blooded killer? One who could take out a long-bladed knife and charge at an enemy screaming "Kill!... Kill!..."? Of course the enemy in this case was a sack of straw and the killer was a draftee whose only real concern, in a time when our country was totally at peace, was how to get out of KP duty. An ironic twist: when it began raining half-way through the exercise, the officer in charge blew his whistle, loaded us into our trucks, and took us back to our dry barracks. The last thing our Commanding Officer needed was a complaint from some concerned parents' congressperson about how he was treating their boy!

The point of my "war story" is that I wasn't a killer at all (far from it!) and the officer who let us off easy was actually a good soldier. But what if there had been a real war? Maybe I would have acted on my army training. Then what would I have been?

The Genius and Fault of Modern Psychology

In Module 20 Rod Plotnik continues his survey of four dominant personality theories (psychoanalytic, humanistic, social cognitive, and trait) and raises one of the most fundamental questions in psychology: how stable is personality? (See Rod's discussion of person-situation interaction.) If the concept of personality is real, people must show a certain degree of consistency over a wide range of situations. But if people exhibit significantly different behavior in varying situations, how real is the idea of personality?

The genius of modern psychology is to help us see inside. You might say psychoanalytic theory reveals the dark side of human nature and humanistic the positive, but both place the truth inside. Trait theories also assume inner tendencies that guide our behavior. Social cognitive theory, based on the interaction of beliefs and past experience, introduces a dangerous question: could it be the other way around, with the situation determining the person?

The tendency to find the problem inside is also the fault of modern psychology. We become so good at digging out the "real" reasons for psychological problems, as Freud taught us, that we can overlook obvious situational causes like unemployment or discrimination or even environmental pollution. We learn to manage stress, discover dysfunctions, and blame ourselves. Sometimes we miss the real problem.

By the way, I fudged at that bayonet drill years ago. I was too embarrassed to actually scream "Kill!... Kill!...," so I just pretended to yell. Does that added detail ruin the point I was trying to make?

Effective Student Tip 20

What Moves You?

When Delores scored her exam paper, she marked down how many questions she got right (32) and the corresponding letter grade ('D'). She handed me her answer sheet and fled. I began recording her score and grade, and then it hit me: by the grading standards I had written on the board, 32 was a 'C', not a 'D'.

A classmate chased her down the hall and when I showed Delores her mistake and asked her why, she said, "I guess because I always get a 'D'."

Like many students, Delores never did quite as well as I thought she would. Was her "slip of the pen" an indication of mixed motivation? Many students are not really sure why they are in school, why they have taken a certain class, or why they aren't doing as well as their abilities would suggest. All of these questions involve motivation, the basic forces that account for our actions.

Are you in college for your parents? Taking a course to "get it out of the way?" Cutting class without much idea why? These are common cases of mixed or poorly understood motivation. Don't let it happen to you. Try to discover your true motivation. Watch for clues that alert you to possible confusion. You will be more successful, more easily, when you get your motivations and your goals in line. Honesty is the best policy.

Your response...

Try making a totally honest [and private] list of the reasons why you are in college.

Key Terms

These key terms from personality theory are somewhat less common that those in the previous module, but look how few of them there are to learn. Piece of cake!

Bandura's social cognitive theory
Barnum principle
behavioral genetics
cognitive factors
collectivistic culture
delay of gratification
environmental factors
factor analysis
five-factor model
heritability

individualistic culture
interpersonal conflict
locus of control (internal and external)
Minnesota Multiphasic Personality Inventory (MMPI-2)
objective personality tests [self-report questionnaires]
person-situation interaction
personal factors

quantum personality change
reliability
self-efficacy
social cognitive theory
structured interviews
trait
trait theory
validity

Outline

- *Introduction*
    1. Power of beliefs: Nelson Mandela's strength and persistence
    2. Determination: Beverly Harvard's skills and resolution
    ☐ How do Rod Plotnik's two examples illuminate the concept and question of personality?

A. *Social Cognitive Theory*
    1. Review and definition: **social cognitive theory**
    2. Interaction of three factors
        a. Cognitive-personal factors
            (1) **Cognitive factors**
            (2) **Personal factors**
        b. Behaviors
        c. **Environmental factors**
    3. **Bandura's social cognitive theory**
        a. Four cognitive factors that influence personality
            (1) Language ability
            (2) Observational learning
            (3) Purposeful behavior
            (4) Self-analysis

4. Three specific *beliefs* that influence *behavior*
   a. **Locus of control** (Julian Rotter)
      (1) Internal locus of control
      (2) External locus of control
   b. **Delay of gratification** (Walter Mischel)
      (1) Preferred rewards and delay
      (2) Personality variables
   c. **Self-efficacy** (Albert Bandura)
      (1) Sources of information
      (2) Self-efficacy and performance
5. Evaluation of social cognitive theory
   a. Comprehensive approach
   b. Experimentally based
   c. Programs for change
   d. Criticisms and conclusions

B. *Trait Theory*
   1. Definition
      a. **Trait theory** (Gordon Allport)
      b. **Trait**
   2. Identifying traits
      a. How many traits can there be?
         (1) Allport's 18,000 terms
         (2) Reduced to 4,500 traits
      b. Aren't some traits related?
         (1) **Factor analysis** (Raymond Cattell)
         (2) Reduced list to 35 traits
   3. Finding traits: Big Five
      a. **Five-factor model** (OCEAN)
         (1) **O**penness
         (2) **C**onscientiousness
         (3) **E**xtraversion
         (4) **A**greeableness
         (5) **N**euroticism
      b. Importance of the Big Five
      c. Big Five in the real world

4. Person versus situation (Walter Mischel)
    a. Experiment: person-situation
        (1) Failure of traits to predict behaviors across different situations
        (2) **Person-situation interaction**
    b. Conclusions
        (1) Descriptions
        (2) Predictions
5. Stability versus change
☐ *What is your age, relative to the Big Three-Oh? What does this suggest about your personality?*
    a. 13-18 years old
    b. 20-80 years old

C. *Genetic Influences on Traits*
    1. **Behavioral genetics**
    2. Studying genetic influences
        a. Twin studies
        b. **Heritability**
    3. Data from twin studies
    4. Influences on personality
        a. Genetic factors (40%)
        b. Nonshared environmental factors (27%)
        c. Error (26%)
        d. Shared environmental factors (7%)

D. *Evaluation of Trait Theory*
    1. How good is list?
    2. Can traits predict?
    3. What influences traits?

E. *Research Focus: 180 Degree Change*
    1. How much can people change in a day (**quantum personality change**)?
    2. A study of personality change
        a. Method: **structured interviews**
        b. Results
        c. Conclusions

F. *Cultural Diversity: Resolving Conflicts*
   1. **Interpersonal conflict**
   2. Cultural differences
      a. **Individualistic culture** (United States)
      b. **Collectivistic culture** (Japan)
   3. Using different strategies
      a. Avoidance (Japan)
      b. Persuasion (United States)

G. *Four Theories of Personality*
   ❏ Rod Plotnik gives you a beautiful summary of the important but complex material of Modules 19 and 20. Take advantage of his chart. Can you describe each theory and its key concepts?
   1. Psychodynamic theory (Sigmund Freud)
      a. Unconscious motivation
      b. Divisions of the mind
      c. Psychosexual stages
   2. Humanistic theories
      a. Self-actualization
      b. Abraham Maslow's hierarchy of needs
      c. Carl Rogers' self theory
   3. Social cognitive theory (Albert Bandura)
      a. Cognitive factors
      b. Locus of control
      c. Delay of gratification
      d. Self-efficacy
   4. Trait theory
      a. Traits (Gordon Allport)
      b. Five-factor model (the Big Five or OCEAN)
      c. Genetic factors

H. *Application: Assessment — Objective Tests*
   1. Definition
      a. **Objective personality tests [self-report questionnaires]**
      b. Structured (specific questions and answers)
   2. Examples of objective tests
      a. Integrity tests
      b. **Minnesota Multiphasic Personality Inventory (MMPI-2)**

3. Reliability and validity
   a. **Barnum principle**
   b. **Validity**
   c. **Reliability**
4. Usefulness
   a. Disadvantages
   b. Advantages

For Psych Majors Only...

Pioneers in Personality Theory: Psych majors should know the famous pioneers of personality theory discussed Modules 19 and 20. Can you match these psychologists to the phrase that fits their work or ideas?

____ 1. Sigmund Freud   a. individual psychology
____ 2. Carl Jung   b. "penis envy" is nonsense
____ 3. Alfred Adler   c. hierarchy of needs
____ 4. Karen Horney   d. personality traits
____ 5. Abraham Maslow   e. delay of gratification
____ 6. Carl Rogers   f. locus of control
____ 7. Albert Bandura   g. collective unconscious
____ 8. Walter Mischel   h. unconditional positive regard
____ 9. Gordon Allport   i. observational learning
____ 10. Julian Rotter   j. unconscious motivation

Language Workout

What's That?

p. 457 guilty of **plotting** against the government = secretly planning harm
fought against white **domination** = control
I have **cherished** the ideal = valued greatly
if need be = if necessary
provided that he make no public speeches = with this condition
lost no time in resuming = immediately returned to
female police **recruits** = newcomers, new employees
they have **what it takes** to be good cops = the necessary qualities

p. 458 **perseverance** = ability to continue, despite problems
ruthless and determined = completely without mercy or sympathy

p. 459 **locus** of control = center, location
preventive health measures = actions to prevent illness (exercise, diet)

p. 460 a single **marshmallow** = soft white candy

p. 461 the role of **Superman** = comic book hero with extraordinary powers
I'm just trying to **cope** = find ways to solve problems

p. 462 **domestic abuse** = violent fighting within family
street **thugs** = criminals
macho males = exaggerated sense of masculine power
diplomatic = solving problems with respect for both sides
two characteristics seemed **mutually exclusive** = cannot both be correct
this **elusive** list = hard to find

p. 463 **coming up with** the Big Five = identifying
climb **Mount Everest** = highest mountain in the world
defusing potentially dangerous situations = removing tension or power

p. 464 **Dean** = supervisor at college or university
Divinity School = professional school to train religious leaders
hard-core pornography = clearly detailed pictures of sexual behavior
the **faculty handbook** = rules for professors and teachers
There is no question that = It is certain, agreed by everyone
you might very well **draw the line** = refuse to continue
you must **take into account** = consider, judge

p. 465 being **reckless** = careless about danger or consequences
thrill seekers = people who value excitement and danger
an eager **liberal** = U.S. political position, valuing individual freedom
an eager **conservative** = U.S. political position, valuing tradition

p. 466 **chain-smoked** = smoked one cigarette after another without stopping
they were **flabbergasted** = shocked, very surprised

p. 467 **there is no use worrying** = worrying is useless, a waste of time

p. 468 too **simplistic** a picture = overly simple, ignoring important factors
a little **shady** = possibly illegal
should not be **blown out of proportion** = emphasized too much

p. 470 **Alcoholics Anonymous** = organization to help alcoholics stop drinking
a **sober** and dedicated worker = not drinking
the **battery** of personality tests = group, set
relieved of a mental **burden** = worry

p. 471 maintain **harmonious** relationships = balanced, with agreement

p. 472 **go after** one's dream = pursue, work to achieve
a socially acceptable **outlet** = way to release pressure

p. 474 has become **big business** = profitable, resulting in new companies
a **parole board** = official group who decide if a prisoner is ready for release
plots whether these traits are normal = identifies, decides position
I am being **plotted** against = my enemies are planning to hurt me

p. 475 **P. T. Barnum** = American circus creator, famous for fooling the public
relatively **straightforward** = clear, with no special needs or problems

p. 478 **white collar** workers = office workers
a **resume** = short statement of education and work history
landing a job = winning, being hired for

medical malpractice insurance = lawsuits by patients against doctors
intangible skills = difficult to see
a good **reality check** = comparison of one's judgment with objective conditions

See It and Say It

p. 457 **apartheid** = uh-PAHR-tayt

p. 460 **self-efficacy** = self-EFF-ih-kuh-see

p. 466 **heritability** = hair-ih-tuh-BILL-ih-tee

p. 470 **quantum** = KWAHN-tumm

p. 474 **multiphasic** = mull-tee-FAYZ-ik

Why a Semi-Colon?

When you see a semi-colon, it is probably telling you that one complete sentence has some connection with the next complete sentence. Look at this example:

>   Jack is stupid ; his dog is smart.

A common example seen in advertisements is:

>   Buy now ; pay later.

Both sides of the semi-colon are strong, complete sentences. Both can stand alone, but the semi-colon links them together.

So, the semi-colon **separates**, like a period (full stop), because it ends a complete sentence. But it also **connects** like a colon because it shows a relationship. Look at another example:

>   Farhad always carries his Walkman, his cell phone, and his Palm Pilot ; let's hope he isn't hit by lightning!

Did you notice the following examples in the text? Look at how the semi-colon connects the meanings of the two sentences in the following examples:

>   Unlike friends and families, pets never pass judgment ; they provide endless amounts of positive regard no matter how their owners look, feel, dress, or talk (p. 445).

>   For example, when children were told to picture the marshmallows in their minds, they waited an average of over 15 minutes ; however, when they could see the real marshmallows, they could wait an average of only six minutes (p. 460).

In the last example, the writer added the word "however" to further signal to us that the second sentence will show a difference from the first.

How about using semi-colons to connect <u>three</u> sentences? Look at the connections in the following examples:

>   Almost all of us "people watch" ; we observe parents, brothers, sisters, peers, friends, and teachers ; by doing so, we learn a great deal (p. 459).

Most (87%) said that, during the quantum experience, an important truth was revealed to them ; 78% said that they were relieved of a mental burden ; and 60% said that they felt completely loved (p. 470).

NOW TRY IT

Where do you think a semi-colon should go in the sentences below? *Write in a semi-colon:*

Jack's dog is really smart in fact, he's smarter than Jack.

The family was flying to Seattle their luggage was sent to Moscow.

Veronica applied for a job at Big Capitalist National Bank in addition, she filled out applications at Shady Assets Savings and at Dollars-R-Us.

"Wagyu", which comes from Japan, must be the most expensive beef in the world butchers in New York City sell it for $150 a pound.

Jaffar planned to have a nice, relaxing bike ride in reality dogs chased him everywhere he went.

Yan Yan is a big fan of Leonardo Di Caprio for example, she has seen **Titanic** thirty-seven times.

Check your answers in the Answer Key. Then, look at the following passage. This one needs more than one semi-colon. *Write in the semi-colons where they are needed:*

Ronald Reagan started as a sports announcer then he moved to Hollywood for a career in acting finally he changed to politics, becoming governor of California and then president of the United States.

Answer Key:

Jack's dog is really smart ; in fact, he's smarter than Jack.
The family was flying to Seattle ; their luggage was sent to Moscow.
Veronica applied for a job at Big Capitalist National Bank ; in addition, she filled out applications at Shady Assets Savings and at Dollars-R-Us.
"Wagyu", which comes from Japan, must be the most expensive beef in the world ; butchers in New York City sell it for $150 a pound.
Jaffar planned to have a nice, relaxing bike ride ; in reality, dogs chased him everywhere he went.
Yan Yan is a big fan of Leonardo Di Caprio ; for example, she has seen **Titanic** thirty-seven times.
Ronald Reagan started as a sports announcer ; then he moved to Hollywood for a career in acting ; finally he changed to politics, becoming governor of California and then president of the United States.

The Big Picture

Which statement below offers the best summary of the larger significance of this module?

A   Social cognitive and trait theories of personality are coming together in a single, persuasive description of human behavior. The central idea of this new, unified theory is well represented in the acronym OCEAN.

B   For all the efforts of psychology to work out a convincing explanation of personality, the newly discovered phenomenon of quantum personality change (often in a single day) makes nonsense of any single theory of personality.

C   The most important fact presented in this module is the "cultural diversity" discussion of collectivistic and individualistic cultures (Japan and the United States). The point is that all important personality variables are cultural.

D   This module must be read in conjunction with the previous one. Together they describe the four major theoretical approaches to our understanding of personality. The study of personality shows how we are alike, yet individuals.

E   So what if I have no will power. I don't like marshmallows anyway!

True-False

_____ 1. Social cognitive theory combines learning and behavior with ideas about how we think.

_____ 2. Gordon Allport and Raymond Cattell were early pioneers of social cognitive theory.

_____ 3. One of the key ideas of Albert Bandura's social cognitive theory is observational learning.

_____ 4. College students who think they "can't beat the system" ought to study the concept of locus of control.

_____ 5. The most important measure of self-efficacy is the ability to delay gratification.

_____ 6. A trait is a personal quirk — something that makes you different from everyone else in the world.

_____ 7. After a long search, researchers now believe that there are as many as 4,500 different personality traits.

_____ 8. One problem with the concept of traits is that traits are not always consistent across situations.

_____ 9. Most changes in personality occur before the age of thirty.

_____ 10. Genetic influences can determine physical factors like height, but not psychological factors like personality.

Flashcards 1

____ 1. behavioral genetics
____ 2. delay of gratification
____ 3. factor analysis
____ 4. five-factor model
____ 5. heritability
____ 6. locus of control
____ 7. self-efficacy
____ 8. social cognitive theory
____ 9. trait
____ 10. trait theory

a. a statistical measure that estimates how much of a trait is influenced by genetic factors
b. beliefs concerning how much control (internal or external) we have over situations or rewards
c. your personal belief concerning how capable you are in controlling events and situations in your life
d. voluntarily postponing an immediate reward to continue a task for the promise of a future reward
e. says personality is shaped by environmental conditions, cognitive-personal factors, and behavior
f. a relatively stable and enduring tendency to behave in a particular way
g. a complicated statistical method; finds relationships among many diverse items and groups them
h. personality categories: openness, conscientiousness, extraversion, agreeableness, and neuroticism
i. an approach for analyzing structure of personality by measuring, identifying, and classifying similarities
j. study of how inherited or genetic factors affect personality, intelligence, emotions, behavior

Flashcards 2

____ 1. Barnum principle
____ 2. collectivistic culture
____ 3. individualistic culture
____ 4. interpersonal conflict
____ 5. Minnesota Multiphasic Personality Inventory
____ 6. objective personality tests [self-report ques]
____ 7. quantum personality change
____ 8. reliability
____ 9. structured interviews
____ 10. validity

a. asking each individual same set of focused questions so same information is obtained from everyone
b. consistency; a person's test score at one time should be similar to score on a similar test later
c. places a high priority on attaining personal goals and striving for personal satisfaction; competitive; US
d. places a high priority on group goals and norms over personal goals and values; harmony; Japan
e. sudden (in a single day) and radical or dramatic shift in one's personality, beliefs, or values
f. your disagreeing with another person who opposes your getting some wish, goal, or expectation
g. listing a number of traits in such a general way (horoscope) that everyone sees self in it
h. degree to which a test measures what it is supposed to measure
i. true-false self report questionnaire (567 items) describing normal and abnormal behaviors
j. specific written statements requiring subjects to respond ("true" or "false") about applicability

Multiple-Choice

_____ 1. One of the key concepts in Albert Bandura's social cognitive theory is
   a. need for social approval
   b. observational learning
   c. self-actualization
   d. unconscious conflict

_____ 2. The only statement below that shows *internal* locus of control is
   a. often exam questions are so unrelated to course work that studying is useless
   b. no matter how hard you try, some people just don't like you
   c. it is not always wise to plan too far ahead, because many things just turn out to be a matter of good or bad fortune
   d. when I make plans, I am almost certain I can make them work

_____ 3. Walter Mischel used children and marshmallows in his study of
   a. delay of gratification
   b. locus of control
   c. observational learning
   d. traits

_____ 4. Which one of the following is *not* included by Bandura in the keys to determining our sense of self-efficacy?
   a. successes and failures we have experienced in the past
   b. comparing ourselves to others
   c. what others say about our capabilities
   d. the power of our conscience to make us feel guilty

_____ 5. One of the major contributions of social-learning theory to understanding personality is
   a. going beyond symptoms to the deeper emotional or unconscious causes of problems
   b. the development of successful programs for changing behavior and personality
   c. explaining the emotional and genetic causes of behavior
   d. offering a complete theory of personality and human nature

_____ 6. Do women make better cops? Evidence suggests that the answer is
   a. yes, at least for now, because women have a greater determination to succeed
   b. no, because women in our society tend to have a lower sense of self-efficacy
   c. yes, because personality traits shared by many women are useful in police work
   d. no, because the performance of male and female officers is about the same

_____ 7. A trait is defined as a
   a. relatively stable and enduring tendency to behave in a particular way
   b. personal idiosyncrasy that distinguishes us from all others
   c. behavioral tendency that is genetically determined
   d. specific belief about the world which influences our personality

_____ 8. For years, research in personality has tried to identify the
   a. single trait that all humans share
   b. particular traits that make up a healthy personality
   c. most complete list of terms that deal with personality differences
   d. fewest number of traits that cover the largest range of human behaviors

9. The result of this effort (above) is the current belief that human personality is best described by
   a. five supertraits
   b. 35 basic traits
   c. 4,500 personality traits
   d. 18,000 descriptive terms

10. One of the sharpest attacks on the concept of traits was
    a. Mischel's argument that behavior changes in different situations
    b. Bandura's theory that we learn by observing others
    c. Maslow's discovery that needs are arranged in a hierarchy
    d. Allport's list of 18,000 terms that deal with personality differences

11. When are you most likely to make changes in your personality? Research says
    a. by age five
    b. before age 30
    c. after age 30
    d. when the end is near

12. The new area of psychology called behavioral genetics is providing evidence that
    a. twins are very different from single-birth children
    b. twins may appear outwardly similar, but in most respects they are quite different
    c. sharing a family environment is the major influence on personality
    d. inheritance sets a range of behaviors for many aspects of personality

13. It is now believed that _____ of the development of personality traits is explained by genetics
    a. about half
    b. about one-fifth
    c. almost all
    d. almost none

14. Some people experience a very sudden (in a single day) and radical or dramatic shift in personality, beliefs, or values; psychology calls this a
    a. flash of insight, or "ah ha" experience
    b. born again spiritual experience
    c. quantum personality change
    d. quantitative personality change

15. A good example of a highly structured, objective personality test is the
    a. Minnesota Multiphasic Personality Inventory (MMPI-2)
    b. Rorschach Inkblot Test
    c. Thematic Apperception Test (TAT)
    d. traditional psychological interview

Answers for Module 20

True-False
1. T
2. F
3. T
4. T
5. F
6. F
7. F
8. T
9. T
10. F

Flashcards 1
1. j
2. d
3. g
4. h
5. a
6. b
7. c
8. e
9. f
10. i

Flashcards 2
1. g
2. d
3. c
4. f
5. i
6. j
7. e
8. b
9. a
10. h

Multiple-Choice
1. b
2. d
3. a
4. d
5. b
6. c
7. a
8. d
9. a
10. a
11. b
12. d
13. a
14. c
15. a

The Big Picture

Statement D

"Pioneers in Personality Theory" quiz

1. j 2. g 3. a 4. b 5. c 6. h 7. i 8. e 9. d 10. f

College Study

The longer you are in college, the more you will appreciate the great overlap in all fields of study. The way we have them neatly arranged in the college catalog is artificial. Therefore, whether you are a business major or English major, congratulate yourself on having had the wisdom to enroll in psychology. You'll find that there are many connections and tie-ins between psychology and other fields of study.

Module 21

Health, Stress, & Coping

This Module Could Save Your Life!

O.K., maybe I'm exaggerating. Then again, maybe not. Remember Rod Plotnik's discussion of the relationship between illness and stress (in the section on psychosomatic symptoms)? Go back and check how much illness doctors estimate results from stress. The percentages are staggering.

It is becoming clear that stress is one of the greatest health hazards we face. We all feel it. Sometimes it seems that modern life not only is more stressful than 'the good old days' were, but that the number of our daily stressors continues to increase.

Does it have to be this way?

Ironically, considering its prevalence, stress is the one health hazard that is not inevitable, at least not in theory. Old age, if nothing else, is going to get each of us. Accidents will happen. We can't eliminate all disease. You won't solve the problem of environmental pollution all by yourself. Yet you are not doomed to be ravaged by stress.

What can you do about it? First, you can adopt a positive attitude and a healthy life style that will tend to protect you against stress. Second, you can learn how to manage the stress you can't escape. Module 21 explains how both of these safeguards work.

Never mind the grade on the test. Study this module to learn how to live a long and healthy life!

Should Stress Be Managed?

What about stress in *your* life? Do you enjoy a good balance between the demands of your environment and your mental and physical abilities to meet them? Or do you see signs in your behavior or your physical health that suggest too much stress in your life?

Often the suggestion of psychology seems to be that in order to avoid physical and psychological problems, we should learn how to "manage" the stress that is causing them. A different approach would be to think of stress as clues to aspects of life that aren't working effectively. While a heart attack certainly qualifies as a "clue," most stress clues are much more commonplace, and therefore are easy to overlook. Search for the small distortions in your everyday behavior (like swearing, irritation, speeding, and headaches) that could be evidence of stress. Look for feelings, thoughts, and actions that may betray problems in your life and suggest connections to pressures from your environment. Meditation and relaxation certainly are valuable, but changing your life and solving your problems, where possible, would be better.

Effective Student Tip 21

No One Is Lazy

All right, go ahead and call yourself "lazy," if it makes you feel better, but it's not good psychology. First, it may be what cognitive psychologists call a self-handicapping strategy, where you excuse yourself in advance for poor performance. ("I probably won't pass the test..., I'm too lazy to study!") Well, at least they can't say you're dumb! Just lazy.

Second, I would argue that no one is lazy. Oh, sure, we humans like to lie around and we goof off a lot, but that probably has more to do with defending our freedom and autonomy against the regimentation of organized work. The natural tendency of all animals is activity. Watch children at play. Look at the time and energy we put into second jobs, hobbies, sports, and social activities. Normally, we prefer to be doing something, because only activity creates the opportunity to feed our constant hunger to be effective.

When we feel lazy we really are feeling ineffective. The task before us seems too difficult, too unrewarding, or too lacking in novelty and challenge. When you feel 'too lazy' to tackle your schoolwork, the real problem is that you haven't figured out how to handle it effectively, or how to make it deliver positive feedback attesting to your effectiveness.

Your response...

Many of my own students violently disagree with me on this Tip. What do you think?

Key Terms

Many of these key terms are as immediate as the morning newspaper, where, in fact, you may find them. Others are psychological terms that take the discussion of stress and coping a bit deeper. All are relevant to your daily life and important to your health and welfare.

alarm stage
anxiety
anxiety (Freud)
approach-approach conflict
approach-avoidance conflict
autonomic nervous system
avoidance-avoidance conflict
biofeedback
burnout
case study
challenge appraisal
conditioned emotional response
conflict
emotion-focused coping
exhaustion stage
experiment
fight-flight response
frustration
galvanic skin response
general adaptation syndrome (GAS)
hardiness
harm/loss appraisal
hassles
immune system
locus of control
major life events
mind-body connection
mind-body therapy
observational learning
optimism
pessimism
posttraumatic stress disorder (PTSD)
primary appraisal
problem-focused coping
progressive relaxation
psychoneuroimmunology
psychosomatic symptoms
relaxation response
resistance stage
secondary appraisal
social support
stress
stress management program
threat appraisal
transcendental meditation (TM)
Type A behavior
uplifts

Outline

- *Introduction*
    1. **Stress**
    2. Coping

    A. *Appraisal*

    1. **Primary appraisal**
    2. Three ways to appraise a stressful situation
        a. **Harm/loss appraisal**
        b. **Threat appraisal**
        c. **Challenge appraisal**
    3. Situations and primary appraisals
    4. Appraisal and stress levels
        a. **Galvanic skin response**
        b. Stress experiment
    5. Same situation, different appraisals
    6. Sequence: appraisal to arousal

B. *Physiological Responses*
- ☐ *Can you explain why the fight-flight response was so valuable in our early evolution but has become such a problem in modern life? (See "For Psych Majors Only..." box.)*
    1. Fight-flight response
        a. **Fight-flight response**
        b. Physical and psychological stimuli
    2. Sequence for activation of the fight-flight response
        a. Appraisal
        b. Hypothalamus
        c. Sympathetic division
        d. Fight-flight response
    3. Fight-flight: physiological responses
        a. Stress appraisal
        b. Respiration
        c. Heart rate
        d. Liver
        e. Pupils
        f. Hair
        g. Adrenal glands
        h. Muscle tension
    4. **Psychosomatic symptoms**
    - ☐ *Have you ever experienced psychosomatic symptoms?*
    5. Kinds of symptoms
        a. Common psychosomatic symptoms
        b. Development of psychosomatic symptoms
    6. **General adaptation syndrome (GAS)** (Hans Selye)
        a. **Alarm stage**
        b. **Resistance stage**
        c. **Exhaustion stage**
    7. Mind-body connection
        a. **Mind-body connection**
        b. **Mind-body therapy**
    8. **Immune system**
        a. **Psychoneuroimmunology**
        b. Evidence for psychoneuroimmunology
        c. Conditioning the immune system
            (1) Classical conditioning experiment
            (2) History of psychoneuroimmunology

C. *Stressful Experiences*
1. Kinds of stressors
   a. **Hassles**
   b. **Uplifts**
   b. **Major life events** (Social Readjustment Rating Scale)
2. Situational stressors
   a. **Frustration**
   b. **Burnout**
   c. Interpersonal violence: **posttraumatic stress disorder (PTSD)**
3. **Conflict**
   a. **Approach-approach conflict**
   b. **Avoidance-avoidance conflict**
   c. **Approach-avoidance conflict**
4. Five styles of dealing with conflict
   a. Avoidance
   b. Accommodation
   c. Domination
   d. Compromise
   e. Integration
5. **Anxiety**
   a. Developing anxiety
      (1) Classical conditioning: **conditioned emotional response**
      (2) **Observational learning**
      (3) Unconscious conflict: **anxiety (Freud)**
   b. Coping with anxiety
      (1) Extinction
      (2) Freudian defense mechanisms

D. *Personality & Social Factors*
1. **Hardiness**
   a. Definition
   b. Function
2. **Locus of control**
   a. External locus of control
   b. Internal locus of control
3. Optimism versus pessimism
   a. **Optimism**
   b. **Pessimism**
   c. Negative emotion

4. **Type A behavior**
   a. Personality and heart attacks
   b. Revised definition of Type A behavior over three decades
5. **Social support**
   a. Buffer against stress
   b. Maintaining mental health

E. *Kinds of Coping*
   1. Appraisal: **secondary appraisal**
   2. Kinds of coping
      a. **Problem-focused coping**
      b. **Emotion-focused coping**
   3. Choosing a coping strategy

F. *Research Focus: Coping with Trauma*
   1. How do people cope with severe burns?
   2. Research methods
      a. **Experiment**
      b. **Case study**
   3. Coping with initial stressful effects
   4. Coping with long-term stressful effects
   5. Conclusions

G. *Cultural Diversity: Tibetan Monks*
   1. Monks' amazing claims (**autonomic nervous system**)
   ☐ Does Rod Plotnik's example of Tibetan monks mean that modern science is flawed?
   2. Mind-body interaction
      a. Voluntary control
      b. Explanation
      c. Application

H. *Application: Stress Management Programs*
   1. Definition: **stress management program**
   ☐ Could you apply the basic principles of a stress management program to your own life?
   2. Changing thoughts
      a. Use challenge appraisals
      b. Substitute positive self-statements
   3. Changing behaviors
   4. Changing physiological responses
      a. **Biofeedback**
      b. **Progressive relaxation**
      c. Meditation

(1) **Transcendental meditation (TM)**
(2) **Relaxation response**

> *For Psych Majors Only...*
>
> **It's a Jungle Out There!** Imagine two of your prehuman ancestors venturing away from the trees looking for food. Suddenly they hear a low growling and see a huge cat with enormous fangs coming toward them. One (an early scientist) is delighted with the new creature and decides to go up and pet it. The other, feeling awful but also all charged up, makes an instant decision to run for the nearest tree and climb like never before. The survivor, whose makeup contained a little more of what became our fight-flight response, lived to contribute genes to the next generation. The other one made a contribution to the genes of the saber-toothed tiger.
>
> Fast forward to today at the office. Suddenly the boss is standing over your desk saying something about a project that was supposed to be finished. Should you calmly explain that one of the reports you need hasn't arrived yet, or should you run for the nearest tree, like your ancestor did? Is it just another problem, or is it a real saber-toothed tiger? You get all charged up just trying to decide.
>
> The situation in today's jungle of school, work, and relationships is much more complicated than it was for our ancestors. It's hard to tell the real emergencies, so we exhaust ourselves with constant false alerts. The fight-flight response was supposed to be for the rare enemy or tiger, not for the simple problems of daily life.

Language Workout

What's That?

p. 481 as I **come to** = become conscious again
smelling salts = ammonia material used to awaken unconscious people
What's the big deal = This is not so important
grimacing at herself = frowning, making unhappy face
she **ducks into** the shower = enters
bundles up the kids = puts coats on, dresses for outdoors
food stamps = government help for poor people to buy food
to **make ends meet** = have enough money for all necessities
husband had **forged** a check = signed false name (crime)
she had come to the **end of her rope** = limit of her strength
a homeless **shelter** = temporary housing for homeless people

p. 482 **overreact** = react too strongly
need to **mobilize** your physical energy = gather, activate

p. 483 not to **identify with** the injured = feel sympathy for
threat appraisal **versus** challenge appraisal = compared to, against

p. 484 stomach **knotting** = uncomfortable tight feeling
situations that are **novel** = new
getting angry over a **putdown** = a shaming or critical remark

p. 485 (blood is) **rerouted** to muscles = redirected
pupils are **dilated** = enlarged

p. 486 being **behind in** the rent = late in paying
prolonged stress = continuing for a long time

p. 487 **coed** Joan = college student (female)
taking a toll on her stomach = hurting, causing harm
detrimental to your health = clearly harmful
has **given rise to** a new area = produced

p. 488 **coming down with something** = beginning to feel sick from illness
surveillance network = watching, supervision
launched the new field = created
engulf and destroy the cell = surround completely
they **tackled** this question **head-on** = tried to solve it directly
quarantined for a week = isolated, not allowed to mix with others
folk wisdom = popular beliefs

p. 490 **grin and bear it** = smile and do what's necessary (don't resist)

p. 491 **checked into** a hospital = entered, registered as a patient
a **graphic** example = dramatic, clear
cynical people = who mistrust other people

p. 492 **on second thought** = reconsidering the first opinion
you **agonize** = struggle, feel suffering
individuals **go to any lengths** to win = do anything necessary, even bad actions
aggressive and **manipulative** = controlling other people unfairly

p. 493 **highly resistant to extinction** = hard to kill

p. 494 **hardiness** = strength to resist harm

p. 495 if I study hard and **apply myself** = use my abilities

p. 496 being a **workaholic** = person who lives for work
100 **relevant** Type A behavior studies = related to the problem or question

p. 497 families of Roseto **prospered** = became rich and comfortable
friendly **get-togethers** = informal social meetings

p. 500 traveling the wrong way on the **freeway** = highway
painful changes of their **dressings** = bandages
going out for football = participating, joining team

p. 501 the monks sat in **the lotus position** = legs folded under
meditating = clearing the mind of thoughts
winds **scattered** in consciousness = blown in different directions

p. 503 relax **at will** = anytime it is desired
a machine that records, **amplifies** = increases, makes louder

p. 506 a lump **turned up** = appeared
a **biopsy** was taken = removal of cells for examination
totally **benign** = harmless
the **pathologist** = doctor who examines cells and tissues for disease
would bet his children's lives = is 99% certain
explore **my inner drag queen** = possibilities to play with clothing styles
other **Pollyana** things = overly optimistic
pass the Kleenex = (I'm going to cry)

What's the Difference?

provided means **if**, with a positive result:

> **Provided** you change your religion, I **will** marry you. This means that you <u>must</u> change your religion if you want me to marry you. It is a necessary condition.

even if means **even though**, usually with a negative result:

> **Even if** you change your religion, I **won't** marry you.

This means that <u>nothing</u> you do will change my decision: I refuse to marry you. Changing your religion is <u>not</u> enough: it is useless for changing the result.

> Jack **will** go to the movie with you **provided** you buy the ticket.
> Jack **will not** go to the movie **even if** you buy the ticket.

Will or **won't**? Write in the word that fits in the sentences below:

I _____ marry you **provided** you pay me a million dollars.

I _____ marry you **even if** you pay me a hundred million dollars.

A baby _____ usually go to sleep provided he is comfortable and well-fed.

A baby _____ usually go to sleep provided he is not hungry.

Greg _____ pass the exam even if he cheats.

Greg _____ pass the exam provided he cheats.

Even if you don't like science-fiction movies, you _____ enjoy *The Matrix*.

Provided no one tells you the ending, you _____ be surprised.

That alligator _____ bite you, provided you don't step on its tail.

That toothless old alligator _____ bite you, even if you step on its tail.

Provided or **even if**? Try it yourself. Write in the word/words that fit in the sentences below:

The liquor store agreed to sell Dan a bottle of beer _____ he had proof of his age.

304   STUDY GUIDE

Nobody really wants to go to war _____ it sounds like fun at first.

Mike refuses to listen to his boss _____ his job is in danger.

Aisha can get her driver's license _____ she passes the driving test.

_____ he practiced night and day, Sakda could never play golf as well as a professional like Tiger Woods.

_____ our plane arrives on time, Jun can meet us at the airport.

_____ an earthquake destroys the college, the professor will never postpone the midterm exam.

_____ they visit Moscow before the end of the month, tourists can see a museum show called "Underwear in the Soviet Era".

Check your answers in the Answer Key.

Did you notice these sentences using **provided** and **even if** in the text? Read them again, and see if you understand them better:

Many times [Mandela] was offered his release from prison **provided** that he make no public speeches and cease his freedom-fighting activities (p. 457).

The person-situation interaction explains that **even if** you were an extravert, you would behave differently at a wedding than at a funeral because each of these situations creates different cues to which you respond (p. 464).

Answer Key:

I **will** marry you **provided** you pay me a million dollars.
I **won't** marry you **even if** you pay me a hundred million dollars.
A baby **will** usually go to sleep provided he is comfortable and well-fed.
A baby **will** usually go to sleep provided he is not hungry.
Greg **won't** pass the exam even if he cheats.
Greg **will** pass the exam provided he cheats.
Even if you don't like science-fiction movies, you **will** enjoy *The Matrix*.
Provided no one tells you the ending, you **will** be surprised.
That alligator **won't** bite you, provided you don't step on its tail.
That toothless old alligator **won't** bite you, even if you step on its tail.
The liquor store agreed to sell Dan a bottle of beer **provided** he had proof of his age.
Nobody really wants to go to war **even if** it sounds like fun at first.
Mike refuses to listen to his boss **even if** his job is in danger.
Aisha can get her driver's license **provided** she passes the driving test.
Even if he practiced night and day, Sakda could never play golf as well as a professional like Tiger Woods.
Provided our plane arrives on time, Jun can meet us at the airport.
Even if an earthquake destroys the college, the professor will never postpone the midterm exam.
Provided they visit Moscow before the end of the month, tourists can see a museum show called "Underwear in the Soviet Era".

Module 21: Health, Stress, & Coping

The Big Picture

Which statement below offers the best summary of the larger significance of this module?

    A   With the creation of the new field of psychoneuroimmunolgy, psychology has at last proved the truth of the old motto "mind over matter." We now know that any physical problem can be solved by using mental processes.

    B   Although Western science tends to treat mind and body as separate entities, obviously they are part of the same whole. This module brings together our current understanding of stress and the many new techniques for coping with stress in our lives.

    C   The purpose of this module is to alert psychology students to the many misuses of science fostered by the holistic health movement and to warn them not to be fooled by stress management courses, Tibetan monks, meditation tapes, and other mind-body fakery.

    D   Psychology is learning how to build stress-resistant people. By using discoveries like hardiness, coping mechanisms, locus of control, Type A behavior, and the fight-flight syndrome, everyone can be stress-free.

    E   *Stress! Stress!* You want to talk about *stress!* Just cancel that %$&# exam!

True-False

_____ 1. Stress depends partly on how we evaluate a situation.

_____ 2. To "appraise" something means to feel very positive about it.

_____ 3. The fight-flight response goes back to the earliest days of the human species.

_____ 4. Some Tibetan monks have developed a type of yoga that allows them to levitate their bodies several inches off the ground.

_____ 5. One of the main ingredients of a stress management program is learning how to relax.

_____ 6. Research shows that small daily hassles are far more stressful than major life events.

_____ 7. The way we respond to frustration influences our levels of stress.

_____ 8. Conflict means the inevitable run-ins that occur when you have to work with someone else.

_____ 9. Your personality can influence how well you deal with stress.

_____ 10. One of the best prescriptions for successfully handling stress is to have many relationships that confer social support.

Flashcards 1

____ 1. anxiety

____ 2. fight-flight response

____ 3. general adaptation syndrome (GAS)

____ 4. locus of control

____ 5. mind-body connection

____ 6. posttraumatic stress disorder (PTSD)

____ 7. primary appraisal

____ 8. psychosomatic symptoms

____ 9. stress

____ 10. Type A behavior

a. body reacting to stressful situations by going through three stages: alarm, resistance, exhaustion

b. continuum of beliefs about the extent to which one is in control of one's own future

c. how your thoughts, beliefs, and emotions produce beneficial or detrimental physiological changes

d. anxious or threatening feeling of a situation being more than our resources can adequately handle

e. real, often painful symptoms which are caused by psychological factors such as worry, tension, stress

f. theory that traits of aggressive workaholism, anger, competition, hostility, can lead to a heart attack

g. directs great sources of energy to muscles and brain creating preparation of body for action

h. result of direct personal experience of an event involving actual or threatened injury or death

i. initial, subjective evaluation of a situation in which you balance demands against your abilities

j. an unpleasant state characterized by feelings of uneasiness and apprehension, physiological arousal

Flashcards 2

____ 1. burnout

____ 2. emotion-focused coping

____ 3. exhaustion stage

____ 4. hardiness

____ 5. hassles

____ 6. major life events

____ 7. problem-focused coping

____ 8. psychoneuro-immunology

____ 9. social support

____ 10. transcendental meditation (TM)

a. combination of three personality traits (control, commitment, challenge) that protect us from stress

b. moderation of stress by having groups, family, and friends who provide attachment and resources

c. small, irritating, frustrating events we face daily and that we appraise or interpret as stressful experiences

d. feelings of doing poorly at one's job, physical and emotional exhaustion, due to very high demands

e. breakdown in internal organs or weakening of immune system due to long-term, continuous stress

f. primarily doing things to deal with emotional distress, such as seeking support, avoiding, denying

g. study of the relationship between central nervous system, endocrine system, and psychosocial factors

h. potentially disturbing or disruptive situations that we appraise as having significant impact on our lives

i. assuming a comfortable position, eyes closed, and repeating a sound to clear one's head of all thoughts

j. solving the problem by seeking information, changing your behavior, or taking whatever action in necessary

Multiple-Choice

___ 1. Which one of the following is *not* a type of primary appraisal?
   a. harm/loss
   b. threat
   c. challenge
   d. advantage/resource

___ 2. Rod Plotnik lists his students' reactions to a number of common stressors in order to illustrate the point that
   a. modern life has become almost unbearably stressful
   b. not everyone appraises these situations the same way
   c. there is a core of common experiences that everyone considers stressful
   d. the one thing everybody hates is waiting

___ 3. The reason why the fight-flight response can harm our health is that
   a. every time it is triggered our bodies go through an automatic process of arousal
   b. overuse is a kind of "crying wolf" that eventually results in letting our guard down
   c. biologically, humans were designed for quiet, peaceful lives
   d. psychologically, humans do not tolerate challenge very well

___ 4. Which one of the following is *not* a stage in the general adaptation syndrome?
   a. alarm
   b. attack
   c. resistance
   d. exhaustion

___ 5. "Psychoneuroimmunology" means the study of
   a. the manner in which physical factors create psychological symptoms
   b. how disease can make a person psychotic or neurotic
   c. the interaction of physical and psychological factors in health
   d. (this is a trick question — that is a made-up word)

___ 6. The total score on the Social Readjustment Rating Scale
   a. subtracts positive life events from negative life changes
   b. gives a precise cut-off point for becoming ill or staying well
   c. reflects how well you cope with stress
   d. reflects how many major life events you have experienced in the past year

___ 7. Having feelings of doing poorly, physically wearing out, or becoming emotionally exhausted because of stress at work is called
   a. frustration
   b. burnout
   c. conflict
   d. stress

___ 8. According to Freud's explanation, we try to reduce anxiety by employing
   a. problem-focused coping at the ego level
   b. defense mechanisms at the unconscious level
   c. approach/avoidance choices at the ego level
   d. "snap out of it" coping messages at the superego level

_____ 9. Which one of the following is *not* an ingredient of hardiness?
   a. control
   b. commitment
   c. contentment
   d. challenge

_____ 10. The famous "Type A behavior" research attempted to relate certain personality traits to
   a. hardy personality
   b. locus of control
   c. increased risk of cancer
   d. increased risk of heart attack

_____ 11. People in Roseto, Pennsylvania didn't follow healthy life styles, but they had lower rates of heart attacks, ulcers, and emotional problems, probably because
   a. the steep Pennsylvania hills forced them to exercise whether they wanted to or not
   b. being the home of the University of Pennsylvania, the town had superb medical facilities
   c. families in this small town were all related to each other, which had built up a good genetic background over many generations
   d. relationships with family and neighbors were extremely close and mutually supportive

_____ 12. Secondary appraisal means
   a. deciding what we can do to manage, cope, or deal with the situation
   b. our subjective evaluation of a situation to decide if we can deal with it
   c. the extent to which we appraise a situation as stressful after we have taken time to think about it objectively
   d. the extent to which we find a situation stressful the second time we encounter it

_____ 13. Solving a problem by seeking information, changing your own behavior, or taking whatever action is necessary is called
   a. problem-focused coping
   b. emotion-focused coping
   c. primary appraisal
   d. secondary appraisal

_____ 14. If Tibetan monks can raise their body temperature through meditation, then perhaps
   a. Western medicine — not Asian — represents the real medical fakery
   b. Western medicine should pay more attention to psychological factors
   c. every culture has a form of medicine that is best for its own members
   d. every culture develops some phenomena that can't be fully explained

_____ 15. The relaxation technique that involves learning to increase or decrease physiological signals from the body is called
   a. the relaxation response
   b. progressive relaxation
   c. biofeedback
   d. Transcendental Meditation (TM)

Answers for Module 21

True-False	Flashcards 1	Flashcards 2	Multiple-Choice
1. T	1. j	1. d	1. d
2. F	2. g	2. f	2. b
3. T	3. a	3. e	3. a
4. F	4. b	4. a	4. b
5. T	5. c	5. c	5. c
6. F	6. h	6. h	6. d
7. T	7. i	7. j	7. b
8. F	8. e	8. g	8. b
9. T	9. d	9. b	9. c
10. T	10. f	10. i	10. d
			11. d
			12. a
			13. a
			14. b
			15. c

The Big Picture

Statement B

One Small Step

If this module got to you at all, now might be a good time to take a step toward modifying your lifestyle. Start by making one small change. Nothing big, just something that takes only a few minutes a day. Take a walk around the block. Spend a few minutes in silent contemplation. Munch veggies instead of chips. What could you do that would be the first step toward a healthier and less stressful lifestyle?

Module 22

Assessment & Anxiety Disorders

What Is Psychological Abnormality?

We can often recognize when a fellow human is psychologically 'abnormal,' but when we try to say exactly what makes the person abnormal, we find that it is not so easy.

Rod Plotnik begins this module with a hard problem for psychology and psychiatry: how to understand and treat mental disorders. In his examples of infamous criminals and everyday problems you will see that psychological science has not yet attained the agreement and precision of medical science. All doctors will agree on the diagnosis of a broken arm, but what about a broken mind? Since psychology has such a long way to go before it can claim a comprehensive and satisfactory definition of abnormality, perhaps I can be forgiven for trying my own definition.

One Try at a Definition of Psychological Abnormality

Psychological abnormality is a typically temporary condition of dysfunction and distress caused by deficits or breakdowns in the universal need to be effective. Lack of effectiveness can occur in any one or more of six areas of human psychological functioning (see Plotnik's six approaches to psychology).

The most damaging results of the loss of effectiveness are the corresponding breakdowns in those processes of regulation and self-regulation that are so crucial to the welfare of human beings, who lack guidance by instincts or reflexes. It is the loss of regulation and self-regulation that seems 'abnormal,' and is so frightening, both to the troubled person and to others.

If we suffer from psychological abnormality, the best thing we can do is begin to take competent action. But this is not so easy. Intervention and treatment may be needed in any one or more of the six realms of psychological functioning. (1) We may need psychoactive drugs to restore the regulation of a biologically based mental function. (2) We may need to explore the past and learn to understand our basic psychological processes, especially emotion. (3) We may need to reverse a negative self-image and learn to think more realistically about ourselves and others. (4) We may need to modify old habits that no longer work and develop new skills and abilities. (5) We may need to project our values and hopes into the future, to discover our true aspirations and real selves. (6) We may need to rebuild and strengthen our ties to others, in order to gain the social support we need to resurrect old competencies and build new ones.

Effective Student Tip 22

What 'Boring' Really Means

Students often complain that they aren't doing well because their classes and schoolwork are boring. I could suggest that *they* are interesting persons, and therefore have a duty to help make their classes interesting, but that wouldn't be fair. It would be more realistic to advise them to reconsider what boring really means.

Most students think certain people (not themselves!) or certain activities are boring, but that is incorrect. Psychologically, boredom means being trapped, not being able to engage in an activity that is good for you. The next time you feel bored, ask yourself if there is anything taking place that allows you to grow and to express what is uniquely you. I'll bet you'll discover that 'boring' means not being able to exercise your urge to be effective.

Nothing is intrinsically boring. Every experienced teacher I've known had something worthwhile to say. Give me any example of activity or knowledge you might consider boring and I'll find someone, somewhere, whose great passion in life is pursuing exactly that activity or acquiring precisely that knowledge. Your schoolwork isn't boring, but perhaps you haven't yet found a way to connect it to the passions in *your* life.

Your response...

Think of something really boring. Now reconsider. Is there a way in which it might *not* be boring?

Key Terms

The key terms in this module ask you to be part lawyer, part historian, and part doctor. They will require more study than many other modules, but hard study will pay off. The next module is worse!

agoraphobia
case study
clinical assessment
clinical diagnosis
clinical interview
cognitive-behavioral approach
cognitive-behavioral therapy
conduct disorder
conversion disorder
Diagnostic and Statistical Manual of Mental Disorders-IV (DSM-IV)

exposure therapy
generalized anxiety disorder
insanity
labeling
maladaptive behavior approach
mass hysteria
medical model approach
mental disorder
obsessive-compulsive disorder
panic attack
panic disorder

personality tests
phobia
psychodynamic approach
social norms approach
social phobias
somatization disorder
somatoform disorders
specific phobias
statistical frequency approach
taijin kyofusho (TKS)

Outline

- *Introduction*
    1. Mental disorder
        a. **Insanity**
        b. **Mental disorder**
    2. Phobia
        a. **Phobia**
        b. Fear of flying
- A. *Three Approaches*
    1. Causes of abnormal behavior
        a. **Medical model approach**
        b. **Cognitive-behavioral approach**
        c. **Psychodynamic approach**
    2. Definitions of abnormal behavior
        a. **Statistical frequency approach**
        b. **Social norms approach**
        c. **Maladaptive behavior approach**

B. Assessing Mental Disorders
   1. Definition of assessment
      a. Case of Susan Smith
      b. **Clinical assessment**
   ☐ *Why is assessment of a mental problem more likely to be controversial than assessment of a problem of physical health?*
   2. Three methods of assessment
      a. Neurological tests
      b. **Clinical interview**
      c. **Personality tests**

C. Diagnosing Mental Disorders
   1. Real life assessment: Susan Smith
      a. Her past
      b. Her present
   2. DSM-IV
      a. **Clinical diagnosis**
      b. **Diagnostic and Statistical Manual of Mental Disorders-IV (DSM-IV)** [Technically, as Rod Plotnik has it in the textbook, the name now includes TR (for Test Revision), so it is DSM-IV-TR. But it is enough for you to learn DSM-IV, as most people call it.]
   3. Nine major problems: Axis I
      a. Disorders usually first diagnosed in infancy, childhood, or adolescence
      b. Organic mental disorders
      c. Substance-related disorders
      d. Schizophrenia and other psychotic disorders
      e. Mood disorders: Susan Smith – diagnosis, mood disorder
      f. Anxiety disorders: Kate Premo – diagnosis, specific phobia
      g. Somatoform disorders
      h. Dissociative disorders
      i. Sexual and gender-identity disorders
   4. Other problems and disorders: Axes II, III, IV, and V
      a. Axis II: Personality Disorders: Jeffrey Dahmer – diagnosis, antisocial personality disorder
      b. Axis III: General Medical Conditions
      c. Axis IV: Psychosocial and Environmental Problems
      d. Axis V: Global Assessment of Functioning Scale
   5. Using all five Axes
   6. Usefulness of DSM-IV

7. Potential problems using DSM-IV
   a. **Labeling** of mental disorders
   b. Social or political implications
   c. Frequency of mental disorders

D. *Anxiety Disorders*
   1. **Generalized anxiety disorder**
      a. Symptoms
      b. Treatment
   ☐ *Do you sometimes experience anxiety? How does it feel?*
   2. **Panic disorder**
      a. Symptoms (**panic attack**)
      b. Treatment
   3. **Phobia**
      a. **Social phobias**
      b. **Specific phobias**
      c. **Agoraphobia**
   4. **Obsessive-compulsive disorder**
   ☐ *No, you don't have the disorder, but what are some of your obsessive-compulsive behaviors?*
      a. Symptoms
      b. Treatment
         (1) **Exposure therapy**
         (2) Antidepressant drugs

E. *Somatoform Disorders*
   1. **Somatoform disorders**
      a. **Somatization disorder**
      b. **Conversion disorder**
   ☐ *Do you worry about your body or your health? Are your worries realistic or exaggerated?*
   2. **Mass hysteria**

F. *Cultural Diversity: An Asian Disorder*
   1. **Taijin kyofusho (TKS)**
      a. Occurrence
      b. Cultural values
   ☐ *What is taijin kyofusho and what are its implications for psychiatry?*
   2. Social customs and cultural differences

G. Research Focus: School Shootings
1. What drove teens to kill fellow students and teachers?
    a. **Conduct disorder**
    b. **Case study**
2. Adolescents involved in school shootings
3. Risks shared by adolescent school shooters

H. Application: Treating Phobias
1. Specific phobia: flying
❑ *Is there anything you are "phobic" about?*
2. **Cognitive-behavioral therapy**
    a. Thoughts
    b. Behaviors
3. **Exposure therapy**
4. Social phobia: public speaking
    a. Explain
    b. Learn and substitute
    c. Expose
    d. Practice
5. Drug treatment of phobias
    a. Tranquilizers
    b. Problems with drug treatments

For Psych Majors Only...

Psychology at its Most Real: Now, boys and girls, can you say "diathesis-stress theory?" You will by the time you are finished with this module and the next.

These two modules are tough partly because the subject involves the technical terminology of medical science and the concept of the medical model of illness. You must learn to think and talk like a doctor. But the main reason is that the subject touches on the most difficult challenge faced by psychology: how to understand why things go wrong for troubled people and how to help them.

Have you noticed how frequently new discoveries about the causes and treatment of mental illnesses are in the news? The field of abnormal psychology is developing right before your eyes. Memorize what you must in these modules, but keep your eyes on the big picture, too.

Yes, these modules are tough, but they present psychology at its most real.

Language Workout

What's That?

p. 509 neither **sinister** nor scary = evil
considered him an **"average Joe"** = ordinary man
guy who **held down** a job = worked
serial killers = criminals who murder again and again in a pattern
a **con man** = criminal who cheats or tricks people
15 **consecutive** life terms = one after another (not at same time)
a **turbulent** flight = bumpy, full of violent movement
a weekend **seminar** = study and discussion group

p. 510 hanged as **witches** = persons (usually women) with power to do evil
mental disorders **run in families** = occur among family members

p. 511 Thompson was **evicted** from his home = removed
living in a **monastery** = house for religious community (monks)
no **adverse** consequences to society = bad, negative

p. 512 confession **stunned** the nation = shocked

p. 513 the **defense** = lawyers who prove innocence
and **prosecution** = lawyers who prove criminality
refused to **press charges** = make formal complaint to police
scarred by her father's suicide = emotionally injured
a **heightened** emotional reaction = stronger than normal
Maybe Susan was **just plain** crazy = simply
Using a more **rigorous** method = careful, accurate

p. 514 **enuresis** = bedwetting (associated with childish lack of control)
delirium = state of mental confusion, with possible hallucinations
dementia = madness, loss of all connection with reality
The **cardinal** feature = most important
palpitations = strong and rapid heartbeats

p. 515 feeling no guilt or **remorse** = sorrow

p. 516 he was having a **mystical** experience = connected to god or spirit world
based on more **empirical** findings = from provable facts

p. 517 **fidgeting** in his chair = moving nervously
quench a never-ending thirst = satisfy
clammy hands = damp, wet
her body **trembled** = started to shake
some clients **relapsed** = returned to old behavior

p. 518 a person **goes to great lengths** to avoid = tries unusually hard
characterized by **marked** and persistent fears = strong, noticeable
caused **stark** terror = total, harsh
an **underlying** fear = basic, below the surface

p. 519 **indicative** of an anxiety problem = a sign of, pointing to
hoarding = collecting and storing supplies (often hidden)

p. 520 problems, such as **paranoia** = excessive distrust of other people
reinforces the occurrence = strengthens
in the **soprano** section = people who sing in the highest voice
no **ruptured** gas line = broken

p. 522 **ridicule** = expose to laughter, shame
result in **a** loss of **face** = dignity, respect in society

p. 523 **wounded** another 79 = injured
violates the established social rules = breaks
he wanted to **get back at** a popular boy = take revenge on
allegedly killed three students = reportedly
fired on **a prayer circle** = group of people who meet to pray together
easy **access** to firearms = freedom to find or use
read a **graphic** journal entry = detailed, clear and direct

p. 524 phobia that **kept her** from flying = prevented, stopped
she was **groggy** for days = weak, unable to think clearly
the landing gear was **retracting** = pulling back into the plane

p. 528 "**Hillside Strangler**" = famous serial killer
to **throw police off** her sweetheart's trail = distract police
She is **disbarred** = officially prevented from working as lawyer (punishment)
those who **fall for** men = fall in love with
Here's the **scenario** = story
an **idealized** version of romantic love = unrealistic
yearnings = feelings of intense desire
ungratified desires = unsatisfied
the daily **tedium** = boring, routine life

See It and Say It

p. 514 **somatoform** = soh-MAT-oh-form

p. 518 **agoraphobia** = uh-GOAR-uh-FOH-bee-yuh

p. 520 **hysteria** = hiss-TAIR-ee-yuh

What about Whom? *Another look*

Do you remember **some of which, all of which,** and **half of which**? We practiced them in Module 13. These forms help us to count and measure objects.

In the same way, with similar forms like **some of whom, all of whom,** and **half of whom**. we can join sentences that count and measure persons

Look at the following pair of sentences:

> The professor gave a surprise quiz to <u>the students</u>.
> None of the students were expecting it.

We can join these sentences together using **none of whom** :

> The professor gave a surprise quiz to the students, **none of whom** were expecting it.

We use a comma here because it is extra information about the students (not necessary for understanding <u>which</u> students).

Look at another example. The two facts are:

> Sixty-one percent of American teenagers surf the internet. Only 14 percent of them admit they have seen something they 'wouldn't want their parents to know about.'

We can compare these facts by joining them in one sentence:

> Sixty-one percent of American teenagers surf the net, **only 14 percent of whom** admit they have seen something they 'wouldn't want their parents to know about.'

Try it: join the sentences below using **whom**, and then check your answers in the Answer Key:

> The meeting was attended by all the employees. **Some of them** arrived late.
> The meeting _____
>
> Rebecca invited 20 people to her birthday party. **All of them** brought gifts.
> Rebecca _____
>
> The experiment used 324 college students. **Half of them** were given placebos.
> The experiment _____
>
> The state of Massachusetts gives tests to all applicants for teaching jobs. **59 percent of them** fail.
> The state _____
>
> The U.S. has 500,000 elected officials. **197 of them** are openly gay.
> The U.S. _____
>
> In August 2000, the Russian nuclear submarine "Kursk" sank with 118 men aboard. **None of them** survived.
> In August 2000, _____
>
> The Macintosh computer was designed by five engineers. **Four of them** were left-handed.
> The Macintosh computer _____
>
> Finland has a population of five million. **The great majority of them** own cell phones.
> Finland _____
>
> The United States has elected 43 presidents. **Not one of them** was named "Bob".
> The United States _____

Did you notice the sentences below in the text:

> Researchers compared two groups of disadvantaged children, **all of whom** had IQ scores below 80 (p. 299).
>
> They tackled this question head-on by giving the same amount of cold virus to 394 subjects, **all of whom** were quarantined for a week (p. 488).

Answer Key

The meeting was attended by all the employees, **some of whom** arrived late.
Rebecca invited 20 people to her birthday party, **all of whom** brought gifts.
The experiment used 324 college students, **half of whom** were given placebos.
The state of Massachusetts gives tests to all applicants for teaching jobs, **59 percent of whom** fail.
The U.S. has 500,000 elected officials, **197 of whom** are openly gay.
In August 2000, the Russian nuclear submarine "Kursk" sank with 118 men aboard, **none of whom** survived.
The Macintosh computer was designed by five engineers, **four of whom** were left-handed.
Finland has a population of five million, **the great majority of whom** own cell phones.
The United States has elected 43 presidents, **not one of whom** was named "Bob".

The Big Picture

Which statement below offers the best summary of the larger significance of this module?

A A major goal of modern psychology is to apply science to the tasks of understanding the causes of mental disorders, developing methods of assessment, and working out effective techniques of treatment.

B Psychology is more an art than a science. Lacking specific guidance, each clinical psychologist or psychiatrist must rely on experience, intuition, and sometimes guesswork in assessing and treating suffering people.

C It is in the area of psychological disorders that modern psychology has encountered its most stubborn difficulties. There are so many specific disorders that it is almost impossible to understand them scientifically.

D Now that psychology has the new, improved fourth edition of the Diagnostic and Statistical Manual of Mental Disorders (DSM-IV), it has become simple to identify a person's problem and prescribe the correct treatment for it.

E When asked why he had placed ten-foot poles with a rope at the top all around his yard, the man responded, "To keep out the giraffes." "But there are no giraffes around here," his astonished neighbor replied. "Sure keeps them out, doesn't it!"

True-False

_____ 1. The psychiatrists who examined him all agreed that Jeffrey Dahmer was insane.

_____ 2. Although no one dreamed she would kill her own children, Susan Smith's neighbors had considered her a ticking bomb likely to explode at any minute.

_____ 3. When psychiatrists need to make diagnoses, they turn to DSM-IV.

_____ 4. Nearly 50% of all Americans report having had at least one mental disorder during their lifetimes.

_____ 5. Anxiety is a general problem that can result in many different disorders.

_____ 6. Panic disorder is more common among women than men.

_____ 7. Don't waste time worrying about your phobias — they usually disappear in a few months.

_____ 8. Experiences like going back inside to check that you turned off the oven show that obsessive-compulsive disorder is quite common.

_____ 9. Taijin kyofusho (TKS) is a social phobia characterized by a morbid fear of offending others.

_____ 10. Research has shown that drug treatment is superior to cognitive-behavior programs for getting rid of phobias.

Flashcards 1

1. clinical interview
2. cognitive-behavioral approach
3. Diagnostic/Statistical Manual... (DSM-IV)
4. insanity
5. labeling
6. maladaptive behavior approach
7. medical model approach
8. psychodynamic approach
9. social norms approach
10. statistical frequency approach

a. legal term meaning not knowing the difference between right and wrong
b. says a behavior is abnormal if it deviates greatly from accepted social standards, values, or norms
c. emphasizes that mental disorders result from deficits in cognitive processes and from behavioral problems
d. one method of gathering information about relevant past and present behaviors, attitudes, emotions
e. says mental disorders are due to unconscious conflicts or problems from the psychosexual stages
f. says a behavior is abnormal if it interferes with the individual's ability to function personally or in society
g. says a behavior is abnormal if it occurs rarely or infrequently relative to the general population
h. views mental disorders as similar to physical diseases, with symptoms to diagnose and treat
i. naming differences among individuals, placing them in specific categories; possible negative associations
j. describes a uniform system for assessing specific symptoms and matching them to 300 disorders

Flashcards 2

1. agoraphobia
2. generalized anxiety disorder
3. mass hysteria
4. mental disorder
5. obsessive-compulsive disorder
6. panic disorder
7. social phobias
8. somatoform disorders
9. specific phobias
10. taijin kyofusho (TKS)

a. characterized by marked and persistent fears that are unreasonable; fear of an object or situation
b. characterized by a terrible fear of offending others through awkward social or physical behavior
c. problem that seriously interferes with ability to live a satisfying personal life, function in society
d. characterized by recurrent and unexpected panic attacks; continued worry about having more attacks
e. characterized by excessive or unrealistic worry about everything; feeling that something bad will happen
f. characterized by irrational, marked, and continuous fear of performing in social situations
g. characterized by anxiety about being in places or situations from which escape might be difficult
h. process in which a group of people develop similar fears, delusions, behaviors, or physical symptoms
i. persistent, recurring irrational thoughts along with irresistible impulses to perform an act repeatedly
j. complaints of a pattern of recurring, multiple, and significant bodily symptoms; no physical causes

Multiple-Choice

___ 1. The main issue in the Jeffrey Dahmer trial was whether Dahmer
   a. actually killed 15 young men, or only the one he was arrested for
   b. was under the influence of drugs when he killed
   c. knew the difference between right and wrong when he killed
   d. really intended to kill the five men who said they got away

___ 2. The difference between the terms insanity and mental disorder is that
   a. insanity is more severe than a mental disorder
   b. insanity is a legal term while mental disorder is a medical term
   c. mental disorders are specific forms of insanity
   d. mental disorders do not qualify for insurance reimbursement

___ 3. Which one of the following is *not* a way of defining abnormal behavior?
   a. statistical frequency
   b. deviation from social norms
   c. maladaptive behavior
   d. slips of the tongue

___ 4. Which one of the following is *not* an approach to understanding and treating mental disorders?
   a. statistical frequency
   b. medical model
   c. cognitive-behavioral
   d. psychoanalytic

___ 5. The method most commonly used to assess abnormal behavior is the
   a. Rorschach inkblot test
   b. neurological examination
   c. personality test
   d. clinical interview

___ 6. Rod Plotnik tells the story of Susan Smith in great detail to make the point that
   a. clinical diagnosis is a complicated yet necessary process
   b. childhood sexual abuse almost always results in adult problems
   c. despite all we know about Susan Smith, we still can't understand why she did it
   d. her friends and neighbors should have seen the tragedy coming

___ 7. The most widely used system of psychological classification is the
   a. Freudian Psychoanalytic System (FPS)
   b. Diagnostic and Statistical Manual of Mental Disorders-IV (DSM-IV)
   c. Disordered Mind Standards-III (DMS-III)
   d. Federal Uniform Code of Psychopathology (UCP)

___ 8. A recent large-scale study showed that _____ of all Americans had at least one mental disorder during their lifetimes
   a. only 15%
   b. almost 50%
   c. fully 80%
   d. almost 100 %

9. The anxiety disorder that causes the greatest terror and suffering is
   a. panic disorder
   b. simple phobia
   c. generalized anxiety disorder
   d. social phobia

10. Rose is so afraid of being out in public that she stays at home all the time now; Rose suffers from
    a. a simple phobia
    b. a social phobia
    c. agoraphobia
    d. claustrophobia

11. Remember the case of Shirley, who had to do everything precisely 17 times? The theory is that she was trying to
    a. reduce or avoid anxiety associated with feeling or being dirty
    b. obey inner voices which told her God loves cleanliness
    c. cleanse her mind of confusing hallucinations
    d. please her mother, who used to punish her severely whenever she got her clothes dirty while playing

12. When half of the 500 children gathered to perform in a concert suddenly became ill, the cause was determined to be
    a. mass hysteria
    b. mass delusion
    c. somatoform disorder
    d. somatization disorder

13. The key feature of somatoform disorders is
    a. pretending to be sick to avoid school or work
    b. real physical symptoms but no physical causes
    c. imagining physical symptoms that aren't really there
    d. psychological problems but no physical symptoms

14. Of all the mental disorders we know, it's a good bet you don't have to worry about getting TKS, mainly because you
    a. are in college, and therefore too old to get it
    b. are in college, and therefore too intelligent to get it
    c. got shots for it as a child
    d. don't live in Japan

15. Which one of the following is *not* a technique for treating phobia?
    a. gradually exposing a client to the feared situation
    b. administering an antidepressant drug to the client
    c. hospitalizing the client until his or her fears begin to diminish
    d. teaching the client to become aware of thoughts about the feared situation

Answers for Module 22

True-False	Flashcards 1	Flashcards 2	Multiple-Choice
1. F	1. d	1. g	1. c
2. F	2. c	2. e	2. b
3. T	3. j	3. h	3. d
4. T	4. a	4. c	4. a
5. T	5. i	5. i	5. d
6. T	6. f	6. d	6. a
7. F	7. h	7. f	7. b
8. F	8. e	8. j	8. b
9. T	9. b	9. a	9. a
10. F	10. g	10. b	10. c
			11. a
			12. a
			13. b
			14. d
			15. c

The Big Picture

Statement A

Your Favorite Web Sites

Have you been exploring the Web sites Rod Plotnik lists in the Links to Learning section at the end of each module of the textbook? Which ones have been most informative and useful? Do you have a favorite psychology Web site? Please tell the publisher or me about it. **Profenos@aol.com**

Module 23

Mood Disorder & Schizophrenia

The Story of a Troubled Person

One of the most perplexing and controversial problems of psychology is how to understand and treat human anguish and suffering. The great danger is that we may classify, label, and prescribe, but without really understanding. Modern psychology has come a long way from the unthinking and often cruel 'treatment' in use not so long ago, but we are still far from having a reliable science of diagnosis and therapy.

I want to suggest an exercise that may help you think about the great complexity of emotional disturbance, yet also show you that your own psychological sensitivity and insight into human suffering may be greater than you realize. The exercise is to write a brief paper about a troubled person you know. I think this would be a good paper to use for an assignment in psychology or English.

An Exercise in Understanding

Write about someone you know fairly well, such as a relative or friend, who seems unable to enjoy the normal human satisfactions of love and work (that was Freud's definition of emotional disturbance). The reasons for the troubled person's distress could be anything from the broad spectrum of mental problems: severe depression or schizophrenia, common problems of anxiety, panic, and phobia, or social problems like alcoholism and child abuse. What you already know about the person is enough for this exercise.

Work hard to draw a clear picture of your troubled person. Include a personality description, tell the life history briefly, and look for significant turning points in the person's life. Bring in ideas from the relevant approaches to psychology and famous theories of personality and treatment.

Your conclusion should reinforce three points: (1) your theory about why the person became troubled, (2) how the person could be helped (what might work), and finally (3) what the story of this troubled person teaches us about human behavior in general — what lessons it has for our own lives.

You could use this exercise as an opportunity to think and write about your own life and problems. Even though you probably aren't a troubled person, you may have private doubts and worries or painful experiences you would benefit from exploring.

Effective Student Tip 23

Try, Try Again

I envied my brilliant classmates. I felt guilty when I read about the successes of others. "How did they do it?" I asked when I read about a new book or scientific breakthrough or business achievement. Now (taking nothing away from the few true geniuses among us) I realize that most successful people just kept trying.

Newly famous stars often ruefully acknowledge their "overnight success." They know they have been waiting tables and taking every part they could get for years before their big break. Perhaps they are uncomfortable with fame because they know it is illusory. The reality is the love for their craft that kept them working at it no matter how few the rewards.

Again and again, when you read about a new discovery or a great accomplishment, you find that a previously unheralded person, probably not much different from you or me, has been working at it for years. What these admirable people do have is persistence, a force psychology could do well to study in greater depth.

The moral is simply this: most great achievements result from a combination of an idea that won't let go of the person, sufficient time to work and rework the idea, and persistence in seeing it through. If at first you don't succeed....

Your response...

Looking back at your life, are there goals you wish you had pursued with greater determination?

Key Terms

You're in med school now. You've really got to work to learn all these key terms, but if you can do it you will gain a whole new world of understanding.

antidepressant drugs
antisocial personality disorder
atypical neuroleptic drugs
Beck's cognitive theory of depression
biological theory of depression
bipolar I disorder
catatonic schizophrenia
dependent personality disorder
diathesis stress theory
disorganized schizophrenia
dissociative amnesia
dissociative disorder
dissociative fugue
dissociative identity disorder
dopamine theory
dysthymic disorder
electroconvulsive therapy (ECT)
genetic marker
hallucinations
histrionic personality disorder
lithium
major depressive disorder
mood disorder
negative symptoms of schizophrenia
neuroleptic drugs
obsessive-compulsive personality disorder
paranoid personality disorder
paranoid schizophrenia
personality disorder
positive symptoms of schizophrenia
psychosocial factors
schizophrenia
schizotypical personality disorder
tardive dyskinesia
Type I schizophrenia
Type II schizophrenia
typical neuroleptic drugs

Outline

- *Introduction*
    1. Mood disorder
    2. Schizophrenia
    ☐ *How do Rod Plotnik's two examples differ qualitatively from those he used in the previous module?*

A. *Mood Disorders*
    1. Kinds of **mood disorder**
        a. Major depression (**major depressive disorder**)
        b. Bipolar disorder (**bipolar I disorder**)
        c. **Dysthymic disorder**
    ☐ *Do you ever feel depressed? How does it affect you? How do you fight it?*
    2. Causes of mood disorders
        a. Biological factors
            (1) **Biological theory of depression**
            (2) Genetic factors
            (3) Neurological factors
            (4) Brain scans
        b. **Psychosocial factors**

3. Treatment of mood disorders
   a. Major depression and dysthymic disorder
      (1) **Antidepressant drugs**
      (2) Selective serotonin reuptake inhibitors
      (3) Effectiveness of antidepressants
      (4) Psychotherapy
      (5) Relapse
   b. Bipolar I disorder
      (1) **Lithium**
      (2) Mania

B. *Electroconvulsive Therapy*
   1. **Electroconvulsive therapy (ECT)**
   2. Usage
   ☐ *Why is ECT, which seems to work, such a controversial form of therapy?*
   3. Effectiveness of ECT
      a. Modern ECT
      b. Memory loss

C. *Personality Disorders*
   1. **Personality disorder**
   ☐ *No, you're not sick, but which personality disorder is closest to your own personality?*
      a. **Paranoid personality disorder**
      b. **Schizotypical personality disorder**
      c. **Histrionic personality disorder**
      d. **Obsessive-compulsive personality disorder**
      e. **Dependent personality disorder**
      f. **Antisocial personality disorder**
   2. Antisocial personality disorder
      a. Delinquent
      b. Serial killer
      c. Two characteristics
   3. Psychopaths: causes and treatment
      a. Causes
         (1) Psychosocial factors
         (2) Biological factors
      b. Treatment

D. Schizophrenia
   1. Definition and types of **schizophrenia**
   2. Subcategories of schizophrenia
      a. **Paranoid schizophrenia**
      b. **Disorganized schizophrenia**
      c. **Catatonic schizophrenia**
   3. Chance of recovery
      a. **Type I schizophrenia**
      b. **Type II schizophrenia**
   4. Symptoms
      a. Disorders of thought
      b. Disorders of attention
      c. Disorders of perception (**hallucinations**)
      d. Motor disorders
      e. Emotional (affective) disorders
   5. Biological causes
      a. Genetic predisposition (the Genain quadruplets)
      b. **Genetic marker**
      c. Breakthrough
   6. Neurological causes
      a. Ventricle size
      b. Frontal lobe: prefrontal cortex
   7. Environmental causes
      a. Environmental risk factors (50%)
      b. **Diathesis stress theory** of schizophrenia
   8. Treatment
      a. **Positive symptoms of schizophrenia**
      b. **Negative symptoms of schizophrenia**
      c. **Neuroleptic drugs**
         (1) **Typical neuroleptic drugs (Dopamine theory)**
         (2) **Atypical neuroleptic drugs** (Clozapine)
   9. Evaluation of neuroleptic drugs
      a. Typical neuroleptics: side effects, relapse, effectiveness
         (1) **Tardive dyskinesia**
         (2) Problem of relapse without drug
      b. Atypical neuroleptics: side effects, effectiveness, second revolution

E. *Dissociative Disorders*
   1. Definition: **dissociative disorder**
   ☐ *What features do all the dissociative disorders have in common? (And don't say you forget.)*
   2. Three common dissociative disorders
      a. **Dissociative amnesia**
      b. **Dissociative fugue**
      c. **Dissociative identity disorder**
         (1) Definition
         (2) Occurrence and causes

F. *Cultural Diversity: Interpreting Symptoms*
   1. Spirit possession
   2. Cultural differences in occurrence
   3. Cultural differences in gender roles

G. *Research Focus: Exercise versus Drugs*
   1. Choices of therapy for depression?
   2. Major depressive disorder
   3. Exercise experiment: 7 rules
      a. Method and results
      b. Relapse
      c. Conclusion

H. *Application: Dealing with Mild Depression*
   1. Mild versus major depression
      a. Continuum
      b. Similarities
      c. Vulnerability
   2. Beck's theory of depression
      a. **Beck's cognitive theory of depression**
      b. Specific negative, maladaptive thoughts
   3. Overcoming mild depression
      a. Improving social skills
      b. Eliminating negative thoughts

Language Workout

What's That?

p. 531 Chuck was **checking out** the exhibits = looking at
every so often = sometimes
it **blasts** him into superactive days = rockets, pushes strongly
he was **going on** 100 hours without sleep = nearing, approaching
the boss fired him **on the spot** = immediately
no better off than he had been before = not improved at all
put into leather **restraints** = devices to prevent movement
Marsha was **at her wit's end** = upset, desperate for a solution

p. 532 **bouts** of severe depression = periods
Chuck **fluctuates** between two extreme moods = moves

p. 534 fight the **stigma** of having a mental disorder = social shame
making his fight with depression **public** = speaking openly about it
he wanted to avoid meeting **at all costs** = [avoiding was extremely important]

p. 535 a **thriving** career = successful
as **a last resort** = a final attempt to solve the problem
causing a **grand-mal seizure** = very strong attack, involving entire body
as if I've just **downed** a frozen margarita = drunk (cocktail)
No more **egregious** highs or lows = terrible
I'm clearheaded and **even-keeled** = balanced
medication **keeps** my illness **in check** = controls

p. 536 **Don't judge a book by its cover** = Look more deeply, go below the surface
killing and **dismembering** 15 people = cutting into pieces
cold-blooded killers = with no sympathy or mercy for victims
being submissive and **clingy** = dependent on other people
sell or **swap** them = trade, exchange
have sex with their **corpses** = dead bodies

p. 537 developed into **full-blown** psychopaths = with complete range of symptoms

p. 538 I was so **high on life** = happy, optimistic
Next thing I knew = suddenly, without warning

p. 539 How in the hell **were we dealt this hand**? = How did this happen to us?

p. 541 puts on a **Bob Marley** record = musician from Jamaica, famous for "reggae"

p. 542 their symptoms reached a **plateau** = period of no change

p. 544 **with much probing** = after many questions
the importance or **extent** of the information forgotten = amount
storm that washed his companions **overboard** = out of the boat
he had **drifted** into town = arrived by chance
the police **ran** a missing persons' check = did
Gene-**alias**-Burt = also called

p. 545 **It's about time** you knew about me = now is the right time
the **trendiness** of the disorder = fashionable popularity
mental health professionals are **skeptical** = doubtful

332 STUDY GUIDE

p. 546 spirit **possession** = control of person by outside force (spirit)
some clinicians **attribute** the higher percentage = identify the cause of

p. 548 now I feel **worn out** = very tired
scrape up enough bucks to pay my rent = find enough money
tired of my **moping around** = acting unhappy, not being active
I should just **get over him** = stop thinking about him
what do I do to get out of **my funk** = my feelings of depression
there is no question that = it is certain, everyone agrees
making a **blanket** judgment = too general

p. 549 we **get "down in the dumps"** = feel depressed
credit for any success **(however small)** = although it might be very small
I've got a lot going for me = I have many advantages and possibilities

p. 552 the disease begins to **warp** reality = distort
shaping up to be a decade of startling progress = becoming
five drugs we expect to be **approved** = (by government for sale to the public)
we have the **ancillary** services = supporting
dishing out meds = giving pills (medicines)
rekindle their ability = rebuild
experts across the nation **bemoan** = complain about
bemoan the **dearth** of reintegration services = lack
vocational as well as social skills training = career preparation
still **wrongheadedly** regards = wrongly
Get me to Supercuts = Take me to a hair salon [I'm ready to re-enter life]

See It and Say It

p. 536 **histrionic** = hiss-tree-AH-nihk

p. 538 **catatonic** = kat-uh-TAH-nihk

p. 538 **neologisms** = nee-oh-LOH-jiz-umz

p. 544 **fugue** = FYOOG

Why a Comma? Another look

When a writer wants to drop some extra information into a sentence, the writer must use commas. These commas tell us that this information is not essential. Look at the following sentences:

The hamburger, **however,** tasted delicious.

The hamburger, **loaded with onions and ketchup,** tasted delicious.

The hamburger, **which was full of fat and cholesterol,** tasted delicious.

The hamburger, **after he picked it up off the floor,** tasted delicious.

The hamburger, **in John's judgment,** tasted delicious.

In all these examples, the sentence remains the same: the hamburger tastes delicious. However, the drop-in parts do different jobs:

they can give organizing information = **however**

or describe the subject = **loaded with onions and ketchup**

or analyze the subject = **which was full of fat and cholesterol**

or place the action in time = **after he picked it up off the floor**

or specify the viewpoint = **in John's judgment**

Look at how this works in the text. Here's an example that gives organizing information, helping us understand how this sentence relates to the sentence before it:

organize = Other individuals, **however,** may not become depressed by the failure of a relationship because they have a different kind of personality (p. 533).

The drop-in information can further identify the subject, always separated by commas:

identify = One group of neurotransmitters, called **the monoamines (especially serotonin and norepinephrine),** are known to be involved in mood problems (p. 533).

The drop-in information can give an example, even a long example with many parts as in the sentence below:

example = Researchers believe that stressful events, such as having hostile **parents, poor social relations, the death of a parent or loved one, and career or personal problems**, can contribute to the development and onset of schizophrenia (p. 540).

In the same way, the drop-in part can identify the place of the action in time:

time = We discussed how, **after treatment for a mental disorder**, a certain percent of patients relapse or again return to having serious symptoms (p. 547).

The writer can drop-in information that specifies exactly who will be affected:

specify = Researchers concluded that, **for more than two-thirds of the patients,** antisocial personality disorders are an ongoing, relatively stable, long-term problem that may need continual treatment (p. 537).

The writer can, using commas to separate, give information that specifies the effect in a particular place:

specify = These studies on the living brains of depressed patients suggest that faulty brain structure or function, **especially in the prefrontal cortex,** contributes to the onset and/or maintenance of mood disorders (p. 533).

Of course, an entire clause can be dropped-in, helping the writer join two sentences (as we practiced in modules 13, 15, 16, and 22). So, the **whom** clause below is an entire sentence joined to the main action:

clause = When his wife called the police, **whom Elliot wanted to avoid meeting at all costs,** he immediately left the house (p. 534).

What about dashes? Dashes — such as these-- are considered more informal. We find dashes more in newspaper and magazine writing, but less in strict academic writing. However, sometimes a writer may use dashes for variety or to avoid extra words. Look at the dropped-in information below, separated with dashes:

informal dashes = These examples show how psychosocial factors — **having a dependent or achievement-oriented personality** — interact with major stressors to increase one's risk of developing a mood disorder, such as depression (p. 533).

This same sentence could be written with commas, but it would need extra words to keep the meaning clear. This is how it would look:

commas = These examples show how psychosocial factors, **such as having a dependent or achievement-oriented personality,** interact with major stressors to increase one's risk of developing a mood disorder, such as depression.

Now, you try it. The following is one sentence from the text (p. 509), but with the commas removed. Can you find the dropped-in information? Underline the part that is dropped-in.

> In other cases mental disorders may involve a relatively common behavior or event that through some learning observation or other process has the power to elicit tremendous anxiety and becomes a phobia.

Now go back and put in commas where you think they are needed. (Plotnik used five commas). You can check your answer in the Answer Key.

Answer Key

In other cases mental disorders may involve a relatively common behavior or event that <u>through some learning observation or other process</u> has the power to elicit tremendous anxiety and becomes a phobia.

In other cases, mental disorders may involve a relatively common behavior or event that, **through some learning, observation, or other process,** has the power to elicit tremendous anxiety and becomes a phobia.

The Big Picture

Which statement below offers the best summary of the larger significance of this module?

A When you see the wide variety of psychological illnesses affecting people, you are tempted to conclude that consciousness may be the fatal weakness of the human species. We think too much, and torture ourselves with fears.

B With every additional discovery in neuroscience, it becomes more obvious that "psychological" disorders are essentially biological. There is not much we can do to prevent or cure these disorders. You either have good genes or you don't.

C There is a class of psychological disorders that are characterized by their crippling effect on a person's ability to function in society. In their extreme forms, they may interfere with a person's contact with reality.

D Psychiatry has discovered a definite hierarchy of disorders. From *least* harmful to *most* harmful, they are: dissociative disorders, schizophrenia, personality disorders, and mood disorders.

E Every time the psychiatrist held up a new Rorschach ink blot card, the subject gave an interpretation that was more disgusting and more vulgar than the last. When the exasperated psychiatrist remarked on this, the subject protested, "But Doc, you're the one showing the dirty pictures!"

True-False

_____ 1. The most serious mood disorder is major depression.

_____ 2. At the opposite pole from depression is mania.

_____ 3. Rod Steiger knew what caused his depression, so he was able to cure it himself.

_____ 4. The treatment of choice for bipolar I disorder and mania is lithium.

_____ 5. The most common treatment for major depression is electroconvulsive therapy (ECT).

_____ 6. People suffering from antisocial personality disorder are extremely shy and attempt to avoid other people.

_____ 7. People suffering from Type I schizophrenia (more positive symptoms) have a better chance for recovery than those suffering from Type II schizophrenia (more negative symptoms).

_____ 8. Antipsychotic drugs are effective, but they also have serious side effects.

_____ 9. Dissociative disorders work like this: dissociative amnesia, forget; dissociative fugue, flee; dissociative identity disorder, split off.

_____ 10. Although many people experience occasional mild depression, there is not much they can do except tough it out.

Flashcards 1

1. antisocial personality disorder
2. bipolar I disorder
3. catatonic schizophrenia
4. disorganized schizophrenia
5. dysthymic disorder
6. histrionic personality disorder
7. major depressive disorder
8. obsessive-compulsive personality disorder
9. paranoid personality disorder
10. paranoid schizophrenia

a. being chronically but not continuously depressed for a period of two years; poor appetite, insomnia, fatigue
b. a pattern of disregarding or violating the rights of others without feeling guilt or remorse (usually male)
c. characterized by excessive emotionality and attention seeking
d. characterized by periods of wild excitement or periods of rigid, prolonged immobility; frozen posture
e. a pattern of distrust and suspiciousness and perceiving others as having evil motives
f. continually being in a bad mood, having no interest in anything, or getting no pleasure from activities
g. an intense interest in being orderly, achieving perfection, and having control
h. characterized by fluctuating between episodes of depression and mania
i. characterized by auditory hallucinations or delusions of being persecuted or delusions of grandeur
j. marked by bizarre ideas (often about body), confused speech, childish behavior, great emotional swings

Flashcards 2

1. diathesis stress theory
2. dissociative amnesia
3. dissociative fugue
4. dissociative identity disorder
5. dopamine theory
6. electroconvulsive therapy (ECT)
7. genetic marker
8. lithium
9. neuroleptic drugs
10. tardive dyskinesia

a. says that some people have a genetic predisposition interacting with life stressors to cause schizophrenia
b. says dopamine neurotransmitter system is somehow overactive and causes schizophrenic symptoms
c. suddenly, unexpectedly traveling away from home or place of work and being unable to recall one's past
d. characterized by inability to recall important personal information or events; associated with stress, trauma
e. slow, involuntary, uncontrollable movements: rapid twitching of mouth, lips; from use of neuroleptics
f. presence of two or more distinct identities, each with its own pattern of thinking about, relating to world
g. an identifiable gene, or genes, or a specific segment of chromosome directly linked to a trait or disease
h. treating serious mental disorders like schizophrenia by changing levels of neurotransmitters in brain
i. administration of mild electrical current that passes through the brain and causes a seizure
j. a mineral salt; the most effective treatment of bipolar I disorder because it reduces manic episodes

Multiple-Choice

_____ 1. Rod Plotnik offers the examples of Chuck Elliot and Michael McCabe to show that
   a. people who have used illegal drugs are more likely to become mentally ill
   b. mood disorders and schizophrenia can be terrifying, crippling disorders
   c. anyone can become mentally ill at almost any time
   d. brilliant, creative people are more likely to become mentally ill

_____ 2. Which one of the following is *not* a mood disorder?
   a. major depression
   b. bipolar I disorder
   c. antisocial personality disorder
   d. dysthymic disorder

_____ 3. Science now says the cause of depression is
   a. mainly biological
   b. mainly psychological
   c. mainly personal (optimistic versus pessimistic)
   d. both biological and psychological

_____ 4. The most effective treatment for bipolar I disorder is
   a. ECT
   b. clozapine
   c. lithium
   d. dopamine

_____ 5. ECT is a controversial treatment for depression because it
   a. has serious side effects, such as memory loss
   b. is based on the use of antidepressant drugs
   c. has no effect at all on many patients
   d. is prescribed by psychiatrists but not by clinical psychologists

_____ 6. Jeffrey Dahmer represented an extreme case of _____ personality disorder
   a. histrionic
   b. paranoid
   c. antisocial
   d. schizotypical

_____ 7. The highest percentage of mental hospital inpatients are there because of
   a. major depression
   b. schizophrenia
   c. antisocial personality disorder
   d. dissociative amnesia

_____ 8. Which of the following are *not* symptoms of schizophrenia?
   a. disorders of thought
   b. disorders of attention
   c. disorders of perception
   d. disorders of moral character

9. Rod Plotnik tells us about the famous Genain quadruplets to illustrate the fact that
   a. science is filled with amazing coincidences
   b. there must be a genetic factor in schizophrenia
   c. children can "learn" to be schizophrenic from close contact with family members who are ill
   d. schizophrenia strikes in a random, unpredictable fashion

10. According to the _____ theory, schizophrenia is caused by the overactivity of neurotransmitters in the brain
    a. dopamine
    b. diathesis stress
    c. genetic marker
    d. tardive dyskinesia

11. The difference between dissociative amnesia and dissociative fugue is that
    a. in the former you stay in contact with reality; in the latter you become schizophrenic
    b. in the former you have memory gaps; in the latter you may wander away and assume a new identity
    c. in the former you forget more than in the latter
    d. these are really two different terms for the same experience

12. The case of "Burt Tate," who turned out to be a missing person named Gene Saunders, illustrates
    a. dissociative fugue
    b. dissociative amnesia
    c. dissociative identity disorder
    d. multiple personality disorder

13. An underlying cause often reported in dissociative identity disorder is
    a. physical trauma, such as a head injury
    b. unstable parents who give their children mixed messages about what they expect
    c. a flighty personality along with a tendency to overdramatize every situation
    d. severe physical or sexual abuse during childhood

14. According to Aaron Beck's cognitive theory of depression, depressed people
    a. learn depressive habits from other depressed people in their families
    b. have many relatives who also are depressed, suggesting a genetic link
    c. automatically and continually think negative thoughts that they rarely notice
    d. suffer from repressed feelings of guilt and overactive superegos

15. Which one of the following is *not* good advice if you are trying to break out of the vicious circle of mild depression?
    a. improve your social skills
    b. improve your self-esteem
    c. substitute positive thoughts for depressive thoughts
    d. learn to face the fact that your life is really bad

Answers for Module 23

True-False	Flashcards 1	Flashcards 2	Multiple-Choice
1. T	1. b	1. a	1. b
2. T	2. h	2. d	2. c
3. F	3. d	3. c	3. d
4. T	4. j	4. f	4. c
5. F	5. a	5. b	5. a
6. F	6. c	6. i	6. c
7. T	7. f	7. g	7. b
8. T	8. g	8. j	8. d
9. T	9. e	9. h	9. b
10. F	10. i	10. e	10. a
			11. b
			12. a
			13. d
			14. c
			15. d

The Big Picture

Statement C

Use School to Learn More about Yourself

On the introductory page for this module I suggested writing a paper on understanding emotional illness. Whenever I give this assignment in my classes, the best papers are often autobiographical. I remember an understanding English professor I had many years ago who allowed me to write about something painful in my own life. I learned from it, and gained a measure of peace as well. Write (and learn) about yourself.

Module 24

Therapies

The Contribution of Psychodynamic Psychology to Therapy

Psychotherapy is one of the great inventions of this century. Whether you consider it an art or a science, it is a young and constantly evolving process. Rod Plotnik discusses four current approaches to psychotherapy, each with numerous varieties and special techniques.

At the heart of most forms of psychotherapy lies a basic assumption and a fundamental process that come from psychodynamic psychology and the work of a great pioneer, good old You-Know-Who. Both the assumption and the technique are inherent in his theory of dreams, about which you read way back in Module 7.

A Model for Understanding Psychotherapy... and Life

The key idea is the distinction between manifest content and latent content. The manifest content of a dream is the story (however bizarre) we remember in the morning. The latent content is the disguised, unconscious wish hidden in the apparently meaningless story of the dream. The challenge to the dreamer, perhaps a patient in psychotherapy, is to gain insight into that latent content because it is a direct line [Our Hero called it the *via regia,* or royal road] to the unconscious. With the help of the therapist, the patient examines thoughts and feelings connected to the dream in the expectation that these associations will suggest an underlying meaning, a meaning that provides insight into the patient's 'dynamics,' or psychological life.

This key idea has broad implications. Freud saw dreams and other unconscious acts (slips of the tongue, losing things, forgetting, accidents) as miniature neuroses, reflecting the larger neuroses of which we all have more than a few. Therefore, we can interpret *any* behavior like a dream. Here's the formula. First, examine the behavior (a comment, an act, even a thought) very carefully. Exactly what happened? That's the manifest content. Next, search the manifest content for clues about what the *latent* content might be. Why did you forget the assignment? Lose your keys? Call your Honey the wrong name? Bingo! Insight into how your unconscious mind works.

This fundamental idea of psychodynamic psychology underlies most forms of therapy, and can be used as a model for understanding almost anything in life from the meaning of Shakespeare's plays to why your roommate is driving you crazy. Just answer two questions: What is the manifest content? What is the latent content?

Effective Student Tip 24

Take Teachers, Not Courses

Take at least a few courses far from your major area of study. Some advisors will urge you to take only courses that fit into your major, but that can be a mistake. One of the purposes of higher education is to broaden your horizons and show you worlds you scarcely know exist. When else will you have the opportunity to investigate ancient history, nutrition, figure drawing, astronomy, women's literature, and other fascinating subjects that aren't required for graduation?

Graduate students, who have been through it all and know all there is to know (just ask them), often say you should "take teachers, not courses." What they mean is that you should sign up for professors with reputations as especially stimulating teachers, without too much regard for how well the interesting courses fit into your official program.

You will come to know quite a bit about the faculty at your school. Some professors will begin to stand out as people you would like to study with and get to know. Try to give yourself at least a few of these experiences. You might learn more from an inspired, creative teacher in an unrequired course than from a dull teacher in the course that fits so neatly into your major.

Your response...

If neither time nor money mattered, what courses would you like to take just for your own interest?

Key Terms

Most of the key terms in this module are closely related to terms you have already learned in other modules.

behavior therapy [behavior modification]
client-centered therapy
clinical psychologists
cognitive therapy
cognitive-behavior therapy
common factors
community mental health centers
counseling psychologists
deinstitutionalization

dream interpretation
eclectic approach
eye movement desensitization and reprocessing (EMDR)
free association
insight therapy
intrusive thoughts
medical therapy
meta-analysis
moral therapy

neurosis
phenothiazines
psychiatrists
psychoanalysis
psychotherapy
resistance
short-term dynamic psychotherapy
systematic desensitization
transference

Outline

- *Introduction*
    1. Beginning of psychoanalysis
    2. Beginning of behavior therapy
    ☐ What parts did "Anna O" and "Little Albert" play in the history of psychotherapy?
- A. *Historical Background*
    1. Definition: **psychotherapy**
    2. Early treatments
    3. Reform movement: **moral therapy** (Dorothea Dix)
    4. **Phenothiazines** and **deinstitutionalization**
    5. **Community mental health centers**
- B. *Questions about Psychotherapy*
    1. Do I need professional help?
    2. Are there different kinds of therapists?
        a. **Psychiatrists**
        b. **Clinical psychologists**
        c. **Counseling psychologists**
    3. Are there different approaches?
        a. **Insight therapy**
        b. **Cognitive-behavior therapy**
        c. **Eclectic approach**
        d. **Medical therapy**

4. How effective is psychotherapy?
   a. **Meta-analysis**
   b. Major findings

C. *Insight Therapies*

  ☐ *Rod Plotnik quotes from sessions illustrating the three insight therapies. Can you describe the different emphasis and style of each approach?*

  1. **Psychoanalysis** (Sigmund Freud)
     a. Psychoanalysis: three major assumptions
        (1) Unconscious conflicts
        (2) Techniques of free association, dream interpretation, and analysis of slips of the tongue
        (3) Transfer strong emotions onto therapist
     b. Therapy session
     c. Role of analyst
        (1) Free association
        (2) Interpretation
        (3) Unconscious conflicts
     d. Techniques to reveal the unconscious: **neurosis**
        (1) Rat man: **free association**
        (2) Wolf-man: **dream interpretation**
        (3) Case studies: Anna O., Rat Man and Wolf-Man
     e. Problems during therapy
        (1) Rat man: **transference**
        (2) Wolf-man: **resistance**
        (3) **Short-term dynamic psychotherapy**
     f. Psychoanalysis: evaluation
        (1) Decline in popularity
        (2) Current directions
        (3) Conclusion

  2. **Client-centered therapy** (Carl Rogers)
     a. Therapy session
     b. Therapist's traits
        (1) Empathy
        (2) Positive regard
        (3) Genuineness
     c. Effectiveness

3. **Cognitive therapy** (Aaron Beck)
   a. Therapy session
   b. Important factors
      (1) Overgeneralization
      (2) Polarized thinking
      (3) Selective attention
   c. Cognitive techniques
   d. Effectiveness

D. *Behavior Therapy*
   1. Definition: **behavior therapy [behavior modification]**
      a. Therapy session
      b. Behavioral approach
      c. Two goals
   ☐ *In what ways is behavior therapy radically different from the insight therapies?*
   2. **Systematic desensitization** (Joseph Wolpe)
      a. Relaxation
      b. Stimulus hierarchy
      c. Exposure
      d. Exposure: imagined or in vivo
   3. **Cognitive-behavior therapy**
      a. Combining therapies
      b. Cognitive-behavior approach
   4. Kinds of problems
      a. Problem behaviors
      b. Effectiveness

E. *Review: Evaluation of Approaches*
   ☐ *Another great Plotnik summary! Can you master the basic elements of each approach?*
   1. Assumptions, methods, and techniques
      a. Psychoanalysis
         (1) Background
         (2) Basic assumption
         (3) Techniques
      b. Client-centered therapy
         (1) Background
         (2) Basic assumption
         (3) Techniques

c. Cognitive therapy
   (1) Background
   (2) Basic assumption
   (3) Techniques
d. Behavior therapy
   (1) Background
   (2) Basic assumption
   (3) Techniques
2. Effectiveness of psychotherapy
3. **Common factors**

F. *Cultural Diversity: Different Healer*
   1. Case study: young woman
      a. Western assumptions
      b. The *balian*, a local healer in Bali
   2. Healer's diagnosis and treatment
   3. Healers versus Western therapists

   ❒ *Hmmm... If the* balian *usually obtains cures, what does that suggest about the successes of Western psychotherapy?*

G. *Research Focus: EMDR*
   1. New therapy method to eliminate traumatic memories
      a. **Eye Movement Desensitization and Reprocessing (EMDR)**
      b. Francine Shapiro's discovery
   2. Evidence from case studies
   3. Evidence from experiments

H. *Application: Cognitive-Behavior Techniques*
   1. Thought problems
   2. Thought stopping program (**intrusive thoughts**)
      a. Self-monitoring
      b. Thought stopping
      c. Thought substitution
   3. Thought substitution
      a. Irrational thoughts
      b. Rational thoughts
   4. Treatment for insomnia

Language Workout

What's That?

p. 555 developed a terrible **squint** = habit of keeping eyes partly closed
a **gagging** feeling = choking
her **governess**'s dog = woman working as tutor with family
an **up-and-coming** behaviorist = young
very different **assumptions** = beliefs
how psychotherapy **came about** = began

p. 556 early **barbaric** treatments = cruel, primitive
twirled until they passed out = turned round and round
until they **passed out** = fainted, lost consciousness
a relaxed and **decent** environment = sympathetic
funds became tight = money was hard to find
milled about in a large room = moved without direction or purpose
the **wretched** conditions = terrible, miserable

p. 557 **halfway houses** = rehabilitation centers (halfway between life in an institution and everyday living)
county jails = local
the **underprivileged** = people without advantages (money, education)

p. 558 friend, relative, or **acquaintance** = person one recognizes (but not a friend)
a psychiatric **residency** = medical training through working in hospital
an **applied clinical setting** = practical situation in real conditions
as of yet = until now

p. 559 **comprehensive** theory = complete, explaining everything
laypersons = non-professionals
an **appreciation** of what happens = understanding
Who are you that I should care = Why are you so important
reflected more **tranquilly** = calmly

p. 561 made him **pledge** himself = promise, commit
unimportant or **irrelevant** = not connected, unrelated
the window opened **of its own accord** = by its own power
their ears **pricked** like dogs = standing up straight

p. 562 called Freud a "**filthy swine**" = dirty pig
therapy would **stall** = stop working
the client's **reluctance** = unwillingness
the analyst must use **tact** = sensitive understanding
therapy can proceed and **stay on course** = move toward the goal

p. 563 such a question was **unheard of** = never spoken
a great advantage **in that** they are much quicker = because

p. 564 trouble **letting** her **go** = releasing control
the old **vacuum** = empty feeling

p. 566 gave a real **jump-start** = stimulus, strong push
let people step all over me = allow others to control me
taking it a little bit at a time = making small changes, not too quickly

Module 24: Therapies 347

p. 567   **run through** some of the situations here = practice
she really wants to **speak her mind** = give her opinion directly

p. 567 felt **queasy** [KWEE-zee] = sick

p. 572 general **apathy** = lack of interest or emotion
periods of **fasting** = not eating food
two small human **effigies** = figures (dolls)
any **lingering** evil wind spirits = remaining

p. 573 he experienced terrible **flashbacks** = memories, suddenly remembered images

p. 574 **clasp her hands** = hold her hands together

p. 578 an **evangelical** minister = Christian group emphasizing the bible
witchcraft = the art of doing evil acts
banishing evil demons = driving out, forcing to leave
charismatic ministries = Christian group emphasizing special powers of healing
psychological causes have been **ruled out** = eliminated
Satan's strongholds = places where the devil is powerful
devils were **cast out** = driven out, forced to leave

Flex Your Word Power

Test your way with opposites. Here are some words used in the last few modules. *Draw a line from a word on the left to the word that means its opposite on the right:*

maladjusted	desensitize
overt	dysfunctional
sensitize	extraverted
clear-cut	hidden
functional	ambiguous
introverted	adjusted

Do you want to try some more? Here are some from earlier modules:

stress	aversion
self	deductive
sensitive	other
inductive	terminate
initiate	insensitive
attraction	relaxation

If you're not sure about the answers, check the Answer Key! Okay, if you want more opposites, here they are:

appropriate	subjective
maximize	progress
objective	minimize
passive	irrational
rational	inappropriate
regress	active

Check the Answer Key, just to be sure.

Why a Semi-Colon? Another look

When a writer wants to present a list, each item is separated by a comma. Look at the following example:

> Luis is afraid of only three things : snakes , public speaking , and his mother-in-law.

When each item in the list is more than two or three words, we need semi-colons to keep order in the sentence. A semi-colon is a stronger separation than a comma. Look at the following sentence:

> Ricky rented three films from the video store : <u>Spy Kids</u> because his little sister wanted to see it ; <u>Gladiator</u> because he wanted to watch the fight scenes again ; and <u>Of Mice and Men</u> because he had to read the book for his English class.

Semi-colons are especially important when each item has its own commas. Take a look at the semi-colons doing their job in this example, which is all <u>one</u> sentence:

> One newspaper reporter who was annoyed with the annual marathon race in Chicago took a friend with him to do an "anti-marathon" : first, they drove to a bar and watched the race on television while they drank a beer ; next, they sat on a park bench and smoked several cigarettes ; then they drove to a fast-food joint and ordered french fries ; and so on for 27 miles.

You saw another good example in the text (p. 513):

> She confessed to being so lonely in the months before the killings that she had multiple sexual encounters : with her stepfather, who had molested her as a teenager ; with her estranged husband, whom she was divorcing ; with her current boyfriend, who later wrote the good-bye letter ; and with her boyfriend's father.

Now you try it. The following is a single sentence, but without any punctuation. It needs one colon, three semi-colons, and three commas. Can you find where to put them?

> Four students were registered for the history course a journalist from Vietnam quiet but very smart an American housewife definitely not quiet but also smart an exchange student from Peru carrying a shopping bag full of books and me.

Check your answer in the Answer Key

The following sentence — also <u>one</u> sentence — needs one colon, two semi-colons, and three commas. Put them in where you think they are needed

> Sofia is trying to choose a subject for her research paper the special problems of counseling immigrants which is her main interest also the reasons why immigrants do not use counseling services a subject that would require a lot of research or possibly the influence of religion on immigrant families.

Now check your answer in the Answer Key:

Module 24: Therapies

Answer Key

maladjusted	=	adjusted
overt	=	covert
sensitize	=	desensitize
clear-cut	=	ambiguous
functional	=	dysfunctional
introverted	=	extraverted
stress	=	relaxation
self	=	other
sensitive	=	insensitive
inductive	=	deductive
initiate	=	terminate
attraction	=	aversion
appropriate	=	inappropriate
maximize	=	minimize
objective	=	subjective
passive	=	active
rational	=	irratioal
regress	=	progress

Four students were registered for the history course : a journalist from Vietnam , quiet but very smart ; an American housewife , definitely not quiet but also smart ; an exchange student from Peru , carrying a shopping bag full of books ; and me.

Sofia is trying to choose a subject for her research paper : the special problems of counseling immigrants , which is her main interest ; also , the reasons why immigrants do not use counseling services , a subject that would require a lot of research ; or possibly the influence of religion on immigrant families.

Flashcards for psych majors only...

The Story of Psychotherapy: You met many famous and intriguing characters from the history of psychology in this module, people like Anna O., Rat Man, and Little Albert (almost sounds like a circus, doesn't it?). If you were to arrange these names in historical order (as I have done below) and add what each contributed, you could construct a capsule history of the development of modern psychotherapy.

Try it. Match each name to the most appropriate phrase. As you do so, see if you can tell yourself the story of how the four strands of modern psychotherapy emerged, and how they differ from each other.

_____ 1. Dorothea Dix   a. reduced hysterical symptoms by talking about them

_____ 2. Anna O.   b. publicized the cruel treatment of "lunatics"

_____ 3. Sigmund Freud   c. developed cognitive therapy for depressive thoughts

_____ 4. Rat Man   d. developed a very positive client-centered therapy

_____ 5. Wolf-Man   e. interpretation of his dreams revealed sexual fears

_____ 6. John B. Watson   f. worked out a therapy called systematic desensitization

_____ 7. Little Albert   g. believed emotional problems are conditioned (learned)

_____ 8. Carl Rogers   h. conditioned to fear a rat in a famous experiment

_____ 9. Joseph Wolpe   i. free association revealed his repressed memories

_____ 10. Aaron Beck   j. developed psychoanalysis — the first psychotherapy

The Big Picture

Which statement below offers the best summary of the larger significance of this module?

A   A painful truth: psychotherapy is the witchcraft of the modern Western world. Plotnik's fascinating discussion of the *balian* of Bali shows why we shouldn't take psychotherapy too seriously. It's all based on belief and faith.

B   That there are several competing theories of psychotherapy is not so much an embarrassment as a reflection of the youth and vigor of psychology. The competing psychotherapies reflect the different approaches to psychology.

C   The crowded field of psychotherapy finally is experiencing what economists call a shakeout. One by one the old methods are being abandoned, as more and more psychotherapists adopt EMDR because of its greater effectiveness.

D   Which method of psychotherapy is best? It is mainly a matter of individual preference. All therapies share the common assumption that problems lie buried in the unconscious, and must be exhumed and examined.

E   As the famous movie producer Samuel Goldwyn once observed, "Anyone who goes to a psychiatrist should have his head examined!"

True-False

_____ 1. The history of therapeutic effort is a story of continual improvement in the treatment of the mentally ill.

_____ 2. Psychotherapists today are more likely to see themselves as eclectic than as adhering to one of the traditional approaches to psychotherapy.

_____ 3. The basic assumption of psychoanalysis is that since maladaptive behaviors are *learned*, they can be unlearned through training.

_____ 4. Transference is the process by which a patient carefully describes his or her problems so the therapist can analyze and solve them.

_____ 5. Although Freud is widely criticized, psychoanalytic ideas continue to be a force in psychotherapy today.

_____ 6. Rod Plotnik quotes from therapy sessions representing the major approaches; the point is that they all sound pretty much alike.

_____ 7. The systematic desensitization technique is essentially an unlearning experience.

_____ 8. Aaron Beck's cognitive therapy assumes that we have automatic negative thoughts that we say to ourselves without much notice.

_____ 9. Carl Rogers' client-centered therapy avoids giving directions, advice, or disapproval.

_____ 10. Research suggests that the new technique called Eye Movement Desensitization and Reprocessing (EMDR) will eventually replace all the traditional psychotherapies.

Flashcards 1

1. behavior therapy [behavior modification]
2. client-centered therapy
3. cognitive therapy
4. dream interpretation
5. free association
6. intrusive thoughts
7. psychoanalysis
8. resistance
9. systematic desensitization
10. transference

a. a technique that encourages clients to talk about any thoughts or images that enter their heads
b. therapy in which client is gradually exposed to feared object while simultaneously practicing relaxation
c. core idea is that repressed threatening thoughts in the unconscious cause conflicts and symptoms
d. uses principles of conditioning to change disruptive behaviors and improve human functioning
e. client's reluctance to work through feelings, recognize unconscious conflicts and repressed thoughts
f. the process by which a client expresses strong emotions toward therapist, who is a substitute figure
g. a search for underlying hidden meanings, symbols providing clues to unconscious thoughts and desires
h. therapist shows compassion and positive regard in helping client reach full potential, self-actualization
i. thoughts that we repeatedly experience, are usually unwanted or disruptive, and are very difficult to stop
j. assumes we have automatic negative thoughts that distort our perceptions, influence feelings, behavior

Flashcards 2

1. clinical psychologists
2. common factors
3. counseling psychologists
4. deinstitutionalization
5. eclectic approach
6. insight therapy
7. medical therapy
8. moral therapy
9. phenothiazines
10. psychiatrists

a. release of mental patients from hospitals and their return to the community to develop independent lives
b. go to graduate school of psychology and earn Ph.D., including one year in an applied clinical setting
c. basic set of procedures shared by different therapies (supportive relationship, accepting atmosphere, etc.)
d. involves use of various psychoactive drugs to treat mental disorders by changing biological factors
e. go to medical school, earn MD, take psychiatric residency and additional training in psychotherapy
f. involves therapist and client talking about the client's symptoms, problems, to identify cause of problem
g. involves combining and using techniques and ideas from many different therapeutic approaches
h. the belief that mental patients could be helped to function better by providing humane treatment
i. block or reduce effects of dopamine, thereby reduce schizophrenic symptoms (delusions, hallucinations)
j. go to graduate school of psych or education and earn Ph.D., including work in a counseling setting

Multiple-Choice

_____ 1. Rod Plotnik begins the module with the story of "Anna O." to make the point that
   a. Freud had some notable failures as well as famous successes
   b. talking about your problems seems to help
   c. the real credit for inventing psychoanalysis should go to Dr. Breuer
   d. talking won't help unless the client also does something positive

_____ 2. John B. Watson's famous experiment with Little Albert was designed to show that
   a. ethical standards of psychological research are much more stringent today
   b. psychological problems affect babies as well as children and adults
   c. fear of rats is almost natural and may be inborn
   d. emotional problems can be viewed as learned behavior

_____ 3. In the history of the treatment of mental illness, Dorothea Dix is famous for
   a. charging admission to watch the crazy antics of the "lunatics"
   b. inventing early treatment techniques like the strait jacket and bleeding
   c. publicizing the terrible living conditions and poor treatment of the mentally ill
   d. emptying the mental hospitals of almost half of their patients

_____ 4. The discovery of antipsychotic drugs led directly to
   a. deinstitutionalization
   b. the reform movement
   c. reinstitutionalization
   d. the community mental health center

_____ 5. In order to become a _____ you need a medical degree and a residency with further training in psychopathology and treatment
   a. clinical psychologist
   b. counseling psychologist
   c. social worker
   d. psychiatrist

_____ 6. When asked which approach they use in therapy, a majority of psychologists indicated a preference for the _____ approach
   a. psychodynamic
   b. behavioral
   c. eclectic
   d. cognitive

_____ 7. How effective is psychotherapy? Studies suggest that psychotherapy is
   a. an effective treatment for many mental disorders
   b. no more effective than just waiting
   c. no more effective than doing nothing
   d. an effective treatment, but only if continued for more than a year

_____ 8. The only one of the following who was a patient of Freud's was
   a. Anna O.
   b. Rat Man
   c. Dorothea Dix
   d. Joseph Breuer

_____ 9. Which one of the following is *not* a technique used in psychoanalysis?
   a. free association
   b. dream analysis
   c. analysis of performance
   d. analysis of transference

_____ 10. Rod Plotnik's fascinating example of the balian, a local healer in Bali, suggests that the success of Western psychotherapy
   a. demonstrates the superiority of modern medicine
   b. results from its assumption that the problem lies inside the sufferer
   c. depends on having intelligent and educated patients
   d. owes much to what are called common factors in psychotherapy

_____ 11. Which one of the following is *not* a step in the systematic desensitization procedure?
   a. relaxation
   b. stimulus hierarchy
   c. stimulus sensitizing
   d. exposure

_____ 12. Aaron Beck discovered that depressed people tend to interpret the world through
   a. carefully planned negative statements
   b. thoughtless repetitions of what other people believe
   c. secretly hostile beliefs
   d. automatic negative thoughts

_____ 13. In his cognitive therapy, Beck attempts to make clients aware of
   a. the importance of education in the contemporary world
   b. adaptive thought patterns like open-mindedness, acceptance, love, and will power
   c. maladaptive thought patterns like overgeneralization, polarized thinking, and selective attention
   d. how much better they could be if they would just "think about it"

_____ 14. The central assumption of Carl Rogers' client-centered therapy is that
   a. each person has the tendency and capacity to develop his or her full potential
   b. psychotherapy must be freely available in community mental health centers
   c. we must struggle to overcome our basic human selfishness and hostility
   d. therapy should focus on real behavior, not vague thoughts and feelings.

_____ 15. Which one of the following is *not* a step in the thought substitution procedure?
   a. through self-monitoring, write a list of your irrational thoughts
   b. compose a matching list of rational thoughts
   c. practice substituting rational thoughts whenever you have irrational ones
   d. if you catch yourself thinking irrationally, administer a predetermined punishment, like no TV that night

Answers for Module 24

True-False	Flashcards 1	Flashcards 2	Multiple-Choice
1. F	1. d	1. b	1. b
2. T	2. h	2. c	2. d
3. F	3. j	3. j	3. c
4. F	4. g	4. a	4. a
5. T	5. a	5. g	5. d
6. F	6. i	6. f	6. c
7. T	7. c	7. d	7. a
8. T	8. e	8. h	8. b
9. T	9. b	9. i	9. c
10. F	10. f	10. e	10. d
			11. c
			12. d
			13. c
			14. a
			15. d

The Big Picture

Statement B

"The Story of Psychotherapy" quiz

1. b   2. a   3. j   4. i   5. e   6. g   7. h   8. d   9. f   10. c

---

Time to Read

With the end of the term approaching, you will soon have time to read again. One of the paradoxes of education is that just when we should be reading most, we have the least time. This is true for instructors, too. Plan to read a good book you have heard about. Now that you know more psychology, you will find that novels and biographies are more interesting than ever. What will you read over the interim?

Module 25

Social Psychology

The Material That Was Difficult Because It Seemed Easy

Well, not really easy — you'll have to study this module as carefully as the others — but obvious, in a sense. One of the difficulties in studying social psychology is that so many of the facts and ideas it presents seem like things you already know. That makes it hard to get a handle on what to "learn." Here's an idea that may make it easier.

Because you are a human being, you have been a social psychologist all your life. If there is one essential human skill, it is how to live with each other. I don't mean this in a preachy way, but in the sense that our instincts, what few we have, tell us very little about interacting with others. Therefore, we must learn to observe, understand, and predict what other people will do (and what we will do) in any given situation. We soon become experts in human interaction. See? You've been studying this stuff all your life.

The beauty of social psychology is that it can take us outside ourselves and help us see our behavior more objectively, and hence more clearly. Such awareness, which social psychology owes to anthropology and sociology, helps correct the tendency of psychology to focus too much on individual, internal factors. There's a price you pay for this insight, however. Theories in social psychology typically involve fancy names and complicated explanations. Don't be afraid. The social psychologists you'll study are talking about what you do every day. Try to understand it that way. Give yourself credit for understanding what seems obvious. Translate what does not seem clear into the language of your own experience.

The Cross-Cultural Approach to Psychology

If you counted them, you would discover that there are more key terms in this module than almost any other. Another module with almost the same number of key terms is Rod Plotnik's presentation of "The Incredible Nervous System." And that's no accident. Just as Module 4 helped define the psychobiological approach to psychology, Module 25 defines the other end of the spectrum — the cross-cultural approach (some might call it the sociocultural approach). In the earlier module, we were almost off the chart into biology, hence the need for many new terms. Here, we are deep into sociology, and once again need a whole new vocabulary.

One problem sociologists have is that they are talking about things that are utterly familiar, like attitudes, helping, groups, and aggression. Sometimes it almost seems like they invent fancy names for their concepts because what they are describing is so familiar. But they wouldn't do that, would they?

Effective Student Tip 25

Honor Your Need to be Effective

Most of my tips have been quite specific, because I wanted them to be actions you could take immediately. If they worked, you won a victory here and there and perhaps did better in the course. I hope they also contribute to a body of strategies that will make you a stronger student in the courses still to come.

In truth, however, I have an even larger goal in mind. That goal is for you to begin to understand that the need to be effective is the essence of your human motivation. If I am right, you feel a need to be effective not only in your schoolwork but more importantly in everything you do.

My argument is simply this: We humans have almost no instincts to guide us. The only way we can tell whether what we are doing is right is the extent to which it works for us. We know our actions are working when they make the world give back what we want and need. In other words, the extent to which the actions we take are effective becomes the measure of our happiness and satisfaction in life.

Whatever situation you may be in, school or employment or relationship, honor your need to be effective by paying attention to how well your actions are working for you and how good you feel about what you are doing.

Your response...

I am convinced that we all have a constant need to be effective. Do you feel that need in yourself?

Key Terms

These terms are especially important because they help define the cross-cultural approach to psychology.

actor-observer effect	diffusion of responsibility theory	peripheral route for persuasion
aggressive behavior	discrimination	person perception
altruism	distinctiveness	person schemas
arousal-cost-reward model of helping	evaluative function	predisposing function
attitude	event schemas [scripts]	prejudice
attributions	external attributions	prosocial behavior [helping]
bystander effect	foot-in-the-door technique	rape myths
catharsis	frustration-aggression hypothesis	role schemas
central route for persuasion	fundamental attribution error	schemas
cognitive dissonance		self schemas
cognitive miser model	group cohesion	self-perception theory
compliance	group norms	self-serving bias
conformity	group polarization	social cognition
consensus	groups	social cognitive theory
consistency	groupthink	social comparison theory
counterattitudinal behavior	informational influence theory	social facilitation
covariation model	internal attributions	social inhibition
crowd	interpreting function	social psychology
debriefing	modified frustration-aggression hypothesis	socially oriented group
decision stage model of helping	obedience	stereotypes
deindividuation		task oriented group

Outline

- *Introduction*
  - *What basic areas of social psychology does Rod Plotnik illustrate with his examples of Lawrence Graham and David Koresh?*
  1. Stereotypes
     a. **Social psychology**
     b. **Social cognition**
  2. Behavior in groups
  A. *Perceiving Others*
     1. **Person perception**
        a. Physical appearance
        b. Need to explain
        c. Influence on behavior
        d. Effects of race

2. Physical appearance
   a. Attractiveness
   b. Psychological characteristics
3. **Stereotypes**
   a. Development of stereotypes
      (1) **Prejudice**
      (2) **Discrimination**
   b. Functions of stereotypes
      (1) Source of information
      (2) Thought-saving device
4. **Schemas**
   a. Kinds of schemas
      (1) **Person schemas**
      (2) **Role schemas**
      (3) **Event schemas [scripts]**
      (4) **Self schemas**
   b. Advantages and disadvantages

B. *Attributions*
   1. Definition: **attributions**
   2. Internal versus external (Fritz Heider)
      a. **Internal attributions**
      b. **External attributions**
   3. Kelley's model of covariation
      a. **Covariation model** (Harold Kelley)
         (1) **Consensus**
         (2) **Consistency**
         (3) **Distinctiveness**
      b. Applying Kelley's covariation model
   4. Biases and errors
      a. **Cognitive miser model**
      b. Common biases in making attributions
         (1) **Fundamental attribution error**
         (2) **Actor-observer effect**
         (3) **Self-serving bias**

C. Research Focus: Attributions & Grades
1. Can changing attributions change grades?
2. Kinds of attributions
3. Method: changing attributions
4. Results and conclusions

D. Attitudes
1. Definition: **attitude**
    a. Evaluative
    b. Targeted
    c. Predisposes behavior
2. Components of attitudes
    a. Cognitive component
    b. Affective component
    c. Behavioral component
3. Functions of attitudes
    a. **Predisposing function**
    b. **Interpreting function**
    c. **Evaluative function**
☐ What was your attitude toward Shannon Faulkner and her goal?
4. Attitude change
    a. **Cognitive dissonance** (Leon Festinger)
        (1) Adding or changing beliefs
        (2) **Counterattitudinal behavior**
☐ Read the famous 'boring task' experiment several times, until you really understand it.
    b. **Self-perception theory** (Daryl Bem)
5. Persuasion
    a. Two routes to persuasion
        (1) **Central route for persuasion**
        (2) **Peripheral route for persuasion**
☐ Can you think of examples from current events for the two routes?
    b. Elements of persuasion
        (1) Source
        (2) Message
        (3) Audience

E. **Social & Group Influences**
  1. Tragedy in Waco
  2. **Conformity**
      a. Conformity
      b. Solomon Asch's experiment
          (1) Procedure
          (2) Results
  3. **Compliance**
      a. Conformity and compliance
      b. **Foot-in-the-door technique**
  4. **Obedience** (Stanley Milgram)
      a. Milgram's experiment
          (1) The set up
          (2) The conflict
      b. Milgram's results
      c. Why do people obey?
      d. Were Milgram's experiments ethical?
          (1) **Debriefing**
          (2) Experiments today
  5. Helping: prosocial behavior
      a. **Prosocial behavior [helping]**
      b. **Altruism**
  6. Why people help
      a. Empathy, personal distress, norms or values
      b. **Decision stage model of helping**
      c. **Arousal-cost-reward model of helping**
  7. Group dynamics: **groups**
      a. Group cohesion and norms
          (1) **Group cohesion**
          (2) **Group norms**
      b. Why do we form groups?
          (1) **Social comparison theory**
          (2) **Task oriented group**
          (3) **Socially oriented group**
  8. Behavior in crowds (**crowd**)
      a. Facilitation and inhibition
          (1) **Social facilitation**
          (2) **Social inhibition**

b. Deindividuation in crowds
- (1) **Deindividuation**
- (2) Internal standards

c. The bystander effect
- (1) **Bystander effect**
- (2) **Informational influence theory**
- (3) **Diffusion of responsibility theory**

9. Group decisions
   a. **Group polarization**
   - (1) Risky shift
   - (2) Polarization

   b. **Groupthink**

F. Aggression

1. Definition
   a. **Aggressive behavior**
   b. Model of aggressive behavior

☐ *Do you believe that human beings are naturally aggressive?*

2. Biological factors
   a. Aggression and neurotransmitters
   b. Mutant mice

3. Social cognitive and personality factors
   a. **Social cognitive theory** (Albert Bandura)
   b. Three factors
   c. Television/video games

4. Environmental factors
   a. **Frustration-aggression hypothesis** (John Dollard)
   b. **Modified frustration-aggression hypothesis** (Leonard Berkowitz)
   c. Three factors

5. Sexual harassment and aggression
   a. Characteristics and kinds of rapists
   - (1) Power rapist
   - (2) Sadistic rapist
   - (3) Anger rapist
   - (4) Acquaintance or date rapist

   b. **Rape myths**

G. *Cultural Diversity: National Attitudes and Behaviors*
   1. Niger: beauty ideal
   2. Japan: organ transplants
   3. Egypt: women's rights

H. *Application: Controlling Aggression*
   1. Case study
   2. Controlling aggression in children
      a. Cognitive-behavioral deficits
      b. Programs to control aggression
   3. Controlling anger in adults
      a. **Catharsis**
      b. Cognitive-behavioral program
   4. Controlling sexual aggression
      a. Socialization
      b. Knowing the risk factors

For Psych Majors Only...

Classic Experiments: The classic experiments in social psychology are among the most elegant in psychology, if not in all of science, but they may seem complicated on first reading. Go through the explanations in the textbook more than once, and make sure you understand the logic of each experiment. The research Rod Plotnik writes about is well worth understanding and remembering. These experiments are important building blocks of modern psychology, and you will come across them repeatedly in your further studies.

There is a great irony surrounding these famous experiments: most of them could not be conducted today. Plotnik explains why in his discussion of the ethics of psychological research.

Language Workout

What's That?

p. 581 a **country club** = private suburban recreation center
I will have to call **security** = a guard
the **exclusive** Greenwich Country Club = limited to rich upper class people
very **affluent** = rich, wealthy
Fortune 500 executives = from the 500 largest corporations in the U.S. (from the financial magazine, *Fortune*)
hired to be a **busboy** = waiter's assistant who removes dirty dishes
diction like an educated white person = clear pronunciation
an **associate** in a New York law firm = partner
move up the social ladder = rise to a higher social position
rose to **prominence** = attention
polygamist = man with more than one wife
armed fortress = group of buildings with guns and weapons for defense against attack
he will be **resurrected** = reborn after death
MTV = rock music television channel
had to **turn over** all their money to him = give
stash of weapons = hidden collection
tear gas = gas that burns the eyes, used by police
sifted through the burned rubble = examined

p. 582 required little conscious **deliberation** = thinking
did not **reveal** that he was actually a graduate = say
a widely **cited** early conclusion = used, discussed
first impressions are **confirmed** = proven to be true
factors that **come to light** = emerge, come to attention

p. 583 **sophisticated** medical tests = advanced, complex
not as intelligent, **competent** = able to do a job
rave parties = large dance music parties, especially with drug use
ways to **conserve** time = save

p. 584 a **board-certified** neurosurgeon = licensed, officially approved
she was repeatedly **propositioned** = given sexual invitations
primarily **for effect** = to impress others (other men)

p. 585 games in the **minor leagues** = baseball clubs that are less successful
this **umpire** = judge in baseball games
passed over for promotion = not considered

p. 586 **perseverance** = quality of continuing work despite problems and obstacles
people **of color** = non-white
he **got to** his car = arrived at

p. 587 I **got my act together** = resolved the problems that were preventing success

p. 588 **skinheads** = antisocial young men (usually with shaved heads) in violent gangs
insubordination = refusal to obey authority
45-page appearance **code manual** = guidebook of rules for employees
dog meat is considered a **delicacy** = exceptionally rare and tasty food

p. 589 she **challenged** the Citadel's all-male attitude = defied, questioned
    on legal grounds = through existing laws
    hate mail = letters expressing extreme hate and threats
    she was **escorted** = accompanied for protection
    federal **marshals** = police officers
    battle **dragged on** for two years = continued very slowly
    having to take **scalding** showers = burning hot
    she was **jeered** = booed, insulted
    excessive **hazing** = unpleasant rituals
    magna cum laude = with great honor

p. 590 an **out-and-out** hatemonger = open, not hidden
    hatemonger = person who encourages hate
    Ku Klux Klan = secret terrorist organization in U.S. South opposed to non-whites, Catholics, and Jews.
    total **extermination** = killing
    bashed and robbed Japanese tourists = physically attacked
    white supremacist notions = general belief that whites are superior to non-whites
    renouncing his previous white supremacist values = giving up
    beliefs **clashed** = conflicted, fought
    a very troubling **inconsistency** = conflict between theory and practice

p. 591 candidate should appear **credible** = believable
    expertise = great skill at a job (expert knowledge)
    national **newscasters** = news readers

p. 592 **armored vehicles** = tanks, specially protected cars
    pick out the line equal in length = choose

p. 593 conforming **drastically** declined = very greatly, dramatically
    used by **telemarketers** = telephone salespersons
    drivers who **run** red lights = drive through
    commands that were clearly **inhumane** = against human values, cruel
    an **accomplice** of the experimenter = partner, helper
    ask the learner **over an intercom** = using an electrical speaker system
    plead with the researcher to stop = beg

p. 594 to the surprise and **dismay** of many = reaction of horror

p. 595 mouth-to-mouth **resuscitation** = reviving from near-death
    donated most of her life savings = gave
    help **perfect** strangers = complete
    Most **onlookers** stopped = people watching, bystanders

p. 596 he had **stumbled** drunk = walked in an unsteady way
    can **exert** powerful influences = produce

p. 597 a runner has a **spotty** history = uneven, inconsistent
    arrested for **looting** = stealing during riots
    a crowd **conceals** a person's identity = hides
    a **rowdy** crowd = behaving in rough way, almost out of control

p. 598 the **brink** of nuclear war = edge, border
    the **escalation** of war = increase (more soldiers and weapons)
    the **Watergate cover-up** = series of scandals in 1973 concerning illegal actions

by government authorities during the Nixon presidency
the **Challenger disaster** = explosion of U.S. space ship in 1986, killing all the astronauts

p. 600 **drive-by killings** = shootings from a moving car
guns will **surpass** traffic accidents = become greater than
mutant mice = physically changed

p. 601 **ramming** = one car purposely hitting another car
the link between the two is not **absolute** = completely proven, always true

p. 602 **nonconsensual** sexual intercourse = unwilling (forced)
penal institutions = punishment (especially prison)
intimidate the victim = frighten
sexuality and aggression have become **fused** = joined together
physical **coercion** = force
demeaning attitudes toward women = shaming, insulting
necking and petting = kissing and beginning love-making
things **get out of hand** = go out of control
the **perpetuation of** rape myths = continuing belief in

p. 603 being very **rotund** = round (heavy)

p. 605 **rant and rave** = complain loudly
take their anger out on whoever = release anger on innocent persons
pent-up emotions = unreleased, not expressed, stored
vent cathartic aggression = express, release

p. 608 **obstetrics** = medical specialty treating childbirth
gynecology = medical specialty treating women's problems
eager to **set up shop** = start working
opened a **Pandora's box** = source of troubles and hidden problems
values that parents **impart** to children = teach
a **self-fulfilling prophecy** = action that, once predicted, will then happen because the predictor makes it happen
chiding themselves = criticizing
for **coddling** teen mothers = treating too lightly, not giving discipline
educators **fret** = worry
the administration has **cracked down on** necking = started to punish, stop
wish that teens would **abstain** = not have sex

Flex Your Word Power

Here are some more opposites, from this module and earlier ones. *Draw a line connecting each word on the left with its opposite on the right.* (You can check your answers in the Answer Key)

flee   con
facilitate   opponent
participant   antisocial
proponent   spectator
prosocial   inhibit
pro   stay

Now try some more:

peripheral
permanent
polarization
passive
rebel
reinforce

aggressive
consensus
central
conform
transient
weaken

The Language Workout Marathon

Are you ready to test yourself? Try the following questions to run through some of the topics we have practiced in the Language Workout. In the sentences below, write in the appropriate form of the **word**, as in the example:

The information you **perceive** is your *perception*.

Someone who **deceives** is guilty of _____.

If you are **deprived** of sleep, you experience sleep _____.

An individual who has a **bias** is a _____ person.

A person who **abstains** from food is described as _____.

An experience that **affects** many people has a great _____.

Now try some plurals. In the sentences below, write the correct form in the blank. The first one is done for you:

One **datum** was not enough, so I looked for more *data*.

One single **phenomenon** caused many more _____.

If one **stimulus** is not successful, different _____ can be tried.

The first **crisis** was harder than all the later _____.

We chose one **criterion** out of many _____.

Are you an expert on seeing the difference between one and many? Look at the phrases below and circle your choice of one or many:

the group**'s** members = one group? many groups?

the student**s'** research = one student? many students?

his brother**s'** lies = one brother? many brothers?

the analyst**'s** techniques = one analyst? many analysts?

her counselor**s'** advice = one counselor? many counselors?

Do you remember our practice in joining sentences with phrases like **to which** and **some of which** and **with whom** and **all of whom**? Join the sentences below in the same way:

The bank kept control of the money. None of the money could be used for daily expenses.
_____

The therapist saw seven patients. Two of the patients arrived late.
_____

Runners trained six months for the marathon. They participated in this marathon.
_____

The professor will arrive soon. All the students are waiting for her.
_____

Now let's try some connecting (or organizing) words. Choose the word that best fits each sentence below, then write the **word** in the blank:

once *or* **while**: _____ the research was published, the public reacted.

once *or* **while**: _____ the research was published, no one read it.

thus *or* **however**: The experiment was a success. _____, the scientific evidence was proven.

thus *or* **however**: The operation was a success. _____, the patient died.

Provided *or* **Even if**: _____ you finish your vegetables, you can have some chocolate ice cream.

Provided *or* **Even if**: _____ you buy a new engine, your old car will never run like a brand new car.

Don't give up now! We're almost finished. This last part reviews choosing the right punctuation mark. The sentences below have no punctuation, so you have to decide which mark(s) to use: a **comma** or a **colon** or a **semi-colon**. Put the correct mark(s) in the suitable place(s) in the sentence.

Americans call the sport soccer conversely the rest of the world calls it football.

Now it is easier to understand the different meanings of the following terms a concept a principle and a theory.

The more she reads the bigger her vocabulary grows.

Seven people were seated at the table one of whom was the murderer.

The explanation although it was clear to the professor was quite hazy to the students.

From the first page to the last the book was full of valuable information.

368 STUDY GUIDE

      Distorted self-statements such as negative judgments and polarized thinking need to be monitored and changed.

      The runners reported numerous good effects an initial feeling of well-being a sense of control over their bodies as well as their lives and an improved self-image.

You finished! Now check your answers in the Answer Key.

Answer Key

flee	=	stay
facilitate	=	inhibit
participant	=	spectator
proponent	=	opponent
prosocial	=	antisocial
pro	=	con
peripheral	=	central
permanent	=	transient
polarization	=	consensus
passive	=	aggressive
rebel	=	conform
reinforce	=	weaken

Someone who **deceives** is guilty of **deception**.
If you are **deprived** of sleep, you experience sleep **deprivation**.
An individual who has a **bias** is a **biased** person.
A person who **abstains** from food is described as **abstinent**.
An experience that **affects** many people has a great **effect**.

One single **phenomenon** caused many more **phenomena**.
If one **stimulus** is not successful, different **stimuli** can be tried.
The first **crisis** was harder than all the later **crises**.
We chose one **criterion** out of many **criteria**.

the group**'s** members = **one**
the students**'** research = **many**
his brothers**'** lies = **many**
the analyst**'s** techniques = **one**
her counselors**'** advice = **many**

The bank kept control of the money, **none of which** could be used for daily expenses.
The therapist saw seven patients, **two of whom** arrived late.
Runners trained six months for the marathon **in which** they participated.
The professor **for whom** all the students are waiting will arrive soon.

Once the research was published, the public reacted.
While the research was published, no one read it.
The experiment was a success. **Thus**, the scientific evidence was proven.
The operation was a success. **However**, the patient died.
Provided you finish your vegetables, you can have some chocolate ice cream.
Even if you buy a new engine, your old car will never run like a brand new car.

Americans call the sport soccer ; conversely , the rest of the world calls it football.
Now it is easier to understand the different meanings of the following terms : a concept , a principle , and a theory.
The more she reads , the bigger her vocabulary grows.
Seven people were seated at the table , one of whom was the murderer.
The explanation , although it was clear to the professor , was quite hazy to the students.
From the first page to the last , the book was full of valuable information.
Distorted self-statements , such as negative judgments and polarized thinking , need to be monitored and changed.
The runners reported numerous good effects : an initial feeling of well-being ; a sense of control over their bodies as well as their lives ; and an improved self-image.

The Big Picture

Which statement below offers the best summary of the larger significance of this module?

A   Understanding the behavior of people in group situations involves a complicated mathematics of combining all the individual tendencies to arrive at an average that will determine how the individuals will behave.

B   Rod Plotnik has discussed the famous nature-nurture debate in several modules of this textbook. With his description of the many elegant experiments in social psychology, the answer finally becomes clear: our behavior owes most to nature.

C   No matter how many experiments social psychologists conduct on group influence, the fact remains that we are unique individuals. If we exercise our freedom of choice, no one can make us do anything against our will.

D   We like to think of ourselves as rugged individuals, but social psychology has demonstrated that our behavior, and even our thinking, is highly sensitive to group pressures and the social situations we are in.

E   How many social psychologists does it take to change a light bulb? Three: one to give the order, one to change the bulb, and one to record whether the order was obeyed! [And so we end as we began.]

True-False

_____ 1. The words "prejudice" and "discrimination" mean the same thing.

_____ 2. A schema is an unfair stereotype we apply to a person who is different.

_____ 3. Attributions are our attempts to understand and explain people's behavior.

_____ 4. An attitude is a tendency to respond to others in a quirky, overly-sensitive manner.

_____ 5. Cognitive dissonance occurs when an audience hears so many contradictory arguments that they lose sight of the main issue.

_____ 6. Advice for all you budding politicians: if the facts are on your side, take the central route to persuasion; if they aren't, take the peripheral route.

_____ 7. The famous "electric shock" experiment showed that if you pay people enough they will follow just about any orders.

_____ 8. It is the social-psychological phenomenon of deindividuation that can make a crowd dangerous.

_____ 9. Because of the pooling of many talents and ideas, group decisions are usually superior to individual decisions.

_____ 10. Good advice on how to avoid date rape: meet unwanted advances with increasing forcefulness and know the risk factors.

Flashcards 1

____ 1. actor-observer effect
____ 2. cognitive dissonance
____ 3. event schemas [scripts]
____ 4. external attributions
____ 5. fundamental attribution error
____ 6. internal attributions
____ 7. person schemas
____ 8. role schemas
____ 9. self-serving bias
____ 10. social cognition

a. a state of tension that motivates us to reduce our cognitive inconsistencies by making beliefs consistent
b. tendency to attribute our own behavior to situation, others' to their personality traits or dispositions
c. focuses on cognitive processes, e.g., how we perceive, store and retrieve information about social life
d. are based on the jobs people perform or the social positions they hold
e. explaining a person by focusing on disposition or personality traits and overlooking the situation
f. attributing our successes to our dispositions and traits, but attributing our failures to the situations
g. explanations of behavior based on the internal characteristics or dispositions of the person
h. include our judgments about the traits that we and others possess
i. explanations of behavior based on the external circumstances or situations; situational attributions
j. contain behaviors that we associate with familiar activities, events, or procedures

Flashcards 2

____ 1. altruism
____ 2. bystander effect
____ 3. central route for persuasion
____ 4. conformity
____ 5. deindividuation
____ 6. foot-in-the-door technique
____ 7. group cohesion
____ 8. groupthink
____ 9. obedience
____ 10. peripheral route for persuasion

a. any behavior you perform because of group pressure, even though it might not involve direct requests
b. behavior performed in response to an order given by someone in a position of power or authority
c. emphasizes emotional appeal, focuses on personal traits, and generates positive feelings
d. increased tendency for irrational or antisocial behavior when there is less chance of being identified
e. helping, often at a cost or risk, for reasons other than the expectation of a material or social reward
f. says that an individual may feel inhibited from taking some action because of the presence of others
g. presents information with strong arguments, analyses, facts, and logic
h. occurs when group discussions emphasize sticking together and agreement over use of critical thinking
i. increased probability of compliance to a second request if person complies with a small, first request
j. group togetherness, determined by how much group members perceive they share common attributes

Multiple-Choice

_____ 1. Rod Plotnik introduces us to Harvard Law School student Lawrence Graham to make the point that
   a. anyone who has the guts to start at the bottom can work his way up
   b. African-American men are overly sensitive to good natured kidding
   c. how people behave is more significant than what they believe
   d. how we perceive and evaluate others has powerful consequences

_____ 2. When we ask someone, "What do you do?" we are trying to get more information about the person by drawing on our
   a. person schemas
   b. role schemas
   c. event schemas
   d. scripts

_____ 3. If I look for the causes of your behavior in your disposition and personality traits, and overlook how the situation influenced your behavior, I am guilty of the
   a. fundamental attribution error
   b. covariation model factor
   c. actor-observer effect
   d. self-serving bias

_____ 4. "I aced the chem exam because I studied my butt off! The psych exam I flunked? Well, you know he always asks tricky questions." Sounds like the _____ in action, doesn't it?
   a. fundamental attribution error
   b. actor-observer effect
   c. self-serving bias
   d. whiner effect

_____ 5. Which one of the following is *not* a component of an attitude?
   a. cognitive
   b. genetic
   c. affective
   d. behavioral

_____ 6. In Leon Festinger's "boring task" experiment, the subjects who were paid only $1 to tell other students it was interesting (a lie) dealt with their cognitive dissonance by
   a. convincing themselves that it was somewhat interesting after all
   b. hoping the students they lied to realized it was just part of the experiment
   c. insisting that they should also be paid $20 for telling the lie
   d. begging Festinger and his assistants not to reveal their names

_____ 7. Daryl Bem (self-perception theory) interprets the above experiment somewhat differently; Bem believes we
   a. consult our attitudes, then adjust our behavior accordingly
   b. observe our behavior, then infer what our attitudes must be, given that behavior
   c. observe our emotional state and adjust our attitudes according to our feelings
   d. govern our behavior according to the kind of person we think we are

_____ 8. Candidate Roberta Reformer, who has an excellent plan for better government, will take the _____ route to persuasion; her opponent Boss Bluster, who plans to label Roberta an hysterical feminist, will take the _____ route
  a. direct ... indirect
  b. honest ... dishonest
  c. central ... peripheral
  d. logical ... emotional

_____ 9. When Solomon Asch had his confederates deliberately choose an obviously incorrect matching line, the lone naive subject _____ went along with the group
  a. always
  b. never
  c. often
  d. rarely

_____ 10. Tell you what... before you quit just do one more of these questions, O.K.? [I'm using the _____ technique on you in my efforts to get you to do all the questions.]
  a. foot-in-the-door
  b. compliance
  c. conformity
  d. soft-soaping

_____ 11. In Stanley Milgram's electric shock experiment, most subjects continued to give shocks
  a. only up to the point they considered dangerous
  b. even beyond the point they believed was dangerous
  c. only if they had been paid a considerable amount to participate in the experiment
  d. only as long as the shocks seemed to be helping the "learner" do better

_____ 12. Milgram's famous experiment could not be conducted today because
  a. a new code of ethics screens experiments for potential harm to the subjects
  b. the experiment has been so widely written about that everyone is in on the secret
  c. few would be fooled by the fake lab, since psychologists are known for deception
  d. people today are too rational and scientific to obey orders they don't agree with

_____ 13. Which one of the following decisions was a classic example of groupthink?
  a. atomic bombing of Japan in World War II
  b. assassination of President Kennedy
  c. Bay of Pigs invasion of Cuba
  d. withdrawal of Shannon Faulkner from the Citadel military college

_____ 14. Contemporary social psychologists would be highly unlikely to agree that aggression
  a. occurs when our goals are blocked and we become frustrated and angry
  b. is learned through observation and imitation
  c. can be controlled by draining off or releasing emotional tension
  d. is directed by mental scripts stored in memory and used as guides for behavior

_____ 15. Why is rape so common? Researchers point to the fact that
  a. there are other motivations for rape, like aggression, power, and control, that may be more important than sex
  b. women are much bolder today, yet still like to be actively pursued, a situation that leaves men confused about what women really want
  c. Hollywood movies keep our sexual urges in a state of almost constant arousal
  d. unfortunately, rape is as natural as male hormones and female flirtatiousness — but it probably gets reported more often today

Answers for Module 25

True-False
1. F
2. F
3. T
4. F
5. F
6. T
7. F
8. T
9. F
10. T

Flashcards 1
1. b
2. a
3. j
4. i
5. e
6. g
7. h
8. d
9. f
10. c

Flashcards 2
1. e
2. f
3. g
4. a
5. d
6. i
7. j
8. h
9. b
10. c

Multiple-Choice
1. d
2. b
3. a
4. c
5. b
6. a
7. b
8. c
9. c
10. a
11. b
12. a
13. c
14. c
15. a

The Big Picture

Statement D

Congratulations!

Here you are, working on the self-tests for the last module. You have worked through a big textbook and a long Study Guide. That means you have done a ton of work this term, and I'm proud of you! Be sure to give yourself the praise you deserve (maybe a reward, too!). You have earned it.

Now that it's over, I would love to know what you thought of your introductory psychology class. Are you glad you took psychology? Did it change you in any way? What was the most important thing you learned? Please tell me by e-mail! **Profenos@aol.com**

TO THE OWNER OF THIS BOOK

May I ask a favor? It would be very helpful to know how well the Study Guide worked for you. I would like to have your reactions to the different features of the guide and your suggestions for making improvements. Please fill out this form, fold and seal it, and drop it in the mail. Thanks!

Matthew Enos

School _____

Instructor's name _____

Used the Study Guide because: Required _____ Optional _____ Comment _____

What did you like *most* about the Study Guide? _____
_____

What did you like *least* about the Study Guide? _____
_____

Was the Study Guide interesting and informative? _____
_____

Did the Study Guide help you with the course? _____
_____

Did you use the Language Workout sections (by Robert F. Keser)? _____

    Were they helpful? _____

Please check ☑ the parts of the Study Guide you used and tell me how useful they were:

    ☐ Module introductions _____

    ☐ Effective Student Tips _____

    ☐ Key Terms lists _____

    ☐ Outlines _____

    ☐ The Big Picture quizzes _____

    ☐ True-False questions _____

    ☐ Flashcards matching questions _____

    ☐ Multiple-Choice questions _____

Additional comments about the Study Guide _____
_____
_____

OPTIONAL

Your name _____ Date _____

May Wadsworth, the publisher, quote you in promotions for the Study Guide or in future publishing ventures?

    Yes _____ No _____

    Note: You can also send me comments by e-mail! **Profenos@aol.com**